Napoleon's Sorcerers

Napoleon's Sorcerers

The Sophisians

Darius A. Spieth

Newark: University of Delaware Press

Associated University Presses
2010 Eastpark Boulevard
Cranbury, NJ 08512

The paper used in this publication meets the requirements of the American National Standard for Permanence of Paper for Printed Library Materials Z39.48-1984.

Library of Congress Cataloging-in-Publication Data

Spieth, Darius Alexander, 1970–
    Napoleon's sorcerers : the Sophisians / Darius A. Spieth.
        p. cm.
    Includes bibliographical references and index.
    ISBN-13: 978-0-87413-957-0 (alk. paper)
    ISBN-10: 0-87413-957-0 (alk. paper)
    1. Sacred Order of Sophisians—Rituals. 2. Freemasonry—France—History—17th century. 3. Freemasonry—France—History—18th century. 4 Egyptology—France—History. 5. Isis (Egyptian deity)—Cult. I. Sacred Order of Sophisians. II. Title.
HS929.F8S75   2007
366'1—dc22
                                                                        2007010884

PRINTED IN THE UNITED STATES OF AMERICA

To my mother, with love

Contents

Acknowledgments

To unravel the long forgotten history of the "Sacred Order of the Sophisians" proved to be a project of far greater intellectual and practical complexity than I could have foreseen when I first discovered this society's *Livre d'or* (Golden Book) in the manuscript department of the Bibliothèque Nationale de France in 1999. Since then, numerous individuals and organizations have brought critical support to the project at various stages of its evolution. This book would not exist in its current form without the help and insights of Jean-Mathieu Robine, whose friendship developed from the very moment of my discovery of the Sophisians. Since 1999 his untiring efforts were invaluable for establishing connections with the Grand Orient de France, pointing out archival resources, interpreting findings, critically commenting on the manuscript itself, and, last but not least, providing logistic support during my extended research ventures in Paris.

I would like to express my most sincere gratitude to the Graham Foundation for Advanced Studies in the Fine Arts, Chicago, which partly sponsored this project. Financial support was also provided by a Summer Stipend I obtained in 2005 from the Office of Research at Louisiana State University. In Paris, I wish to acknowledge in particular the assistance of Pierre Mollier, archivist and librarian of the Grand Orient de France, who has encouraged the project enthusiastically from the moment when I first approached him. Monsieur Raymond Meyer opened his rich private collection of Masonic materials from the turn of the nineteenth century to my critical inquiry and pointed out the possible connection between the Sophisians and Alexandre Lenoir. At the manuscript department of the Bibliothèque Nationale, Sylvie Bourrel was kind enough to grant permission to have the Golden Book photographed and researched into its provenance, while at the Archives Nationales, Monsieur Poivre showed patience beyond the call of duty in helping to reconstruct Sophisian identities. In The Hague I was most graciously received by Evert P. Kwaadgras and Wim van Keulen at the Archives of the Grand East of the Netherlands during my research trips in 2004 and 2006. Christian Hogrefe of the Herzog August Bibliothek in Wolfenbüttel, Germany, was most obliging in providing illustrations that could not have been obtained otherwise.

On the LSU home front, I enjoyed the support of many wonderful colleagues, foremost among them Mark Zucker, whose editorial skills left their mark on every page of this book. Patricia Lawrence helped solve the mysteries of Sophisian philhellene connections by translating whole articles from Greek into English. David Cronrath, Dean of the College of Art and Design, came to the rescue on more than one occasion and helped cut through red tape. I also wish to acknowledge the many intellectual and practical contributions of the following individuals on campus: Michael Carpenter, Kevin Cope, C. Barrett Kennedy, Suzanne Marchand, Marchita Mauck, Todd Pourciau, Elaine Smyth, and the staff of LSU Special Collections. Special thanks go to Jerry Cohn, formerly curator of prints and acting director of Harvard University's Fogg Art Museum, for commenting on the manuscript and for being the patron saint of my academic life for so long. I am also grateful to Donald C. Mell at the University of Delaware Press for recognizing the potential of this book, to the anonymous peer reviewers for their commentaries, and to Julien Yoseloff for his care in the production process of the book. Finally, I wish to thank my patient parents in Germany, who were all too often deprived of my presence due to summer research obligations, and Hans Peter Schubert for his ongoing support for my endeavors.

Photograph Credits

Archives départmentales du Pas-de-Calais: Fig. 20; Author: Figs. 2, 5, 7–9, 15, 42, 44, 46; Bibliothèque Nationale de France, Paris: Pls. 1–15, 17, Figs. 10–13, 26–30, 32–34, 36–37, 39–41, 43, 45, 47–48; © Bildarchiv Preussischer Kulturbesitz, Berlin, 2005: Fig. 16; Collection Royal Army Museum, Brussels: Fig. 49;

Grand Orient de France, Paris: Fig. 18; Herzog August Bibliothek, Wolfenbüttel: Figs. 23, 31, 38; © PHOTO-THÈQUE des Musées de la Ville de Paris: Figs. 21–22 (Photos: Toumazet); Rare Book and Manuscript Library, University of Illinois at Urbana-Champaign: Fig. 14; © Réunion des Musées Nationaux/Art Resource, NY: Pl. 16, Figs. 1, 3–4, 6, 17, 24–25, 35.

Illustrations

FIGURES

Library and Archive Locations

AAE	Archives des Affaires Étrangères, Paris
ADG	Archives Départementales de la Gironde, Bordeaux
ADPC	Archives Départementales du Pas-de-Calais, Arras
AN	Archives Nationales, Paris
BML	Bibliothèque Municipale de Lyon, Lyons
BN-ASP	Bibliothèque Nationale, Site Richelieu, Département des Arts du Spectacle, Paris
BN-EST	Bibliothèque Nationale, Site Richelieu, Département des Estampes, Paris
BN-MSS, FM	Bibliothèque Nationale, Site Richelieu, Département des Manuscrits, Division occidentale, Fonds Maçonniques, Paris
BN-MUS	Bibliothèque Nationale, Site Richelieu, Département de la Musique, Paris
BN-MUS, RÉS	Bibliothèque Nationale, Site Richelieu, Département de la Musique, Réserve, Paris
BN-RDJ	Bibliothèque Nationale, Site François-Mitterand/Tolbiac, Rez-de-Jardin, Paris
BN-RDJ, RÉS	Bibliothèque Nationale, Site François-Mitterand/Tolbiac, Rez-de-Jardin, Réserve des livres rares, Paris
BVP	Bibliothèque de la Ville de Paris, Paris
CMC	Cultureel Maçonniek Centrum "Prins Frederik," Library and Archives, The Hague
ENSBA	Bibliothèque de l'École Nationale Supérieure des Beaux-Arts, Paris
GODF	Grand Orient de France, Library and Archives, Paris
MAT	Médiathèque de l'Agglomération Troyenne, Troyes
SHD-DAT	Service Historique de la Défense, Département de l'Armée de Terre, Vincennes
SHD-DM	Service Historique de la Défense, Département de la Marine, Vincennes

Introduction: The Sophisians

The official Egyptologist does not like to talk about the "enigmatic" character of Egyptian culture. He shrugs his shoulders. "Enigma? What enigma, if you please?"
—Grégoire Kolpaktchy[1]

NAPOLEON BONAPARTE'S EGYPTIAN CAMPAIGN (1798–1801) was the first systematic colonial conquest of a non-European country justified entirely by the alleged superiority of the Western social, political, and moral value system.[2] Ordered by the post-Revolutionary Directory government of France, it differentiated itself from any previous conquest in that reason and scientific scrutiny—as opposed to religion—validated the expedition intellectually. The logic and arguments advanced to justify the invasion of Egypt set the tone for a long succession of similar colonial endeavors throughout the nineteenth and early twentieth centuries.[3] In retrospect, there can be no doubt that the modern age of colonialism dawned when Napoleon first set foot on African soil near Alexandria on July 1, 1798 (fig. 1).

Despite its disastrous failure in military terms, the Egyptian campaign proved to be an enormously influential catalyst for nineteenth-century French culture. Its difficult political legacy, however, was determined by accounts of French plague deaths, the poisoning of sick soldiers on Bonaparte's personal order, and the unexpected ferocity of native resistance against the Western occupiers.[4] These "image problems" were compounded by Bonaparte's secretly abandoning his troops under the cover of darkness with a small coterie of faithful, only to overthrow the Directory government in a matter of weeks after his return in 1799 to Paris. He successfully mesmerized the French public into a collective ecstasy for all things Egyptian, which cast a veil of oblivion over the loss of his navy under the fire of Lord Nelson's British fleet in the sea battle of Aboukir, and the subsequent isolation of his invasion force consisting of military personnel, scientists, and suppliers. Roughly one-third of the 32,200 men and women who set sail for Egypt together with Bonaparte in 1798 would never return alive to Europe.[5] After securing his power base, Napoleon and his administration set out in 1802 to systematically destroy any official document related to the events of the Egyptian and Syrian campaigns.[6] While the real historical memory was thus purged, a substitute needed to be invented to take the place of the often unflattering and gruesome reality. A solution to this problem presented itself in a shift of focus from the military to the cultural conquest of Egypt. In due course, the Empire's propaganda apparatus managed not only to deflect public attention away from the military disaster at the origins of Bonaparte's political career, but also to initiate an enduring Western fascination with ancient Egyptian monuments and art. Hazed in a profound sense of mystery and incomprehension for the Western beholder, hieroglyphics, papyrus rolls, and mummies became magic fetishes in the nineteenth-century frenzy of Egyptomania. As Jurgis Baltrušaitis has pointed out, the intellectual pillars of this cultural phenomenon comprised "a vast erudition, a nostalgic passion, and the resurrection of a primordial world, where antique splendor mingles with secret and sacred writing."[7] A protean cultural event, Egyptomania first spawned an avalanche of travel descriptions penned down hastily by eyewitnesses of the campaign, then spread to official Salon paintings elevating Napoleon's Oriental conquests to the status of history painting, before metastasizing into such popular paraphernalia as theater plays and stylish decorations for chinaware.

In what follows I will be concerned with a distinct epiphenomenon of Egyptomania, namely its role as a catalyst for the revival of so-called Egyptian-rite Freemasonry in the aftermath of Napoleon's ascent to power.[8] Almost completely ignored, even by specialists in the art and political life of the Consulate, Empire, and the Restoration, surviving documents of the Egyptian-rite lodges, established in France by returning veteran military personnel and scholars from the defunct Institut d'Égypte in Cairo, cast a revealing light on how colonialism, cultural politics, and esoteric mysticism came to define the episteme of Napoleonic power.

At the cusp of the passion for Egyptianizing hermeticism and the legitimatization of Napoleon's rule through cultural conquest was the *Ordre Sacré des Sophisiens*, founded in Paris in 1800/1801. Whereas specialists in Masonic history would describe the Sophisian order as a system of rituals analogous to the "higher degrees" (*hauts grades*) of mainstream Freemasonry, it is easier to think of it as an esoteric society concerned with the mysteries of Isis.[9] At least initially,

Fig. 1 Charles Lemire, *The Disembarkation of Bonaparte in Egypt*, after 1798, black-and-white chalk drawing on blue paper, 35.5 × 45.6 cm. Lille, Musée des Beaux-Arts, inv. Pl. 1526.

so the Sophisians claimed, members were exclusively recruited from the ranks of soldiers and scholars who participated in Bonaparte's Egyptian expedition.

Almost all knowledge about the order can be gleaned from its Golden Books (*Livres d'or*), which come in the form of manuscript copies established after a now lost original document from the turn of the nineteenth century. Of the three extant transcripts, the richly illuminated Egyptian-style Golden Book of the Bibliothèque Nationale in Paris stands out for its visual splendor.[10] As will be shown in chapter 3, the manuscript was the handiwork of Marie-Nicolas Ponce-Camus, a skilled specialist in miniature painting and set designs, who frequented Jacques-Louis David's studio during the 1790s. Mimicking the "Bembine Tablet of Isis" on its cover design (pl. 1, fig. 23), it outlines in poetical conundrums and lavish gouache and ink drawings the initiation rites (pl. 4), foundation myths (pl. 2), and ethical principles of the organization (fig. 28). The BN *Livre d'or*, which grants a unique insider view of the Sophisians' Egyptianizing fantasy spectacles and Hermetic mystery rites, dates from a rather late point in the order's history of about 1819–21. By this time, the Restoration of the Bourbon monarchy had stripped many of the fervently pro-Napoleonic adepts of their positions and titles, making the Sophisian rituals effectively exercises in Bonapartist nostalgia. An inserted list of all initiates since the foundation of the order affords the opportunity to reconstruct a scholarly, artistic, and military milieu drawn from the politically, socially, and intellectually most influential circles of the Empire.

By contrast, the oldest surviving version of the *Livre d'or* is a visually unpretentious document preserved in the archives of the Grand Orient de France in Paris.[11] It was drawn when the Sophisian "Grand Pyramid" (main temple) in Paris granted charter rights to a satellite chapter in the southern port city of Toulon. The Sophisians had made provisions to spread their rituals to other cities in France by issuing charters certified as identical copies of the original Golden Book.[12] However, the charter conferred to the Toulon "Pyramid" seems to have remained an isolated case. Toulon was certainly no incidental choice for establishing a Sophisian chapter, since it was from here that Napoleon's invasion force embarked, communication with Egypt was maintained, and the returning troops were received. Although devoid of the illustrations that make the later BN version so appealing, the Golden Book in the Grand Orient collection holds significant historical interest, because it is an example of a Sophisian document that can be dated to the Empire. A *terminus ante quem* of 1813 can be established for the manuscript, based on the observation that one of the signing grand officers, Delmas de la Coste, had died following Napoleon's retreat from the Russian campaign. A comparison of the corpus of texts in the Grand Orient manuscript with that in the BN *Livre d'or* reveals a similar internal organization. But while some rare passages are identical, it is clear that the Grand Orient book presents a different and presumably earlier version of the manuscript, frequently using simpler formulations and omitting all of the highly esoteric texts from the Professorship of the Grand Mysteries degree, along with the pseudo-historical observations about ancient Egypt. The Toulon charter also lacks the extensive descriptions of Sophisian mystery rites and attributes of high officers that fill so many of the pages in the BN *Livre d'or*. A plausible explanation for these differences in canon is that the Grand Orient manuscript is a copy conforming to the no longer extant "original" Golden Book. If this hypothesis holds true, it would confirm the initiate Guerrier de Dumast's late nineteenth-century memoirs describing how the military overtones of the order under Napoleon's rule gave way to the festive and polite mystery cult of the Restoration that Ponce-Camus portrayed by 1819.[13]

A third manuscript repeats almost verbatim the corpus of texts in the BN *Livre d'or*, albeit in a somewhat different order. It was written in Ponce-Camus's hand, and its title, *cahier d'études*, or study guide for aspiring initiates, suggests a ritual purpose different from the previous two manuscripts. The *cahier d'études* is part of the *mélanges Lerouge*, a cache of Sophisian documents, presumably from the early 1820s, that was assembled by the namesake nineteenth-century Parisian collector of Masonic materials. André-Joseph-Étienne Lerouge's collection was dispersed at auction in 1835, when the *mélanges* were acquired by the German collector Georg Kloss. Upon his death, the documents were sold to Prince Frederik of the The Netherlands, who gave them to the archives of the Grand East in The Hague.[14] Besides the study guide, the *mélanges Lerouge* contain printed invitations for banquets in celebration of Sophisian women (*Fête de la Sophisienne*, February 21, 1821) and the goddess Isis (*Agape Sophisienne pour la fête d'Isis*, August 30, 1821), sample imprints of seals used by various Sophisian officers (fig. 44), and an abbreviated, handwritten history of the order. The latter component in particular is of great interest, because it was written, presumably by Lerouge himself, in the form of a memoir summarizing the contents of a personal interview with the founder of the order in Paris, Cuvelier de Trie. It remains the only testimonial of the Sophisians to an outsider about the origins and objectives of their order and its rituals.

There also exist a number of miscellaneous publications related to the order, the most important of which is the *Règlement* approved by the "Seven Sages" in September 1800.[15] This sixteen-page, pocket-format pamphlet outlines the responsibilities for aspiring members and lists the functions of Sophisian officers in an appended *Nomenclature*. Written in a harsh military style, the opuscule has the distinction of probably being the earliest surviving document related to the order.

Mention also has to be made of the Sophisians' special ties with the Masonic lodge of the *Frères Artistes*. Cuvelier de Trie had founded the lodge in 1796/97 with the help of his friends from the world of the Parisian theater. Lerouge tells us that, beginning in the early 1800s, the *Frères Artistes* were used merely as a legitimating façade to recruit new members for the Sophisians. The truth of this assertion remains difficult to determine, but unquestionably the Sophisians were, to all intents and purposes, a quirky offshoot of the *Frères Artistes*. Both groups shared the same pool of adepts, as is evident in the similarities of their membership rolls (*tableaux*), which were all but identical during the critical years around 1819.[16] The Sophisians, however, excluded those members of the regular group who failed to impress Cuvelier and his associates by their zeal, while they welcomed foreigners and travelers among their ranks—something the *Frères Artistes* did only exceptionally.

The archives of the *Frères Artistes* lodge in the Bibliothèque Nationale are of great importance for studying the Sophisians, because it was only the *Frères Artistes* who kept annual rolls of their members. The

Sophisians, on the other hand, only once, in 1819, took a census for a tableau included with the then newly established BN Golden Book. This roll lists all members since the foundation of the order, active or inactive, dead or alive. From an analysis of the *Frères Artistes* tableaux, the conclusion emerges that Cuvelier's two groups were active during the Empire period until 1813, when the impending collapse of Napoleonic rule put an end to their reunions. After a lapse of about five years, both groups were revived in 1818, but while the Sophisians fade into oblivion after Cuvelier's death in 1824, the *Frères Artistes* continued to be active until 1840. Given the extremely close ties between both groups from 1800/1801 through 1824, the *Frères Artistes* tableaux can effectively be used as a proxy to observe membership fluctuations in the Sophisian order.

This closeness also transpires from a book-length prose poem with extensive annotations entitled *La Maçonnerie*, published in 1820 by Guerrier de Dumast, a member of both the *Frères Artistes* lodge and the Sophisians, who found his cues in the Egyptianizing contents and social life of Cuvelier de Trie's organizations.[17] An army administrator and scholar of Oriental languages in the early nineteenth century, the author made himself a name in 1854, when he helped "restore" the university of Nancy. His poem was intended to cleanse Freemasonry from allegations of having sponsored the French Revolution and destroying religion, advanced by such anti-Masonic detractors as the Abbé Barruel.[18] Guerrier de Dumast's objectives amounted to an apology of Freemasonry under the Restoration, since they solicited the official support of the reinstalled Bourbon monarchy and sought to reconcile Masonic purposes with the revival of Catholicism, which frequently bordered on bigotry during these years. Later in life, Guerrier de Dumast, whose devotion to Catholicism only deepened over the years, came to regret his involvement with Cuvelier's societies and most particularly the contents of his publication. Subsequently, he would spend a great deal of time and money to buy and burn any available copies of his own book.[19] In the early 1820s, however, Cuvelier de Trie and his associates celebrated the author of *La Maçonnerie* with a gold medal and considered the book a semiofficial utterance of their organizations. Copies of the poem were given out as a prize to reward members for special achievements.[20] One rare example of such a book, inscribed with a dedication by Cuvelier de Trie to the composer of Sophisian music, Louis-Alexandre Piccinni, is preserved at the Bibliothèque Nationale. Although it was sold publicly and discussed the status of Freemasonry under the reactionary climate of

the Restoration in general terms, *La Maçonnerie* remained specific enough in its choice of themes and examples to be linked intimately to the activities of both the *Frères Artistes* lodge and the Sophisians.

The *Frères Artistes* hold a unique position in the history of Masonic organizations for yet another reason. The group presented itself as an immediate successor of the *Neuf Soeurs*, a lodge which had famously initiated Voltaire in April 1778 and elected Benjamin Franklin its *Vénérable* in May 1779, thereby giving Freemasonry the imprimatur of Enlightenment thought.[21] This prestigious derivation seems especially convincing, since at least two Sophisians, the Comte de Lacépède and Louis-Alexandre Piccinni, had ties with the *Neuf Soeurs*. The *Frères Artistes* also gained notoriety for their liberal practice of mixed male and female initiation, gallantly breaking with Masonic gender codes:

> Although the rule which forbids women admission to lodges is absolute, yet it has once been infringed under very remarkable circumstances. The lodge of *Les Frères Artistes*, presided over by Bro. Cuvelier de Trie, was giving a *fête d'Adoption*. Before the introduction of the ladies, the Brethren had begun their ordinary work. Among the visitors who were waiting in the ante-chamber was a young officer in the uniform of a major of cavalry. He was asked for his certificate. After hesitating for a moment, he handed a folded paper to the senior Deacon, who, without opening it, proceeded to take it to the Orator. This paper was an aide-de-camp's commission issued to Madame de Xaintrailles, wife of the general of that name, who, like the Demoiselles de Fernig and other Republican heroines, had distinguished herself in the wars of the sword. When the Orator read to the lodge the contents of the commission the astonishment was general. They grew excited and it was decided unanimously that the bearer should be admitted at once to the order. Madame de Xaintrailles was acquainted with the decision of the lodge and asked if she would accept the hitherto unprecedented favor. Her reply was in the affirmative. "I am a man for my country," she said, "I will be a man for my Brethren." The initiation took place, and from that time Madame de Xaintrailles often assisted in the work of the lodge.[22]

A Prussian lady whose real name was Marie Henriette Heiniken, Mme de Xaintrailles became in 1791 the common-law wife of a French general stationed in Germany, Charles-Dominique de Lauthier de Xaintrailles.[23] In 1792 she accompanied de Xaintrailles to the Sixth Batallion of Light Infantry in the Army of the Rhine and one year later was appointed his unofficial aide-de-camp. By that time she had made herself a name for military bravery. Allegedly, she helped in the capture of Prussian artillery, swam across the Rhine river, and had her left breast amputated after a fall from a horse during a cavalry exercise in 1799. When her companion was decommissioned, the two separated in 1798. On March 16, 1801 (Ventôse 15, year IX), Mme de Xaintrailles appeared before Bonaparte in the uniform of an aide-de-camp to General Abdallah Jacques de Menou, a Sophisian who commanded the Armée de l'Orient during the last phase of the Egyptian campaign. On this occasion the First Consul gave her instructions for a secret mission in Egypt and an allowance of one thousand francs. She subsequently embarked for Alexandria on board of the vessel of rear admiral Honoré Ganteaume, another Sophisian initiate, whose attempt to land in Egypt and bring relief to the beleaguered French forces was thwarted by the British. Despite this failure, Mme de Xaintrailles participated in the siege of Elba, organized by Ganteaume's squadron, and fought in an ensuing naval combat with British vessels. Upon her return to Paris and retirement from the military in the fall of 1801, she settled in the Temple district and was received about a year later by Cuvelier de Trie's lodge.

Like the *Frères Artistes*, the Sophisians admitted women as fully integrated members (pl. 5).[24] There was a female equivalent for most male officer ranks in the order, such as the five female *Isiades* corresponding to an equal number of male *Isiarques*. The BN Golden Book contains specific instructions for female initiations, which differed slightly from those administered to male candidates. Most *Sophisiennes*, however, appear to have been related to a male member, or were professionally associated with the stages of the Parisian boulevard theaters, the most likely venue for Sophisian reunions. The reverential treatment of female initiates is already implicit in the name of the order, since Sophia, the female personification of secret Gnostic wisdom, and the Isis cult of which she was part, provided the spiritual tenets of its rituals.[25]

General information about the Sophisians outside the above-mentioned sources is sparse. Nineteenth-century Masonic dictionaries frequently mention the order in passing as a curious but dusty footnote in the tangled history of secret societies during the Napoleonic age.[26] Despite the paucity of outside sources, a look at the Sophisians' tableaux confirms the group's significant cultural and political clout in early nineteenth-century Europe. The order counted within its ranks a cross-section of the intellectual élite of Bonapartist France: generals, Egyptologists, engineers, artists, architects, linguists, composers, and natural scientists.[27] Even two Marshals of the Empire, or members of Bona-

parte's shadow cabinet—Jean-Baptiste Bessière and Guillaume-Marie-Anne Brune—figured on their rolls. Notwithstanding their origins in Napoleonic militarism, the Sophisians were an eminently cosmopolitan group of Egyptophiles. They enlisted in their ranks the director of the Berlin National Theater, August Wilhelm Iffland, right along with a retired Creek Indian tribal leader of French descent named Louis Milfort, also known by his *nom de guerre* as Tastanegy, who had spent his better days as "chief of war" in Louisiana. Adventurers and soldiers of fortune from any walk of life seem to have been welcome, provided their personalities were interesting enough.[28] Even a muckraking British journalist and pamphleteer like Lewis Goldsmith, turning coat too many times to count during the early nineteenth-century propaganda wars between France and England, found an intellectual home with the Sophisians.

Perhaps the most exotic faction within the Sophisians consisted of five exiled Greek professors and intellectuals from the defunct Princely Academy of Bucharest, led by Nicolos Sava Piccolos.[29] In the early 1820s the group was canvassing French and British literary circles to muster support for the cause of Greek political independence from the Ottoman empire. Presumably introduced by the philhellenic sympathizer Guerrier de Dumast to Cuvelier's groups, Piccolos and his associates immediately sparked the French initiates' passions for the freedom fight of the culturally and politically oppressed Greeks.[30] After the outbreak of the independence war in 1821, members of Cuvelier's groups attempted to raise funds to help the Greeks purchase arms and recruit mercenaries. The engagement in the philhellenic cause, popular in French liberal and pro-Napoleonic circles alike during the Restoration, was politically sensitive, since the governments of Louis XVIII and Charles X officially supported the Ottoman Turks and supplied their armies.

The Greek émigré presence certainly added yet another colorful and exotic touch to Sophisian spectacles. A humorous snapshot of a similar gathering of Greek patriotic professors and Western philhellenic supporters comes from Sir Charles James Napier, a British military officer stationed on the Ionian islands in the Mediterranean. Napier described a reception organized in March 1819 by the English philhellenic Lord Guilford, founder of the Ionian Academy on Corfu, where Piccolos intermittently taught:

> Lord Guilford is here, a queer fish, but very pleasant. He dined with Sir Thomas, and entered the room at the head of twelve little men, professors in black, with powdered

heads, bandy legs, cocked hats under their short arms, and snuff-boxes in hand. They "louted out," flinging and scraping their little crooked legs about with great formality; then waddling, each to a chair, snuffed, coughed, hawked, blowed noses, all fiery red, gave loud umphs! stuffed their dirty colored handkerchiefs into their pockets, and sat silent, though brimful of snuff and Greek, and hoping to be full of dinner and claret. Ogling the door they remained until grub was announced, and then such scraping, such bowing, such Greek, Italian, French and German compliments! All the Greeks would speak Italian, the Italians English, the English French and Italian mixed, the French all the five languages together. . . . Here Babel began again with the confusion of tongues.[31]

Sophisians agapes of the early 1820s may not have been much different after the joining of the Greek faction, although the general confusion was certainly further enhanced by Cuvelier's Egyptianizing mysteries. Indeed, support for the Greek cause was consistent with the order's intellectual interests, since the Sophisians eagerly studied Hellenistic sources embellishing the mysterious aspects of ancient Egyptian cults and religions.

The creative mind behind the Sophisians was the playwright Cuvelier de Trie, an ex-lawyer and former military commander of an élite unit of interpreter-scouts attached directly to Napoleon's headquarters.[32] Despite his enthusiastic support for Napoleonic militarism, Cuvelier de Trie did not take part in the Egyptian expedition. Decommissioned during the Napoleonic campaign in Poland for health reasons, he returned in 1807 full-time to his established career as a prolific author of boulevard theater pieces. Cuvelier's involvement with the subcultures of stage life dated back to the early 1790s, when he wrote propaganda pieces to uphold republican morale at the most tumultuous moment of the French Revolution.[33] Later on, public opinion labeled Cuvelier de Trie a modern "Crébillon of the Boulevards," in reference to the wide popular appeal his plays enjoyed during the Empire and Restoration at the Théâtre de l'Ambigu-Comique and the Cirque Olympique in Paris.[34] Among his many claims to theatrical fame were the inventions of melodrama and its today mostly forgotten relative, mimodrama, a term describing pantomime plays with minimal text reenacting historical scenes, preferably inspired by well-documented military events such as the Egyptian campaign.[35]

Cuvelier de Trie's personal impact on the social makeup of the Sophisians is thoroughly attested by the circumstance that many initiates from the Napoleonic era were recruited from the military, while neophytes joining during the Bourbon Restoration were typically associated with the Parisian stage. Thus, for instance, in 1819 the Sophisians welcomed among their full members the co-owner of the popularly acclaimed Théâtre de l'Ambigu-Comique, Nicolas Audinot-D'Aussy, who brought along the establishment's *régisseur général*, François Varez. The Ambigu-Comique's composer, Louis-Alexandre Piccinni, was already a long-standing Sophisian, who had joined the order in 1813. There was also the professor of music, Jacques Foignet père, a retired former director of both the Théâtre des Jeunes Artistes and the Théâtre des Victoires nationales, located along the "theater mile" in the Temple district.

Cuvelier de Trie presided over the order as self-appointed "Grand Isiarque." In this capacity he commissioned Ponce-Camus to paint the Egyptianizing illustrations in the BN *Livre d'or*, which render the activities of the Sophisians during the Restoration so vivid. As they joined in greater numbers, playwrights, composers, and artists left the distinct aesthetic mark of the popular theaters on the order. The directions, stage-like settings, and décor of some of the more elaborate rituals described in the BN Golden Book therefore amalgamated the subculture of Parisian boulevard plays with Masonic traditions and Greco-Egyptian iconography.

The theatrical context of the Bourbon Restoration should not detract from the historical significance of the Sophisians as a product of the intellectual climate and officially sanctioned structures sustaining the revival of Egyptian-rite Masonry in Napoleonic France. This context raises a number of interesting problems touching on the changing fortunes of the Egyptian rite in the late eighteenth and early nineteenth centuries. The Sophisians inserted themselves into a Masonic tradition of questionable pedigree, which would have tested the tolerance of the French Masonic umbrella organization, the Grand Orient de France. Their insistence on reviving a rite of Egyptian derivation raised the specter of one of the most infamous Masonic manipulators and charlatans of the eighteenth century, Giuseppe Balsamo, better known under his alias Comte de Cagliostro, the "great Cophte."

Any historical account of Egyptian-rite Masonry will have to address Cagliostro and his dabbling in alchemy, mystery healings, and the conjuring of spirits.[36] Born and raised in one of Palermo's popular Arabic quarters, the Albergheria, Cagliostro had only cursory firsthand experience with the Near East, yet styled himself convincingly as an Oriental sage. As he toured the cities of Europe, mesmerizing rich burghers and nobility alike, he discovered that Masonic circles provided him easy access to the rich and politically influential. In 1784 Cagliostro arrived in Lyons, where he founded the first Egyptian-rite lodge by the name of *Sagesse triomphante*. During a subsequent sojourn in Strasbourg his role as self-appointed grand master of the rite earned him the confidence of Cardinal de Rohan, who made him his spiritual adviser.

The timing of Cagliostro's involvement with de Rohan was certainly unfortunate, since the cardinal would soon become embroiled in the infamous necklace affair, a scam in which de Rohan was duped into serving as middleman in the fraudulent sale of a vastly overpriced piece of jewelry to Marie-Antoinette. When the scandal broke, both Cagliostro and his patron were incarcerated in the Bastille. It took a lengthy, high-profile investigation by the *parlement* court of Paris before their innocence was established and both men were released. But the damage was done.

The aftermath of the necklace affair proved painful for all parties involved. While de Rohan retired a ruined and dishonored clergyman to Strasbourg, Marie-Antoinette's spendthrift reputation, which made the case for her execution in 1793, was henceforth permanently established with the French public. Cagliostro's infamy became legion and spread quickly across Europe by means of calumnious pamphlets, many of which satirized the Egyptian rite in order to unmask the adventurer (fig. 2). Growing debts, endless litigations, and public slander made Cagliostro a persona non grata during an odyssey that led him from London to Basel. In a desperate move, he and his wife finally turned to Rome, where Cagliostro hoped to receive the pope's blessing for the amalgamation of Roman Catholicism with his Egyptian rite. The move had tragic consequences for him, since he was arrested and tried by the Holy Inquisition. His death penalty was commuted to life imprisonment in the Castel San Leo near Urbino, where Cagliostro died in 1795 as a mad prisoner of the Vatican, leaving behind the quack legacy of Egyptian-rite masonry.

The fortunes of the Egyptian rite took an unexpected turn in 1798, when the Directory government sent Bonaparte to invade Egypt in a move to weaken Great Britain by cutting her off from India. The colonizing of Egypt was chosen as a military alternative to attacking Britain directly, a strategy ultimately dismissed as too risky. Instead, the planners of the Egyptian campaign dusted off speculative theories by Enlightenment thinkers such as Leibniz and Voltaire, who envisioned Egypt as a model colony where the rule of alleged Oriental despotism could be broken by replacing it with a Western value system based on rea-

son, rationalism, and positivism.[37] The benefits of the enterprise were twofold: a colonized Egypt was supposed to improve the quality of life of its subjects and promised economic rewards to the colonizer. But first, to quote Edward Said, Egypt had to be rendered "completely open to make it totally accessible to European scrutiny."[38]

To this end Bonaparte took along more than 150 of France's most distinguished mathematicians, zoologists, geologists, geographers, architects, artists, antiquarians, and archeologists when he embarked for Egypt.[39] Soon after the initial phase of the invasion, these *savants* were organized to form the Institut d'Égypte, which assumed the role of a clearinghouse for the intellectual conquest of Egypt that was to parallel the military occupation. The investigative activities of the institute, however, were cut short by the campaign's military failure. When General Abdallah Jacques de Menou negotiated the conditions for the surrender of Egypt to the allied British-Ottoman forces in 1801, he insisted that the remaining *savants* be allowed to take along the collections and documents of the Institut d'Égypte during the evacuation.[40]

As the veteran soldiers and scholars trickled back into France between 1799 and 1801, some of their most prominent leaders revived the secret Masonic societies and rituals that they had created in Egypt based on their discoveries of Pharaonic monuments, artifacts, and documents. They encountered a cultural climate supportive of their interests. During the Empire, Masonry rose from clandestine obscurity to the rank of a protected, semiofficial institution. As François Collaveri points out, Napoleon himself saw to it that Masonry enjoyed a "prosperity and prestige that it never previously could have claimed."[41] Ever since Bonaparte's return from Egypt in 1799, rumors circulated that the First Consul and later Emperor had joined Masonry during his campaigns in the Near East. Allegedly, both he and his designated successor, General Jean-Baptiste Kléber, founded in 1798 the Isis Lodge in Cairo, which catered to officers, scholars, and high-ranking Egyptian collaborators.[42] Whether or not such rumors were correct to the letter mattered little as long as the public believed in them. In any case, Napoleon and his administration had no interest in dispelling the hearsay, since they took an active interest in rallying the political support of Masonic organizations for the Napoleonic cause.

While Bonaparte thus polished his image as the new patron saint of Freemasonry, a panoply of lodges, rites, and orders emerged that paralleled or competed with the Sophisians' claim to ancient Oriental descent. The

Fig. 2 James Gillray, *A Masonic Anecdote*, [Satire on Cagliostro's Attempt to Found an Egyptian Masonic Lodge in London], 1786, etching, 50.4 × 44.8 cm.

Fig. 3 Antoine-Jean Gros, *Bonaparte among the Plague-Stricken at Jaffa*, 1804, oil on canvas, 532 × 720 cm. Paris, Musée du Louvre.

Loge Impérial des Chevaliers de Saint-Jean-d'Acre, for instance, derived its appeal from deliberately conflating Crusader mysticism with military nostalgia for the siege of Acre that had stalled Napoleon's campaign into Syria. At the installation of the lodge in 1806, its second orator, one Roettier de Montaleau, recalled the miraculous rescue of the head of the lodge, a soldier named Jeanin, by none other than Napoleon himself: "It was during the attack of this famous place [Acre] that the brave Jeanin was covered with injuries; injuries which would have been fatal, if the hand of a genius had not rescued him. It was the benevolent hand of a brother, the hand of a general, the hand of the French Emperor, the great Napoleon, who dispelled through his care the tenebrous veil that threatened to deprive us of our brother, our friend, our honorary *Vénérable* Jeanin."[43] The scene of Jeanin's miraculous rescue and healing is evocative of Jean-Antoine Gros's masterwork *Bonaparte among the Plague-Stricken at Jaffa* (fig. 3), presented to the pub-

lic in the Salon of 1804, two years prior to the lodge's installation. In Gros's composition "the sick among the French seem almost to rise by magic to make contact with their leader; dominating the foreground, by contrast, are the shadowed figures of those dead and dying deprived of that touch."[44] Napoleon's dramatic appearance as thaumaturgical savior suggests the possibility of a miraculous rescue from the bubonic plague by his healing touch, much like Jeanin was saved before Acre from succumbing to his wounds. As the example of the Knights of Acre shows, the legend of Napoleon's Near Eastern conquests was woven into the very fabric of the rituals of many of these newly established Masonic organizations.

The *Loge Impérial des Chevaliers de Saint-Jean-d'Acre* shared an ephemeral fate with other Orientalizing secret societies that sprang up at the time, such as the *Souveraine Pyramide des Amis du Désert*, founded by the archeologist Alexandre Dumègue in

Toulouse in the early 1800s, or the *Disciples de Memphis*, established in Montauban in 1814 as an alleged successor to the Isis Lodge of Cairo.[45] It is only with the Sophisians that the revival of Egyptian-rite Masonry during the Empire as a distinct cultural phenomenon comes into clearer focus across the distance of time. Given the social standing of its members, the Sophisians emerge not only as the most prestigious Egyptian-rite esoteric society, but also the earliest and longest-lived, ceasing activity only sometime during the Restoration in the mid-1820s. The relative longevity of the Sophisians may perhaps be explained by the visual splendor of their rituals, as conveyed to us through the BN Golden Book, which helped promote the loyalty of its members.

From the perspective of Orientalism the emergence of Egyptian-style mystery rites represents an interesting phenomenon. Here, suddenly, the positivist discourse of the Orientalist scholar and colonial administrator is disrupted by an undercurrent of superstition and irrationality. Some of the Sophisians have written, drawn, and published the most tersely factual travel descriptions conceivable for the genre. They were members of learned societies whose objective discourse pretended to make the scientific penetration and opening of the Orient possible. Yet, after hours, they used this knowledge to bestow authenticity upon secret societies that inverted positivist transparency and celebrated an occult mysticism.

The practical experiences of the Egyptian campaign may account for this unexpected re-enchantment with metaphysics. Even for the members of the Institut d'Égypte, founded for the express purpose of "promoting progress and Enlightenment in Egypt,"[46] the daily challenges of cultural misunderstandings blurred the strict division between reason and superstition. Consider for instance the following passage from Antoine Galland's *Tableau de l'Égypte pendant le séjour de l'armée française* describing the difficulties of the artist and *savant* Michel Rigo in introducing Western portrait painting to Egypt:

A while ago a caravan from Nubia arrived in Cairo, which habitually carries, other than the slaves for commercial dealings, ostrich feathers, ivory tusks, tamarind, and gold powder. The citizen Rigo resolved to paint its chieftain, whose Nubian character was strongly imprinted on his appearance. He used all possible means to lure him to his studio, and finally succeeded in doing so. Initially, the Nubian seemed much content with his pencil drawing; he pointed out with his finger those parts of the design that corresponded to his face, while crying out: "Tayeb!"—"Good!" But when the painter proceeded to put color to the drawing, the sitter hardly looked at it before stepping back repulsed, emitting terrible screams. It was impossible to calm him down, and he ran away head over heels, telling everywhere that he came from a house where one had taken away his head and half of his body. A female slave from the same region, who belonged to a Frenchman, was made by her master to have her portrait painted. As the artist completed the head, the shoulders, etc., she asked him incensed: "Why do you take away my head? Why do you remove my shoulders?" These people are convinced that any part of the body represented on canvas will dry out. Those who had been to the studio of the citizen Rigo spread the rumor that they had seen cut-off heads and body parts at a Frenchman's place. These things helped to promote the impression among the Egyptians that the members of the Institute were Bonaparte's sorcerers.[47]

Rigo accompanied the expedition as its official portrait painter and was admitted in this capacity to the literature and arts section of the Institut d'Egypte. Upon the artist's arrival in Cairo Napoleon commissioned him to paint a series of oil portraits of allied Arabic chieftains to decorate his headquarters housed in the palace of an ousted Mameluke by the name of Elfy-bey, which display a distinct interest in ethnographic typology (fig. 4).[48] As trophies of colonial conquest these portraits were intended to serve as both scientific evidence and historical records, since we have similar studies of racial types reproduced in etchings from Vivant Denon's *Voyage dans la Basse et la Haute Egypte* that catalog and explain the ethnographic diversity of the country (fig. 5).

To the extent that the scientific purpose of Rigo's portrait sessions was perverted by native cultural resistance into exercises of Bonapartist sorcery, epistemological certainties began to evaporate. The Sophisians represent a similar moment in the cultural history of colonialism where Western reason, rationality, and empiricism live in a dangerously close symbiosis with the superstition, mysticism, and occultism typically identified with the Oriental "Other." As such, the study of their order affords an opportunity to investigate one of those "borderline engagements of cultural difference," which, according to Homi K. Bhabha, "may as often be consensual as conflictual; they may confound our definitions of tradition and modernity; realign the customary boundaries between the private and the public, high and low; and challenge normative expectations of development and progress."[49]

Although the Sophisians were without exception part of a socially, economically, and politically privileged class, their deliberate meddling in cultural subtexts for

Fig. 4 Michel Rigo, *Sheikh Guerguess El-Gohari*, after 1798, oil on canvas, 80 × 66 cm. Rueil-Malmaison, Musée National des Châteaux de Malmaison et Bois-Préau.

their own sake—inclusion of women in a men's society, cave dwellings reminiscent of primitive Egyptian abodes, magic as a means for achieving Enlightenment—tells a story different from that of official Orientalist discourse. Underneath the self-assured veneer of colonial pomp and circumstance, latent psychological trapdoors of loss, uncertainty of purpose, and shifting identities are lurking. In a revealing confessional addendum towards the very end of the BN Golden Book, radical doubts gain the upper hand. After the anonymous author—almost certainly Cuvelier de Trie himself—finishes explaining the secret rebuses and mottos of the order, he concludes by striking a tone of Gnostic pessimism about the human condition:

Fig. 5 Vivant Denon, *Head Studies*, etchings, 9.8 × 17.8 and 8.9 × 17.0 cm. From *Voyage dans la Basse et la Haute Égypte*, Pl. 107.i–ii., 1802.

If life is nothing but a test, a passage; if Nature's great movements are to destroy and reconstruct in preparation for things to come; if death is the true guide; if every bit of matter returns inevitably to feed on the mass of its similars: Why does the spark called spirit or soul not enjoy the same privilege? . . . Disciple, follow me, form the triangle of initiation with your fingers so that your companion may put his index finger there. This is the figure of the Hierogrammatist: fire, matter, spirit or movement, the triangle of creation; theos, one in three, in the center . . . do you understand me? No. Well, Agent, Patient, Product . . . Osiris, Isis, Horus—These should be your words.[50]

The anticlimax comes at the least expected moment, when tension is at the highest pitch for the ultimate revelation. Upon realizing his inability to communicate the ancient Egyptian mysteries in all their profundity, the anachronism of his quest simply collapsed on the author. What is left from the rubble is not so much greater spiritual insight, but the painful vacuity of an unfulfilled promise to implant ancient Oriental mysticism in a modern world order that validated knowledge primarily as a function of political and economic interests.

1

Some Sophisian Precursors: Comte de Cagliostro, Vivant Denon, and Benjamin de Laborde

All light comes from the Orient;
all initiation from Egypt.
—Cagliostro, *Mémoire*[1]

EARLY IN SEPTEMBER 1783 THE FRENCH *CHARGÉ D'AFFAIRES* at the court of Naples, Vivant Denon, received a difficult guest. With barely disguised pride he reported to his superiors in the remote Parisian Ministry of Foreign Affairs that "Comte de Cagliostro, famous for his unique ways and praiseworthy for the healings he administers and his generosity in dispensing medicine, has been in town for some days. Until now he has avoided all contact and wanted to see no one but the *chargé d'affaires* of France."[2] Inconspicuously inserted among diplomatic gossip, Denon's note seems oddly out of place and self-contradictory. If Cagliostro is indeed famous, praiseworthy, and generous, why is he hiding? And why did he want to see just Denon and nobody else?

The official reprimand was quick, terse, and acerbic. It came from none other than the French foreign minister, the Comte de Vergennes, a long-standing personal friend of Denon and himself an ardent admirer of Cagliostro not too long before: "From what you are telling me about your connection to this person [Cagliostro], I understand that it would be in his best interest to appear in good standing with a man reporting to the Minister of France and that you could have abetted one of his dirty tricks. You could have avoided this inconvenience if you had heeded in your attitude towards him the basic rule for everybody employed in the foreign services of the King not to receive any visitors, except for those recommended, whose entreaties one is allowed to answer."[3] Caught off guard, Denon tried to play down the incident as well as he could. He pointed out that Cagliostro had been to Naples for "relaxation" and that his guest wanted to see only him and "some patients I introduced to him in my own quarters and in secret."[4] Besides, he asserted, the count had already left Naples and was now en route to Paris. Whether out of ignorance or by calculation, Denon was mistaken about the true destination of Cagliostro, who resurfaced next in Antibes, Montpellier, and

Bordeaux. From there he continued on to the "capital of Freemasonry," Lyons, where on October 26, 1784, he would found the mother lodge of the Egyptian rite called *Sagesse triomphante*.[5]

De Vergennes was right, of course, in that Comte de Cagliostro meant trouble. When he arrived in Naples from Strasbourg in 1783, the magician was already implicated in the events that would culminate before long in the necklace affair, which incriminated his protector, the Cardinal de Rohan, and incensed the compromised Queen Marie-Antoinette. Although Cagliostro had no direct dealings with Mme de la Motte, who conspired to steal the necklace, he found himself imprisoned in the Bastille, together with de Rohan, for nine long months based on her accusations. Only a lengthy investigation in 1785 revealed that de la Motte had tricked de Rohan into secretly buying the diamond necklace in the queen's name from the court jewelers, Böhmer and Bassange, for the unheard-of sum of 1,600,000 livres, and that she had arranged for a female impersonator of Marie-Antoinette to perfect the cardinal's deception.[6] The scandal broke at the moment when Cagliostro had just graduated from mystery healer to self-proclaimed "Grand Cophte" of the Egyptian rite, and so his recent dabbling in Near Eastern mysticism made him an easy scapegoat in the proceedings initiated by Louis XVI and his wife. Inevitably, as Cagliostro's reputation was tainted, the Egyptian rite itself became associated with charlatanism and shady manipulations, which led to an exodus of his newly acquired converts.

As for Denon, Cagliostro probably fascinated him for the same reasons that attracted him to Sophisian Masonic circles at the very end of his life. Always elusive but always close to the centers of power, Denon never hesitated to explore fringe experiences. Like Cagliostro, he was a polymath accustomed to wearing many masks: diplomat, writer, traveler, printmaker, collector, museum administrator, and finally Mason.[7] A courtier under Louis XV and a spying diplomat under

Louis XVI, Denon was inscribed in the list of artisto-cratic émigrés during the early phase of the Revolution, which he experienced from safe exile as an independent graphic artist in Venice. But his peace of mind did not last for long. The spies of the Serenissima's State Inquisition accused him of Revolutionary sympathies, Masonic activities, and contacts with the dissenting Enlightenment circles of local patricians, which resulted in his expulsion from Venice by 1793. (Oddly enough, they never seem to have bothered with his flourishing production of pornographic prints.) Through the intervention of the Revolutionary painter Jacques-Louis David, Denon's name was cleared in France, and he began to work as *graveur de la République* in the service of Robespierre's Terror regime. After the fall of the tyrant, he resurfaced during the Directory as one of the *savants* of the Egyptian campaign, an experience that inspired him to publish one of the earliest travel accounts of the expedition. A grateful Napoleon rewarded him in 1802 with an appointment as director general of the Louvre and all French museums, which quickly earned Denon the nickname *emballeur de l'Europe*, owing to his efficiency in despoiling Europe's princely art collections wherever Napoleon's troops marched. The emperor's fall from power divested him of his official positions but left his social reputation unharmed. Denon died in 1825 as a celebrated writer and art collector in Paris.

At the beginning of Denon's twisted career path across the antechambers of kings and dictators, artists' studios, and Masonic temples stood a man who could pass for a personification of the ancien régime itself. Jean-Benjamin de Laborde was a *fermier général* and the first valet to Louis XV's chamber at Versailles, but he spent most of his days neither collecting taxes nor rendering services to the king. An amateur composer and musicologist with a considerable publication record, Laborde harbored a penchant for a life of unbridled luxury far beyond his means, which he only occasionally interrupted for bouts of experiments in alchemy. While passing through Strasbourg in 1781, the latter foible drove him directly into Cagliostro's arms.[8] Under the spell of the Grand Cophte's charisma Laborde jettisoned common sense with remarkable bravura:

> Nobody knows where he [Cagliostro] comes from, what he is, where he is going. Beloved, cherished, and respected by the local commanders and the heads of town, adored by the destitute and the little people, [he] spends his life seeing the sick, above all the poor, to whom he distributes medicine for free. He eats very little, mostly Italian pasta; he never goes to bed and only sleeps about two to three hours in his chair. Finally, always ready to fly to the rescue of the sick at whatever time of the day, he has no other pleasure but to help his fellows. This man lives an incredible lifestyle, which is the more surprising since he pays for everything in advance, and one neither knows the source of his revenues nor who provides him with money. . . . It is easy to see why one cracks jokes at his expense: he is at least the Anti-Christ; he is five or six hundred years old; he is in possession of the philosopher's stone, the universal medicine. . . . Nobody has more *esprit* and knowledge than he does; he speaks almost all the languages of Europe and Asia and his eloquence is amazing and convincing, even in those he commands less well.[9]

Soon the conversation with Cagliostro turned to the mysteries of the pyramids of ancient Egypt, a particular interest of Laborde's, who believed that a Rosicrucian assembly used to be held annually inside the monuments.[10] Cagliostro, for his part, appreciated the influential position of his interlocutor at least as much as his esoteric insights, and remembered him when he extended his network of Egyptian-rite lodges beyond Lyons. Key to this plan was the Parisian lodge, which was installed in 1785 with Laborde as "grand inspector in the Supreme Council" and his brother-in-law, Jacques de Vismes de Valgay, as its "grand secretary." Although the necklace affair made the name Cagliostro synonymous with royal vexation, Laborde remained loyal to his "dear master" until 1787. In April of that year, together with de Valgay, he undertook a trip to London, where he intended to question Cagliostro about recent revelations in the press identifying him as Giuseppe Balsamo, a shady adventurer born in Palermo in 1743. Clearly Laborde and his travel companion preferred not to believe in these allegations, but upon arriving in England they learned that Cagliostro had recently fled the country under mysterious circumstances. He had left behind his poverty-stricken wife, who confirmed their worst suspicions. Disabused of the Grand Cophte's freely invented pseudo-Oriental biography, they returned to Paris where they joined the ranks of Cagliostro's royal persecutors. With Laborde and his brother-in-law, the Egyptian rite lost its two most influential promoters in France, whose defection would bring about the collapse of the rite's pivotal Paris chapter.[11]

VIVANT DENON

During the ancien régime Denon was Laborde's protégé at Versailles. Legend has it that Denon found a particularly ingenious way of attracting Louis XV's

Fig. 6 Noël Halle, *The Race of Hippomenes and Atalanta*, 1765, oil on panel, 320 × 700 cm. Paris, Musée du Louvre.

attention. The king seldom granted audiences, but petitioners could readily address him as he walked through the large *Galerie des Glaces* of Versailles twice a day at a set time. Denon would position himself repeatedly at the same spot but refrained from accosting the king.[12] Finally Louis XV stopped and asked what he wanted. "To see you, Sire," was the audacious answer, which baffled the king. "What! You have nothing to ask of me; you desire nothing?" "No, Sire, unless it is to be able to escape from the bayonets and guards who prevent me from approaching you." Denon's rhetorical trap had snapped, and it turned the tables in the discourse of power. By starting the conversation and asking the questions, the king had unwittingly assumed the role of the supplicant that Denon so strongly disavowed.

Although almost certainly fictitious, the legend is compelling to the last detail because the Hall of Mirrors at Versailles was a performance ground for those seeking advancement by currying royal favors. Mme de la Motte, for instance, refined to perfection her skills at fainting on cue upon Marie-Antoinette's passage until the queen's sister-in-law, Madame Élisabeth, put an end to the spectacle by having the finance minister double the supplicant's pension.[13] By contrast, a prosaic, yet more convincing account of Denon's debut at court maintains that Laborde simply introduced him to Louis XV in 1769.[14]

At the beginning of the next stage of Denon's career at Versailles, we find Laborde issuing him a passport for the royal gardens and apartments. As the scene unfolds, Denon received the mellifluous title *Gentil-*

homme ordinaire du roi and was appointed Royal Curator of the recently deceased Mme de Pompadour's collection of minerals, antique gems, and medals. The king had assembled the collection for his mistress in order to help along her experiments as amateur engraver and decided to keep it for sentimental reasons after her death in 1764. Denon's ambitions as an artist and printmaker, along with a short stint in the studio of the painter Noël Halle in the late 1760s, provided him with the minimum qualifications for the charge. Halle's facility at bridging the gap between Rococo style and classical iconography (Fig. 6), enhanced by the antiquarian connoisseurship and exposure to printmaking techniques acquired in Mme de Pompadour's *cabinet*, defined Denon's aesthetic sensibility during the 1770s.[15]

Under Laborde's tutelage Denon used these opportunities for political advancement. His ability to recast boring, factual narratives into humorous anecdotes endeared him to the morose king, who used to snap at less gifted courtiers: "Tell that to Denon, he will repeat it to me this evening."[16] But Denon must have sensed that Louis XV's reign would soon come to an end. In 1772 he arranged to join the French mission at Catherine II's court at Saint Petersburg, which resulted in the first of his misadventures in diplomacy. Expelled from Russia after an ill-fated attempt to liberate an imprisoned actress, Denon returned to France in 1774 endowed with a pension from the recently deceased king.[17]

In the years to come the relationship between the two courtiers, Denon and Laborde, remained close.

When the latter published a selection of his prolific output of operas, epigrams, and songs, the frontispiece of his *Choix de chansons* featured a portrait of the author with the poetic title *Laborde à la lyre* (fig. 7).[18] The print was based on a Denon drawing, which had been engraved in 1774 by François-Denis Née and Louis-Joseph Masquelier. A vanity publication, the *Choix de chansons* volumes contained Laborde's compositions for the musical society of the *Caveau*, or Cave, "an illustrious and Bacchic society for singing" originally founded in 1733 by the popular playwrights Alexis Piron and Crébillon fils.[19] The Caveau's social activities centered on communal meals held in the cabaret of Landel that assured filled stomachs and helped sustain the Bohemian lifestyle of its more destitute members. The playwright and *encyclopédiste* Jean-François Marmontel, for instance, invoked the spirit of the Caveau in his description of the bon-vivant singer Panard, who "forgot about the past as easily as he neglected the future. In his misfortune [he had] more of the tranquility of a child than the indifference of a philosopher. Worries about food, lodging, or clothing did not concern him; this was the business of his friends, and they were good enough that he could count on them."[20] The Caveau indeed deserved the epithet illustrious, because it counted among its members the Rococo painter François Boucher, along with the influential connoisseur and antiquarian Comte de Caylus, a self-proclaimed initiate to the mysteries of Isis and Osiris, whose company Denon had sought out in the 1760s as a first step in advancing his artistic ambitions.[21] In the spirit of the Masonic societies introduced to France from Britain in 1725, the Caveau excluded women from its meals and celebrated music as a bond among its members. Denon's ingenious idea of framing his benefactor's portrait by a lyre—a well-known Masonic symbol for universal harmony—thus seems to anticipate Laborde's later involvement with Masonry in more than one respect.[22]

By August 1775 Denon had another one of his drawings engraved by Née and Masquelier, this time depicting Laborde's pregnant wife in a landscape setting (fig. 8). The print's unusual iconography shows her accompanied by a lap dog, symbol of marital fidelity, thereby demonstrating Denon's intimate familiarity with the Laborde household.[23] The work emerged in the aftermath of Denon's infamous visit to the exiled philosopher Voltaire in Switzerland, which Laborde had helped to arrange in July 1775. Upon completion of a secret diplomatic mission in that country, Denon contrived from Geneva an ingenious plan to gain access to the ailing Enlightenment thinker, who resided nearby on his Ferney estate. Denon had asked Laborde

Fig. 7 Louis-Joseph Masquelier after a drawing by Vivant Denon from 1770, *Laborde à la lyre*, 1774, engraving, 14.3 × 9.5 cm. From Jean-Benjamin de Laborde, *Choix de chansons mises en musique*, second ed., vol. 1, Rouen, 1881. Baton Rouge, Special Collections, LSU Libraries.

for a letter of introduction to the philosopher, whom the composer had befriended when setting one of his theater pieces to music.[24] Impatience for the arrival of Laborde's letter, however, inspired Denon to write directly to Voltaire:

Monsieur,

I have an infinite desire to render you homage. You may be sick, and that is exactly what I fear: I feel also that frequently you want to be [sick], and this is what I do not want you to be at this moment. I am Gentleman in Ordinance to the King, and you know better than anybody that one never refuses us an [open] door. I am claiming herefore every privilege to have the padlocks removed.[25]

Flavored with a tone of insolence, Denon's insistence on being received by Voltaire was inspired by the will to

Fig. 8 François-Denis Née and Louis-Joseph Masquelier after Vivant Denon, *Madame Laborde Pregnant*, 1775, engraving, 15.7 × 10.2 cm. From Jean-Benjamin de Laborde, *Choix de chansons mises en musique*, second ed., vol. 2, Rouen, 1881. Baton Rouge, Special Collections, LSU Libraries.

associate his name with that of the famous philosopher, an asset of social prestige that did not fail to impress Napoleon, among others, later in Denon's career. The ruse succeeded. Voltaire welcomed the diplomat-courtier at Ferney on July 4, 1777, but he soon came to regret his hospitality. Upon Laborde's request, Denon sketched portraits of the philosopher, which he had engraved after his return to Paris. There, they gained instant notoriety because of their caricature-like qualities.[26]

Voltaire was not amused to see himself depicted as an "emaciated monkey."[27] Vanity obsessed him in his old age more than ever, as he fought a losing battle against the numerous prints and pamphlets that portrayed him as an anorexic skeleton. One print in particular enraged the philosopher: Denon's *Déjeuné de Ferney* features an oval composition that depicts Voltaire in bed dressed in a nightgown and surrounded by his entourage (fig. 9). He is flanked on the left by Père Adam, an "enlightened" Jesuit who lived on the Ferney estate, and on the right by Mme Denis, Voltaire's niece and mistress, as well as their chambermaid Agathe. In the foreground, lounging in a salon chair, the artist introduced a feisty Laborde, who conspicuously replaces Denon as Voltaire's visitor in the composition.[28] Denon left the disgruntled Enlightenment philosopher no other choice but to accept the fait accompli of the print.

BENJAMIN DE LABORDE

Meanwhile, Laborde had arranged a new job for Denon that would take him to southern Italy before the end of the year. The death of Louis XV in 1774 and the subsequent loss of his official position at court had left Laborde, a notoriously indebted gambler, with much reduced revenues. To remedy this situation, he envisioned a future as an entrepreneur, editing, publishing, and writing illustrated travel descriptions. He conceived of a grandiose project for *Tableaux topographiques, pittoresques, historiques, moraux, politiques, littéraires, de la Suisse et de l'Italie* containing no fewer than twelve hundred engravings—two hundred per volume—executed "after drawings by MM. Robert, Pérignon, Fragonard, Paris, Poyet, Raymond, Le Barbier, Barthélemy, Ménagot, Le May, Houel, etc., and the most able masters of Italy."[29] The publication was ambitious not only in its geographical scope, but also in the range of subjects covered, which included classical archeology, political economy, and natural sciences. For a man who had recently emerged from a particularly tangled case of personal bankruptcy, the project was indeed audacious. To realize it, Laborde needed financially potent partners who could advance the money needed to send the artists to Italy, to provide them with materials, and to satisfy the demands of the printers.

Laborde found a solution to this dilemma in the persons of the Abbé de Saint-Non and his older brother Louis-Richard de la Bretèche.[30] Saint-Non enjoyed a distinct notoriety in France as a clergyman who tended to foresake at his convenience the teachings of the church for those of the philosophes. In 1752 he had been exiled to Poitiers, together with other oppositional *parlementaires*, for his resistance to registering a papal bull. His political ambitions frustrated, Saint-Non turned his attention to traveling and to publishing philosophically inspired travelogues. After visiting Britain, Holland, and Flanders, he set out between 1759

Fig. 9 François-Denis Née and Louis-Joseph Masquelier after a watercolor by Vivant Denon, *Le Déjeuné de Ferney*, 1775, engraving, 13.7 × 17.3 cm. From Gustave Desnoiresterres, *Iconographie Voltairienne*, 1879.

and 1761 on an extended sojourn to Italy in the company of his favored painters, Jean-Honoré Fragonard and Hubert Robert. On this trip he passed through Ferney and joined the seemingly endless stream of foreign visitors paying homage to Voltaire. A skilled draftsman and printmaker, Saint-Non was in a privileged position to appreciate the rich visual potential of an illustrated Italian travel description.

Saint-Non was exactly the kind of business partner for which Laborde was looking. The abbé had both the intellectual background and the means to support his project. Saint-Non's financial position was secured by the banking interest of his family and a *commendam* (annuity) he received from his abbey in Poultères. In fact, the revenues generated by this abbey alone were

sufficient to cover the entirety of the expenditures incurred by the costly enterprise of sending an expedition of artists to Italy. The entrepreneurs agreed to begin the Italian volumes of the series with scenes from the southern Italian kingdom of Naples and Sicily.

Upon Laborde's suggestion, Denon was appointed artistic director of the expedition. Endowed with thirty thousand livres from Saint-Non's family, Denon left Marseilles for Naples in the fall of 1777. He was accompanied by his aged private teacher, the Abbé Buisson, who would be the interpreter for the expedition, and the painter Claude-Louis Châtelet. Upon arrival, he assembled Laborde's hand-picked crew of graphic artists, including Fragonard, Robert, and Claude-Joseph Vernet, and, after exploring the newly excavated sites

Fig. 10 Vivant Denon after Jean-Honoré Fragonard, *Satyr and Goat*, ca. 1778–85, etching, 7.7 × 10.8 cm. Paris, Bibliothèque National de France, Département de l'Estampe.

of Pompeii and Herculaneum, then ventured into the terra incognita of Sicily's hinterland, before concluding with a trip to Malta.

For Denon the experience was fruitful on more than one account. He expanded his artistic skills by learning how to etch copper plates, frequently reproducing Fragonard's compositions, as in the rendition of a classical fresco uncovered in Herculaneum of a satyr and goat in sexual congress (fig. 10).[31] The idea of using a wide selection of plates to breathe visual life into a travel account with claims to scientific exactitude certainly influenced the formal presentation of his own *Voyage dans la Basse et la Haute Égypte*, published in 1802 after his return from the Egyptian campaign. The expedition to southern Italy also gave Denon an understanding of how a large, cooperative enterprise involving a multitude of artists should be organized, which later qualified him as Napoleon's premier art administrator.

Denon's accomplishments notwithstanding, the project was riddled with problems that originated from the increasingly troubled relationship between Laborde and his financers back in France. Saint-Non and his brother quickly realized that the benefits in their partnership were skewed to Laborde's advantage. The latter had contributed a pittance of ten thousand livres to finance the project but was supposed to draw half of the projected revenues. Laborde's reasoning that his "in-kind contributions" of previously executed drawings would make up for his default in matching the brothers' venture capital became difficult to maintain as the financial burden from the project grew. Moreover, Laborde was initially supposed to write the text for the volumes, which would have assured him all the intellectual credit associated with the enterprise.[32] Laborde, however, had relied on Denon to keep a diary as the source for the text he agreed to provide. Saint-Non, in turn, rejected

Denon's travelogue, allegedly because it was crude and lacked proper editing.

ENCOUNTER IN NAPLES

At this point the falling out was inevitable. Saint-Non was in a stronger position because he continued to hold the purse strings. Beginning in 1780, the abbé published under his own name five volumes entitled *Voyage pittoresque dans les royaumes de Naples et de Sicile*, this time showing no scruples when it came to plagiarizing Denon's text.[33] Back in Naples, meanwhile, Denon had depleted the seed money for the expedition, but managed to secure a new job as secretary to the French embassy by the spring of 1779.[34] At least initially he seems to have tolerated Saint-Non's appropriation out of respect for his new diplomatic charge. During the following years, however, he published, to Saint-Non's dismay, two books to restore his claim to the authorship of the travel description. In the first instance Laborde played a pivotal role, indicating that the friendship between the two courtiers emerged intact from the controversy with the financers. Upon Laborde's instigation Denon hired the English traveler Henry Swinburne to translate and edit his travel diaries, which were published in London between 1783 and 1784 as *Travels in the Two Sicilies*.[35] Not content with the French-language edition that Laborde began to market under Swinburne's name a year later, Denon redressed the situation in 1788 by publishing his text for a fourth time in Paris—now under his own name as *Voyage en Sicile*.[36] Since Saint-Non retained access and rights to the illustrations and plates, both Swinburne's translation and Denon's Paris edition lacked the prints that made Saint-Non's publication so visually appealing.

The resumption of Denon's diplomatic career in Naples rekindled his interest in the art and culture of classical antiquity and introduced him to southern Italian Masonic circles. The cultural and political situation Denon encountered in Naples was in many ways unique. An extensive selection of eighteenth-century "enlightened" travel literature on the Kingdom of the Two Sicilies invariably depicted the punchinello monarchy at the court of Naples as an observatory for the governmental and social evils of old regime absolutism.[37] For the better part of the eighteenth century, Naples had been ruled remotely by either Austria or Spain, and both administrations thought it sufficient to appoint viceroys to govern the city and its hinterland. This arrangement came to an end in 1759, when Ferdi-

nand IV, then eight years of age, acceded to the throne of the Kingdom of the Two Sicilies. During Ferdinand's minority the law professor and jurist Bernardo Tanucci managed everyday governmental affairs and oversaw the upbringing of the king. To protect his power base as de facto vice-monarch, Tanucci treated the king's education with deliberate negligence. Socially inept, barely literate, and unable to express himself other than in the base Neapolitan jargon of the local underclass, the adult king preferred hunting over interfering with Tanucci's government business. His oversized, deformed nose made him an easy target for caricaturists and earned him the nickname "il nasone."

Tanucci's corrupt and socially repressive regime came to an end only after Ferdinand married Marie-Antoinette's older sister, Marie-Caroline of Austria, who succeeded in disposing of her husband's eminence grise in October 1776.[38] The queen's desperation over her coarse husband and the general backwardness of her kingdom translated into raging envy of her younger sister's lot and a passionate hatred for France. To Tanucci's dismay, Marie-Caroline explored Freemasonry as one of the few outlets available for intellectual diversion and the exchange of Enlightenment ideas. Instrumental in the queen's discovery of Freemasonry may have been her lover, Sir John Acton. The son of an Irish surgeon practicing in Besançon, Acton shared Marie-Caroline's hatred for the French because he had been dishonorably discharged from their navy. After selling his services to various small Italian principalities, Acton arrived in 1778 in Naples, where he introduced Masonry and convinced the queen to have him appointed Minister of the Neapolitan navy. Marie-Caroline's patronage of Masonic societies secured them from the violent persecutions prevalent in other parts of Italy, turning Naples into an unlikely haven for Masonic tolerance.

In this situation Paris withdrew its ambassador, Clermont d'Amboise, from Naples and left it to Denon as interim diplomatic representative to manage the rapidly deteriorating Franco-Neapolitan relations. His promotion to the office of French *chargé d'affaires* in 1782 was a losing proposition from the beginning. As a scapegoat for Marie-Caroline's and Acton's intrigues, Denon was excluded from state dinners and could not otherwise gain access to court. Frustrated, he found fulfillment in extracurricular activities. He traded in antiquities, honed his skills as an etcher, and joined *La Vittoria*, the most influential Neapolitan Masonic lodge at the time.[39]

Two of Denon's earliest autograph prints are reminders of his involvement with southern Italian Masonic

Fig. 11 Vivant Denon, *Marquis Caracciolo, Neapolitan Ambassador to France*, ca. 1780–85, etching, diameter 8.0 cm. Paris, Bibliothèque National de France, Département de l'Estampe.

circles in the early 1780s. One plate depicts Marquis Domenico Caracciolo, the former Neapolitan ambassador to London and Paris, who was appointed viceroy of Sicily after the end of his diplomatic career in 1781 (fig. 11).[40] Caracciolo's *tondo* profile, etched in stark whiteness against a black background in imitation of an antique marble bust or cameo, celebrates Caracciolo's Masonic virtues, which are supposedly reflected in his physiognomy ("Spirat adhuc, vultu bono, maconica virtus"). When the French traveler Jean Gorani encountered Caracciolo in southern Italy at about the time that Denon etched the politician's portrait, he characterized him as an enlightened philosophe, a savior of the popular classes, and an outspoken opponent of the arbitrary power of the landowners in his province, as well as an uncompromising proponent of anticlericalism in a society steeped in superstition:

> This function, to be Sicily's viceroy, was quite a difficult charge for a philosophe, an intellectual [homme d'esprit], such as Caracciolo; a man who knew better than anybody else what to think of the clergy and, above all, the monks. . . . Caracciolo succeeded in improving the life of the common people in town and countryside. Unable to abolish the onerous privileges of the lords [seigneurs], he prevented them from indulging in the abuse of committing a thousand vexations by firmly announcing severe punishment for those who deviated from the precise terms of the law. . . . Several Madonna statues thought to produce miracles were removed by his orders in plain daylight. The priests and the monks emitted loud cries that he had destroyed religion; the usual language of this type of people. "It is you," he told them, "who, by your fraud and ridiculous superstition, do the greatest damage to religion; and you render stupid a people who, without you, would be among the brightest [un des plus spirituels] in Europe. I will never allow the display of images whose miracles are unconfirmed by authentic proof for worship by the people."[41]

In a subsequent entry Gorani qualified this positive judgment of Caracciolo. Despite the persistence of his Francophile feelings, Caracciolo had too easily readapted himself to the local customs, which expressed themselves in a previously unnoticed vulgarity of manners and a negligence of his outer appearance.[42] In Denon's print, however, there is no trace of this "négligence de sa personne" decried by Gorani, as the artist is entirely absorbed with capturing the spiritual nobility of his sitter.

Another Masonic *tondo* etching by Denon commemorates the election of Charles-François Dauptain père, treasurer of the French Royal Lottery, as *Vénérable* of the great lodge of *la Douce Union* in Paris on October 23, 1780 (fig. 12).[43] The Dauptain print could almost pass for a pendant of Caracciolo's imitation-marble bust shown in profile. In both compositions the sitter's head is turned to the right and an annular inscription explains the Masonic inspiration of the portrait.

The two prints are roughly contemporary with a visit Denon received from Laborde late in the summer of 1781.[44] En route to Italy, Laborde had encountered Cagliostro for the first time, and he undoubtedly shared with his old friend Denon the mystical experiences of his meeting with the magician in Strasbourg, which he recounted, one may assume, using the same flowery language as in his writings. Laborde's Neapolitan interlude almost certainly helped prepare the ground for Cagliostro's return to southern Italy two years later. Vergennes may have issued recommendations to Cagliostro, as Denon later claimed in his defense, but what really opened the door of the French embassy to the Grand Cophte in 1783 was probably Laborde's involvement with the nascent Egyptian rite.

GIUSEPPE BALSAMO, COMTE DE CAGLIOSTRO

The precise circumstances of Cagliostro's Neapolitan stint still remain shrouded in mystery. According to Denyse Dalbian, Cagliostro's friend Luigi d'Aquino was dying in Naples and had asked him to use his skills in a last-ditch attempt to save his life.[45] The scion of one of Naples's oldest aristocratic families, d'Aquino was also a member of the Knights of Malta. In the latter capacity he had arranged for Cagliostro's apprenticeship to an apothecary on the island during the adventurer's youth. The ties to the Maltese Order always remained important for Cagliostro, because it was during his training with the Knights that he had learned the scientific foundations for his later activities as an alchemist and miracle healer. Although permanently banned from the Kingdom of the Two Sicilies, he simply could not fail his old friend and protector on his deathbed. As Dalbian points out, "the Chevalier d'Aquino requested this last visit for more than just being treated by Cagliostro and seeing him one last time; he wanted to confide in him the spiritual directives for their common Masonic mission." In this situation the diplomatic immunity of Denon's embassy promised a safe refuge in case of need. Neapolitan lore maintains to the present day that Cagliostro stayed at d'Aquino's residence during the sojourn, while he would have used the French legation for his miracle healings. This type of arrangement was not unusual for him, since from the very beginning of his career he had carefully separated the venues of his public performances from his private living quarters.[46]

Denon shared with Cagliostro not only a passion for Masonic spiritual revelations, but also an involvement in a thriving market for reproductions of Rembrandt etchings. Ironically, word about Cagliostro's involvement with the graphic arts and the reason for abandoning his artistic pursuits comes from his fellow

Fig. 12 Vivant Denon, *C. F. Dauptain, Vénérable of the Lodge La Douce Union*, ca. 1780, etching, diameter 8.1 cm. Paris, Bibliothèque National de France, Département de l'Estampe.

adventurer Giacomo Casanova, who encountered him accidentally in 1769 while recovering from a serious bout of pneumonia at the Three Dolphins Inn in Aix-en-Provence:

At breakfast I asked the pilgrim [Cagliostro] what he did, and he replied that he was an artist. He could not design a picture, but he could copy it, and he assured me that he could copy an engraving so exactly that none could tell the copy from the original. "I congratulate you. If you are not a rich man, you are, at least, certain of earning a living with this talent." "Everybody says the same, but it is a mistake. I have pursued this craft at Rome and at Naples, and found I had to work all day to make half a tester, and

that's not enough to live on." He then showed me some fans he had done, and I thought of them most beautiful. They were done in pen and ink, and the finest copper plate could not have surpassed them. Next he showed me a copy from a Rembrandt, which if anything, was finer than the original. In spite of all he swore that the work he got barely supported him, but I did not believe what he said. He was a weak genius [*génie fainéant*] who preferred a vagabond life to methodical labor.[47]

Copying Rembrandt prints was in fact a profitable business in Italy, as Denon was about to discover in the 1780s. Original etchings sold at considerable prices, and skillful imitations, some of them fraudulently brought

Fig. 13 Vivant Denon after an etching by Rembrandt Van Rijn, *The Resurrection of Lazarus*, before 1784, etching, 36.3 × 25.3 cm. Paris, Bibliothèque National de France, Département de l'Estampe.

he even printed a sales catalog that was supposed to prop up the high asking prices for these prints.

On September 22, 1783, d'Aquino died, prompting Cagliostro to leave Naples for good only five days later. Although Denon's path never crossed Cagliostro's again, his diplomatic correspondence underscores the lasting impression of their encounter in no uncertain terms, which may help explain his continuous fascination with all aspects of Egyptian culture in the years to come.

Egyptian Freemasonry

Cagliostro, in turn, may have recalled Denon's hospitality when in 1789 he was invited by the painters and sculptors of the French Academy in Rome to attend the reunions of their lodge.[51] Driven by curiosity, the expatriate French artists welcomed Cagliostro with open arms, blissfully oblivious to their guest's reputation for freebooting and converting regular-rite lodges, such as their own, to the revelations of Isis. Cagliostro certainly also appreciated the finer points of Roman diplomatic etiquette, which extended immunity to members of the French Academy, especially since, as he confided to the painter Philippe-Auguste Hennequin, he felt the Holy Inquisition closing in on him. Once again, Cagliostro's timing was anything but judicious. From the very onset of Freemasonry's expansion across Europe, the papacy had branded it as heretical and anti-Christian in bulls issued in 1738 and 1751.[52] The political events in France only reinforced the pressure from official persecution and repression by the Vatican. For Pius VI, Masonry and revolution were all but synonymous when Cagliostro arrived in Rome, a view eagerly shared by the activists of the French Academy rallying in support of Republicanism. Cagliostro's presence in the lodge of the *Amis Sincères* only strengthened the pope's resolve to make an example of the French artists and their new spiritual leader. The Holy Inquisition relied on a small army of underemployed monks and priests who freelanced as spies to make the case against Cagliostro. The keystone for their indictment of the *Amis Sincères* was a banquet the French artists had secretly organized in the Grand Cophte's honor, which for security reasons was held in a country house outside of Rome. Shortly after the banquet the authorities struck in two concerted raids. On December 27, 1789, Cagliostro was arrested and transferred to the Castel Sant'Angelo, never to regain his freedom. The evening of the same day a party of soldiers and monks ransacked the studios of those French artists living outside the confines

into circulation as originals, could easily approach the figures paid for originals. One of the earliest examples of Denon's Rembrandt copies is his *Resurrection of Lazarus*, which he etched during the leisure time from his diplomatic obligations in Naples (fig. 13).[48] On one occasion he presented Sir William Hamilton, the British ambassador and antiques dealer in Naples, with an impression of the plate, which Hamilton is said to have later resold for the price of an original.[49] While for Cagliostro printmaking was a dead end in his career—a circumstance incidentally confirmed by the absence of any extant works of art firmly attributable to him—for Denon it provided the kind of mainstay in times of need that Casanova outlined. When the French Revolution surprised Denon years later in Venice, he added dozens of new plates to his selection of Rembrandt copies, which he reproduced in his studio-apartment on a semi-industrial scale that required the help of three native apprentices.[50] Ever conscious of marketing and hagglers, of the academy. Unable to incriminate any of them, the inquisitors confiscated papers, Masonic paraphernalia, and a draped mannequin, once the prized possession of the painter Louis-Augustin Belle, which a desperate Hennequin watched them carry triumphantly from the top-floor studio in the mistaken belief of having discovered an effigy used in "magic operations." Only five years after its launch, the Egyptian rite was thus squashed by a band of superstitious Roman clergymen, who rightly interpreted it as a portent of the changes to come.

Similar problems with Italian authorities began to trouble Denon in Venice upon the outbreak of the Revolution. Other than selling reproductions of Rembrandt etchings, Denon filled the *otium* of a prematurely retired diplomat by frequenting a select group of Enlightenment sympathizers clustered around the ousted Venetian Senator Angelo Querini. Denon had originally made the senator's acquaintance in Naples in 1781. Now, in Venice, Querini introduced the peripatetic connoisseur to Isabella Teotochi-Marini, whose *Salon* attracted patrician politicians and men of letters alike.[53] Her marriage to Carlo Antonio Marini, a commander in the Venetian navy, was unhappy, and, for a while, she and Denon discreetly carried on a love affair.

Even among Teotochi-Marini's distinguished acquaintances Querini held a unique position. A member of one of the Serenissima's oldest patrician families, the senator is mostly remembered as an unruly judicial and constitutional reformer, whose failure precipitated the fall of the Venetian Republic in 1797 under the onslaught of Napoleon's army.[54] To accommodate Venetian traditionalism, he refrained from promoting reforms in the name of Voltaire, Rousseau, Bacon, or Montesquieu, whose writings he admired, but tried to revive the ancient laws of the *Liber Magnus*. Shortly after his election as Public Attorney (*Avogador di Commun*) of Venice in 1758, Querini rose to become the nemesis of the ruling Council of the Ten and its repressive police apparatus, the State Inquisition. The situation escalated when Querini ordered the arrest and deportation of a maidservant from Brescia accused of theft, and his decision was overturned by the State Inquisitors.[55] Querini retaliated by voiding the arrest warrant against two blacksmiths accused of theft in the *Arsenale* shipyards. The power struggle between the two parties of the *Tribunalisti* and *Querinisti* culminated in the senator's arrest on August 12, 1761. Subsequently, he was charged with attempting to overthrow the government, for which he served a two-year prison term in Verona. The dispute left Venetian society deeply divided, especially since Querini

styled himself as the people's tribune, who defended the rights of commoners against the arbitrary rule of the Ten and their henchmen. By portraying Venice as an Old Regime dictatorship, Querini inadvertently furnished Napoleon with a cogent argument for invading the Serenissima and eradicating the Venetian Republic after more than a thousand years of existence. Most modern historians, however, believe that the lower Venetian nobility, which was largely excluded from the oligarchic clique of the Ten, provided Querini's true constituency.[56] In a situation of general crisis, it found in the senator a defender of its eroding power base and declining personal fortunes.

After Querini's release from jail in October 1763, his open political involvement became more and more sporadic. Upon returning to Venice he decided to channel his Enlightenment activism in new directions, for which Freemasonry would deliver the blueprint. By the early 1780s Querini appears on the membership lists of the Masonic lodge *de la Fidelité* on the Rio Marin, the very first such establishment founded in the Serenissima. The other members of the group were a cross-section of illustrious and politically influential individuals, who figured prominently in the public life of the city state. The lodge brought together "persons of diverse interests; philanthropists and humanists; hermeticists as well as spiritualists."[57] Most importantly, a significant number of *la Fidelité*'s followers were also regulars of Isabella Teotochi-Marini's literary salon.

The objective of the lodge was to promote French Enlightenment thought, conveyed by such officially indexed authors as Voltaire, Rousseau, Diderot, and d'Holbach, on the highest social and political level. According to the mid-nineteenth-century Venetian historian Fabio Mutinelli, the goal of Querini's involvement with Masonry was the implementation of humanism, social liberty, public welfare, and "cleansed" religion and mores, sustained by the belief that "God created man in a state of plain natural liberty, in which we are all equal."[58] Owing to his nostalgia for the political order of the Venetian Republic, Mutinelli certainly had an ax to grind with Querini, the Freemason who opened the city gates to Napoleon's barbarian hordes; yet behind his reactionary polemics lurks a precious opportunity for a glimpse of how the history of ideas shaped political events.

Mutinelli was of course mistaken in claiming that Querini's lodge brought about the downfall of the Venetian Republic single-handedly. No conspiracy attempt would have escaped the attention of the numerous and diligent spies of the State Inquisition, who had infiltrated every aspect of public life in the city. They quickly learned about the existence of the lodge and kept the authorities au courant concerning its activities. Armed with a freshly issued decree banning Masonic temples from the city, the State Inquisitors proceeded to raid the lodge's premises on the Rio Marin on March 9, 1785. By autumn, the persecution culminated in a public auto-da-fé of seized Masonic paraphernalia in the interior courtyard of the doge's palace.[59]

When Denon met Querini these eventful years already belonged to the past. Withdrawn to the *terra ferma*, the senator resided on his country estate at Alticchiero, near Padua, which he had inherited in 1765. By all appearances politics no longer interested him. Instead, he lived the reclusive life of an eccentric art connoisseur. What distinguished Alticchiero, with its seventeenth-century Palladian-style villa, from other patrician estates in the Veneto was its surrounding park, designed by Querini according to philosophical principles and filled with symbolic statuary amassed mostly during the 1770s and 1780s. A recent study by Giuliana Ericani has revealed that the overall garden design was conceived in large part as a Masonic allegory, concealed under a veneer of classical learning and a pretense of vast erudition.[60] Among Alticchiero's most noteworthy outdoor monuments were three altars dedicated to Friendship, Fortune, and the Furies. A casual *flâneur* might also have encountered such arcana as a "Cabin of Madness," a coffeehouse, a Chinese pavilion, a pair of phallic Etruscan grave markers, a labyrinth, the "Woods of Young," and temples to Venus and Apollo, as well as a dovecote and aviaries. Querini had assigned a special place within this idiosyncratic layout to a group of ten authentic ancient Egyptian sculptures, designated by the generic term *canope* (fig. 14).

Although the senator's collection has long since been dispersed, a detailed record of it survives in the form of an illustrated book-length description by Querini's companion Justiniana Wynne, Comtesse de Rosenberg-Orsini.[61] Of Anglo-Greek descent, Wynne had gained notoriety in 1759, when she enlisted Casanova's help in procuring an illegal abortion in Paris.[62] In her old age, destitute from gambling debts, she found a refuge with Querini and, in gratitude, wrote a description of his garden, for which she relied on the help of the scholars, writers, and artists who frequented her literary salon at Alticchiero. Her account is a synthesis of opinions on the monuments in Querini's garden collected from the amateur academy of the senator's friends. In terms of social, economic, and cultural background, then, the contributors, named and unnamed, of her *Alticchiero* opuscule move in the same oxymoronic sphere of

Fig. 14 Giovanni del Piano and Antonio Sandi, *Canope: Encased Isis*, engraving, 23.8 × 16.8 cm. From Justiniana Wynne Comtesse de Rosenberg, *Alticchiero*, second ed., 1787. Urbana, Rare Books and Manuscript Library, University of Illinois at Urbana-Champaign.

pseudo-mysterious Enlightenment thought as the Sophisians. It is worth quoting from the comtesse's description of the *canope* because her discussion of the Pharaonic sculptures in the garden confirms the central role Egyptian civilization played in the spiritual outlook of the Rosenberg-Querini circle:

The amateurs and connoisseurs of Antiquities, the more they are profound & erudite, the more they experience a predilection for things Egyptian. The rarity of monuments that remain to us, the primacy that they hold in the chronological order, the mysteries & sciences that they contain; all these qualities make them infinitely precious . . . The nations that flourished after the Egyptians owe them everything up to the ABCs: they derived from them their Religion, whether it concerns the objects of their cult or the content of the cult itself. In every researched study about the Arts & Sciences, I always read & hear that one has to go back to the Egyptians, to

Fig. 15 Vivant Denon (after Johann Heinrich Rambert ?), *Conversazione Rosenberg,* **ca. 1778–91, etching, 11.0 × 16.0 cm. Venice, Museo Civico Correr, Gabinetto di Disegni e Stampe.**

whom historians & philosophers in the old days turned to receive instructions, in order to acquire knowledge which they disseminated in their place of origin. . . . I attained [my knowledge] easily and with great pleasure from leafing through the works of Montfaucon & de Caylus & looking off to the side into good interpreters, such as [Athanasius] Kircher. Mr. Querini's study is filled with the works of classical writers, whose reading or handling one appreciates more, as one inspects first hand part of the objects they point out & describe. As a passionate antiquarian & even more importantly as an enlightened amateur of all erudite or religious mysteries, of all moral or physical allegories, our friend [Querini] knew how to elevate the dignity of this place [Alticchiero] by endowing it with a small number of the rarest & most interesting works of Egyptian origin.[63]

In the interpretative description of the individual sculptures to be found in the park that follows, references to Isis and her cult abound. Both Wynne's account and the cosmogony of the Sophisians rightly identified the

goddess of Nature as a generic reference employed by antiquarian circles and Enlightenment philosophers alike to harness the esoteric powers emanating from ancient Egypt.

Since Denon was a frequent guest at Alticchiero (fig. 15), he would certainly have enjoyed the rarefied aesthetic pleasures of the estate's garden design and could have consulted the exceptional print collection of his host. Most importantly, however, he took part in the type of speculative contemplations about the esoteric aspects of Egyptian art and culture that Wynne so vividly conveyed.

The aftermath of Denon's involvement with the diverse currents of Egypticizing mystery teachings in Italy during the 1780s took a rather unexpected turn about a decade later in France. Unlike the luckless Comte de Cagliostro, Denon succeeded in making a career and a fortune out of his fascination with Egypt, while securing for himself a permanent place in the annals of the new discipline of Egyptology. In the spring of 1798 Denon appears to have gained insider knowledge of the preparations for the Egyptian campaign; otherwise, doubts about the possible destination of the Armée de l'Orient would have alloyed his enthusiasm. When the fleet left Toulon, many less privileged members of the expedition were still speculating about whether the general would lead them to the coasts of "the Nile or the Euphrates; the Ganges or the Thames."[64] Denon knew better and had moved heaven and earth to be asked to join the expedition. His participation was exceptional on more than one count. Members of the military had no choice but to comply with the order to join the invasion force, regardless of their widespread reservations. By contrast, the scholars were free to decline Napoleon's invitation, although doing so could result in some heavy psychological arm twisting and, if they insisted on their resolution, professional disadvantages down the line. When Napoleon recruited the scholars for the Institut d'Égypte, Denon was already past fifty years of age and could only present a spotty record of amateur dabbling in Egyptian art. Consequently, Napoleon's first choice for the position later to be filled by Denon was the philosopher and historian Constantin-François de Chasseboeuf Comte de Volney, whose apocalyptic vision of overthrowing the decaying, tyrannical monarchies of the state and religion in order to found a new order based on reason and equality appealed to the revolutionary generation. A friend from the time of Napoleon's youth on Corsica, Volney possessed the distinct advantage of having recently traveled to and written about Egypt and Syria, which earned him an uncontested national reputation as the foremost authority on the Near East.[65] While the author of the *Voyage en Syrie et en Egypte* politely declined the offer to accompany the Armée de l'Orient, Denon had to rely on the political intervention of Josephine de Beauharnais, and borrowed money from his mistress in Venice to submit his competitive bid to accompany Napoleon.[66] The general himself would most likely never have given the aging courtier-antiquarian a second thought. Ultimately, Bonaparte settled for Denon and resigned himself to taking along Volney's book on the expedition. As far as Denon was concerned, one has to wonder whether his contacts with Cagliostro, Laborde, and Querini during the 1780s predestined him to seek the truth about a land whose mysteries had continued to haunt him in the Masonic and antiquarian circles that were his intellectual home.

In the context of the Sophisians, Denon's career provides an exemplar for the type of influences and experiences that induced individuals to associate themselves with the order. But in other respects Denon presents an unusual case. Although his name does not appear on the tableau of the founding members of the order, he has often been cited in Masonic literature as one of the most prominent Sophisians—a circumstance which spurred the fancy of even the post-structuralist writer Philippe Sollers in his Denon biography.[67] From a broader perspective, however, Denon's physical and intellectual wanderings closed the circle between Cagliostro's Egyptian rite, Napoleon's Egyptian campaign, and Freemasonry during the Restoration. On this account he remains a historically unique figure.

In contrast to Cagliostro, who made the Egyptian rite his life's vocation, Denon understood Masonry as a form of social entertainment. Like many of his contemporaries he drifted in and out of lodges for most of his life, but seldom left evidence for firm commitments. This attitude is confirmed by an intriguing character portrait of Denon written by Sydney Lady Morgan, an Irish writer of Continental travel descriptions who met Denon twice in Paris during the Restoration. The retired Louvre director gave her a tour through his famed private collection of Egyptian antiquities and introduced her to his wide circle of friends. By her own admission, the most memorable event of Lady Morgan's second visit to France in 1818/19 was her initiation into the female lodge *Belle et Bonne*, which the Sophisians, according the Guerrier de Dumast, marked out as the subject of their chivalric adulation.[68] The reception was organized mainly by Lady Morgan's friend Mme de Villette ("the dear 'belle et bonne' of Voltaire"), but according to the Irish writer's *Passages from My Autobiography*, Denon also played a key role in the preparation of the ritual:

> Denon took both [Mme de Villette's] hands and kissed them in silence; then turning to me she said, "I am come to make you a proposition: will you be a FREEMASON? Yes; don't be frightened, I want to install you in the 'Loge Ecossaise, Belle et Bonne,' established last year, a branch of the vieille souche, and in which 'les femmes vont pour quelque chose.' I am grande maîtresse for the present, and your friend, the Countesse Gaiton de la Rochefoucault, is sécretaire." . . . I at once entered into the spirit of the proposition, whilst Denon's face would have made a cat laugh; he is so *grimacier*! At this point enter—my husband—whose permission I had not waited for; he immediately proposed himself, and was admitted *par acclamation*. He saw at once that the "Loge Belle et Bonne" was an anti-Bourbon société, for which he is always primed. So much for our conspiracy. . . . I should have thought that the "Loge Belle et Bonne" was a mystification of Madame de Villette's, if Denon had not just dropped in and showed us his invitation to our initiation

in the "Loge Belle et Bonne"—here it is; and I pin it into my journal with my own, as curious traits of these times of transition, when all is doubt and "nothing is, but what is not." ... Madame La Générale Foy ... ; His Royal Highness Prince Paul of Wurtemberg; the Bishop of Jerusalem; Talma; Count de la Rochefoucault ... ; Denon; the Count de Cazes ... and many others whom we knew, were assembled, and muttered their conversation in little groups. At half past eight they all proceeded to hold the Chapter for the installation of the "Dames Ecossaises du Temple," according to the programme, we, *les dames postulantes*, remaining behind till we were called for. ... When the battants were thrown open, a spectacle of great magnificence presented itself. A profusion of crimson and gold, marble busts, a decorated throne and altar, a profusion of flowers, incense of the finest odour filling the air, and, in fact, a spectacle of the most scenic and dramatic effect presented itself.[69]

Appropriately, for a participant of Denon's intellectual pedigree, the specialty of the lodge *Belle et Bonne*'s rituals was the celebration of Voltaire and the cult of reason.[70] Except for details in procedure and décor, an initiation among the Sophisians would not have been experienced much differently by the neophyte. The emphasis on theatricality and cosmopolitanism, enjoyed by a socially and intellectually stratified audience, is a recurrent theme in French Masonic circles during the late 1810s and 1820s that did not remain confined to the Sophisians. Outer form and spectacle now supplemented the contemplative contents of the ritual. To see and to be seen were of primary importance. Fashion ranked equal with philosophy, while archeological exactitude was drafted into the service of Orientalism's popular appeal.

Lady Morgan was certainly right when she associated such pageantries with deep-seated feelings of loss and ambiguity experienced by a society in transition. But where did these emotions have their roots, and why did Egyptian symbolism become a privileged form to represent the ineffable? To answer these questions it will be insightful to look at two conflicting interpretative models, reason and mysticism, that shaped the views of Egypt held by Napoleon's soldiers and scholars, but which they were at loss to reconcile with their experience as colonizers.

2

The Laboratory of Reason: Egypt from the Philosophes to Napoleon's "Oriental Dream"

Search for illumination at the bosom of the sacred mysteries.
—Golden Book of the Sophisian Order[1]

WHEN FIFTY-TWO-YEAR-OLD SCIENTIST GASPARD MONGE embarked on the Egyptian campaign in 1798, he deliberately failed to apprise his wife of his plans. Before the distinguished mathematician and physicist could leave Europe, however, matrimonial discontent caught up with him in the Italian port city of Civitavecchia, where he received an indignant letter from home: "Old fool, aren't you tired of running all over the world? Don't you have a good wife, daughters who love you dearly, sufficient means, and a reputation that should suffice for your happiness? Shouldn't you be content and, instead of going to who-knows-where, think about ending your days peacefully while relishing the things you possess?"[2]

Monge was not just any scientist, but one of the pre-eminent mathematicians of the eighteenth century. He had pioneered descriptive geometry, published widely on his specialty, was a member of the Institut de France in Paris, and held a chair in physics at the École militaire. An ardent supporter of the Revolution, he came to admire Napoleon by the late 1790s. Since Napoleon himself liked to dabble in mathematics, the respect was mutual: Monge received a personal invitation from the general to join the Egyptian expedition on board the flagship vessel *L'Orient*. He had the option to decline the offer, as in fact many of his colleagues from the scientific world did. The professional rewards at stake, however, were significant, even for a man of Monge's standing. In his case, the allegiance to Bonaparte would pay off quickly. Once the expedition had arrived in North Africa, he was appointed first director of the Institut d'Égypte in Cairo by Napoleonic fiat. In this capacity he was put in charge of organizing the archeological excursions launched by this learned society. When Napoleon decided to secretly abandon Egypt a few months later, Monge was again invited to join the general on his ship, the *Murion*. After Napoleon's coup d'état against the Directory, Monge entered the political arena in France. He received an appointment to the

Sénat and later rose to become its president. Somewhere in between these events, he also joined the Sophisians.

But apart from professional advancement, why would a man like Monge volunteer for the Egyptian campaign, which remained, even in its most lucid moments, a questionable political adventure with uncertain outcome? A personal letter the mathematician wrote to Bonaparte a few days prior to the departure of the invasion force gives a rare inside view of the higher goals that motivated scholars and soldiers alike:

My Dear General,

Today we received your last orders. . . . Here I am thus transformed into an Argonaut! This is one of the miracles of our new Jason, who will not tire of riding the oceans in the conquest of a fleece . . . but who will bring the flame of reason to a country where its light has not shone for ages and who will extend the domain of philosophy and further promote national glory.[3]

Monge was one of many participants in the expedition who understood its goals as a project of the Enlightenment. Bonaparte himself elevated these ideas to the level of quasi-official doctrine when he decreed from Cairo in August 1798 that the three principal objectives of the Institut d'Égypte should be to promote: "1st, The progress and dissemination of the *lumières* in Egypt; 2nd, Research, study, and publication of natural, industrial, and historical facts about Egypt; 3rd, The assistance with advice on different questions for which the Institut will be consulted by the government."[4] Especially among the more educated members of the campaign, these goals were widely approved. There was a widespread consensus that the true purpose of the expedition was to liberate the country from Oriental despotism, and to turn it into a textbook example of how Western ideas of the Enlightenment could be applied for the betterment of humanity.

The political situation of Egypt in 1798 made it easy for the French conquerors to situate the abstract idea of Oriental despotism that had haunted so many eighteenth-century philosophes in an empirical context. The country was under the control of equestrian bands of vagrant Mameluke warriors, who had been tolerated for centuries as de facto rulers by the Ottoman empire in remote Constantinople. The Mamelukes fit the profile of Oriental despots perfectly because of the way they perpetuated their dynasties. Mostly of Georgian or Circassian descent, wealthy and influential Mamelukes bought slaves as boys or adolescents in the slave markets of Constantinople and the Crimean city of Caffa, converted them to Islam by force, and trained them as soldiers.[5] Once their training was complete, the slaves were freed and eventually perpetuated the system by buying and training slaves of their own. To the confusion and disgust of Western observers, being a slave could indeed hold the key for social advancement in precolonial Egypt. Given this political and social context, General Berthier, for instance, found it appropriate to interpret the French conquest of Cairo as a milestone in "tearing Egypt from the despotism of the Mamelukes."[6]

The conviction that Egypt was a laboratory of Reason remained strongly ingrained in the minds of many veteran scholars and military leaders even after Egypt had been evacuated by the French army. A case in point is the memoirs that another Sophisian, General Jean-Louis-Ebénézer Reynier, published in 1802. His treatise *De l'Égypte après la bataille d'Héliopolis* was conceived as an indictment of the incompetence of Napoleon's second (and last) successor as commander-in-chief of Egypt, General Abdallah Jacques Menou, who at one point was also associated with the Sophisians. Because of the book's accusatory tone towards Menou, Napoleon had most copies confiscated and destroyed shortly after publication.[7] Remarkably, Reynier's text outlines a vastly ambitious catalog of social, political, cultural, and economic reforms required to bring the *lumières* to Egypt. Most of these reforms he declared accomplished during the three short years of French rule. For Reynier there existed no doubts that changes had to be imposed from the outside, that is by the European colonizers:

> There are elements in Egyptian society that oppose all improvement; any useful change cannot be brought about but by foreigners called to the government. The French found themselves in this position. . . . It was necessary to organize a justice system, establish municipal authorities, a general police force, an administration uniquely concerned with the public good; to abolish political and religious privileges, to get people of different religious convictions used to obeying the same laws, to change the nature of land property and the status of the fellahs [peasants]. It was necessary to educate farmers about how to improve their harvest, to convince artisans and merchants to become more daring in their undertakings by assuring them of the rewards for their efforts. It was necessary to destroy the errant Arabs, or to undermine by force their prejudice against a sedentary life. It was ultimately necessary to subordinate all private interests to the general interest, to bring the tax system to perfection, to improve the system of water distribution and irrigation, to develop cultures of colonial plants, to build canals for navigation, etc. Finally Egypt will lift itself to the highest degree of prosperity. But it was necessary to study this people perfectly, to destroy its prejudices; to inspire feelings of love and admiration for the legislators, the only ones who could give them a moral force strong enough to establish and consolidate the new institutions. . . . During the expedition of Bonaparte in Egypt one saw, for the first time, sciences and arts unite themselves with the march of a conqueror. Henceforth, the Egyptians will appreciate the power of the Europeans, the kindness of their laws, and the vastness of their Enlightenment (*lumières*).[8]

Reynier's observations are nothing short of a manual for how to convert the theoretical ideas of the Enlightenment into a practical plan of action applicable in the exemplary case of the Egyptian conquest. Understandably, from his perspective as a colonial administrator, Reynier chose to focus on Egypt's present population and not its past civilization. Other members of the expedition, however, found justification for bringing the Enlightenment to the Orient precisely in the architectural remains of Egypt's celebrated Pharaonic grandeur, which assumed the role of monuments to despotism and superstition. Vivant Denon, for instance, was certainly one of the most learned and sophisticated scholars of antiquity to accompany the campaign. Still, even he could not refrain from making it a point to compare, if only implicitly, Pharaonic megalomania to ancien régime political tyranny under the Bourbons:

> In reflecting on the object of the construction of the pyramids, the gigantic pride which gave them birth appears more enormous even than their actual dimensions; and one hardly knows which is the most astonishing, the madness of tyrannical oppression, which dared to order the undertaking, or the stupid servility of obedience in the people who submitted to the labour. . . . But forever temples! Not a single public edifice, not a single house, nor even a royal palace, which had been able to resist the

ravages of time! What then were the people, and who the sovereigns? It should seem that the former were composed of slaves, the latter pious leaders, and the priests humble and hypocritical despots, concealing their tyranny from the people by the name of a vain monarch, and possessing all the science that was then known, which they wrapped up in emblem and mystery, to put a barrier between them and the people. The king was served by priests, counseled by priests, fed by them, instructed by them; every morning, after having dressed up, they read to him the duties of a sovereign towards his people, and towards his religion . . . I should see in the rich country of Egypt nothing but a gloomy and mysterious government, weak kings, and a sad unhappy people. . . . What monotony! What melancholy wisdom! What austere gravity of manners! I still admire with awe the organization of such a government; its stupendous remains yet incite the mingled sensations of respect and dread. The divinity, in sacerdotal habits, holds in one hand a hook [ankh, the "key of life"], and in the other a flail; the former, no doubt, to restrain, and the latter, to punish: everything is measured by the law and enchained by it. . . . Not a single circus, not a single theater, not a single edifice for public recreation; but temples, but mysteries, but initiations, but priests, but sacrifices; ceremonies for pleasure; for luxury, sepulchers. Surely, in the evil hour of France, some demon evoked the gloomy ferocious soul of an Egyptian priest to animate the monster, who imagined, by making us sullen, to render us happy.[9]

In this passage Denon appropriated themes recurrent in Enlightenment literature, where temple priests deliberately manipulate the ignorant masses through doctored miracles, fraudulent secrecy, and the retention of occult wisdom and scientific knowledge in order to secure their dominant political influence.[10] Although the true target in these lines of attack was the clergy in absolutist Europe, the sacerdotal class in ancient Egypt or classical antiquity was often portrayed as the epitome for the degeneration of priestcraft into organized imposture. Interestingly, at least one Sophisian, Guerrier de Dumast, took it upon himself to restore the damaged honor of Egyptian temple priests, whose civilizational importance he underlined. Contrary to the assertions of certain "modern writers," Egyptian priests promoted truth "without pride and without weakness" before the political leadership class.[11] They acted for the "general good," "nourished a patriotic spirit," and even if they kept their knowledge a secret, they did so because they were convinced that "society would be better organized, if the dissemination of knowledge never took place without a commensurate elevation of the soul. . . . Great science, according to Solomon, is almost always the subject of great affliction," which is

why its insights, "denied to the commoners [les vulgaires], would not even be useful to them." Despite its anachronism, this apology for priestcraft is not surprising, since the Sophisians understood themselves as a modern reincarnation of an ancient Egyptian college of temple priests.

In the final analysis, the reading of Egypt by Monge, Reynier, and Denon was remarkably similar. The parallels in their thought patterns do not, however, explain why Monge abandoned his family to bring the Enlightenment to Egypt, why Reynier wanted to uproot contemporary Egyptian culture and society in the name of the *lumières*, or why Denon condemned temples and religion of ancient Egypt in the name of Reason. In fact, none of them conceived these ideas in isolation. Rather, they built on a body of philosophical speculations whose origins extended back deep into the eighteenth century.

EGYPT, AN ENLIGHTENMENT PROJECT

For eighteenth-century Enlightenment philosophes, Egypt embodied the idea of a clean slate, where, after the suppression of Oriental despotism through Western intervention, the material rewards of Reason beaconed to announce the coming of a new age for mankind. The question of what a submissive Egypt could offer Europe was discussed in hundreds of publications over the course of the *âge des lumières*.[12] In one form or another, theories about the prospects of a colonial conquest of the country captured the imagination of such luminaries as Leibniz, Voltaire, Turgot, Montesquieu, and Constantin de Volney.[13] The circumstance that these ideas were primarily entertained by thinkers of the Enlightenment had far-reaching implications for the moral justification proposed in support of Napoleon's Egyptian campaign by the end of the century.

Philosophical speculations about North Africa's political future date back to the seventeenth century. The German writer Gottfried Wilhelm von Leibniz offered perhaps the first concrete plan for the French colonization of Egypt in his *Consilium Aegyptiacum*, commissioned by Louis XIV.[14] While the immediate practical implications of this proposition may have been rather limited (we do not even know whether Louis XIV ever read Leibniz's treatise),[15] its existence demonstrates that the idea of a French military conquest of Egypt was already in circulation by 1672.

Philosophers of the eighteenth century were captivated by speculations about the Orient's (and especially Egypt's) decline and decadence, which they attributed to lethargy stemming from political despotism.[16] Voltaire, in his *Essai sur les moeurs* and other writings, deplored the lack of intellectual curiosity among the Turks, whose indifference, he claimed, prevented them from cultivating the arts and sciences, while despotic and arbitrary rulers eliminated any incentive for commercial development.[17]

Like Voltaire, Turgot attributed the idea of progress to the Occident.[18] Western civilizations, by his account, were superior to those of the Orient because their development came to full blossom at a relatively late point in history and because the mental faculties of Westerners allowed for a more rapid intellectual acquisition. Moreover, Turgot introduced the influential idea that the Orient was caught in a vicious circle in which ignorance (and its concomitant phenomena like slavery, polygamy, and sloth) perpetuated despotism, while despotism perpetuated ignorance.[19]

Montesquieu, in his *Esprit des lois*, attributed the West's embrace of freedom and the Orient's propensity for despotism to climatic differences between the "war-like, brave, and active" Occident and the "effeminate, lazy, and timid" Orient.[20] This dichotomy provided him with an explanatory model when he tried to find reasons for the sharp contrast between the military resistance to the expansion of the Roman Empire by northern Europe compared to the indifferent submission of Asia.[21]

In the area of travel literature, three accounts were of pivotal importance for psychologically and intellectually preparing the ground for Napoleon's invasion of Egypt. Among their authors—Claude-Étienne Savary, Sonnini de Manoncour, and Constantin de Volney—the last certainly proved to be the most influential contributor in the long run because of his considerable social and political clout by the end of the century.

Claude-Étienne Savary's *Lettres d'Égypte* of 1785–86 contained an impressionistic, suave, and bucolic description of a land of Epicurean plenty and erotic pleasures.[22] The *Lettres* probably provided the blueprint for many of the propagandistic accounts of the early successes of the campaign disseminated through the French press. These reports were quickly discredited after incriminating bits and pieces of information about the real hardships of the Armée de l'Orient began to reach Europe. The appeal of Savary's *Lettres*, flavored with erudite references to classical sources, rested on their polished style, which foreshadowed the taste of nineteenth-century Romantic literature.[23] While experts could easily detect that Savary's acquaintance with Egypt was rather superficial and that his observations were frequently anecdotal, the lower

ranks of Napoleon's army devoured this account. Indeed, there was a clear class distinction associated with the readership of Volney and Sonnini, on the one hand, and Savary, on the other. Savary attracted many of the less intellectually minded among the soldiers in the Armée de l'Orient, especially young officers, while most of Volney's readers were recruited from the ranks of the generals and *savants*.[24]

Not surprisingly, Sonnini's and Volney's approach to their Egyptian travel experience was characterized by a greater sense of sobriety, and their accounts were therefore read by a more select and scholarly audience. Sonnini's *Voyage dans la Haute et Basse Égypte* described the country from the point of view of a physician and engineer.[25] Although the author's main objective was to survey the country from the perspective of a natural scientist, he frequently digressed in order to discuss evidence for the alleged decadence of Egypt. Like Denon after him, he took the prevalence of "superstitious" religions as an occasion to give his anticlerical feelings free rein and noted with disgust that contemporary Egyptians literally lived in the ruins of their great past. A moralist and self-appointed hygienist, Sonnini was appalled by the inclinations towards iconoclasm and homosexuality he observed in the native Arab population. Despite his unfavorable perception of the country in which he traveled, Sonnini met a French officer in 1780 in Cairo to discuss the possibility of a conquest of Egypt as an operational base for an invasion of India.[26]

While the scope of Sonnini's work was too narrow to capture a larger audience, and while Savary's book was discredited by the adverse experiences of the campaign itself, Volney's version was largely confirmed, and his authority could no longer be questioned after 1799. During the preparatory stages of the campaign, his *Voyage en Syrie et en Égypte pendant les années 1783, 1784, et 1785* was often cited as the only reliable source of information on Egypt, and its author, at least until the publication of Denon's travel account in 1802, virtually monopolized the intellectual *mise en valeur* of the expedition.[27] Although Volney had declined a personal invitation to join the scholars embarking for Egypt, it was mostly he who inspired Napoleon to conceive of the campaign as both a military and a cultural conquest.[28]

Combining the genres of philosophical treatise and travel description, Volney's *Voyage en Syrie et en Égypte* was not only the single most influential book on Egypt in the late eighteenth century, but also the one that attracted the most learned audience. It was written in a lucid, though blunt and technical style that avoided

the literary flourishes, speculations, and personal anecdotes that characterized so many Oriental travel
descriptions of the time. Since Volney had begun his
literary career as a follower of the *Encyclopédistes*, he
was able to produce a book that anticipated the stylistic
preferences of the Napoleonic age. The Egypt of the past
did not interest Volney, who abstained from indulging
in those speculations about ancient civilization that rendered other travel descriptions so picturesque: the world
of the Pharaohs and early Christians, mummies, temple
priests, Coptic convents, Caliphs and Mamelukes. What
inspired him instead was Realpolitik. For Volney, it
was only a small step from the mid-eighteenth-century
philosophical treatises to the development of plans for
the colonial conquest of the Orient, in which Egypt figured as a particularly promising first target. Speculations about a military conquest of the country and the
political consequences such a move entailed became
Volney's idée fixe, on which he commented in his *Voyage en Syrie et en Égypte* as follows:

> The wish to see Egypt pass into different hands is un-
> doubtedly dictated by the best interests of the [native]
> people, rather than by an interest in [ancient] monuments.
> But even under the second premise, this revolution would
> still remain very desirable. If Egypt were owned by a na-
> tion that is a friend of the fine arts, we would make dis-
> coveries here that the rest of the world refuses us; maybe,
> one day, we will even discover books.[29]

Volney reserved the investigation of Egypt's cultural
past for a moment when the political situation would
allow for such pursuits. For the time being, he settled
for analyzing the military weakness of the Ottoman
Empire in Egypt and for describing in sober words the
hygienic condition of the country, haunted by illnesses
ranging from fever to blindness and from cow pox to
plague.[30] Although Volney's forecast for a successful
French invasion of Egypt was pessimistic, he did implicitly help garner interest in the plans for a military
intervention. Soon, his treatise came to be the standard
reference for those who favored a French colonization
of northern Africa, most notable among them his old
friend Bonaparte.[31]

Esoteric Egypt

Although plans for the colonization of Egypt seemingly evolved in a linear progression from Enlightenment thought, there existed a thriving eighteenth-
century literary subculture promoting Egypt as a land

of mysteries. Of course, for any enlightened philosophe, there were only two ways of dealing with mysteries: either mysteries could be rationally explained
(and hence ceased to be mysteries), or they were part
of religious superstition (and hence to be condemned
and purged by force of Reason). Seen from this perspective, esoteric Egypt would seem like a parallel
universe from the ordered world of rationality that the
Enlightenment envisioned as the country's future. In
literary practice, however, there was always plenty
of overlap between the anachronistic genres. Traces
of the esoteric Egyptian tradition survived even in
Voltaire, who included a chapter on the "Mystères de
l'Égypte" in his *Essai sur les moeurs*. The philosopher
contended that "there is a great deal of evidence that
the Egyptians, once they established these mysteries, preserved their rites faithfully: because, in contrast to their moral flexibility (*extrême légèreté*), they
were constant in their superstition."[32] When it came to
Egypt, the rational and the esoteric scholarly milieus
of the eighteenth and early nineteenth centuries existed in close intellectual proximity.

Egyptosophy, a pseudoscience concerned with "an
imaginary Egypt, perceived as the most profound source
of occult knowledge," has a long history in Western
thought.[33] Its roots go back to the travel writers of Hellenistic Greece and classical Rome, such as Herodotus,
Plutarch, or Diodorus of Sicily. During the Renaissance
this tradition was perpetuated by the Neoplatonic academy in Florence under Marsilio Ficino, who attributed
a body of Egyptian occult texts to a legendary author of
his own invention, Hermes Trismegistus. In Germany,
between 1652 and 1654, the Jesuit scholar Athanasius
Kircher published his *Oedipus aegyptiacus*, in which
he presented a scheme to recover ancient Egyptian sciences and wisdom by means of the study of artifacts,
symbolism, and hieroglyphics. By the mid-seventeenth
century the British proto-Masonic milieu around Elias
Ashmole came under the spell of Egyptosophy, thereby
further tightening the association of ancient Egypt with
occult sciences. In 1731, finally, a certain Abbé Jean
Terrasson published a two-volume novel entitled *Séthos, histoire ou vie tirée des monumens anecdote de
l'ancienne Égypte, traduite d'un manuscrit grec*, which
would resonate so strongly with adepts of Egyptian
esoterica that it became the blueprint for Cagliostro's
rite, the writings of the Jacobin archeologist Alexandre
Lenoir, and the Sophisian order. Despite its long history
and distinguished pedigree, however, the tradition of
Egyptosophy has no other scientific claim than that of
being "a timeless idea, with few connections to historical reality."[34]

In an eighteenth-century context, Terrasson's novel stands out as the most important and influential contribution to this tradition. Both English and German translations became available as early as 1732, followed by an Italian version two years later. Over the course of the century, the French text went through three editions, the last one being released at the height of the Reign of Terror in 1794. Literary spin-offs, such as Étienne-François de Lantier's *Voyages d'Antenor en Grèce et en Asie avec des notions sur l'Égypte*, which copied wholesale Terrasson's esoteric descriptions of initiation rites in ancient Egypt, found avid readers as late as 1797.[35] The eminent importance of the *Séthos* saga in eighteenth-century European culture is also confirmed by the fact that Terrasson's work inspired some of the themes in Emanuel Schikaneder's libretto for Mozart's *Die Zauberflöte* (The Magic Flute).[36] In the early nineteenth century the abbé's novel experienced another surge in popularity. As the editor of the fourth edition of 1813 explained, "the memorable campaigns of Egypt and the publication ordered by His Majesty the Emperor of the volumes summarizing the observations and the research undertaken in this region [i.e., the official *Description de l'Égypte*] have created a great interest in works that represent the country in its ancient condition; and *Séthos* is very satisfying in this respect."[37] Aided by historical circumstances beyond the author's control, Terrasson's *Séthos* enjoyed an unexpectedly long literary life. For roughly one hundred years after its initial publication in 1731, the book held a place as unrivaled best seller on esoteric Egypt.

Historical facts and Egyptosophic fiction are in free flow throughout Terrasson's novel. The author pretends to provide the reader with a translation of a Greek manuscript he had discovered in an unidentified foreign library that was "protecting this kind of treasure extremely jealously."[38] The claim to be a mere translator was especially deceptive, since Terrasson had commented on Homer's *Iliad* in 1715 and worked on a French translation of Diodorus of Sicily's *Universal History* during the 1730s.[39] As a member of the French Academy, Terrasson enjoyed the authority and prestige only a serious scholar of classical antiquity could command.

According to Terrasson, the fictitious manuscript he proposed to study dated to the age of Marcus Aurelius in the second century A.D., when it was written by a Greek monk living in Alexandria. The life story of the Egyptian prince Séthos related therein, however, allegedly took place about fifteen hundred years earlier, during the "century preceding the Trojan war."[40] Séthos's spiritual peregrinations began when, while still a teenager, his mother died, and his

father, the Pharaoh Osoroth, took a second wife, who gave birth to a competing heir. At this point Séthos and his teacher Amédès left the court and departed on an extended trip that led them to explore the principal temples of Egypt. This journey not only concluded Séthos's education through the acquisition of new knowledge in the arts and sciences from Egypt's most eminent priests, but also afforded Terrasson the opportunity to describe how his young hero prevailed over the various secret initiation rites administered in the underground chambers of the temples he visited.

Initiation to the Egyptian mysteries is a central theme of the novel, which Terrasson described over long stretches of the ten books that comprise the *Séthos* saga. The author found an ingenious way to reconcile the irrational world of mysteries with the rational world of the intellect. In ancient Egypt, initiation was consubstantial with learning, mastery of the arts and sciences, and, ultimately, enlightenment. This idea was also the cornerstone of Sophisian initiation rites, as will be seen in the next chapter.

At first, Séthos and his teacher set out on a nocturnal exploration of the great Cheops pyramid. They inspected the outside first, then entered the pyramid's interior by way of a tar-coated well that opened into an underground passage system connecting all of the pyramids. Once inside the great pyramid, Séthos was overcome by a "violent wish for initiation."[41] At long last, he found the following inscription answering to his quest:

WHOEVER DECIDES TO TAKE THIS ROUTE WITHOUT LOOKING BACK SHALL BE PURIFIED BY FIRE, WATER, AND AIR; HE MAY CONQUER FEAR AND DEATH, HE WILL ISSUE FORTH FROM THE BOSOM OF THE SOIL, HE WILL SEE THE LIGHT AGAIN, AND HE WILL HAVE GAINED THE RIGHT TO PREPARE HIS SOUL FOR THE REVELATIONS OF THE MYSTERIES OF THE GREAT GODDESS ISIS.[42]

Thus began the test by the three elements to which Séthos had to submit himself in order to reemerge from the underground maze. For the test of fire, he had to step over a red-hot iron grill, then, for the test of water, swim through a gushing canal, all the while being careful not to extinguish the torch he was carrying.[43] Finally, by pulling a pair of steel rings dangling from the ceiling above a treacherous suspension bridge, he opened a trap door that unleashed a violent gust of wind. Although many later eighteenth-century descriptions of Egyptian-rite initiations included a test by the fourth element, earth, Terrasson chose to omit this reference, probably because he considered it redundant, given that the scene already took place in an underground setting.

The next stage of Séthos's peregrinations led him to Memphis, famous for the worship of the Egyptian trinity of Isis, Osiris, and their son Horus.[44] Here he was instructed in symbolic arcana that allowed him to associate Isis with the veil of mysteries, Osiris with an ibis peeking out from an urn, and Horus with the notion of silence. He was received by a college of high priests and took an oath of secrecy. Séthos learned about the strict hierarchical and social divisions that governed cult practices: while ceremonies held in the temples above ground were administered for "the people," only initiates were admitted to the underground mysteries. The Memphis sojourn served the purpose of purifying the initiate's body and soul. Séthos attained the first objective through an eighty-day fasting period. Purification of the soul, however, required participation in the temple ceremonies and the preparation of a dissertation for the temple college on a moral problem. Following these procedures, Séthos was asked to withdraw for an eighteen-day period of silence, at the end of which he was again examined by the college on three moral questions.

As Séthos began to earn the priests' confidence, they revealed to him that the veiled underground entries of their temples gave access to a maze connecting the pyramids with the Memphis catacombs, an arrangement that served as a means for communicating with the dead. The underground conduits also comprised the so-called syringes, or underground chambers with the columns of Thoth-Hermes preserving all human knowledge from cataclysmic events. Appropriately, for a discussion of the netherworlds, Séthos is told the story of the Greek traveler Orpheus, who came to Africa in search of initiation and to improve his singing. While in Egypt, his wife, the nymph Eurydice, died, and Orpheus submitted to the test of the three elements in order to communicate with her. Like Séthos, Orpheus approached the great pyramid at night, equipped only with a torch and his lyre, found the tar-covered well, and entered the maze. He passed the tests of fire and water, but failed the test of air by retracing his steps. Despite his lapse, the Egyptian priests granted him initiate status on the condition that Orpheus agree to disseminate the Egyptian mysteries at home in Greece. This provision afforded Terrasson (and others who followed in his footsteps) the convenience of consulting Greek sources in order to speak authoritatively about ancient Egyptian occult sciences.

Despite his craving for mysteries and initiation, Séthos was brought up a child of the Enlightenment. Amédès instructed him from early on to denounce the former use of foreign slaves, captured at war, in the construction of the pyramids as a crime against humanity, "because, while it is the condition of slaves to serve, one always needs to bear in mind their being part of mankind."[45] Human sacrifices were another "shameful barbarism" of primordial Egypt, long since abolished in Séthos's day. In the distant past, they had customarily been administered as part of the underground initiation rites in the temple of Osiris at Heliopolis.[46] The legacy of this practice, however, lingered on in the injunction to preserve the secrecy of the rituals at any price.

The Egypt of Séthos's day, by contrast, was run by a civilized and enlightened society that assigned the highest value to the pursuit of knowledge.[47] Under the auspices of the priestly colleges, arts and sciences were in full flower. Thanks to the teachings of Hermes Trismegistus, Egypt was at the forefront of discoveries in chemistry, anatomy, zoology, and botany. Priests taught law publicly in the palaces across the country. Alexandria possessed the richest library of the world, which could be accessed, like the museums and concert halls of the country, by all segments of the population free of charge. There was an academy of sciences and an academy of painting and sculpture in Memphis. The population was industrious, and commerce prospered. In short, Terrasson's Egypt was in almost all respects the exact opposite of the country Napoleon and his army conquered in 1798.

To measure the novel by any kind of political and social reality, however, would be to miss the point. Terrasson's text described a utopian model society, a paragon of virtue and morality to be emulated by his readers. *Séthos* was conceived as a pseudoclassical *Bildungsroman*, a literary genre popularized at the turn of the eighteenth century by François de Salignac de La Mothe-Fénelon, the private tutor of the teenage Duke of Burgundy, grandson of Louis XIV, and heir-apparent to the French throne until his premature death in 1712. Fénelon wrote his *Télémaque* as an educational tool to provide moral guidance for the prince.[48] He framed his moral lessons with a series of adventures, patched together from an array of mythological sources, which his youthful hero had to master as a rite of passage into adulthood. First published in 1699, the book was an instant success that Terrasson attempted to copy by substituting Séthos for Télémaque, and by embellishing the story with tinges of Egyptian exoticism and mystery rites. Compared to

Fénelon, Terrasson was a much more radical reformer and philosophe, who would not hesitate to denounce Christianity as morally corrupt, while celebrating Egyptian paganism as a virtuous precursor to the age of Reason. Over the course of the eighteenth century, Terrasson's novel transcended its fictional origins, as increasing numbers of readers interpreted the description of Séthos's initiations to be genuine testimonials of ancient Egyptian cult practices.[49] For the Sophisian Guerrier de Dumast, for example, invented passages in the novel "could pass for the truth, because they capture the spirit of the matter—it was a good idea [by the author] to sustain the interest through action rather than through research that could be tiring."[50] But just in case that action alone was found to be deficient in authenticity, the imagination of scholarly inclined readers was helped by Terrasson's festooning of his text with footnotes that referenced sources from classical antiquity.

In the context of the Napoleonic age, the conclusion to Séthos's odyssey offered an inadvertent parallel to the outcome of the Egyptian campaign: "Animated by true heroism, [Séthos] used the time of a long exile to visit unknown people that he delivered from the most cruel of superstitions, and whose legislator he became. Upon his return, he saved a powerful republic from an enemy at her gates, and he demanded as reward only the happiness of the people under attack from its king or tyrant. Having returned to his home country, he became the benefactor of those he had reason to consider his enemies and rivals."[51] Early nineteenth-century readers thus had every reason to perceive Séthos as an allegory for Bonaparte, who had delivered the "unknown" people of Egypt from superstition and the cruelty of arbitrary Mameluke despotism in order to introduce the rule of equality before the law. The "powerful republic," of course, could now be read as France besieged by hostile European monarchies—a situation that called for the immediate return of a heroic savior currently engaged in sowing the seeds of the Enlightenment abroad.

Terrasson's novel provided retroactive justification for the Egyptian campaign on two grounds. Not only did it furnish politically motivated excuses for Napoleon's abandoning his troops in North Africa, but it also presented the vision of a prelapsarian Egypt prior to the arrival of Islam and Oriental despotism. Séthos's Egypt was surprisingly well attuned to the ideas of the Enlightenment, which it anticipated by three thousand years. Notwithstanding its compulsive preoccupation with initiations, mysteries, alchemy, and occultism, Terrasson's novel hinted at the possibility that the rule of Reason could be easily restored in Egypt, if only the native population received proper guidance.

THE SOPHISIANS IN EGYPT

During the early stages of the campaign the idea of bringing the Enlightenment to Egypt was often no more than a coded term for letting the native population marvel over Western military might and scientific progress. Of the Mameluke warriors, only a few possessed primitive firearms that, in any case, were no match for French cannons. Still, their guerrilla tactics and better knowledge of the territory made them formidable foes for Napoleon's dehydrated troops. The countryside therefore remained difficult to control. If the Enlightenment were to take root in Egypt, it would have to be in Cairo. But even here, the limitations were painfully obvious. The library that Napoleon had ordered to be brought along from France was made accessible to the population on the premises of the Institut d'Égypte, housed in the palaces of the fugitive Mameluke leaders Hassan bey Kachef, Qacim bey, Ali Youssef, and Ibrahim el-Sennari.[52] Still, it was mainly the French who read the 550 volumes selected from a cross-section of disciplines from the natural sciences to philosophy. The scientific instruments imported for the work of the scholars awed the educated élite of Egypt, but aroused the superstition of the population that vandalized the equipment of the Institut during the revolt of Cairo from October 21–22, 1798.[53] Remarkably, the revolt broke out as a reaction against another measure in the French Enlightenment reform package, the introduction of cadastral offices to raise property taxes. As the native chronicler Al-Jabartî reported, the losses included "many precision instruments, like telescopes and other apparatuses, both astronomical and mathematical. All these instruments had no equal and, as to the value of the objects, only those who made them and knew about their use could have appreciated it. The populace looted all of them and reduced a large number to pieces."[54] Hot air balloon flights, organized by French engineers, triggered panic rather than scientific curiosity in Cairoites.[55] Before long, these experiments, too, had to be abandoned because of technical difficulties. When on July 29, 1799, the French *savants* from the Institut received the Divan, a native puppet government installed by Bonaparte, the chemist Jean-Louis Berthollet showed the sheikhs a number of scientific experiments, including demonstrations that involved the discharge of static electricity and various mixtures of colored liquids. After the lecture, Sheikh

Khalil al-Bakri remarked to Berthollet: "All of this is very nice, but can you make me present both here and in Morocco at the same time?" Berthollet's reaction of shrugging his shoulders encouraged the Sheikh to conclude: "There we go! He is not entirely a sorcerer after all!"[56] Moments like these showed that the intellectual mission of the campaign was in a state of crisis only months after standing the test of reality.

In the wake of such setbacks, many Sophisians played pivotal roles in redefining the intellectual mission of the campaign. While converting natives to Western ways of thinking proved to be a tiring and often dangerous undertaking, preparing Egypt for Western consumption held a much greater promise. A new intellectual objective loomed on the horizon: to unveil Egypt's alleged mysteries by means of scientific methodology and militarily enforced duress. Two institutions became the tools for accomplishing this goal: the Institut d'Égypte and the military. While the latter provided the logistical framework for the necessary explorations, the savants would develop the intellectual content for the new mise en scène of the Egyptian spectacle.

Future Sophisian initiates held key positions in both institutions from the very start of the campaign. Rear Admiral Honoré Ganteaume, for instance, was a Sophisian adept and captain of the *Murion*, the vessel that assured Bonaparte's timely escape from Egypt to France in 1799.[57] Several Sophisians also figured prominently on Napoleon's staff of generals during the campaign, including Maximilien Caffarelli du Falga, who, despite his amputated leg, embarked on the adventure.[58] General Édouard-Pierre-David Baron de Colbert distinguished himself by organizing the peace negotiations with the Mameluke leader Murad-bey, who would subsequently convert from French archenemy to closest ally against the British.[59] Colbert's Arabic language skills greatly helped him in this task. Later, he commanded a regiment of Mameluke warriors who, once subdued and inducted into Bonaparte's service, became Napoleon's personal bodyguards. When General Jean-Baptiste Kléber, Napoleon's designated successor as Egypt's governor, was assassinated by Islamic fundamentalists organized in the al-Azhar mosque, a Sophisian, General Abdallah Jacques Menou, replaced him.[60] Yet another member of the Sophisian order, General Jean-Louis-Ebénézer Reynier, was the head of the military tribunal that judged the culprits. The style and content of the judgment rendered by Reynier's panel reveal that by this point indigenous traditions of cruel and unusual punishments had effaced any high-minded ideals of reforming the justice system in the spirit of the Enlightenment:

The tribunal of executive power decided to impose the death penalty on those defendants who were previously declared guilty. The tribunal then proceeded to decide the manner in which this punishment would be inflicted on those found guilty. It consulted article V of the decree of General Menou, dated yesterday [June 15, 1800], in which it is written: "The tribunal decides the kind of punishment it deems appropriate to inflict on the assassin who committed the crime, as well as his accomplices." The body decided unanimously to select a type of punishment used in this country for the greatest crimes, and, commensurate with the severity of the wrongdoing, sentences Soleyman el-Hhaleby to have his right hand burned, then to be impaled, and to remain on the stake until his body has been eaten by carnivorous birds. This execution shall take place on the mound in the courtyard of the Institut, immediately following the funeral rites for commander-in-chief Kléber, in the presence of the army and the inhabitants assembled for the above-mentioned funeral. The tribunal pronounces the death penalty against Seyd A'bd el-Kadyr el-Ghazzy by default. His belongings shall be confiscated and acquired by the French state. His sentence shall be written on the stake to receive his head. The tribunal also condemns Mohammed el-Ghazzy, A'bd Allah el-Ghazzy, and Ahhmed el-Oulay to have their heads cut off and exposed on the site of their execution. Their bodies shall be burned in a bonfire set up at the above-mentioned place [the courtyard of the Institut d'Égypte] for this purpose. The condemned mentioned above shall be executed in the following order: A'bd-Allah el-Ghazzy, Ahhmed el-Oualy, Mohammed el-Ghazzy, and Soleyman el-Hhabeley last.[61]

Many Sophisians in particular considered the assassination of Kléber and the execution of Soleyman el-Hhabeley's gang a pivotal moment in the collective memory of the campaign. Almost two decades after the fact, the events still inspired Cuvelier de Trie, for instance, to write a *mimodrame* entitled *La mort de Kléber, ou les Français en Égypte*, performed in the Cirque Olympique theater in Paris. Despite the play's overt sentimentality and French bias, Cuvelier followed the historical facts very closely when he first recounted the preparations for the conspiracy from the perspective of the Islamists, then shifted his focus to the assassination of Kléber, and concluded with the trial and execution of the killers. The play finishes by pointing out in a footnote that the skeleton of Soleyman el-Hhabeley was brought to France, where it remained one of the attractions at the Muséum d'histoire naturelle located in the gentrified setting of the Jardin du Roi.[62] Apparently, the display was the idea of another Sophisian, the scientist Geoffroy Saint-Hilaire, former member of the Institut d'Égypte, who had returned, after the end of the campaign, to his post as director of the zoology department at the Muséum in Paris.

Despite the pressure from manifold outward dangers, internal division threatened to rend the unity of the French occupiers in the aftermath of Napoleon's stealthy departure for France. This rift extended even to the inner core of those Sophisian adepts who had participated in the campaign. In 1798, Menou famously converted to Islam, submitted to circumcision, and married an Egyptian woman. An ardent partisan of the idea of making Egypt a self-sufficient French colony, Menou nevertheless suffered the humiliation of surrendering the country to British forces in 1801. Before the evacuation, however, Menou and Reynier had become bitter enemies. In May 1801, Menou had Reynier arrested and forcibly deported from Egypt. Reynier was the champion of the anti-colonist camp after Kléber's assassination and argued in favor of an immediate evacuation of the country, if the safe return of the troops could be guaranteed. With this position he followed in the footsteps of Kléber, who had already ratified the conditions for abandoning Egypt to the British admiral Sidney Smith in the convention of Al-Arich on January 24, 1800, but then learned that the British government was unwilling to honor the brokered agreement. Although Reynier enjoyed wide support in the military and seemed to be the logical successor to Kléber, Napoleon confirmed Menou's appointment from the safety of distant Paris. Menou's pro-colonist position enjoyed Bonaparte's unconditional support, since a surrender of North Africa would have publicly underscored the failure of Napoleon's conquest. A curious but noteworthy point in these developments is that the officer Menou sent to arrest Reynier, one General Destaing, was also a Sophisian.[63] This action had a tragic aftermath, because in 1802, following the return from Egypt, Reynier challenged Destaing to a duel in the Bois de Boulogne and killed his adversary. As these examples show, the clash between the colonist and the anti-colonist camp that so bitterly divided the French troops after Bonaparte's departure did not spare the ranks of the Sophisians.

Perhaps even more than the military, the Institut d'Égypte functioned as a nucleus of the order.[64] There was hardly a section of the Institut that did not count an adept in its ranks. The twelve-member mathematics section, for example, headed by Bonaparte himself, included the Sophisians Gaspard Monge and Étienne-Louis Malus de Mitry. During the ill-fated Syrian campaign, Napoleon had ordered Malus to establish the plague house of Jaffa in a former Greek convent. The setting gained infamy in 1804 with Gros's monumental history painting commemorating the visit of Napoleon to the plague-stricken victims spread out in the building's courtyard (fig. 3). Painted to dispel rumors that Bonaparte had ordered the poisoning of soldiers suffering from the plague, the composition bears no resemblance to the actual convent under Malus's supervision. On the eleventh day after he opened the hospital, Malus himself became afflicted with the disease, but he was fortunate enough to survive. His so-called *Agenda*, or diary, published in the late nineteenth century, contains one of the most shocking descriptions of hygienic conditions in the plague house of Jaffa.[65] Profoundly shaken by these traumatic events, Malus developed a penchant for morally uplifting, socially inspired prose, which he composed, while still in Egypt, in his *Pensées*: "All actions in life need to lead to the perfection of the soul and social harmony. Hope is a source of happiness one should not ignore. One must exercise patience, a virtue absolutely necessary for happiness in social existence."[66] The interesting point about Malus's *Pensées* is that they emphasize themes of central importance to Sophisian teachings, such as the perfection of the soul, social harmony, and a virtuous life. Although Malus was a geographer by training and a philosopher in spirit, he also developed an ardent interest in archeology during his sojourn abroad. He marveled at the bas-reliefs and hieroglyphics that he studied in the catacombs near the great Cheops pyramid, as if to confirm some of the Abbé Terrasson's speculations about how an aspiring initiate experienced Egyptian mysteries.[67] After his return to France, Malus's intellectual interests changed again, and he became a scholar of optics, a field to which he contributed groundbreaking discoveries on the polarization of light.

Another Sophisian, the engineer Michel-Ange Lancret, joined the mathematics section as a replacement for a deceased member on July 4, 1799.[68] After his arrival in Egypt, Lancret was put in charge of securing for the French state the possessions abandoned by the Mamelukes during their flight from the Western invaders. It was also he who first described the discovery of the Rosetta stone to the Institut, and who recognized the importance of the find for the deciphering of hieroglyphics. Subsequently, Lancret became the second editor of the vastly expensive luxury volumes that summarized the findings of the Institut, the official *Description de l'Égypte*, which he supervised between 1805 and the year of his death in 1807. Despite its emphatic insistence on rational objectivity in the presentation of ancient and modern Egypt, the *Description*, with its hundreds of obsessively detailed, decorative engravings, provided the blueprints for Egyptomania in the fine and applied arts during the first half of the nineteenth century.

Geoffroy Saint-Hilaire was the only Sophisian adept in the physics section of the Institut.[69] A zoologist and a professor at the Muséum d'histoire naturelle in Paris, he also became a close collaborator of Lancret in the publication of the *Description* during the opening decade of the nineteenth century. He crossed the Mediterranean in the company of General Reynier's division, and proved to be one of the most prolific scientists of the Institut as measured by the number of lectures delivered. In December 1799, Reynier selected Geoffroy Saint-Hilaire to participate in a scientific expedition to measure the height of the great pyramid of Cheops. After this objective was accomplished, the explorers continued on to Saqqara, where Geoffroy Saint-Hilaire inspected the underground chambers in search of bird mummies. "We lowered ourselves down the well of birds, where, for the first time, I saw mummies in place. These openings led to rather large underground caves, from which a great number of smaller, dead-end excavations branched off at right angles. The excavations extend deep enough to have been filled with Ibis mummies piled up horizontally like the wine bottles in our French cellars."[70] The unraveling of underground secrets is a recurrent theme in archeological reports by members of the Institut that inadvertently gave new currency to the Egyptian esoteric tradition. Sophisian initiation, which included the symbolic exploration of Egyptian underground labyrinths, could build alternatively on both the experience of scholars like Geoffroy Saint-Hilaire and the mystical speculations of Terrasson's novel.

During his Egyptian sojourn, Geoffroy Saint-Hilaire also maintained an active correspondence with other Sophisians, including his colleague in the zoology section of the Muséum, Comte de Lacépède.[71] A widely influential Masonic dignitary of the Empire, Lacépède served as president of the board of overseers (*Sosis*) for Cuvelier de Trie's order. On another occasion, Geoffroy Saint-Hilaire wrote to Charles Norry, a Sophisisan from the arts and letters section of the Institut, about the traumatic events of the revolt of Cairo. Throughout his sojourn in North Africa, Geoffroy never tired of assembling a collection of live animals, biological specimens, and archeological artifacts, which he managed to ship back to the Muséum under great difficulties. Even if Egypt itself would be lost for France, its fauna, flora, and curiosities, once put on display, continued to speak of the country's intellectual conquest by force of reason.

Many members of the military also doubled as *savants* for the Institut. Maximilien Caffarelli du Falga, for example, was both a general under Napoleon's orders and a member of the Institut's political economy section.[72] Prior to the departure of the expedition, he had selected the titles for the library that was to be transported to Egypt. Besides Malus and Monge, Caffarelli was one of the few Sophisians to accompany the campaign to Syria, where he was mortally wounded at the siege of Acre. Since he was the only Sophisian to die during the campaign, his membership in the order after 1801 must be considered purely honorary. However, the fact that Caffarelli was recognized as a Sophisian lends support to Cuvelier de Trie's foundation story of the order, according to which the core of the group bonded on Egyptian soil.

Two members of the Institut's arts and letters section maintained ties with the Sophisians. Vivant Denon, of course, had been exposed to the esoteric tradition of Western thought on Egypt through his encounter with Comte de Cagliostro in Naples and was now eager to test his acquired knowledge against reality. Like Monge, he was fortunate enough to leave Egypt with Bonaparte in 1799, and three years later he published his illustrated travel description, the *Voyage dans la Basse et la Haute Égypte*, which became a popular substitute for the overpriced and endlessly delayed *Description*. Charles Norry was an architect by training and built for Napoleon the first gunpowder factory in Egypt.[73] He was the first to measure Pompey's Pillar in Alexandria, Egypt's highest column, and got involved with hot air balloon experiments near Cairo. Despite these feverish activities, Norry appears to have developed a distinct dislike for Egypt, which he left precipitously in early November 1798.

Even after the French evacuation of Egypt, the Institut experienced a long afterlife, since many of its scholars (and others previously excluded from the Institut's membership roll) reunited in the Commission des Sciences et des Arts, charged with publishing the official *Description de l'Égypte*. One of the members of the Commission was the Sophisian musicologist Guillaume-André Villoteau, who was hired by Bonaparte as a singer for official entertainment functions.[74] Villoteau was also an old friend of Cuvelier de Trie. At the height of Robespierre's Reign of Terror, the aspiring musicologist had played the role of a military commander in Cuvelier's Jacobin play *La Fête de l'Être Suprême*. By 1798, evidently, he had set his sights on higher goals than simply being Napoleon's *artiste musicien*. After he had embarked with the troops destined for Egypt, Villoteau refused to sing for the commander-in-chief, styled himself as a serious scholar of Oriental music, and began to do field research, in the course of which he assembled an impressive selection of native musical instruments. During his sojourn, he acquired a considerable body of knowledge about Egyptian music, which he personally found displeasing. In particular the music of the Coptic minority in Egypt captured his intellectual curiosity. A lot of his discoveries found their way into the journal of the Institut, a publication called the *Décade égyptienne*, and later into the official *Description*. His dream to be admitted as a full member of the Institut, however, never came to be fulfilled. Towards the end of the campaign, Villoteau closely associated himself with General Menou, who appointed him his personal secretary.

As these examples from the life experience of various Sophisians show, the initial intellectual mission of the campaign was compromised soon after the arrival of the French troops in Egypt. Although Napoleon's campaign carried the dawn of the modern age to the Near East, the idea of treating Egypt as a social laboratory to test the ideals of the Enlightenment was riddled with unexpected pitfalls that subverted original intentions. Rather than reshaping Egypt in their likeness, the colonizers' thoughts and actions adjusted to their new cultural environment. The result was a hybrid in which an always inscrutable and mysterious Egypt existed in an uneasy symbiosis with the rationalism of the Enlightenment.

THE EGYPTIAN CAMPAIGN AND THE FRENCH PRESS

Outside Egypt, there existed a second front in Europe, where the events of the campaign were gradually consumed by myth. This second front was the press coverage concerned with the fate of Napoleon's army. The history of the representation of the Egyptian campaign in the French news can be divided into three stages. Immediately after the departure of Napoleon's troops in 1798 reports rife with metaphors reminiscent of Savary's description of the North African land of plenty filled the information void. These reports were soon overshadowed by the political fallout from the proposed indictment of those responsible for the planning of the campaign. Shafik Ghorbal has aptly summarized this second stage as follows: "In spite of the false reports published by the Directory, much anxiety about the Army in the East was felt. Anyone who had anything to do with the Expedition was anxious to disclaim any share of the responsibility."[75] In the wake of the political cabal that ensued in Paris, rumors from Great Britain spread that Napoleon and his troops had

been massacred. The moment of these rumors marked the onset of the second and most intense stage in the press coverage of the campaign. The tone of the reports shifted from hopeful optimism to outright public hysteria. Because the Directory felt that it could no longer control the outpouring of controversial and contradictory information about the fate of the Armée de l'Orient, it decided to curtail the freedom of the press, which had previously been a right guaranteed by the French constitution.

The third stage in this development coincides with Napoleon's unexpected return from Egypt on October 9, 1799, and the first months of the Consulate. Faced with the problematic legacy of the contested public image of the campaign, Napoleon, after his coup d'état, further tightened the censorship measures taken by the Directory to attain total control over the press. The political and military aspects of the campaign were no longer open to public discussion. Instead, "the cultural conquest" of Egypt and the promised revelations about the oldest mysteries of human civilization set the stage for an alternative spectacle, one which thoroughly distracted the public's attention from the reality of the failed conquest.

After the destruction of the French fleet in the roadstead of Aboukir by Admiral Nelson's British fleet, pastoral descriptions of Egypt in the fashion of Savary's travel account made up for the lack of factual information about Napoleon's army. A typical example of this type of report is the *Extrait d'une lettre du Caire du 22 brumaire*, published on February 29, 1799, in the *Moniteur universel*.[76] The unidentified author, who described himself as *un citoyen attaché à Bonaparte*, began his letter by praising the climate of the country, which he likened to a Garden of Eden. He mentioned the unselfish support of the French army by the native Arabs in defeating their Mameluke enemies, and concluded his report by examining the agricultural riches of Egypt in greater detail. However, despite the bucolic overtones of the letter, the author made it clear from the start that the main purpose of the correspondence was to dispel horror stories about the fate of the expedition in circulation in France.

Compared to these "sunshine reports" allegedly sent from Egypt, news from the home front must have been much more disconcerting. Threatened by indictments for promoting the campaign politically, the former foreign ministers Charles Delacroix and Charles-Maurice de Talleyrand-Périgord accused one another in open letters of having planned the bungled military expedition.[77] The crux of the dispute was that each man sought to exculpate himself by blaming the other. Talleyrand-Périgord first challenged Delacroix in the *Rédacteur* by charging him with having encouraged the French consul's lobbying for a military intervention from Alexandria. Delacroix retaliated in the *Moniteur universel* by reminding the public that Talleyrand-Périgord, through his treatise on the *Avantages à retirer des colonies nouvelles*, had gained prominence as the principal proponent of plans for a French colonization of Egypt. The sophistry with which they put their arguments forward should have sufficed to alert the readers of these newspapers that the situation of the French army in Egypt had spun irreversibly out of control.

The arrival in the French capital of English press reports concerning the alleged death of Napoleon and the immolation of the French army put an unexpectedly dramatic twist on reporting about the progress of the campaign.[78] Although the *Moniteur universel* was quick to refute these reports as British propaganda aimed at plunging France into civil war, disquieting pieces of information about the state of affairs in North Africa trickled through with ever greater frequency.[79] While the propaganda machinery of the Directory preferred to publish letters and orders of the day from the Armée de l'Orient, the relative scarcity of these tangible documents often left an embarrassing information vacuum that was readily filled with freely invented anecdotes or insubstantial *historiettes*.[80] Just when many believed that Napoleon and his army were marching victoriously on Constantinople, three half-dead soldiers were brought back to Paris and delivered gruesome oral reports of the siege of Acre, which ended Bonaparte's invasion of Syria. Barely able to articulate his words clearly, one of the soldiers had to be interviewed by Volney to verify his account.[81]

Smaller, more critical newspapers were even more daring and did not hesitate to portray the Egyptian campaign as the cause of France's undoing. *Le Thé, ou le Contrôleur général*, for example, published the following dialogue between an evildoer and his heart (*Dialogue entre un méchant et son coeur*):

> Heart: In whose heart have you carried hope? What are your rights? What are your good deeds?
> Evil-Doer: Liberty.
> Heart: Give it to us the way we received it from heaven. Liberty in its primitive state resembles the inundations of the Nile, which fertilizes the soil by covering it with its waves. But if it overflows in torrents, it carries with it plague, famine, and devastating insects. There goes your liberty.
> Evil-Doer: Miserable moralizer, I will no longer listen to you.

> Heart: At present, I am only your judge, but tomorrow I may be your executioner.[82]

Spreading an atmosphere of doom, ambiguous allusions such as this one were probably regarded as the most devastating part of the press coverage, because they helped to promote feelings of panic within the population at a moment when France was threatened militarily on all fronts.

Similarly esoteric in its approach to criticizing the campaign, *L'Accusateur public* devoted its only two issues in 1799 almost exclusively to denouncing the conquest of Egypt.[83] In the July 24, 1799 (Thermidor 6, year VII) issue, the publisher Auguste Danican tells how he experienced a dreamlike revelation from an ephebic youth to whom he refers as an "angel." The angel's discourse in fact turns out to be a lengthy diatribe against the Egyptian campaign, Napoleon, and the Directory:

> . . . and the Lord has thus spoken, and he has cursed the tyrants of your nation, and he has sent to them a spirit of dizziness that made them turn their heads, and he sent them a vapor of pride that made them drunk; and they became mad, and they said: we are omnipotent, and it is necessary that all gives in to us. . . . They assembled many vessels, and they equipped a great fleet; and they put on this fleet their best soldiers, best officers, and best general. . . . They sent them to the extremity of the world, to the extremity of Africa, to a bad climate, to a sterile earth, and to a barbarian people. They arrived in these foreign lands and disembarked, and the fleet that carried them was attacked by another fleet, and was beaten, destroyed, and annihilated by that other fleet. . . . They could not return and suffered greatly in this remote region . . . many became blind; during the day the sun was scorching, the air was aglow, and the plague ravaged the camps so that several thousands died of the plague. Some died of hunger, others died of thirst, and many were killed in combat, as the people rose and massacred many. A great number were impaled, and the heads of many were planted on pikes. They were thirty thousand who had plans to do great miracles. They wanted to rebuild the temple of Jerusalem, and they wanted to prove the predictions wrong. Here they are, exterminated, and all were devoured by death, and not a single one is still alive.[84]

Danican's angel bears a certain resemblance to the genius of France in the center of Jean-Baptiste Regnault's monumental Revolutionary painting of 1795, *Liberty or Death*, which hung during these years in a prominent, publicly accessible position on the wall of the French Legislative Assembly, the Conseil des

Fig. 16 Jean-Baptiste Regnault, *La Liberté ou la mort*, 1795, oil on canvas, 60 × 49 cm. Hamburg, Kunsthalle.

Cinq-Cents.[85] Although the original canvas is no longer extent, the composition survives in a small copy at the Kunsthalle in Hamburg (fig. 16). In this version, the angelic genius of France presents a choice between the female personification of Liberty, on the left, equipped with a Masonic square rule, and Death, in the form of a skeleton, on the right. While the rhetoric of Regnault's painting suggests that there was no alternative to Liberty, Danican's angel reversed this logic and equated the Egyptian campaign with death meted out in the name of liberty.

The angel's address to the newspaper editor is interesting from a historical perspective because it constitutes a rare instance of a critical commentary on the garbled information policy of the Directory concerning Napoleon's campaign. Upon the messenger's disclosure that all French soldiers in Egypt had died, Danican expresses his surprise as follows:

> And I did not know that they had all been devoured by death, and not a single one had survived. I was greatly surprised to learn about these things, because, on the contrary, I believed they were all alive and victorious, and that they had made great conquests, and that the expressions on their faces instilled terror in their enemies. I did not dare to tell the angel that I was surprised, because he prohibited me from interrupting him. I tried to hide my surprise, but nevertheless it showed on my face. The angel became aware of it and said: "You did not know about these things, and you are surprised to hear about them, because you believed the fables that the tyrants feed to your nation. I am telling you about these events so that you may disabuse the people and that you may acquaint them with these truths, because they were ignorant of them, just like you did not know them. And the tyrants of your nation deceive them, and the tyrants of your nation lie shamelessly, and they declare white for black, and one should not believe one word of what they say."[86]

The prevalence of such writings in the *petite presse* caused the Directory to reluctantly consider measures curtailing freedom of opinion. In the political discussions that ensued over the issue, the Egyptian campaign provided the underlying subtext. An outspoken opponent of censorship measures, the new foreign minister Briot, for instance, saw a correlation between the Egyptian military adventure and the decline of Revolutionary virtues.[87] In his eyes, the campaign directly threatened one of the most essential Revolutionary achievements, precisely because it forced the government to reconsider the freedom of the press. Despite his adamant objections, however, the presses of more than forty newspapers and periodicals were sealed early in September 1799, their circulation suspended, and many of their editors exiled to the notorious penal colony of Guiana.[88]

Napoleon's unexpected return to France in October 1799 marked a turning point in the official information policy, since enough information was now available for a series of articles extending over fifteen issues of the *Moniteur universel*.[89] Written in a matter-of-fact style typical of Napoleon's military administration, these official reports were more efficient in communicating the activities of the Armée de l'Orient, but at the same time they reduced possibilities of reading between the lines in order to differentiate propaganda from fact. Inevitably, the reports were open-ended, disclosing

neither whether the campaign was actually over nor whether it had resulted in triumph or defeat.

Second thoughts about the military enterprise and the troops remaining in Egypt were soon brushed aside by open demonstrations of enthusiasm for the person of Napoleon, whose steps in public were watched closely. Readers submitted laudatory poems in honor of Bonaparte to journals, while newspaper editors asked their subscribers when the first vaudeville play dealing with the heroism of the Armée de l'Orient would be written.[90]

However, beneath the superficial display of public devotion to Napoleon lay a deeply felt ambiguity about the return of the troops. Despite a flat denial that French soldiers had ever been exposed to the plague, reports of which were dismissed as a symptom of mass hysteria, the editors of the *Moniteur universel* found it appropriate to translate a long article by the English physician Mead, originally published in the *Morning Chronicle*, which explained the history, possible causes, and symptoms of the epidemic.[91] The translated article was followed by an addendum, underlining that the purpose of the exposé was to calm the public's anxiety over the possible introduction of the sickness into France by the returning army.

Concerns also remained about the French soldiers left behind on Egyptian soil.[92] Nothing summarized the dilemma of this situation better than two notes appearing next to each other in the *Moniteur universel* just four days prior to Napoleon's coup d'état.[93] The first of these short paragraphs reported that a soldier left behind in Egypt, but who made it to Paris on his own after Napoleon's return, was accusing the military leader of having cravenly abandoned his troops. The second note related the enthusiastic reception of a theater piece inspired by Egyptian themes. Since a genuine Mameluke who had returned with Napoleon's retinue to France was spotted in the audience, the performance assumed an electrifying authenticity. As this example shows, the inconsistency between the euphoria over the person of Napoleon and all things Egyptian, on the one hand, and the harsh reality of the campaign, on the other hand, became increasingly difficult to manage, even for uncritical editors.

The 18th of Brumaire imposed an almost instant and permanent silence on the press coverage of the campaign. The *Moniteur universel* became Bonaparte's official propaganda instrument and as such held a quasi-monopoly on information.[94] In the three years that followed, the deliberate oblivion enshrouding the Egyptian campaign was interrupted only once, when extensive excerpts from Denon's *Voyage* were reprinted in the newspaper.[95] The elevation of Denon's account to the status of a pseudo-official final report on the campaign was no coincidence. The *Voyage* was dedicated to Bonaparte, downplayed negative aspects of the expedition like the plague, and emphasized the revelation of Egypt's secrets through archeological exploration. Although the hardships and brutality of Mameluke battles and desert marches were described at length, they did not register with the reader as criticism of the campaign per se. The *Voyage* reprint complied with the mandate of Napoleonic propaganda by appealing to the reader's imagination through a hybrid of scientific reporting and romantic travel writing. Within the logic of this hybridity, the political controversies surrounding the campaign were effectively neutralized.

As in a prism, Western perceptions of Egypt shifted constantly during the eighteenth and nineteenth centuries, depending on who claimed to speak on behalf of the country, its society, or its history. Two schools of thought stand out in this muddle of voices and pseudo-expertise: the school of Enlightenment philosophes like Voltaire or Volney, and the esoteric school represented by Comte de Cagliostro or Abbé Terrasson, both of which were immediate antecedents to the Sophisians. Far from affording an opportunity for clarification, the events of Napoleon's campaign provided a second chance for the corrupting influences of superstition to gain hold. They crept up on the conquerors in the form of native metaphysics, opportunistic behavior from within the ranks, and hysteria at home kindled by rumors spread in the press. Instead of purging Egypt of impurities through Reason, Napoleon's army and scholars became the first victims of the impurities' resilience. Whereas the Enlightenment's grip on Egypt as a colonial possession always remained fickle and finally slipped completely in 1801, new spaces for negotiating Egypt's mythical past opened up. One such space was the Sophisian order transplanted to Paris.

3

Under the Pyramids of Paris:
Sophisian Rituals and the Golden Book

Nature likes to hide herself.
—Heraclitus[1]

SOMETIME IN 1813 THE PAINTER MARIE-NICOLAS PONCE-Camus joined the Sophisians. Trained in Jacques-Louis David's studio, Ponce-Camus distanced himself in Cuvelier's circle from his acknowledged expertise in miniatures and set design to identify himself solely as a history painter on the rosters he signed for the *Frères Artistes* until he left their lodge in 1824.[2] There was indeed a grain of truth to this assertion. David had accepted the future painter-in-residence of the Sophisians, then barely aged fifteen, in 1791, the very year that the older artist reinvented himself as a Revolutionary painter by agreeing to execute a monumental canvas of the *Tennis Court Oath* at the request of the National Assembly.[3] As for Ponce-Camus, the decision to pursue artistic training openly challenged parental authority, which had sent him before the outbreak of the Revolution to the prestigious Collège des Quatre-Nations, a school attached to the Institut de France, so that he might become a notary.

Brimming with Revolutionary fervor and outstanding artistic talent, the atmosphere of David's studio must have been electrifying for Ponce-Camus. Politically, David's activities during this year focused on lobbying for the abolition of the Royal Academy of Painting and Sculpture, which was to be replaced by the Commission des Arts under his leadership. Eliminating what royal privileges and control mechanisms remained in the production of art, the move was accompanied by the opening of the Salon to all artists, without regard to their membership in the Academy. In 1791, thanks to David, the principle of *égalité* finally arrived within the microcosmos of the Parisian art world.

By all accounts Ponce-Camus was never one of David's most intimate followers, but extant documents show that the master took it upon himself to procure studio space for him and later listed Ponce-Camus among his most talented pupils—although apparently only upon second thought.[4] Ponce-Camus's devotion to David, on the other hand, only grew over the years. When, after Bonaparte's fall, his former master had to withdraw to exile in Brussels as a regicide and supporter of Napoleon, Ponce-Camus sent him an obsequious letter assuring him of his undying loyalty and offered to paint a full-length portrait of his mentor.[5] He then seized the occasion to complain bitterly about his being discriminated against for defending the Davidian school. Indeed, in 1819 this overtly expressed pro-Davidian sentiment brought Ponce-Camus into open conflict with the Bourbon arts administration, which considered his *Alexander Visiting the Studio of Apelles* a disguised homage to Napoleon modeled on David's canvas of the same subject. The suspicion was reason enough to exclude the picture from the Salon, a decision that the artist bitterly resented.

Ponce-Camus's talents first came to the attention of a wider audience at the Salon of 1802 with his *Abbé de l'Epée and the Deaf-Mute Joseph, Comte de Solar*, a commission for the Institute of Deaf-Mutes in Paris, where it is still located. This early work features the institute's founder, the Abbé de l'Epée, who was the first to provide education to deaf-mutes in the eighteenth century, defending the rights of his protégé Joseph, disenfranchised merely because of his handicap. It would be easy to dismiss the work as a celebration of oppressed virtue, comparable to so many other Revolutionary canvases, if it did not anticipate the themes of unselfishness, philanthropy, and speechlessness that figure so prominently on Ponce-Camus's Sophisian artistic agenda by 1819.

In subsequent years, Ponce-Camus's claim to be a history painter came to rest mainly on a suite of large-scale canvases executed in the aftermath of the Napoleonic campaigns in Germany, the most important of which was *Napoleon Meditating before the Coffin of Frederick II of Prussia* (fig. 17), exhibited in the Salon of 1808.[6] This composition holds a particular interest for the study of Sophisian material, since its underground

Fig. 17 Marie-Nicolas Ponce-Camus, *Napoleon Meditating before the Coffin of Frederick II of Prussia in the Crypt of the Garnisonkirche in Potsdam on 25 October 1806*, 1808, oil on canvas, 181 × 232 cm. Versailles, Musée National du Château et de Trianon.

setting, melodramatic lighting, morbidity, and Masonic subtext foreshadow themes dear to Cuvelier de Trie's group. The subject is based on Bonaparte's historically documented visit to the crypt with the tomb of the Prussian soldier king Frederick II, located in the Garnisonkirche in Potsdam near Berlin, on October 25, 1806.[7] On the surface of things a homage from one great military leader to another across the distance of time, the painting would have been easily read by knowledgeable viewers as an allegory of a Masonic temple, featuring a "Column on the North" and a "Column on the South" (the lineup of attendants on either side of the arched gateway to the tomb), while the coffin itself marks the Orient (the direction of enlightenment). The checkered pattern of the floor, moreover, was completely a product of the artist's invention and resembles the type of black and white floor tiling ("Mosaic Pavement") required for

Masonic rituals (fig. 18).[8] If indeed Ponce-Camus's intention was to depict Napoleon as a *Vénérable*, or head of a Masonic lodge, he was harking back to themes in the Napoleonic legend that originally surfaced in the context of the Egyptian campaign.

Some Napoleonic apocrypha claim that one day in 1798 Bonaparte and his deputy General Kléber were ushered into the dark interiors of the Cheops pyramid by a venerable old man, directly descending from the sages of antiquity, who initiated them into the rite of Memphis on this occasion.[9] Contemporary French newspapers expounded this legend in the alternative version of a verbatim *Entretien de Bonaparte dans la grande Pyramide avec plusieurs Imams et Muphtis*, which was also supposed to have taken place in Memphis on August 12, 1798.[10] Praised by the flowery language of the commentator as a "genre of grandeur

Fig. 18 Interior view of the Masonic Temple "Johannis Corneloup" with mosaic pavement, early twentieth century. Paris, Seat of the Grand Orient de France.

and mysteries," the *Entretien* reveals itself upon closer analysis as a simpleminded ploy to justify the French occupation of Egypt in terms palatable to Islamic theology. Speculations about supernatural revelations that members of the Egyptian campaign received in secret underground chambers were also reinforced by the officially published findings of the Institut d'Égypte, which appeared in twenty volumes between 1809 and 1822.[11] Interestingly, the monumental tomes of the allegedly scientific and objective *Description de l'Égypte* were edited during the critical years between 1805 and 1807 by the Sophisian Michel-Ange Lancret. One of the most widely reproduced plates in the *Description* features a group of French *savants* assisted by native guides while they are exploring the intestines of the pyramids with the help of torches and ladders (fig. 19).[12] The maze-like structure, nocturnal setting, and exotic connotations implied by the natives' garments bestow distinctly metaphysical overtones to the archeological investigation of Egypt's key historical monuments.

The appeal of Ponce-Camus's *Napoleon Meditating before the Coffin of Frederick II of Prussia* rests primarily on the painting's claim to historic authenticity.[13] When the artist exhibited the canvas in 1808, it instantly became a favorite of both the Parisian audience and art critics, who praised the "genuine feeling inherent in the choice of a subject matter properly suited for painting."[14] Expressions of gratitude towards the artist turned into triumph when Napoleon acquired the work and had it hung in the dining room of his Trianon country retreat at Versailles. In every respect the painting matched both the emperor's personal preferences for aesthetic modesty and the image he wanted to bequeath to history as a contemplative military leader. Ponce-Camus had previously entered the prestigious (and financially rewarding) official competitions for large Napoleonic battle paintings, but his efforts met with little enthusiasm from the arts administration.[15] Now, the breakthrough seemed at hand, since even Napoleon's "minister for the arts," Vivant Denon, found warm words of appreciation for

VUES DE LA GALERIE HAUTE DE LA GRANDE PYRAMIDE, PRISES DU PALIER SUPÉRIEUR ET DU PALIER INFÉRIEUR.

Fig. 19 François-Michel Cécile and Jean Duplessis-Bertaux (left), Jean-Baptiste Réville and Jean Louis Delignon (right), *The Pyramids of Memphis,* **engraving, 52 × 41 cm. From** *Description de l'Égypte: Antiquités,* **1809–22, Vol. V, Pl. 13. Baton Rouge, Special Collections, LSU Libraries.**

the completed follow-up composition of *Napoleon at Osterode* in 1810: "This canvas enters naturally into the suite of events in the life of His Majesty. It is executed agreeably and with care; it makes a good impression and should be worth 500 francs more than the drawings in the gallery of the Prince de Neuchâtel."[16] Nevertheless, Ponce-Camus apparently encountered obstacles in building upon these short-lived successes.

Between 1802 and 1831 he showed about a dozen works in the Salon, but only sporadically received official commissions. His activities as a painter appear to have been guided above all by his patriotism and political idealism rather than by monetary concerns.

Indeed, Ponce-Camus had a second, very successful career as a set designer and effect specialist employed by various Parisian theaters. In the world of the popular stages he was simply known as Camus, one of the *machinistes* whose talents were "worth their weight in gold" for the entertainment industry of the early nineteenth century.[17] In this capacity he would have arranged for the customary pyrotechnical tricks, moving chariots, and hidden traps that turned theatrical performances and Sophisian rituals alike into special experiences for the spectators. This bread-and-butter job would not only have secured Ponce-Camus's livelihood, but also put him in touch with Cuvelier de Trie, who wrote the plays for the very same theaters that employed the painter. An intriguing side aspect to this theatrical connection was that Ponce-Camus's wife, one of the most prominent *Sophisiennes*, performed frequently in Cuvelier's plays by 1811.[18]

Evidence for the unusual collaboration between the painter and the playwright also comes in the form of Ponce-Camus's portrait of Cuvelier de Trie, preserved only as a lithograph in the departmental archives of the Pas-de-Calais (fig. 20).[19] The print shows Cuvelier as a chubby elderly man in a simple uniform and decked out with the insignia of the Legion of Honor, hinting at yet another shared biographical element between sitter and artist: their extended tours of active duty after the Revolution and during the Empire.

Like Cuvelier, Ponce-Camus served in the National Guard in the early 1790s and eventually rose to the rank of an officer. This military engagement interrupted his studies in David's studio on at least one occasion. During the Empire he may have accompanied Napoleon's armies to Southern Germany, as suggested by his title *Chevalier du Lion de Bavière*, a Bavarian decoration often conferred upon veterans of the German campaigns.[20] Unfortunately, since Ponce-Camus never applied for a pension, his military records remain spotty.

For Cuvelier de Trie, the campaigns in Germany and Poland from 1806 to 1807 brought to a close a long military career that started when he was only twelve years old in the port town of Ambleteuse in his native Calais region.[21] Promoted to the rank of captain in the National Guard, he settled in Paris in 1790. From this moment on, Cuvelier would pursue a parallel career as a prolific playwright for the Parisian popular theaters, changing

Fig. 20 Charles-Étienne-Pierre Motte (lithographer) after a drawing by Marie-Nicolas Ponce-Camus, *Portrait Cuvelier de Trie*, ca. 1824 (drawing prior to 1824), lithograph, 42 × 36 cm. Archives départementales du Pas-de-Calais, 6 Fi C 965.

plots—if political events required—from eulogies of Revolutionary virtue to celebrations of Napoleonic military prowess. Cuvelier rallied to Bonaparte immediately after the 18th of Brumaire and was rewarded with an appointment on March 23, 1800, to the First Consul's personal hussar regiment serving in Switzerland. Later he joined Napoleon's Rhine Army until his promotion in May 1804 to commander of the *guides-interprètes* in the Calais region. The interpreter-scouts were an élite translators' corps attached directly to Napoleon's headquarters and charged with the dual mission of providing translation services during campaigns abroad, while teaching French soldiers the basics of the English language at the camp de Boulogne in anticipation of the perennially delayed invasion of Great Britain. The latter charge, however, proved to be an exercise in futility, since even the best efforts of the *guides-interprètes* did not produce much in terms of desired results.

While still serving as commander of the interpreter-scouts under General Berthier in Poland, Cuvelier's

Fig. 21 Maquette of the Temple Enclosure in 1783, late eighteenth century. Paris, Musée Carnavalet, inv. PM2.

health, already strained from rheumatism and previous injuries sustained in action, further deteriorated. By 1807 he had returned to Paris with an honorable discharge. Yet, even in retirement, he "retained the trappings of his first profession in his outward appearance, and every day one would see him walking along the boulevards accompanied by his mistress, Mlle Dumouchel, a very beautiful actress who wore, like him, a military costume in the Brandenburg fashion, buttoned up from the waist to the neck."[22] Despite this dapper outward display of fashion consciousness and joie de vivre, Cuvelier's life was overshadowed by constant pain owing to his various injuries, and he finished his years a paralytic. Amazingly, none of these multiple handicaps ever seem to have prevented him from taking the lead in organizing Sophisian activities.

During the Napoleonic age, military charges of the type Cuvelier and Ponce-Camus held were prestigious assets that artists, no matter whether they were painters, writers, or actors, would use for their professional advancement.[23] Given the progressive militarization of French society through the Empire, such experiences could be decisive in obtaining official favors or simple tolerance of artistic expression from the powers that be. Not surprisingly, Napoleonic militarism provided the primary context for the Sophisians until the suspension of their activities in 1813. By the time Cuvelier revived the order with the help of Ponce-Camus in 1818, peacetime also had brought about the pacification of French culture.

Another formative influence on the Sophisian order was the urban environment from whence it originated. During the critical years between the last phase of Napoleon's empire and the revival of the Sophisians

under the Bourbons, both Cuvelier and Ponce-Camus lived in the neighborhood of the Temple district in the Marais, adjacent to the boulevard du Temple where the popular theaters were clustered.[24] A recruiting ground for new Sophisian members during the order's heyday, the Marais is located in the eastern part of the *rive droite*, extending roughly from today's Pompidou Center to the Bastille. At the northern end of the Marais was the Temple enclosure, which Cuvelier de Trie listed as his home address on the rosters of the *Frères Artistes.*[25] By the turn of the nineteenth century the Temple district still retained diverse tinges of its original social milieu, which it could only have acquired because of its unique historical place in the urban fabric of Paris (fig. 21). Its name derived from the Knights Templar, a military and religious order founded in Jerusalem during the First Crusade in 1118 to protect Christian pilgrims on their way to the Holy Land. After the crusaders were driven out of Palestine by the Arabs following the fall of Acre in 1291, Paris became the European headquarters of the Templar order. Their Temple enclosure (so named after the order's first establishment next to the site of the legendary Temple of Solomon in Jerusalem) provided its residents with a number of exemptions and special privileges: craftsmen were free from guild restrictions and could practice their trade unencumbered, the Jewish population was sheltered from persecutions, and debtors enjoyed immunity from imprisonment by order of their creditors. A city within the city surrounded by eight-meter-high walls and watch towers, the Temple's maze-like lanes and picturesque medieval architecture defined a neighborhood that attracted distinguished aristocrats of old money and artists alike. Most importantly, however, all of its roughly four thousand inhabitants were traditionally exempt from taxes.

THE GOLDEN BOOK OF THE BIBLIOTHÈQUE NATIONALE

Undoubtedly, the Temple district and its adjacent theater mile along the boulevards was a historically rich environment, whose atmosphere provided the humus for the never-ending quest to unravel the mysteries of lost cultures and civilizations that informed the Sophisian worldview. The illustrated version of the Golden Book in the Bibliothèque Nationale attests to these vastly eclectic influences, as they presented themselves to its creators, Cuvelier de Trie and Ponce-Camus. Perhaps the best way to interpret this complex document is to read it as Ponce-Camus's attempt to give visual form to Cuvelier de Trie's speculative reveries about the ancient Egyptian Isis myth and how it could become a catalyst for radical utopian change in an early modern society. Although physically written and painted by Ponce-Camus's hand, it is intellectually a collective product. Cuvelier de Trie, by his own testimony in the *Mélanges Lerouge*, saw himself as a custodian of the knowledge and aspirations of those members of the Egyptian campaign who had founded the order in Africa for the

> glory to work Masonically on the soil of the most ancient mysteries and on the very grounds where they had been practiced by the sages and skillful leaders of peoples and by kings. United on several occasions in their lodge, these investigators and commissioned interrogators discovered, it is said, in all parts of the classical lands where they traveled, documents according to which they founded the sacred institution of the Sophisians. Upon their return to France, charged with their precious materials, the contemporary successors of the Egyptian priests resolved to implant in their own country a sacred order that they announced as having been discovered under the pyramids. They even showed the ambition to destroy all other secret societies, Masonic or otherwise, to replace them with a new foundation, which, so they said, contained the original blueprint for all mysteries and all religions. The organization of the canon of these mysteries caused many problems, because those who worked to formulate it, rich in sciences, lacked the administrative knowledge indispensable for such a labor. The venerable and very illustrious brother Cuveillier [*sic*], informed about what was happening, presented himself and was immediately admitted to the sacred college. This rich material provided precious nourishment to his inventive genius, by means

of which the formless whole could be devised in a clear fashion and adorned in each one of its parts with emblems proper to attract all possible interests.[26]

Although some of these original pioneers and sages appear in ornamental and honorary roles within the context of Sophisian activities, there are many documented Egyptian campaign veterans from all walks of life, such as the architect Charles Norry, the musicologist Guillaume-André Villoteau, the army colonel Charles Holtz, or the lawyer Henry Royanez, whose appearances as active members occasionally date from as late as the Bourbon Restoration.[27] Moreover, the Sophisian foundation story has precedents in other Masonic organizations that were translated from Egypt to France, such as the lodge *Les Vrais Amis Réunis d'Égypte*, founded in Alexandria on August 20, 1799, and continuously active in Toulon until 1845.[28] Cuvelier de Trie may have been a man with a rich fantasy life, but there is always just enough truth at the bottom of his storylines about the Sophisian origins to make his statements credible.

Given his self-appointed title of Grand Isiarque, Cuvelier de Trie's role in developing the Sophisian canon is self-evident. To establish Ponce-Camus's artistic authorship of the Bibliothèque Nationale's Golden Book, however, requires a more refined analysis. A close comparison of the membership roster inserted in the BN manuscript with the annual rolls of the *Frères Artistes* shows that Ponce-Camus was the only visual artist who ever made an active and sustained commitment to Cuvelier's societies.[29] Given the secret (not to mention sacred) nature of the manuscript's content, it is inconceivable that an outsider could have been commissioned for the work. Moreover, the gouache illustrations in the BN Golden Book are, strictly speaking, miniatures, seldom measuring more than ten centimeters in height. The format and style of the drawings therefore reveal the manuscript to be the product of an artist accustomed to working in this genre, which was certainly the case with Ponce-Camus. Further support for the hypothesis of Ponce-Camus's authorship comes from an analysis of the handwriting found in the BN manuscript. With the exception of a four-page addendum consisting of *autres notices diverses*, the entire document was written by a calligraphic hand that indulged in an almost Mannerist fondness for curving, elongated characters. Comparing the manuscript's distinctive handwriting with extant letters by Ponce-Camus leaves no doubt that indeed he wrote the BN Golden Book.

These conclusions can be corroborated by retracing the artist's career within the order between 1813 and 1824, again using the *Frères Artistes* records as a proxy for organizational and administrative changes affecting the Sophisians. Ponce-Camus's joining of the organization in 1813 coincided with the aftermath of Bonaparte's Russian campaign, which marked the decline of the Napoleonic era. At that moment, Ponce-Camus was listed as a simple member. Shortly before the fall of the Empire, the Sophisians appear to have ceased all activities; at least there are no *tableaux* preserved for the period between 1814 and 1817 in the archives of the *Frères Artistes*. However, by 1818 Cuvelier de Trie revived both groups, and the years until the Grand Isiarque's death in 1824 saw the highest level of Sophisian activities yet. After the restoration of the order in 1818, military overtones gave way to a growing influence from the popular theaters, evident in the influx of new members from the world of the stage and an increased interest in festive activities. The order's intellectual profile thus reverted to the original self-definition of the *Frères Artistes* during the Directory, when the term *artistes* referred primarily to individuals associated with the theater.

Ponce-Camus's name reappears in the context of the restoration of the Sophisians in 1818, but again only as a simple member. This time he listed his profession for the first time as *peintre d'histoire*, a semantic detail that may already indicate higher ambitions for both his art and his role within the organization. By the following year, 1819, Ponce-Camus had risen through the ranks of the order and was now designated as *garde des sceaux et des archives*, the guardian of seals and archives.[30] This new appointment as scribe and record keeper can only be interpreted as a consequence of Cuvelier's request to paint the Bibliothèque Nationale's Golden Book since the previous roster was drawn.

The Golden Book's membership roll is dated, according to the Sophisian calendar, "the first day of the first month of the year 15,819."[31] Interpreting Sophisian dates can at times be a daunting task because of a changing base date after France's switch back from a Revolutionary to a Christian calendar in the early 1800s. By the late 1810s, however, the Sophisians surely used an almanac that simply added fourteen thousand years to the Christian calendar to signify the symbolic age of their mystery cult. It is therefore a fair assumption that the BN Golden Book was begun in 1819, the year all archives and seals were entrusted to Ponce-Camus, possibly to facilitate his work on what was conceived as a magnum opus summarizing the Sophisian canon of secret Egyptian knowledge. The last dated entries in the manuscript indicate a Sophisian year of 15,821, which suggests that Ponce-Camus

worked on the Golden Book over a three-year period, roughly between 1819 and 1821.

In the early 1820s Ponce-Camus had obtained the additional title of *Maître des Fêtes*, a charge which, given the nature of Sophisian initiations, would have drawn on all his skills as a set designer and effect specialist. In this capacity he would not only have organized initiations, but also the sumptuous *Fête Sophisienne (Hommage aux Dames)* held on February 2, 1821, in honor of all female members, followed only four months later by the *Agape Sophisienne* on May 29, celebrating the Egyptian deity Isis.[32] Décor, choreography, and costumes for these events were almost certainly all of Ponce-Camus's invention. Although many more festivities of this type may have taken place, only the events mentioned above can still be documented, thanks to the printed invitations preserved with the *Mélanges Lerouge* in The Hague. For those members who had lived through the years of the French Revolution, the Sophisian celebrations probably evoked lingering memories of those *fêtes révolutionnaires* that Ponce-Camus's master David had choreographed for the Parisian public during Robespierre's Terror regime. Although organized on a much more intimate scale and for a very specific audience, the *fêtes Sophisiennes* shared with the Revolutionary *fêtes* a predilection for such Egyptian décor as the Pharaonic Fountain of Regeneration erected on the Place de la Bastille for the *Fête de l'Unité et l'Indivisibilité de la République* on August 10, 1793 (fig. 22).[33] Ponce-Camus served the Sophisians faithfully until Cuvelier's death in 1824, when he abruptly left the order. The Grand Isiarque's passing marked a terminal crisis for the Sophisians, whose scope can only be compared with the temporary suspension of all activities prior to Napoleon's fall from power. Although the *Frères Artistes* continued to be active until 1840 under the leadership of Jean-Antoine-Joseph Fauchet, former Isiarque and Prefect of the Var department, the Sophisians never recovered from the exodus of members following Cuvelier's death. (It so happened that Fauchet had served in 1809 as Prefect of the Arno in Italy and in this capacity assisted Vivant Denon in plundering Italian art collections to "enrich" the Louvre in the name of Napoleon's glory.)[34] One way of interpreting the disappearance of the Sophisians in 1824 would be to ascribe the order's viability to Cuvelier's charisma, so that, with the playwright's death, the appeal of their Egyptian mysteries also vanished.

In the years following the restoration of the Sophisians in the late 1810s, the newly commissioned Golden Book must have played a central role in the

Fig. 22 Joseph Tassy, *Design for the Fountain of Regeneration, Place de la Bastille, Fête de l'Unité et de l'Indivisibilité de la République, August 10, 1793*, 1793, watercolor drawing, 22.6 × 37.0 cm. Paris, Musée Carnavalet, inv. D2414.

group's rituals. The *Livre d'or* served multiple functions: it was a repository of knowledge about ancient Egypt, an outline of rituals to be performed, a book of laws and moral principles to be followed, and finally a blueprint for exams and exercises to which aspiring initiates submitted.

Ponce-Camus's BN version of the Golden Book features a parchment binding, adorned on both recto and verso with three registers of Egyptianizing figures performing rituals against a sky-blue background surrounded by a decorative border containing pseudo-hieroglyphics (pl. 1). The artist's design choice was inspired by an attempt to imitate the "Bembine Tablet of Isis," whose composition features an identical distribution of compartments (fig. 23).[35] Also known as "Mensa Isiaca," this curious artifact, presumably created for an Isis temple of ancient Rome, is made of bronze with silver inlays. It was uncovered after the sack of Rome in 1527, whence it passed into the collection of Cardinal Pietro Bembo. After the Napoleonic conquest of Italy, the Bembine Tablet was brought to Paris in 1799, where Alexandre Lenoir reported it on display at the Bibliothèque Nationale in 1809. Following the appearance of a reproductive engraving by Enea Vico in 1559 and the publication of a succinct iconographic analysis by Athanasius Kircher in 1654, the tablet remained a standard reference in compendia of ancient art and Egyptosophic literature alike.[36] It was only in the late nineteenth century that scholarly opinions assigning the work to the Roman mystery cult of Isis prevailed. In the early nineteenth century, however,

the tablet was still widely believed to be genuine and of the greatest Egyptian antiquity, which inspired endless speculations about its iconography and symbolic meaning, sometimes even relating the work to numerology and Tarot.

A genuine Egyptian artifact may also be cited to explain the style of figure drawing on the covers of the BN Golden Book. This was a polychrome Ptolemaic or Roman-Egyptian funerary chest, made of stuccoed wood, that Vivant Denon had brought along from Egypt and which the painter Antoine-Jean Gros owned after 1824, before it entered the collections of the Louvre (fig. 24).[37] Prominently displayed in Denon's dining room on the Quai Voltaire during the 1810s and early 1820s, the chest's narrative describes an owl sacrifice. It features the same summary, cartoon-like style of figure drawing as the *Livre d'or* binding. Although less finely crafted than many artworks from the dynastic periods, the coffin is important for the study of Egyptian art because of its unique decoration and drawing style not seen in any other artifact, even from this relatively late point in Egyptian history. Given Ponce-Camus's excellent relationship with Denon, it seems reasonable that the artist would have enjoyed privileged access to the object during the critical years between 1819 and 1821.

The Golden Book's manuscript proper opens with a frontispiece depicting a veiled Isis figure wearing a blue skirt embossed with crescent moons against the backdrop of a partially obscured pyramid on the left side of the composition (pl. 2). In her hands she holds a ring and a hooked cross, the hieroglyphic *ankh*, symbol for the key of the Nile or, more generally, the key to life and fertility.[38] All these elements—the veil, crescent moon, and the hooked cross—are standard attributes that served to identify the goddess. To Isis's right, a pedestal inscribed with the words "I am all there was, all there is, and all there will be—no mortal till now has lifted my veil" lends a voice to the solitary figure. Although in no way identified as such, the motto is quoted from Plutarch, who reported that a statue of Neïth at Saïs, associated in the context of local worship with Athena and Isis, carried this inscription.[39] In slightly altered form the saying resurfaced in later classical texts, such as Proclus's commentary on Plato's *Timaeus*, or in eighteenth-century Egyptosophic literature.[40] A second inscription, however, located at the bottom of the page—"Guided by Isis, do not be afraid to make use, / To live according to the law is to live well, / But to abuse is a transgression"—seems to be of genuinely Sophisian derivation and highlights the importance of maintaining a Masonic regiment of self-improvement.

Fig. 23 *The Bembine Tablet of Isis*, engraving, 47 × 62.5 cm. From Athanasius Kircher, *Oedipus Aegyptiacus*, vol. 3, Rome, 1654. Wolfenbüttel, Herzog August Bibliothek Wolfenbüttel, 25.3 Quod. 2°.

The Isis mysteries are unquestionably the cornerstone of the Sophisian cosmogony. At the center of this Hellenized body of ancient Egyptian cults and myths stands the trinity of Isis, Osiris, and their son Harpocrates.[41] The divine family's fate is recounted in an epic struggle pitching the siblings and royal consorts Isis and Osiris against Seth, identical with Typhon in his Greek form. Seth is not only Osiris's brother but also the embodiment of the evil principle, whose attributes contrast sharply with those of Osiris, regulator of the Nile's inundations and protector of nature and fecundity. Osiris is also one of several Egyptian deities cited for the invention of hieroglyphics, which makes him a proponent of civilization in general. His female consort Isis is the mistress of magic and the goddess of the royal throne. In its classical form, the Isis legend relates how Seth organized a banquet for his brother returning from battle, following which he lured Osiris

to lie in a magnificent, custom-made casket that turned out to be a lethal trap. The incapacitated Osiris was then killed by Seth, his body cut in pieces, and the remains of his corpse scattered along the Nile. Upon learning of her husband's death, Isis set out to gather and reconstitute his remains. She managed to assemble his body, save for his phallus, which she proceeded to revive in its recreated form to impregnate herself. Following these events she gave birth to Horus, represented in countless Egyptian statuettes in his infantile form of Harpocrates seated on his mother's lap (fig. 25). As the "feeble" Harpocrates grew up to become Horus, he avenged his father and assumed rule over a country unified for the first time. For this reason Horus came to be regarded as the mythical ancestor of all Pharaohs.

As a coherent narrative, the Isis legend is a product of Greek and Latin writers active over a period from the early fifth century B.C. to the second century A.D.

Fig. 24 Funerary Chest, Ptolemaic or Roman-Egyptian period, ca. fourth to first century B.C., wood, stucco, and polychrome paint, H: 27.0 cm, Base: 20.0 cm. Paris, Musée du Louvre, département des Antiquités égyptiennes, inv. AF 427.

Fig. 25 *Isis Breastfeeding Harpocrates*, Late Period, 712–332 B.C., bronze. Paris, Musée du Louvre, département des Antiquités égyptiennes, inv. H 1704.

Fig. 26 Marie-Nicolas Ponce-Camus, *Golden Book of the Sophisian Order, Apophthegms: The Book of Hermes Trismegistus*, ca. 1819–21, pen, ink, and gouache on paper, 5.2 × 11.0 cm (illustration). Paris, Bibliothèque Nationale de France, MSS FM 4.15, fol. 5v.

The most important source certainly remains Plutarch's *De Iside et Osiride*, but variations on the saga also abound in the texts of Herodotus, Apuleius, and Diodorus of Sicily, among others.[42] Plutarch's treatise is of particular interest in connection with the Sophisians, not only because it concerns itself exclusively with the Isis myth, but also because it was part of the *Corpus Hermeticum*, attributed by Italian Neoplatonic compilers of the Renaissance to the legendary author Hermes Trismegistus. Although the Sophisians were notoriously shy in divulging their sources, the order's high esteem for the semidivine sage is made explicit in one illustration from the BN *Livre d'or*, which features a book inscribed with the name of Hermes Trismegistus displayed on a mound (fig. 26). As we shall presently see, the Hermetica turned out to be a treasure trove of mystery knowledge for the Sophisians, who freely borrowed elements from these writings and adjusted their contents as they deemed fit for their rituals. This approach should not necessarily be dismissed as the work of amateurs, because it was only in 1822, when the ink of the last entries in the Golden Book was hardly dry, that Jean-François Champollion presented his groundbreaking method for deciphering

Egyptian hieroglyphics and unlocking the secrets of genuine Egyptian inscriptions and papyri.

In the absence of this information, the Sophisians present the reader with an (admittedly skewed) survey of received knowledge and popular notions about ancient Egypt on the eve of modern Egyptology, enhanced by the recent discoveries of the Napoleonic campaign. Despite their fundamental differences, it needs to be kept in mind that both Champollion and the Sophisians sprang from the same Napoleonic scholarly milieu that was originally spawned by the Institut d'Égypte in Cairo. Typically, members of these circles held staunchly republican and anticlerical views during the 1790s, before rallying to the Bonapartist cause by the turn of the century.[43] As for the Sophisians, they never concealed their indebtedness to the Greek view of Egypt during classical antiquity. They also aired their philhellenic sentiments by actively recruiting Greek refugees in Paris, or by openly siding with the Greek movement for independence from the Ottoman empire.[44] Philhellenism in the context of French politics of the 1820s was synonymous with opposition to the Bourbon Restoration that supported the Turks, and implied a liberal and intellectual position that could easily blend in with Napoleonic nostalgia. The most eloquent partisan among the Sophisians for the cause of Greek liberation was certainly Guerrier de Dumast. During the April 1821 reception ceremonies in honor of four Greek exiles admitted to the *Frères Artistes*, he encouraged the "children of Greece to come to us. You need a fatherland [*patrie*]: you will find it with the French. . . . You need affectionate consolation: you will find it among the Masons, since they consider all mortals as brothers."[45] Later in life, he confessed that the event reminded him of "the Aurora of a new day that seems to dawn on Mt. Athos." Sophisian-style Greco-Egyptian scholarship therefore always also carried politically charged meanings underneath its placid and philanthropic surface.

After the frontispiece of the BN Golden Book, there follows a membership list or *tableau* drawn up in 1819 (15,819 according to the Sophisian calendar), reflecting the order's profile at the moment when Ponce-Camus set to work on the manuscript (see appendix). Written in the artist's hand, the introductory text to the *tableau* informs the reader that:

> The ancient Golden Book shall be closed, sealed with a hieroglyphic Scarabaeus, finished, and deposited in the archives of the Conclave. A new Golden Book shall be established on Papyrus leaves; ornamented with hieroglyphics; it shall carry at its head the complete list of the members [*colonne des membres*] of the order since the elevation of the Grand Pyramid in France, with remarks about those dead or alive. The new Golden Book shall be signed by all former members who were a part of the order to this day and by those absent, who shall be re-admitted in due form, and finally by those [new] aspiring members after their admission to the second-class level.
>
> ☞ By order[46]

While this preamble neatly establishes the new Golden Book as a product of the Sophisian renaissance of the late 1810s, the whereabouts of the first Golden Book remains shrouded in mystery. One may perhaps gain a feeling for its contents from the certified copy issued to the Sophisian chapter in Toulon sometime prior to 1813 and now preserved in the Grand Orient collection in Paris. The Grand Orient manuscript is devoid of illustrations and repeats in simplified form the texts and rituals outlined in the BN version. The transcripts of Golden Book texts in the *Mélanges Lerouge* in The Hague, on the other hand, are clearly marked as copies of an original in the Grand Pyramid (a Sophisian term for temple) of Paris and follow the BN manuscript verbatim, strongly suggesting a post-1819 date. If indeed

an original first Golden Book existed, no traces of it remain today. Even so, one can conclude that it would have lacked a rich apparatus of illustrations, because its creation predated Ponce-Camus's joining of the group. One can further speculate whether the missing first *livre d'or* was created in Egypt during the Napoleonic campaign or written in Paris after the evacuation of the French colony in 1801. Either way, the conclusion will depend on the credibility one is willing to assign to the foundation story that the Sophisians crafted for themselves.

In the section that follows in the BN *livre d'or*, Ponce-Camus introduces the reader to twelve *Apophthegms* or sayings of wise men from antiquity, conveyed in the form of pictorial rebuses and literary conundrums. The *Apophthegms* open with a second frontispiece depicting a strangely androgynous Harpocrates, who carries a cornucopia while holding his left index finger to his lips. The Sophisians interpreted this hallmark gesture as a command of silence (fig. 27), which they found congenial to their rituals based on a regime of muteness.[47] The emphasis on silence is reinforced by the related maxim, exceptionally inscribed directly underneath the miniature, which reads "close your mouth, so that the honey flowing from your half-opened lips be more suave than the balmy breath of Harpocrates." By subscribing to this interpretation of the Harpocrates iconography, the Sophisians inadvertently perpetuated a misconception originating with Plutarch, who, as a Greek foreigner, had failed to recognize the pose's native Egyptian context, which stressed the youthful immaturity of a puerile god still sucking his fingers.[48] Other Hermetic writers firmly cemented the association of Hermes with silence as a commonplace of initiation, such as Asclepius, who, in his discourse "Hermes Trismegistus to His Son Tat," makes the semidivine sage say: "My child, intelligent wisdom is [enjoyed] in silence, and the seeds sown are the true Good."[49] The frontispiece is then followed by a dedication to "the Seven Immortal Sages, the Sovereign Patriarch, and the Five Virtuous Mortals, known under the name of Isiarques," reflecting the structure of Sophisian hierarchies, where Egyptian pseudonyms concealed the identities of dignitaries.

Each one of the twelve *Apophthegms* consists of a spread in the Golden Book that features a miniature painting on the left-hand folio and a poetic adage, frequently exhorting philanthropy, on the right-hand folio. The individual sayings and their attendant illustrations (called "hieroglyphics" in Sophisian lingo), as well as the solutions to the rebuses obtained from a manual annexed to the main texts in the Golden Book, can be summarized as follows:

Description of "Hieroglyphic"	Apophthegm on Facing Page	Interpretation in Solutions Manual
Lyre (fol. 4v.)	"Be attentive to the Voice of Wisdom, / that it may not be a vain sound in your ears, / that it may penetrate and captivate your souls like the chords / of the harmonious Lyre"	"Lyre, emblem of harmony in the words of wisdom. The ancients put all morals in the form of music"
Book of Hermes Trismegistus on a Knoll—Fig. 26 (fol. 5v.)	"Metal polished by a skillful hand / reflects luminous rays; / [thou shalt] convey in the same way the Lessons of Wisdom"	"Book, symbol of the first depository of human knowledge"
Pot of Gold (fol. 6v.)	"The Rich [person] owes to the Poor [person], / the Strong [person owes] to the Weak [person], / the Seer to the Blind"	"Purse, embodiment of active good deeds; formerly this was the hand always ready to give"
Hand Sieving (fol. 7v.)	"Sow on Sand and Rock / The Seeds may encounter a place which they fecundate"	"Winnowing basket, it separates the chaff from the sweet grain; this is what initiation does to morals"
Flame on Altar— Fig. 28 (fol. 8v.)	"Continue to spread good deeds / Even if ungrateful people will turn against you. / Does the flame not devour the substance which keeps it alive?"	"Burning fire, explained by the motto, which, in its positive sense, says that ungratefulness should not discourage the benevolent being"
Bending Reed/ Lightning Breaks Oak Tree (fol. 9v.)	"Respect the Unfortunate. / As the reed bends under the northerly gale, / so can lightning uproot the oak tree tomorrow"	"Oak and Reed, the facing motto [already] offers a clear explanation"
~~Two Hemispheres of the World~~ (fol. 10v.)	~~"You are Five, make not but one, / Be like the Zones whose five Parallels embrace the Globe"~~	~~"Globe of the World, this geological image demonstrates that the division into zones was not as unknown to the ancients as one believed; as far as morals are concerned, it expresses the hope of spreading throughout the world the Seeds of Wisdom"~~
Five symbols as follows: 1. Sun & Eye 2. Mouth 3. Thunder 4. Heart 5. Phallus & Hand (fol. 11v.)	"Let the Sovereign Patriarch be the Sun that warms and fertilizes, the head that / commands and inspires to move: The First Isiarque, the eye which surveys; / The Second [Isiarque], the Mouth that teaches; / The Third [Isiarque], the Thunder that Illuminates and Strikes; / The Fourth [Isiarque], the Heart that receives and gives; / and the Fifth Isiarque, the Hand that points and traces"	"The Sun (Solus) identifies the unique leader ruled by the Superior and Immutable Laws; the Eye designates Surveillance, the Mouth Teaching, the Heart the equal distribution of vital forces by its double-movement: to receive, to give by means of the Hand of the Execution"
Coiling Snake (fol. 12v.)	"Your tasks are the same. / Run without variation along the points / on the circle traced for us"	"The Snake is but the emblem of the divine circle"
Sphinx-hooded Sophisian "Ark" with Isiarque emblems Sun/ Eye/Heart— Fig. 29 (fol. 13v.)	"Search the Light in the bosom of sacred Mysteries: / But that no mystery you were made a part of ever leaves / the Tabernacle without our express will"	"Ark, emblem of the alliance between divine and human morals; here, it also signifies that the secrets confided to the adepts may never be violated"
Standard Pole with Cat-Faced Pinnacle (Cat of Bubastis), Flying Banner with a Bull's Head (Apis) (fol. 14v.)	"If your Lights turn insufficient, / If uncertainty for one instant shakes your decisions, / then suddenly the symbolic sign of the call [to order] floats above the summit of the Pyramid; / as quick as the light we shall be with you"	"Egyptian Banner, mounted symbolically above the pyramid when the secret conclave (whose decisions rule the order sovereignly) is assembled. The conclave is formed by the reunion of seven inivisible governors and five invisible governors"
Giving Tree— Fig. 45 (fol. 15v.)	"The man doing good deeds, like the Alma, gives both fruits and / flowers, which will be replaced to the extent that they / fall"	"Alma, tree of India that carries flower and fruit at the same time"

Maxime.

Clos ta bouche, ou que le miel coulant de tes levres
entrouvertes, soit plus suave que l'haleine embaumée)
g^d harpocrate.

Fig. 27 Marie-Nicolas Ponce-Camus, *Golden Book of the Sophisian Order, Harpocrates Commanding Silence,* ca. 1819–21, pen, ink, and gouache on paper, 9.8 × 8.5 cm (illustration). Paris, Bibliothèque Nationale de France, MSS FM 4.15, fol. 3v.

Fig. 28 Marie-Nicolas Ponce-Camus, *Golden Book of the Sophisian Order, Apophthegms: Flame on Altar Devouring its Own Substance,* ca. 1819–21, pen, ink, and gouache on paper, 9.5 × 7.3 cm (illustration). Paris, Bibliothèque Nationale de France, MSS FM 4.15, fol. 8v.

The *Apophthegms* survey a wide range of typically Sophisian interests and themes, including Egyptology, hermetic mysticism, enlightenment, learnedness, deism, nature worship, and altruism. A transitional note to the next chapter of the BN Golden Book declares the *Apophthegms* instruments to reinforce Sophisian notions of moral superiority, and encourages the initiate "to conserve the moral empire given to us by the Constitutional Charter."[50]

This Constitutional Charter (fig. 30) marks a pivotal chapter in the Golden Book. Commensurate with its status, the charter is preceded by an ample apparatus of prolegomena, opening with another frontispiece (pl. 3) described in the solutions manual as "Osiris with the head of Anubis stepping with his feet on Typhon [represented] in the figure of a crocodile, (id est) virtue subduing vice, the probable archetype of St. Michael with his Dragon."[51] Obviously, the painting was intended as an allegory of the eternal fight between the

principles of good and evil, rendered in terms of the Isis legend, where Osiris appears as the regulator of the Nile's inundations and the inventor of hieroglyphics, hence his association with nature, fecundity, reason, and the dawn of civilization. Typhon, or Seth, as he is known by his native Egyptian name, is Osiris's evil stepbrother, the instigator of crime and the principle of both evil and unreason.

Although sculptures with the effigy of Horus treading on a crocodile are known to have been carved in Ptolemaic and Roman Egypt, the prototype for the stele in the Golden Book is of Hellenistic Greek origin (fig. 31).[52] This antiquity, originally published in the sixteenth century by Jean-Jacques Boissard, was reproduced and commented upon in the eighteenth century by Bernard de Montfaucon, followed by another illustrated exegesis by Alexandre Lenoir in 1808.[53] According to Montfaucon, the scene depicts the dog-headed god Anubis, guard of Isis and Osiris, flanked

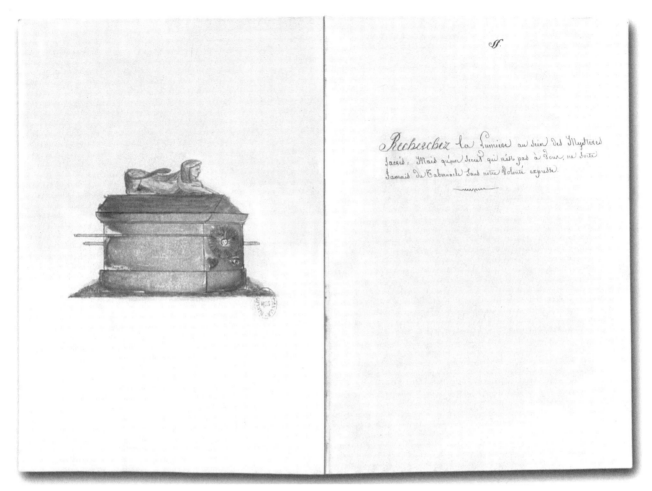

Fig. 29 Marie-Nicolas Ponce-Camus, *Golden Book of the Sophisian Order, Apophthegms: Sphinx-Hooded Sophisian Ark with Isiarque Emblems,* **ca. 1819–21, pen, ink, and gouache on paper, 5.8 × 8.8 cm (illustration). Paris, Bibliothèque Nationale de France, MSS FM 4.15, fol. 13v.**

by the floating head of Serapis with the horns of Jupiter Ammon on the left, and the bull's head of Apis on the right. Anubis holds a caduceus and a sistrum, which, in the Golden Book drawing, turn into a globe and winged staff featuring the rising thunder-bird Phoenix, another privileged deity in the Sophisian pantheon. The Greek inscription of the original stele described Anubis and Apis in a typically Hellenistic fashion as "Brother Gods." Lenoir mostly agreed with this interpretation, but provided a more detailed analysis of the lateral symbols. For him, the palm branch on the left is a reminder that Anubis was the inventor of astrology, while the laurel leaf on the right describes his eloquence. The Egyptian deity also presided over commerce and the inundations of the Nile, which is signified by a package of merchandise and the amphora in the lower left-hand corner. The Sophisians liked such eclecticism, because it added ever new levels of complexity to the game of interpreting the Golden Book.

The intellectual challenge of finding satisfactory interpretations for these rebuses was an integral part of Sophisian rituals, in which initiates were asked to present their own solutions to the riddles presented.

Lenoir, director of the Musée des monuments français, which functioned as a repository for religious art and artifacts looted during the French Revolution, returned to the theme of the animal-headed figure in Egyptian art in 1814, when he published *La Franche-Maçonnerie rendue à sa véritable origine*, a book celebrating the Egyptian origins of not only Freemasonry, but all world religions. The publication contained numerous engravings by the fashionable printmaker Jean-Michel Moreau le jeune of Pharaonic initiation rites, Isis mystery processions, and portraits of the most important mythological figures in the Egyptian and Greco-Egyptian pantheon. One of the plates (fig. 32) depicts, according to Lenoir, "Anubis with his jackal's head holding, in one hand, a staff with a coiling serpent

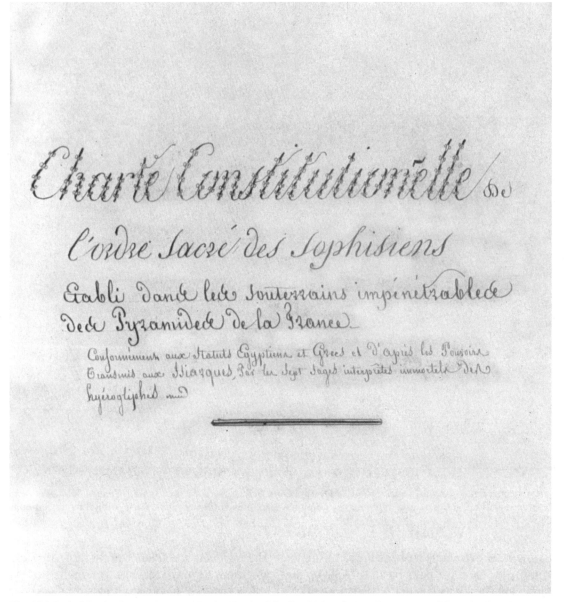

Fig. 30 Marie-Nicolas Ponce-Camus, *Golden Book of the Sophisian Order, Cover page of Constitutional Charter,* ca. 1819–21, pen and ink on paper, 29.2 × 20.5 cm (page). Paris, Bibliothèque Nationale de France, MSS FM 4.15, fol. 71r.

and, in the other, the key of the Nile; his head is adorned with solar rays. It was under this guise that one of the ministers of Osiris presented himself to the initiate at the moment when he was to take the first step towards initiation, in the voyage through the underground that he had to go through before continuing to submit to the tests."[54] The passage presents an interesting shift in interpretation away from a purely symbolic and mythological figure in a static environment, descriptive of the world of scholarly antiquarians, to a setting in which the protagonists of the Egyptian pantheon come to life and play an active part in the events unfolding, which

characterizes the world of Egyptosophy. Lenoir's decision to install a jackal-headed Osiris priest at the entry to the underground passage to initiation is consistent with the place of the analoguous illustration in the liturgy of the Golden Book. The placement of Osiris before the Constitutional Charter has symbolic meaning above all, because it is he who who ushers the reader cum initiate into the main body of the mysteries.

According to its preamble, the Constitutional Charter was promulgated "in the name of the Grand Goddess," that is Isis herself, and put "under the auspices of Harpocrates."[55] The Isis evocation is juxtaposed with

Pl. 1 Marie-Nicolas Ponce-Camus, *Golden Book of the Sophisian Order, Cover Imitating the Bembine Tablet of Isis,* ca. 1819–21, pen, ink, and gouache on parchment, 29.9 × 21.2 cm. Paris, Bibliothèque Nationale de France, MSS FM 4.15.

Pl. 2 Marie-Nicolas Ponce-Camus, *Golden Book of the Sophisian Order, The Great Goddess Isis (Nature) under a Veil That Can Never Be Lifted, except During the Grand Mysteries,* ca. 1819–21, pen, ink, and gouache on paper, 26.2 × 16.2 cm. Paris, Bibliothèque Nationale de France, MSS FM 4.15, fol. 1v.

foⁿᵈ du Temple d'la Sagesse
inᵛⁿⁱ Pierre Sacré, Duⁿclaβa

Pl. 3 Marie-Nicolas Ponce-Camus, *Golden Book of the Sophisian Order, Rebus for the Class-Two Scholar of Hieroglyphics Degree: Osiris with the Head of Anubis Treading on a Crocodile,* ca. 1819–21, pen, ink, and gouache on paper, 19.8 × 16.1 cm (illustration). Paris, Bibliothèque Nationale de France, MSS FM 4.15, fol. 16v.

Pl. 4 Marie-Nicolas Ponce-Camus, *Golden Book of the Sophisian Order, Class-One Initiation to the Aspirant Degree: Underground Cave Scene with a Sword Suspended by a Hair from a Lion's Head in the Ceiling above the Neophyte,* **ca. 1819–21, pen, ink, and gouache on paper, 22.2 × 18.3 cm (illustration). Paris, Bibliothèque Nationale de France, MSS FM 4.15, fol. 66v.**

Tableau figuratif.
Chambre des Sépultures.

Pl. 5 Marie-Nicolas Ponce-Camus, *Golden Book of the Sophisian Order, Class-Two Initiation to the Aspirant Degree: Underground Cave Scene with Mummies; Initiation Ritual with Mixed Male (Black Tunic) and Female (White Tunic) Participants,* ca. 1819–21, pen, ink, and gouache on paper, 17.6 × 15.2 cm (illustration). Paris, Bibliothèque Nationale de France, MSS FM 4.15, fol. 68v.

Pl. 6 Marie-Nicolas Ponce-Camus, *Golden Book of the Sophisian Order, Rebus for the Class-One Scholar of Hieroglyphics Degree: Syringe with Columns of Thoth-Hermes (Mercurii Columnae)*, ca. 1819–21, pen, ink, and gouache on paper, 14.5 × 18.0 cm (illustration). Paris, Bibliothèque Nationale de France, MSS FM 4.15, fol. 37r.

No. 2

Trinus, unus.

Phta, *Neith,* *Cneph,*

Maxime à Interpréter.

Tu impera velut omnium ara.

Pl. 7 Marie-Nicolas Ponce-Camus, *Golden Book of the Sophisian Order, Rebus for the*
Class-One Scholar of Hieroglyphics Degree: Sophisian Triad with Ptah, Neith, and Kneph,
ca. 1819–21, pen, ink, and gouache on paper, 13.7 × 4.2 cm (illustration). Paris, Bibliothèque
Nationale de France, MSS FM 4.15, fol. 39r

Pls. 8–9 Marie-Nicolas Ponce-Camus, *Golden Book of the Sophisian Order, Rebus for the Class-One Scholar of Hieroglyphics Degree (two views): 'Moral Triangle' with Sun, Goat, Hidden (left)/Exposed (right) Phallus and Hooked Cross of Isis*, ca. 1819–21, pen, ink, and gouache on paper, diameter 5.0 cm; 6.2 × 17.4 cm (illustrations). Paris, Bibliothèque Nationale de France, MSS FM 4.15, fol. 40r.

Pl. 10 Marie-Nicolas Ponce-Camus, *Golden Book of the Sophisian Order, Rebus for the Class-Two Scholar of Hieroglyphics Degree: Horus, Jupiter Ammon, Osiris, Serapis as Allegorical Figures for the Seasons and the Ages of Man*, **ca. 1819–21, pen, ink, and gouache on paper, 19.4 × 19.2 cm (illustration). Paris, Bibliothèque Nationale de France, MSS FM 4.15, fol. 42r.**

Pl. 11 Marie-Nicolas Ponce-Camus, *Golden Book of the Sophisian Order, Class-One Initiation to the Scholar of Hieroglyphics Degree: Stage Setting with the 'Temple of Wisdom' to Receive the Neophyte,* **ca. 1819–21, pen, ink, and gouache on paper, 18.0 × 17.8 cm (illustration). Paris, Bibliothèque Nationale de France, MSS FM 4.15, fol. 72v.**

Pl. 12 Marie-Nicolas Ponce-Camus, *Golden Book of the Sophisian Order, Class-Two Initiation to the Scholar of Hieroglyphics Degree: Stage Setting with Isis Throne to Receive the Neophyte,* ca. 1819–21, pen, ink, and gouache on paper, 16.7 × 18.3 cm (illustration). Paris, Bibliothèque Nationale de France, MSS FM 4.15, fol. 75v.

alpha.

Nº 2.

Quies, Justitia Sané ambæ in Deo.

Pl. 13 Marie-Nicolas Ponce-Camus, *Golden Book of the Sophisian Order, Rebus for the Class-One Professorship of the Grand Mysteries Degree: Egyptian Landscape 'Alpha'*, ca. 1819–21, pen, ink, and gouache on paper, 14.7 × 18.3 cm (illustration). Paris, Bibliothèque Nationale de France, MSS FM 4.15, fol. 47r.

Omega.
N° 3.

Pl. 14 Marie-Nicolas Ponce-Camus, *Golden Book of the Sophisian Order, Rebus for the Class-Two Professorship of the Grand Mysteries Degree: Alchemical Apparatus 'Omega'*, ca. 1819–21, pen, ink, and gouache on paper, 14.2 × 18.7 cm (illustration). Paris, Bibliothèque Nationale de France, MSS FM 4.15, fol. 48r.

Pl. 15 Marie-Nicolas Ponce-Camus, *Golden Book of the Sophisian Order, 'The Triumph,'
or Class-Three Initiation to the Professorship of the Grand Mysteries Degree: Admission of
a Sophisian to the Highest Order of Wisdom in an Idealized Egyptian Setting,* ca. 1819–21,
pen, ink, and gouache on paper, 18.5 × 20.4 cm (illustration). Paris, Bibliothèque Nationale
de France, MSS FM 4.15, fol. 79v.

Pl. 16 Louis Léopold Boilly, *The Entrance to the Théâtre de l'Ambigu-Comique before a Free Performance*, 1819, oil on canvas, 66 × 80.5 cm. Paris, Musée du Louvre.

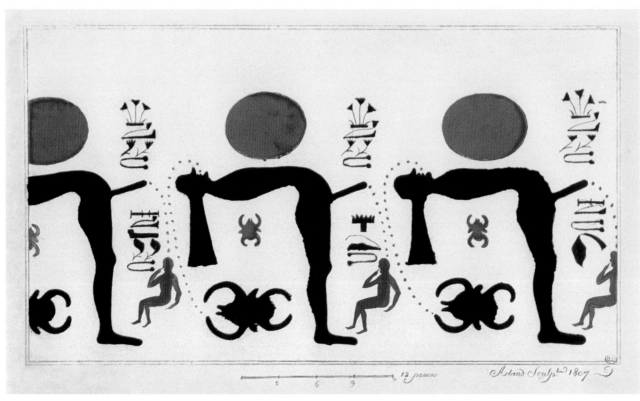

Pl. 17 Artaud after a drawing by Jean-François Pugnet, *Hieroglyphic Tableau from the Temple of Denderah, tomb of King Bab-el-Melouk*, copied from the frontispiece in Jean-François-Xavier Pugnet's *Mémoires sur les fièvres pestilentielles*, ca. 1807, hand-colored engraving, 13.7 × 24.2 cm. From Fabien Richelme, *Mémoire rélatif aux monumens de l'Égypte, considérés dans le sens hermético-maçonnique*, 1807. Paris, Bibliothèque Nationale de France, Rés. P. R.1084.

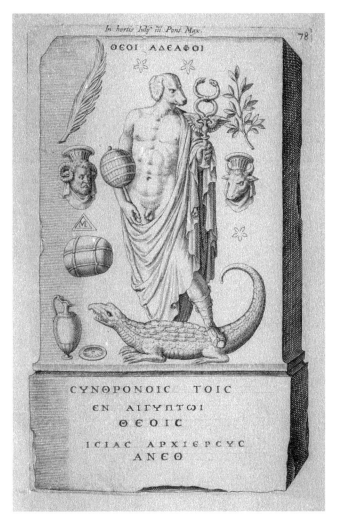

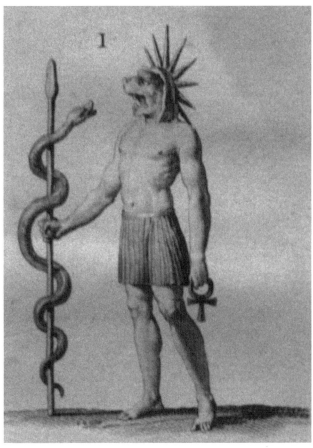

Fig. 32 Jean-Michel Moreau le jeune, *Anubis, Egyptian Divinity*, 1791, engraving, 8.5 × 6.5 cm. From Alexandre Lenoir, *La Franche-Maçonnerie rendue à sa veritable origine*, 1814. Paris, Bibliothèque Nationale de France, Réserve.

Fig. 31 Theodor de Bry, *The God Anubis*, 1602, engraving, 26.2 × 16.1 cm. From Jean-Jacques Boissard and Theodor de Bry, *Antiquitatum romanorum*, Vol. 3/II (Pt. VI), Plate 78, 1597–1602. Wolfenbüttel, Herzog August Bibliothek Wolfenbüttel, 185.3 Hist. 2°.

the illustration of a twenty-two-step pyramid, identified in the solutions manual as "the Great Cheops pyramid, where the order is symbolically assembled."[56] It is followed by five *Paragons* or comparisons, which are simply continuations of the miniature-painted rebuses already encountered in the *Apophthegms* section. The reader here successively encounters a sphinx, a Gallic cock, a phoenix, an urn with the head of an ibis peeking out, and a pelican.

Devoid of illustrations, the charter is divided into four sections with up to fourteen articles each. The sections outline in great detail the responsibilities of Sophisian officers according to their rank, the costumes and insignia to be worn, the degrees within the order, and the accreditation procedures for satellite "pyramids" outside Paris, as well as the rights and obligations of individual

members. The charter concludes with the text of an oath of allegiance to be sworn by aspiring Sophisians. An addendum itemizes formulas for how Sophisian officers were to be correctly addressed according to their rank, along with a painstakingly detailed decree on Sophisian costumes and jewelry, issued by the "Secret Conclave on the 10th day of the 12th month, 15,820 [December 10, 1820]."[57] The addendum highlights a manifest shift towards festive and confraternal activities in the early 1820s, which stood in striking contrast to the traditional initiation rituals based on intimidation and fear, the typical features of the Egyptian rite after 1789.

Two hieroglyphics for Sophisian women constitute the transition to the exams and study manuals for the three principal levels of Sophisian initiation, mimicking the Masonic degrees of Apprentice, Fellow Craft, and Master Mason. The first of these two *hyérogliphes des Sophisiennes* depicts "Youth Supporting Blindness," in the form of a young woman guiding an old one walking with a stick, and the second, "Innocence

Fig. 33 Marie-Nicolas Ponce-Camus, *Golden Book of the Sophisian Order, Hieroglyphics for the Sophisiennes: Innocence Prevailing over Power*, ca. 1819–21, pen, ink, and gouache on paper, 5.8 × 13.0 cm (illustration). Paris, Bibliothèque Nationale de France, MSS FM 4.15, fol. 31v.

Fig. 34 Marie-Nicolas Ponce-Camus, *Golden Book of the Sophisian Order, Rebus for the Class-One Aspirant Degree: Pyramid with Sphinx, Phoenix, and Gallic Cock; Harpocrates Commanding Silence*, ca. 1819–21, pen, ink, and gouache on paper, 14.3 × 18.4 cm (illustration). Paris, Bibliothèque Nationale de France, MSS FM 4.15, fol. 34r.

Prevailing over Power," features a blindfolded woman commanding a lion on a chain (fig. 33).[58]

The three degrees of the Sophisian order—Aspirant, Scholar of Hieroglyphics, and Professorship of the Grand Mysteries—are each divided into two classes. The corresponding study and solution manuals comprise the visually most appealing passages of the Golden Book. The need for sumptuous illustrations emerged from the specific function of the manuals in the context of the initiation rituals, since "the Aspirants cannot proceed with the initiation unless they have studied and explained the hieroglyphics of aspiration and practiced philanthropy and good deeds, the essential virtues of a Sophisian."[59]

ASPIRANTS

Presided over by an occluded sun (motto: *non omnibus lucet*), the first-class "study of Aspiration" opens with an alpha-numerical riddle which asks the apprentice to explain the Greek name for the Nile, *Nilos*, in terms of the numerical order of the corresponding letters in the Greek alphabet. Another rebus features the image of the coiling snake from the *Apophthegm*, but inscribed

with the Latin motto *videbunt et non videbunt*—they can see and they cannot see. Among the prescribed exercises for aspirants was the interpretation of an Egyptian landscape painted in gouache with a large pyramid in its center, the base of which is flanked by representations of a sphinx, a phoenix rising from the ashes, and a Gallic cock (fig. 34). In the lower right corner of the composition, a Harpocrates is giving the sign of *silentium*. When confronted with the image, a neophyte would have identified the pyramid as a symbol for the order, and the sphinx and the cock as emblems of Egypt and France, respectively, while the phoenix would have stood for rebirth through initiation and purification.[60] Below the illustration, a Latin motto, *Fodias invenies*, exhorted the aspirant to "excavate in order to find." The painting is the first instance of an illustration in the Golden Book where Ponce-Camus moves away from the vignette format and presents the viewer with one of his framed full-page compositions.

In the separate section at the end of the Golden Book, a more detailed description provides insight into how these symbols were used in actual cult practices. Under the heading *Place of Assembly and Materials* the Sophisian pyramid cum temple is described in the following terms:

A cavern in the countryside: above the vault, a lamp with seven branches; in the background a stone table and a circular bench for the Supreme Tribunal. On the table, the heart of Ch_ and S_ [Charity and Silence] covered with a black veil, a stylus, and a tablet for writing. Above the tribunal, the sun veiled by clouds with the inscription *Non omnibus lucet* [it does not shine everywhere]. Above the entryway to the interior, a serpent, biting its own tail, amidst vaporous rays with the inscription *videbunt, non videbunt*. In the middle, a rock forming a seat, above a large and long sword, airborne and cutting, suspended from a hair coming out of the mouth of a lion affixed to the vault. Outside the entryway, a large mechanical pyramid in wood: when touched by the Recipient, it will swing open and one reads in fiery words: *Enter, if you dare*. An iron barrier padlocked from the outside, distant from the pyramid by 6, 8, or 10 feet at least. Around the cavern, before arriving at the barrier, a recess without a door, being the cabinet of retreat; inside, a rock as a seat, no light at all.[61]

The description is accompanied by one of Ponce-Camus's full-page gouache illustrations (pl. 4), which replicates the written description with a few variations. Presiding over the assembly on an elevated platform in a vaulted recess are the five unmasked governors of the Supreme Council, also known as Isiarques. Below the tribune sit two Sophisian officers, identified as Harpocrates and Nomarque. While the former is in charge of "maintaining order and silence," the latter functions as a spokesperson for the Grand Isiarque, a protocol officer, and an instructor.[62] Along the rusticated walls of the vault, hooded members of the order have taken their seats on benches surrounding the neophyte in the center. The only embellishment to their austere black tunics consists of a bird-shaped headdress, alluding to membership in the Sophisian Order of the Phoenix. On the ceiling of the vault, the two Latin mottos, *Non omnibus lucet* and *Videbunt et non Videbunt*, are repeated. In the foreground a so-called Mystophor (literally: mystery bearer), armed with a sword, guards the secrecy of the initiation. According to the Golden Book, he has an invisible homologue outside the cavern called

Naophilax, or lover of the temple interior. Ponce-Camus took artistic liberty by moving the barrier and the recess for the cabinet of retreat inside the cavern, where he labeled them for the sake of clarity with the inscription *entre, si tu oses*—enter if you dare.

Perhaps the most fascinating aspect of the composition is the central, seated figure of the neophyte, who turns his back upon the viewer, while above the vault a sword, suspended on a hair from a lion's mouth, hovers above his head. The ordeal is an obvious allusion to the sword of Damocles in Greek legend, which had gained renewed iconographic currency during the French Revolution through one of Jacques-Louis David's masterworks (fig. 35). On January 20, 1793, a former royal bodyguard had mortally stabbed a Jacobin deputy and regicide of aristocratic descent by the name of Lepeletier de Saint-Fargeau in the Palais Royal. David rose to the occasion and organized the elaborate public funerary ceremonies for the fallen hero of liberty held at the Place Vendôme. Within only two months of the body's lying-in-state, David had completed a life-size canvas after his Vendôme display. It depicted the deputy's reclining corpse with its ostentatiously displayed wound, while a menacing sword of Damocles, hovering above, pierces Saint-Fargeau's ballot for Louis XVI's death. Although the original oil painting is reputed to have been destroyed, its composition survives in the form of a contemporary black-chalk drawing by David's collaborator Anatole Devosge.[63] From this copy, one learns that David suspended the sword precariously on a hair-like thread attached somewhere on an imaginary ceiling beyond the viewer's field of vision. The first of David's portraits in a series of "Revolutionary Martyr" paintings, the *Death of Lepeletier de Saint-Fargeau* was a widely known and indeed a very public work of art. On March 29 David had presented the canvas as a gift to the Convention, where it would remain installed above the speaker's rostrum along with its pendant piece, the *Death of Marat*, until February 1795. As a student of David during these years, Ponce-Camus would certainly have been familiar with the work on more than just a superficial level. He could have observed the progress on the painting while still in David's studio, and he would have known its iconography and its home in the Convention. Lingering memories of the work quite possibly informed the content of Ponce-Camus's Sophisian cavern scene more than a quarter of a century later.

But did the cavern setting described in the Golden Book really exist? It is above all the Sophisians' close association with the Parisian popular stages that makes the enactment of such an elaborate initiation

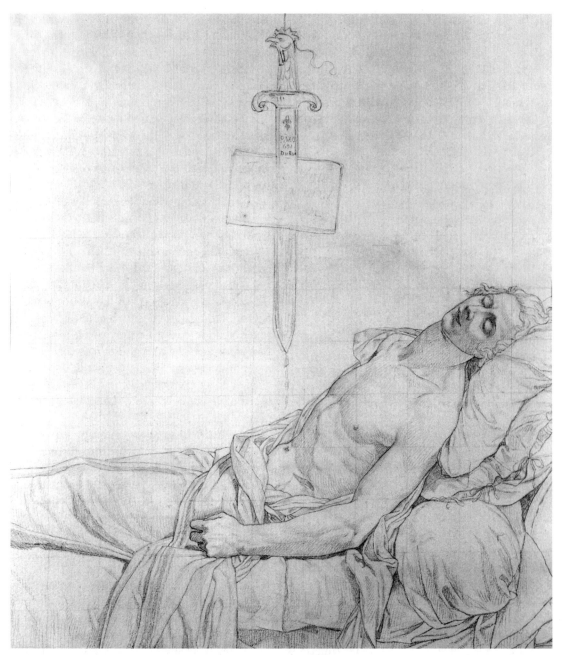

Fig. 35 Anatole Devosge after Jacques-Louis David, *The Death of Lepeletier de Saint-Fargeau*, 1793, black chalk on paper, 46.7 × 40.0 cm. Dijon, Musée des Beaux-Arts.

more plausible. If rituals of this type did in fact take place, their most likely setting would have been the popular theaters along the boulevard du Temple in Paris, where Sophisian activities were concentrated over so many years.

The Golden Book contains yet another drawing for the more advanced class-two initiation of the Aspirant, which took place in the granite-lined "Chamber of Sepulchers" (pl. 5). This time, the interior accom-modates a mixed audience of male and female aco-lytes. The chamber is decidedly more sumptuous than the cavern, and the texts make no mention of an un-derground setting. Nevertheless, morbid overtones resound prominently in the décor. Both the ceiling with its three-pronged candelabrum and the six niches along the walls housing "mummies and ibis urns" are painted in monochrome black.[64] A faint shadow in the background, Ponce-Camus's Egyptian landscape composition with a pyramid, sphinx, phoenix, cock, and the figure of Harpocrates (fig. 34) makes a surprise return as a full-fledged painting hung at the rear of the meeting hall. Behind the tribunal on the stage, a sarcophagus symbolically represents the tomb of Ozymandias, a corrupted form of the Greek name for Ramses popularized in the early nineteenth century by one of Shelley's poems. With the inclusion of female members, the number of Isiarques in the Supreme Council doubled to ten; female Isiades are easily recognizable by their headgear in the form of a crescent moon, as well as the white dress with a black veil prescribed for all *Sophisiennes*. The group is seated around an elongated table on which "the golden heart covered in black" is displayed.

Below the raised tribune, before the Isiarques, a prop supposedly representing the "Ark . . . covered with a heavy black veil" is depicted. Contrary to the written description, however, the artist painted a diaphanous veil, so as to allow the viewer to see the Ark underneath. Despite frequent references to this symbolism in Sophisian rituals, the Golden Book provides no solution for its meaning. Apuleius relates in his *Metamorphoses* how a casket containing "secret attributes, concealing hidden objects of magnificent sanctity inside," was carried in the procession of Isis.[65] This description was a code for Osiris's genitals. In the Jewish tradition, on the other hand, the Ark of the Covenant (the "Holy of the Holies") contained the Tablets of the Law and was placed by King Solomon himself in the inner sanctuary of his temple. Cuvelier de Trie was certainly aware of the importance of the Ark in both its Old Testament and Masonic contexts, since in 1817 he wrote a play dealing with the profanation of the Temple of Solomon and the destruction of the Ark by the Syrian king Antiochus IV Epiphanes.[66]

In the foreground of the initiation scene one finds the neophyte surrounded by an assembly of eight regular Sophisian dignitaries of both sexes seated on lateral "red granite benches." He is prominently exposed on a pyramidal, stepped pedestal in the center. Apparently, the purpose of the reunion is the examination of a candidate, who is quizzed on matters such as the "explanation of hieroglyphics and maxims." The supplicant was then required to deliver a discourse about the "hieroglyphic" painting of a female cadaver and a rosebush he or she had studied in the "cabinet of retreat." Understandably, no trace of the painting remains, but the Golden Book contains a trustworthy vignette-type copy of the composition (fig. 36). This illustration was inserted towards the end of the study manual for the Aspirant degree, where the vignette appears above the motto

ex morte vita—from death, life. The session terminated with an admonition to the neophyte that: "The one who renounces or withdraws, no matter in which degree, is considered dead, and his name shall be inscribed without honor on a funerary column. Nobody shall advance a degree without having explained, by dint of his spirit and reason, the hieroglyphics and enigmatic sentences of the previous degree."[67] To confirm the resolve to become a Sophisian, the neophyte was then asked to swear on the ashes of his or her hair, a sample of which was deposited in an urn.[68] In return for the oath, he or she received a white veil in honor of Isis.

SCHOLAR OF HIEROGLYPHICS

The procedures to attain the "Scholar of Hieroglyphics" degree were even more elaborate and complex than those prescribed for the Aspirants. The corresponding study manual opens with a drawing of an Egyptianizing underground maze rendered entirely in gray and black gouache with ink (pl. 6). The caves are accessed from a staircase on the right side of the composition leading to a dizzying succession of vaults, chambers, doors, niches, columns, and pilasters. The setting is entirely devoid of human presence, but remarkably, all the columns are inscribed with fantasy hieroglyphics so as to highlight the special importance of the place. A further hint as to the meaning of the illustration is provided by the identification of the maze as a *syringe*, a specialized architectural term describing underground burial chambers in the Valley of the Kings, and particularly at Thebes, where long, narrow passageways precede the tombs.[69] The solutions manual goes to even greater length in interpreting the rebus: "*Syringe*. Labyrinth dug by the Hierophants after the deluge for fear of a new cataclysm and to lock away the hieroglyphic columns destined to preserve for posterity all human knowledge; the syringes served for the celebration of mysteries; here Plato and Pythagoras acquainted themselves with the study of [hieroglyphic] columns."[70] From the cultural perspective of the turn of the nineteenth century, an obvious starting point for interpreting this iconography and its commentary is the *Encyclopédie*. Under Diderot's entry for *Égyptiens*, one indeed finds the Hierophant introduced as a temple guardian and specialist for hieroglyphic inscriptions, who "made perceptive to the imagination of natives and the curiosity of strangers all that they needed to see for the glory of the nation and in their own interest."[71] As a writer whose intellectual orientation was thoroughly consistent with the Enlightenment's view on Egypt,

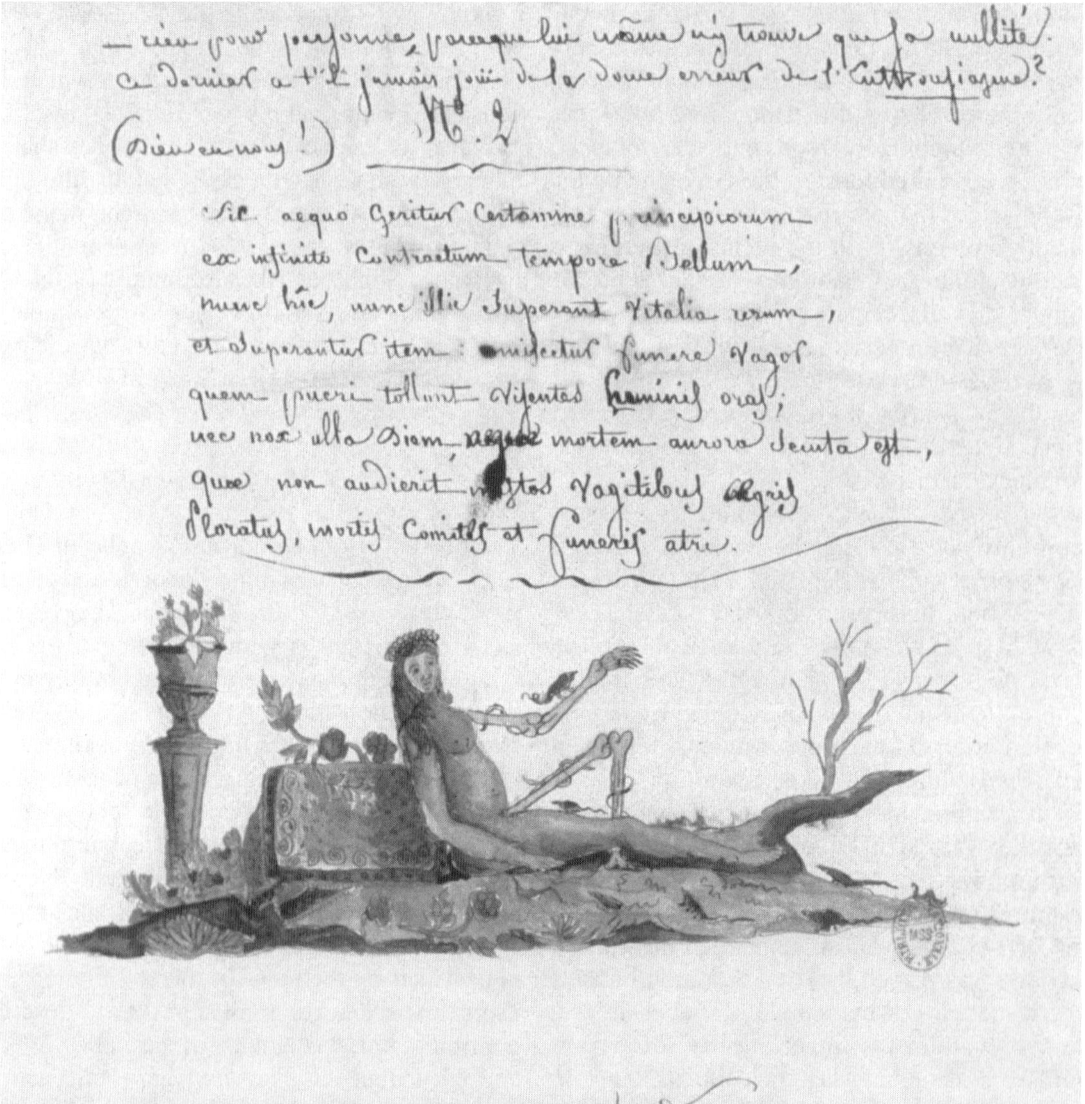

Fig. 36 Marie-Nicolas Ponce-Camus, *Golden Book of the Sophisian Order, Rebus for the Class-Two Aspirant Degree: Female Cadaver and Rosebush*, ca. 1819–21, pen, ink, and gouache on paper, 6.8 × 17.0 cm (illustration). Paris, Bibliothèque Nationale de France, MSS FM 4.15, fol. 36r.

Diderot envisioned the Hierophant in Herodotus's time as a mediator between the native temple priests and the Greek philosophers exploring Egyptian mysteries in the place where they originated.[72] Based on Eusebius, his essay also relates the following rather fanciful history of the inscribed columns erected by the Greco-Egyptian composite deity Thoth-Hermes:

> Hermes, the son of Agathos Daimon & father of Tat, or the second Mercury, succeeded Thoth in the historical or legendary annals of Egypt. Thoth had perfected theology; discovered the first principles of arithmetic and geometry. Struck by the inconvenience of symbolic images, he replaced them with hieroglyphics and elevated columns on which he had engraved the new characters that he had invented, [describing] the things he felt necessary to pass on to posterity. It was thus that he tried to overcome the inconsistencies of tradition; the people erected altars and organized celebrations in his honor. Egypt was then ravaged by internal and external wars. The Nile broke its levies; it made vast openings that submerged a large part of the country. The columns of Agathos Daimon were overturned, and science and art were lost. Egypt almost fell back to its first state of Barbarism, when a man of genius took it upon himself to collect the debris of ancient wisdom, to assemble the dispersed monuments, to research the key to the hieroglyphics, to increase their numbers, and to confide their intelligence and caretaking to a college of priests. This man was the third founder of the wisdom of the *Egyptians*. The people counted him at once among the number of the Gods and worshipped him through the name of *Hermes Trismegistus*.[73]

Diderot faithfully summarized in this passage a recurrent topos of Hermetic theurgy, according to which the native Egyptian god Thoth, traditionally credited with the invention of writing and the protection of magic, was the grandfather of the Greco-Egyptian Hermes Trismegistus. One of the more esoteric classical writers of Hermetica, the pseudo-Manetho, concludes the saga by recounting that "after the Flood [the hieroglyphic texts inscribed by Thoth] were translated from the sacred language into Greek, and deposited in books in the sanctuaries of Egyptian temples by the second Hermes [Hermes Trismegistus], the son of Agathos Daimon and father of Tat."[74] Confusion between Hermes Trismegistus and his father Agathos Daimon—Hermetic literature almost randomly identified one or the other as translator of the Egyptian hieroglyphics into Greek—creates recurrent genealogical problems in the saga that not even Diderot knew how to resolve. More often than not this confusion was deliberate. For the classical Hermetists, the grafting of a second (or even a third) Hermes upon the figure of

Thoth served a dual function. For one, they "wished it to be believed that their compositions were books of Thoth rendered from Egyptian into Greek." Secondly, to lay claim to "the legitimacy and prestige of these books" required "plausible explanations of how this translation had been brought about."[75] The Thoth-Hermes saga fulfilled both purposes. As a literary product of the hybrid cultures of Ptolemaic and Roman Egypt, the Hermetica pursued similar strategic ends as the Sophisian documents in that they sought to usurp the prestige of established ancient traditions in order to obscure their own more recent derivation.

Cuvelier's mention of Plato and Pythagoras studying together the inscriptions on the columns of Thoth-Hermes suggests acquaintance with yet another text from the *Corpus Hermeticum*, namely Iamblichus of Apamea's *De Mysteriis Aegyptiorum*, written at the turn of the fourth century A.D. in Syria. A thoroughbred product of Greco-Egyptian syncretism in late antiquity, Iamblichus's treatise on the mysteries of the Egyptians, Chaldeans, and Assyrians opens with a scene in which the philosopher-tourists Plato and Pythagoras "read through" a stele of Hermes with the help of native priests in order to export the wisdom contained therein to Greece.[76] By all evidence, even this obscure episode did not escape the attention of the Sophisian pageant masters.

Nor did they ignore the existence of texts from the Hermetic milieu of late antiquity that provided specific instructions concerning the underground cache of the *Mercurii Columnae*, as the columns of Thoth-Hermes were also known. Here is what the mid-fourth-century historian Ammianus Marcellinus, a friend of the apostate Emperor Julian, had to say on this subject: "There are certain underground galleries and passages full of windings, called syringes, which, it is said, the adepts of the ancient rites (knowing that the flood was coming, and fearing that the memory of the sacred ceremonies would be obliterated) constructed in various places, distributed in the interior [of the caverns], which were mined out with great labor. And leveling the walls, they engraved on them numerous kinds of birds and animals, and countless varieties [of creatures] of another world, which they called hieroglyphic characters."[77] Marcellinus's testimony may offer the most plausible explanation for the Sophisians' insistence on calling their Golden Book rebuses "hieroglyphics," when in fact they were nothing but humble gouache drawings. Moreover, as will emerge shortly, the Sophisians harbored a distinct predilection for images of birds, animals, and fantasy creatures in these "hieroglyphic" rebuses. As all these examples demonstrate, some members of the order were more profound scholars of classical antiquity than one would have expected from their deliberately confusing indulgence in obscure references.

The Thoth-Hermes saga appealed to Cuvelier's group for an obvious reason: like the Greek philosophers of the Hellenistic age, the founding fathers of the Sophisians had been foreigners who came to Egypt in order to study theology, literature, hieroglyphics, and art—at least this was the myth gleefully perpetuated by apologists of Napoleonic nostalgia seeking to divert attention from the military fiasco of the Egyptian campaign. By extension, the Sophisians could bask in the light of being Hermes Trismegistus's epigones, because, like the legendary hero and author, they could claim to have collected and preserved the threatened remains of Egyptian greatness for the benefit of all humanity.

Sophisian rituals must have shifted constantly between iconological interpretations, hermeneutics, and performance. Not surprisingly, therefore, the *syringe* image is followed in the BN Golden Book by a number of textual and musical exercises, including the *Hymne Sacré pour l'Initiation* and the *Chant d'Orphée*. Since musical interludes were an integral part of Sophisian pageantry, both poems were presumably set to music by one of the renowned composers in the order, such as Louis-Alexandre Piccinni, grandson of the Italian composer Nicolò Piccinni, who was famously brought to Paris in 1776 as Marie-Antoinette's teacher of song. Another prominent Sophisian musician was Jacques Foignet père, a theater director and professor of solfeggio, harpsichord, and harp. Interestingly, some musical scores of Sophisian inspiration do survive, such as the *Hymne Sacré des Anciens Mystères*, composed by Foignet père for the previously mentioned *Fête d'Isis* in August 1821.[78] The *Conseils de Mentor dans l'Asile du Silence*, a song composed for a play with strong Sophisian overtones written by Cuvelier in 1811, was set to music by Piccinni, the "artist retained by His Majesty the Emperor and King Napoleon Bonaparte for private musical entertainment."[79] Despite its esoteric contents, the *Asile du Silence* was a popular success on stage since it celebrated the birth of Napoleon's son. It is worth quoting the *Chant d'Orphée* of the Golden Book at this point, not only because the poem conveys the flavor of these interludes, but also because it serves as an introduction to one of the most intriguing illustrations of the Golden Book, the Sophisian trinity:

> This god, people of the Nile, who rules over your
>   masters,
> is in himself alone the root and the branch of beings;
> The hand upholds the Sky, the Earth, and Hell,

> Matter and Spirit share in its essence;
> He unites the rings of this immense oak tree
> that, from the star to the atom, encompasses the
>   universe;
> of the being assembled [from its parts] his voice
>   produces the germ,
> and is thereof the principle as much as it is the term;
> The Sage of Memphis becomes gradually cognizant
>   thereof:
> within the flame of the nights and the morning star;
> The earth below fully unfolding its ornament,
> The wave that restores the luster of greenery,
> The fire that through our senses maintains the vigor,
> All, to the lightened eyes, paints [the view of] an
>   original motor:
> God comes like a husband to fecundate nature;
> he announces himself to the unthankful [beings], but by
>   striking them,
> he speaks, and his decrees make the passage without
>   murmur
> from nothingness to being and from being to
>   nothingness.[80]

The chant's attribution to Orpheus is fitting, because it is predicated on the god's role as singer, lyre player, poet, and charmer of animals, which qualified him as a titular deity for a sung poem. Orphic associations with Egypt had existed since antiquity, but were reinforced after the mid-seventeenth century by the success of Kircher's *Oedipus aegyptiacus* publication.[81] Abbé Terrasson's novel *Séthos*, moreover, had helped establish Orpheus as one of the earliest initiates who submitted to the Egyptian-rite tests by the elements administered under the Cheops pyramid, from whence he brought the Isis mysteries to Greece. A few years later, the Abbé Pluche in his *Historie du ciel* even asserted that Orpheus and Horus were essentially identical, thus further bolstering the myth of an "Egyptian Orpheus."[82] The Sophisians proved to be sensitive again when it came to grafting their rituals onto existing textual sources dealing with Hellenized Egyptian materials. For instance, the reference to a monotheistic God is rare in the Golden Book. The vast majority of the Sophisians belonged to a generation that had grown up under the ancien régime, in an intellectual climate tinged with the often virulently anticlerical writings of philosophes such as the Baron d'Holbach or Diderot. They had witnessed or participated in the overthrow of established religious institutions in the name of Reason during the Revolution, and entered the Napoleonic age as Deists and Naturalists. Members of the Egyptian campaign in particular were also infamous for their atheism, which raised immediate suspicion among the native population when Napoleon hinted at the possibility that he and his army could convert en bloc to Islam.[83] The offer was widely interpreted as further proof of the colonizers' hypocrisy and disrespect for local culture and customs.

The allusion to a monotheistic creator God in the Golden Book, however, is entirely consistent with the structure of genuine Orphic hymns of late classical antiquity, in which the formula "there is *one* god," quoted originally after Xenophanes, is a recurrent trope.[84] As scholars of this type of literature have pointed out, "the hymns were used by a religious association of people who called themselves mystic initiates and who, through prayer, libation, sacrifice, and, presumably, secret ceremonies invoked a deity and asked for its presence or for the gift of some blessing, such as wealth, peace, health, and not infrequently 'a blameless end to a good life.'"[85] All of these concerns are addressed, for example, in the *Hymn to Kronos:*

> Everlasting father of blessed gods and men,
> resourceful, pure, mighty, and powerful Titan,
> you consume all things and replenish them, too.
> Unbreakable is the hold you have on the boundless
>   cosmos,
> O Kronos, begetter of life, Kronos of contrasting
>   discourse,
> child of earth and starry sky.
> In you there is birth and decline, august and prudent
>   lord of Rhea,
> who, as progenitor, dwell in every part of the world.
> Hear my suppliant voice, o wily and brave one,
> and bring an ever blameless end to a good life.[86]

Orphic hymns could variably invoke Greek gods, such as Zeus, Hera, or Poseidon, or natural elements, such clouds, the sea, the sun, or even death. The literary structures and cosmogonies they espouse are in all respects compatible with those of the Sophisians, since both groups maintained the essential unity of nature and a supreme being as creative principles of the universe, while sharing a general sense of pessimism about human existence.[87] The Sophisians, however, distinguished themselves from the Greek Orphists by situating the classical hero in the context of Egyptian mysteries. In doing so, they relied on an extensive body of eighteenth-century literature on classical mythology and religious history that promoted the hypothesis of an Egyptian Orpheus as a figure allegedly linked to the cult of Isis.[88]

With the depiction of the Sophisian Trinity (pl. 7), facing the Orphic hymn, one is back on the nebulously polytheistic ground where the Sophisians are properly at home. The vignette for this rebus consists of a bull's head, mounted on a Rococo-style pedestal, which provides a platform for a figure group consisting of a male genius, an owl, and a female figure; snakes coil around the anthropomorphic figures and support the world egg at the pinnacle. Underneath, the protagonists are identified as the Egyptian deities Ptah, Neith, and Kneph, and at the bottom of the page appears the Latin motto *Tu impera velut omnium arae,* a reminder that the triad rules over all altars. Again, the solutions manual provides some helpful hints for interpreting the meaning of the allegory: "*Triad.* A. Kneph (god of goodness) B. Ptah (power of god) C. Neith (god's wisdom). Three names for divinity, Kneph holds in her mouth an egg, emblem for the creation of the globe; Ptah, god of fire, the Greek Vulcan, issues therefrom, to animate everything; Helios (Sun) is the son of Ptah; after the Sun follows Agathos Daimon or good genius, providence."[89] While one's first impulse is to associate the Sophisian trinity with Isis, Osiris, and Horus, it needs to be remembered that ever-changing variations of divine triads were common coin from the lowly magician to the august temple priest of Hellenized Egypt.[90] Guerrier de Dumast, for one, was convinced that Ptah, Kneph, and Neith formed the "first Egyptian trinity, prior to that of Isis, Osiris, and Horus, [which are] allegorical divinities."[91] Despite such speculations, neither Egyptian mythology nor Hermetic texts show an inclination to group Ptah, Neith, and Kneph together, which suggests a heavy dose of modern-day ingenuity and editing efforts in order to arrive at the divine triad.[92] Individually, however, Ptah, Neith, and Kneph are firmly established members of the Egyptian pantheon.

Ptah was a deity closely associated with the temples at Memphis, renowned until Ptolemaic and even Roman times for their traditionalism.[93] For the Memphites, Ptah was the divine artist and craftsman, a role that earned him the attribute of a close-fitting blue cap of the type smiths, craftsmen, and other workmen sometimes wore in the mastabas of the Old Kingdom. A primal creator and inventor of the world's egg, he was the first of all the gods. In the Golden Book, Ponce-Camus faithfully introduced the identifying cap surmounted by a small flame, but otherwise followed the canon of idealized nudity prescribed by neoclassical aesthetics. The bull's head, serving as a pedestal, probably also belonged to Ptah. The great temple of Memphis, for instance, contained enclosures for the Apis bull, which was revered, among other animals, as one of the embodiments of Ptah.

Another chthonic Egyptian deity was Neith, the female figure on the far right of the Sophisian triad, who was worshipped at Saïs and, during the Ptolemaic era, at Esna.[94] She was the goddess of hunt and war, but her typical attributes of bow and arrow are absent from Ponce-Camus's depiction. Neith has been described as the Egyptian *Urgöttin*, since she was regarded as the mother of the sun god Re, the Greek Helios, which established her as one of the ancestors of Thoth-Hermes. The owl that appears on the base of the Sophisian trinity belongs to Neith, although her association with wisdom is of course a purely Greek, indeed Attic, convention.

Kneph is also known as the serpent-deity of Thebes, who was an embodiment of Amûn.[95] First mentioned in Ptolemaic literature, Kneph was known to Plutarch, who associated her with agelessness. A primordial creature, the cobra is said to have emerged from the waters at the beginning of the earth's existence. There is frequent confusion of Kneph with that other important snake persona of the Egyptian pantheon, Agathos Daimon, especially in Alexandria, home to the latter deity.

The egg at the pinnacle of the triad, we are told, is an emblem for the creation of the world. This idea has a colorful mythological history. At one time or another, the world egg may have been associated with Osiris and Kronos, according to Diodorus of Sicily, or with Orpheus, who, in the Hermetica, "likens Chaos to an Egg in which was the confusion of the primordial elements."[96] The Golden Book's juxtaposition of the Sophisian triad with the *Chant d'Orphée* was thus certainly not a scriptural coincidence, since Orphic legends conceived of the undeveloped world as a mystic egg.[97] If one takes these cues for what they are worth, it may seem plausible to read the entire composition as a competing version of the creation story, rendered in Greco-Egyptian terms. Support for this theory comes from one of the Sophisians' uncanny contemporaries in France, Alexandre Lenoir, whose influential book *La Franche-Maçonnerie rendue à sa véritable origine* appeared in 1814. A convoluted and openly syncretistic apology for the Egyptian origin of all civilization, the publication has the merit of establishing the missing context for the three deities Ptah, Neith, and Kneph, as well as for the bull and the egg of creation:

> According to Diderot, the Egyptians had two theologies, the Esoteric or secret one, and the Exoteric or external one. The first one admitted no other gods than the universe; no other principles of being but matter and movement. Nevertheless they [the Egyptians] recognized an intelligent being distinct from matter that they called Ptah; this was the fabricator of the universe, the living god, whose wisdom they personified under the name of Neith, represented as a woman emerging from the body of a lion, just as, in Greek mythology, Minerva issued forth from the head of Jupiter. The god Kneph of the Egyptians, mentioned by Plutarch, is an eternal god who neither ever had a beginning, nor will he ever have an end. They maintained that this all-powerful god, to create the world, had united two co-eternal principles existing in him, *matter* and *soul*, which engender movement and life. This god Kneph, or the primal and all-powerful god, is represented by the serpent producing an egg with its mouth. This symbolic egg, broken by a touch from the horns of the celestial bull, according to the religion of the Persians and the Japanese, is the symbol of the world.[98]

Although entirely contrived, Lenoir's account provides a coherent mythological narrative for the Sophisian triad, where Ptah and Neith are, respectively, the physical and the spiritual creators of the world presided over by Kneph, the divine principle.

Creation and fertility are ongoing concerns in the initiations accompanying the Scholar of Hieroglyphics degree. The rebus, described as *triangle moral* or moral triangle, comprises a sun, a goat, an erect phallus hidden behind a nondescript coat of arms, and the "hieroglyphic cross of the Phallus, general emblem of the sun and of [Isis's] divinity" (pls. 8–9).[99] The last symbol is identical with the Egyptian hooked cross or hieroglyphic *ankh*, the key of life. As usual, some additional cues are provided by the inscriptions ("What is Nature? Wisdom, Truth?") and the Latin motto, *Sol generat, Terra recipit, natura vivit.* Pagan authors of classical antiquity invariably mention that phallic worship in ancient times was an integral part of the Isis mysteries, which ultimately traced their origins to the foundation myth of Egyptian civilization. Plutarch, for instance, made this connection explicit when he wrote: "Further, the story which is added to the myth tells how Typhon threw the male member of Osiris into the river and how Isis failed to find it, but after producing and preparing an identical image instructed that it should be honored and carried in phallic procession; and this virtually teaches that the procreative and seminal aspect of the god from the very beginning used moisture as its material and through moisture was fused with the elements that naturally take part in generation."[100] Interestingly, when Alexandre Lenoir included a large fold-out plate of an Isis procession in his book *La Franche-Maçonnerie rendue à sa véritable origine* (fig. 37), he carefully omitted the phallic detail. By contrast, the Golden Book was a private document accessible to only a select group of members, allegedly with the right kind of intellectual preparation, for whom such permissiveness would be acceptable.[101] Although church fathers like Eusebius unconditionally

Fig. 37 Jean-Michel Moreau le jeune, *Procession in Honor of Isis*, engraving and etching, 1791, 22.3 × 58.5 cm. From Alexandre Lenoir, *La Franche-Maçonnerie rendue à sa véritable origine*, 1814. Paris, Bibliothèque Nationale, Réserve.

condemned the phallic worship associated with Isis as an example of pagan orgiastic debauchery, the practice needs to be considered within the wider framework of Isis's association with Nature.[102]

This association gained prominence through the writings of the early third-century author Diogenes Laertius, who reported an anecdote that continued to fascinate philosophically inclined commentators for centuries to come. In 500 B.C., according to this source, Heraclitus, one of the oldest Greek thinkers, deposited a book in the temple of Artemis at Ephesos, one of the seven wonders of the ancient world. This book was said to have contained the aphorism "Nature likes to hide herself (φύσις δὲ καθ᾽ Ἡράκλειτον κρύπτεσθαι φιλεῖ)."[103] Since a connection could be established in the syncretistic milieu of Asia Minor between the "hidden" Artemis and the veiled Isis, the figure of the Greek fertility goddess from Ephesos subsequently merged with that of the Egyptian Isis. The saying attributed to Heraclitus proved surprisingly resilient to oblivion and the vicissitudes of time, and has been commented on by almost every philosopher of stature from Plato and Aristotle to Nietzsche and Heidegger. However, as Pierre Hadot has recently argued, the idea that Nature likes to hide herself experienced a paradigm shift beginning in the Renaissance, when the classical Orphic conception of Nature, respecting her secrets out of feelings of awe, was replaced by a Promethean calling exemplified by Francis Bacon, who proposed to have Nature reveal her secrets under the "torture of experiment."[104] For this reason alone Isis managed to preserve her intellectual

appeal in the modern era, because, "Paradoxically, it was at the beginning of the seventeenth century, in the age of the scientific revolution . . . , at the moment when Nature lost its value as autonomous subject and stopped being imagined as a goddess, that she appeared under the guise of Isis unveiling herself on a large number of frontispieces of scientific manuals."[105] With a few exceptions, Isis's career as embodiment of Nature (fig. 38) progressed relatively smoothly from the metaphysics embraced by the Hermetists of the Hellenistic world to the "hard sciences" of the *savants* accompanying Napoleon Bonaparte to Egypt in 1798. Ponce-Camus, however, added a particularly ingenious twist to this tradition by quite literally hiding the phallus—symbol for Isis and, by extension, for Nature—under a partly detachable coat of arms functioning as a fig leaf in the Golden Book (pls. 8–9). The reader thus physically "uncovers" Nature in the very act of flipping over the loose lower right end of the coat of arms and beholding the phallus underneath. In spite of the fascination such details may hold, it needs to be borne in mind that the Sophisians were not only adepts of Isis, but also of Jean-Jacques Rousseau, the eighteenth-century philosophe and founder of the modern cult of Nature. Rousseau would certainly have approved of the Sophisians' concluding motto, *Natura duce itendum est; idem est beate vivere, et secundum naturam*—to be guided by Nature is the same as to live blessedly according to Her laws.

There follow a number of pages in the Golden Book's study guide with multiple-vignette illustrations that

Fig. 38 Jan Lyken, *Science Unveiling Nature,* **1681, engraving, 23.0 × 17.3 cm. Frontispiece from Gerhard Blasius's** *Anatome animalium,* **Amsterdam, 1681. Wolfenbüttel, Herzog August Bibliothek Wolfenbüttel, Nh 4° 46.**

would have been used to quiz candidates on numerological riddles and simple semiotic analogies. The aspiring Scholar of Hieroglyphics would have been required to explain, for instance, why Apis defined the length of a solar period to be twenty-five years or why the alleged number of works by Hermes amount to 36,525. (The answer? Consult Iamblichus of Apamea's *De Mysteriis Aegyptiorum*, which ransacked the third-century B.C. Egyptian historian Manetho's *Sacred Book*.[106]) Other exercises asked for the association of animals with specific character traits, ranging from the by-now familiar egg as symbol for birth to the crocodile as embodiment of viciousness. An analogous plate with seven mostly human figures asked for the correspondence of Greek and Egyptian deities with "planets or celestial bodies" (fig. 39). On this astrological laundry list, Isis stands for the moon (A), Anubis for Mercury (B), Venus for Athor (C), Ares for Mars (D), and Sothis for the dog-star Canicula or Sirius (F).[107] At the very bottom of the page, one finds a representation of the Scarabaeus beetle (G), symbol for God the Creator.

The most visually rewarding gouache drawing from this section of the Golden Book is a fantastic landscape composition with multiple figures, which was intended to establish a correspondence between the seasons of the year, the ages of man, and Egyptian mythological figures (pl. 10). On the left half of the composition, in a papyrus basket, we find the "feeble" infant Horus, symbol for the winter solstice and for childhood. He is surmounted by the floating head of the composite Roman-Libyan deity Jupiter Ammon, identified by a sun-crown and a trident. For the Sophisians, Jupiter Ammon was invested with the double connotations of the summer solstice and maturity. Dionysian elements dominate the center of the composition, where a figure group of Bacchus and two satyrs sets out to "conquer the world."[108] They are synonymous with Osiris, who stands for the fall equinox. At the far right, a bearded pseudo-Phoenician figure, seated on an ornate throne carved out of stone, is supposed to allude to the "winter sun, old age, and debility."

Not surprisingly, the cult of Isis and Osiris was fraught with pseudo-knowledge for the Greco-Egyptian mind, gained from astronomical observations and astrological interpretations. The following passage from Diodorus of Sicily, for instance, could easily have struck Cuvelier's and Ponce-Camus's fancy when they elaborated the Sophisian cosmogony:

And of the ancient Greek writers of mythology some give to Osiris the name Dionysus or, with a slight change in form, Sirius. . . . Some say that Osiris is also represented

with the cloak of fawn-skin about his shoulders as imitating the sky spangled with the stars. As for Isis, . . . they put horns on her head both because of the appearance which she has to the eye when the moon is crescent-shaped, and because among the Egyptians a cow is held sacred to her. These two gods, they hold, regulate the entire universe, giving both nourishment and increase to all things by means of a system of three seasons which complete the full cycle through an unobservable movement, these being spring, summer, and winter; and these seasons, though in nature most opposed to one another, complete the cycle of the year in fullest harmony.[109]

Such cryptic remarks were not lost on the fervid imagination of contemporaries at the turn of the nineteenth century. Alexandre Lenoir, for one, took this type of speculation to an extreme when, in 1814, he published an overly detailed chart consisting of concentric circles that establishes a comprehensive series of correspondences between the seasons, the zodiac, the legendary ages of Egypt, the stars and their equivalent Egyptian deities, the sounds and the numbers, Greek and Roman gods, Jewish prophets, minerals, aridity or humidity levels, natural elements, hemispheres, solstices and equinoxes (fig. 40). There seems to be nothing this chart leaves unexplained, which renders it, for all intents and purposes, an unintelligible marvel of erudition.

Deliberate or not, the Sophisian approach was much less sophisticated. There is no claim to comprehensiveness and scientific correctness in the Golden Book. Rather, the Egyptian gods retain their anthropomorphic form, even though they remain strangely stiff, like theater props. For the Sophisians, mythology, like nature, belonged to the realm of their mysteries, and for this reason it did not lend itself to overt scientific analysis.

The theatrical context emerges with even greater urgency when one considers the two illustrations of props and décor for the initiation to the Scholar of Hieroglyphics (pls. 11–12). In both cases one enters a proscenium flanked in the foreground by two columns supporting a wide and, in one instance, curtained arch that opens onto a stage-like setting. On a formal level, this device of spatial separation is reminiscent of Ponce-Camus's *Napoleon Meditating before the Coffin of Frederick II of Prussia* (fig. 17), where a similar arch kept the crypt with the soldier king's tomb separate from the gathered spectators. Only Napoleon was allowed to cross over from the world of the living to that of the dead.

For the class-one initiation Ponce-Camus envisioned a pseudo-Egyptian landscape dominated by a small Greek temple prop (pl. 11). Its pediment inscription pretentiously declares the structure to be the Temple

Fig. 39 Marie-Nicolas Ponce-Camus, *Golden Book of the Sophisian Order, Rebus for the Class-Two Scholar of Hieroglyphics Degree: Egyptian Deities and Their Correspondences with Planets and Celestial Bodies*, ca. 1819–21, pen, ink, and gouache on paper, 7.0 × 7.0 cm (largest illustration). Paris, Bibliothèque Nationale de France, MSS FM 4.15, fol. 44r.

of Wisdom, while in fact it cannot pass for more than a shell for the stool in the central recess that was designed to receive the initiate at the end of the ceremonies. In the background of this recess one can faintly discern a painting that repeats the composition of Osiris with the head of Anubis standing on a crocodile and a floating canopic head (pl. 3). The image had figured prominently among the rebuses to be interpreted by the

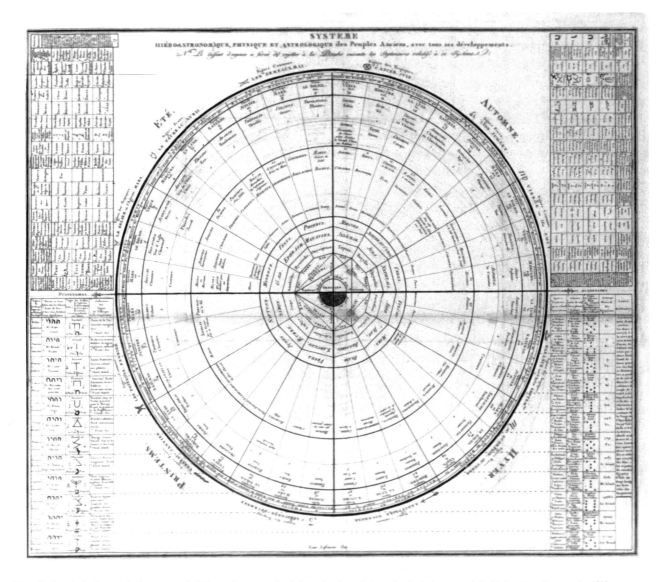

Fig. 40 Louis Lefrançois (engraver), *Hiero-Astronomical, Physical, and Astrological System with All Its Developments of the Ancient People,* **engraving and letter print, 55 × 65 cm. From Alexandre Lenoir,** *La Franche-Maçonnerie rendue à sa véritable origine,* **1814. Paris, Bibliothèque Nationale de France, Réserve.**

aspiring Scholar of Hieroglyphics, which qualified it as an emblem for this level of initiation at-large. Dramatic thunder invades the foreground of the scene from the left, while in the background on the right, pyramids function as geographical and cultural markers for Egypt. Other noteworthy details include the symbolic covered passageway to the underground of the temple in the left foreground and the sphinx-hooded Ark on the right. The Grand Isiarque, whose absence is marked by an augural staff, would occupy the round, central stand, located behind the crocodile prop in the foreground. After passing the various tests of initiation, a neophyte would be seated in the recess of the Temple of Wisdom,

in order to be received into the Sophisian community rallying around Cuvelier de Trie in the center.

Not surprisingly, the setting for the class-two initiation is somewhat more sumptuous (pl. 12). Here, three richly decorated wall props of "red granite" define the space of the stage in the background.[110] A gallery behind these walls would have allowed the Tribunal of the Isiarques to watch over the ceremonies below. In the center of the stage, an altar, half uncovered from its "blue and golden veil," represents the Ark. Above it, a throne adorned with the horns of the Apis bull and decorated with the image of Isis suckling Harpocrates was erected to receive the initiate. This altar is flanked by Corinthian columns and caryatid figures of Isis and Osiris surmounted by flagpoles. The left flagpole is tipped with a sculpture of a golden cat, "symbol of Diana of Bubastis, or Chastity," while the corresponding pole on the right features a golden crocodile, "Savior of Menes, or symbol of Fertility." The lateral wall props are adorned, against a star-spangled background of zodiacal constellations, with the whole panoply of Sophisian sacred animals, both fantastic and real. On the left screen, the heads of a dog (Anubis) and a ram float next to the figures of an ibis, an eagle, and a hare. They have counterparts on the right screen in the shape of a lion, a pelican, a hawk (Horus), a falcon, and a bull's head. The central stand for the Grand Isiarque and his staff remains unchanged from the previous scene, but two sphinx-like fantasy figures now appear at the left and right sides of the proscenium. Pierced by the banners and finials, the sky in the background is illuminated by an expansive rainbow and a glaring African sun, presumably associated with Osiris.

The apparently idyllic aspect of this décor is deceiving. In contrast to the first degree, the Sophisians have left a detailed description of the prescribed exercises to attain the second-class rank of Scholar of Hieroglyphics. This description is worth quoting not only for its psychological density, but also because Sophisian initiation at its best could easily compete with the late twentieth-century adventures of an Indiana Jones. After the male initiate is led to the chamber of retreat, he beholds:

A cave illuminated by a lamp affixed to the vault. As soon as the recipient has entered, the stone-cut door shuts with a shattering noise, and he finds himself locked in. On a rock, tablets have been left that contain the following words:

"Neophyte:

You entered the Pyramid by your own free will and you will finish your life in it, unless you find the Sanctuary of Truth . . . Search, but watch out! The vault is narrow, treacherous, and difficult . . . ; water, air and fire, all the elements you conjured, will block your passage; if you do not have the courage to face these perils, remain here where you are in safety . . . ; instead of triumphing in the eyes of the world, live unspectacularly in solitude . . . ; what glory is to the eagle, who challenges the air to behold nature's king of stars [the sun], nourishment is to the owl, who avoids the light of the sun by hiding itself in the hole of a solitary and rotting tree . . . ; make your choice . . . but consider that you need to conquer alone, without counsel, by dint of your spirit, by your courage, by your prudence. . . . Think well . . . ; three slaps with your hand of equal length and the word 'Hermes' enunciated three times with a high voice will be the signal of your resolution, and will open for you the secret and dangerous exit

passage, where you will need to crawl in order to elevate yourself." After the recipient has given the signal, the first underground conduit will be uncovered; he enters by bending over. Soon the canal will become narrower; the neophyte drags himself on his hands and knees, sometimes going uphill, sometimes going downhill. During this difficult crawl the sound of rumbling boulders in lateral conduits inspires fear in his soul, and an odious stench troubles his sense of smell. One by one he experiences the tests of the three elements, and amidst the fourth test he arrives at the well at the bottom of which is Truth. He climbs into the well by finding holds in the openings of the decaying walls, and at the bottom of the gaping mouth encounters a unique access opened by his pushing a protruding block that activates [an unlocking mechanism]. He finds himself in the sanctuary of fantastic illusions: Typhon and his terrible following block the passage by vomiting fire and flames. The neophyte cannot dissipate the magic spell, but by pronouncing with a raised voice all the sacred words of the previous classes [Nusiba-Sosiri-Siis/Kaïze-Demeter-Cereri-Horus], finally the phantoms vanish completely upon the recipient's pronouncing the name Hermes last. After this triumph he catches his breath for a moment as the netherworld recedes to obscurity. A voice shouts, "get rest," and a chair approaches the recipient; he sits down. Immediately, invisible hands cover his eyes, a swift chariot carries him away, and thunder accompanies his course. When the chariot stops, the neophyte hears a vague melody; he inhales an air embalmed with perfumes, and remote voices resound with the opening Hymn of the Mysteries: "In vain, Demiurge, you veil your essence, etc." At the end of the song, the blindfold falls, and he finds himself on a flower throne facing the assembled heads of the order in the Temple of Wisdom. All *Sophisiens* and *Sophisiennes* decked out in their splendid costumes surround him and congratulate him.[111]

The only conceivable setting to accommodate such elaborate special effects would have been the popular theaters on the boulevard du Temple with their labyrinthine stage mechanisms, fantastic papier-mâché sets, animal menageries, and richly furnished storage rooms filled with theater props of all kinds. The reference to the movable chariot especially is revealing, since similar vehicles, operated on hidden, inclined tracks across the proscenium, defined the cutting edge of stagecraft in the early nineteenth century.[112] Another detail in the above account also seems to confirm its authenticity: the actual musical score for the "Hymn of the Mysteries" that concluded the ritual was published in 1821. It is identical with the *Hymne Sacré de l'Initiation* transcribed in the BN Golden book and the already mentioned *Hymne Sacré des Anciens Mystères*, composed by Jacques Foignet, which both open with the words "In vain, Demiurge [Isis/Nature], you veil your essence."[113]

While male initiations tempted the pride and bravado of the candidate, the procedures for female initiation were predicated on a different set of psychological dispositions. In this case, the instructions were altered so as to tempt the allegedly innate curiosity of the *Sophisiennes*:

> One leads the female neophyte to the cabinet; one gives her the golden key while telling her that it is the one that opens the little door. But open it she is not allowed to do. She is then left alone. Soon one will know whether her curiosity leads her to use the key; one does everything to let [curiosity] gain the upper hand, whether by means of a ballad, accompanied by harps and guitars, sung in the Secret Cabinet, or by sending in a female friend, who convinces her to use the key, or by a remote voice, or by having a [male] Sophisian talk to her through the closed door, urging her to use the key. If she insists on her refusal to open the secret door, two ladies will enter the cabinet. They congratulate her on her discretion and tell her that she will be given a prize. They blindfold her and take her to the rolling chariot. [Otherwise,] if she opens [the door], there issues forth with great noise a winged monster; two masked male members of the Aspirant degree appear; they dress her down with reproaches over her perjury, put her in chains, cover her eyes, and spirit her away with the same chariot. In either case, the reception continues like the one for the men, but one does not ask her to explain the hieroglyphics and maxims to the letter. One modifies them by making them sweeter, by making them likable and spiritual. Immediately after this explanation, one accuses the female recipient of a mistake; one demands that she show the courage to punish herself, if she is guilty, or to tolerate her punishment, when she thinks her conscience to be beyond reproach. As soon as she has promised to do so, one presents her with the dagger so that she may slash herself: but hardly has she touched the hilt than the blade changes into a bouquet of flowers.[114]

The mechanical tricks required to make this type of performance possible will probably forever remain the Sophisians' secret, but what is perhaps of even greater interest here is the intellectual context that made such rituals appealing. As Louis Amiable already underscored as early as 1887, the emergence of a violent and treacherous "Egyptian" strain in Masonic rituals coincided with the events of the French Revolution. Comparing Guillemain de Saint-Victor's 1783 edition of the *Recueil précieux de la Maçonnerie Adonhiramite* to follow-up publications by the same author in 1789 and 1803, Amiable concluded that prior to 1789 admission

rituals remained "extremely simple, and in no way served the later ends of intimidation and purification." Only a few years later, however, the Saint-Victor publication recited a whole catalog of tortures, including such items as "a walk on hot frames or across a diaphragm, the chaining of the candidate in irons, intimidating speech, obstruction of the walk by means of dangerous obstacles put in the way of a temporarily blinded candidate, passage across flames, bitter drink, purification by water and fire, simulation of branding, administered or simulated blood-letting."[115] Responsible for the emerging interest in these radical exercises were the horrors of the French Revolution and the spectacular success of Mozart's *Die Zauberflöte* (The Magic Flute), which was first presented in Vienna in 1791. Mozart's Masonic opera established the notion of purification by the four elements as a mainstay of pseudo-Egyptian ritual among spectators across Europe. Perhaps the most drastic depiction of these rituals comes from an engraving by Moreau le Jeune that was published in Alexandre Lenoir's *La Franche-Maçonnerie rendue à sa véritable origine* in 1814 (fig. 41). Here, in a frighteningly somber underground interior reminiscent of an Arabian bath house, candidates suspend their bodies from rings in the ceiling to open trapdoors, unleashing violent gusts of wind; they walk through fire or swim with a lighted torch across a gushing river. By all appearances, the illustration took its cue from the description of Séthos's tests by the four elements under the great pyramid of Cheops described in Abbé Terrasson's adventure novel. Like the abbé, Lenoir maintained in his accompanying text that the tests originated in ancient Egypt as expiation and purification exercises prescribed after involuntary manslaughter, which explains the punitive, if not sadomasochistic, aspect of Egyptian-type initiation. Both authors also skip a discussion of the test by the fourth element, earth, presumably because its dangers were already implied by the underground setting. The following excerpt from a treatise on the four tests, published in 1863 by Henri Cauchois as *Cours oral de Franc-Maçonnerie*, clarifies the importance of earth in the Egyptian rite:

> Passage underneath the earth—*Ancient Initiation*—The Aspirant to the Mysteries of Isis, equipped with a lamp and the necessary means to light its flame, should it become extinguished, moves on a long and winding path, which one cannot pursue without overcoming obstacles. At the end of this path, he finds a well, to the bottom of which he descends, first by means of a ladder with sixty steps, then by means of steps carved in the rock,

La seule inspection de cette Planche, dont le sujet est tiré de Séthos, suffit pour montrer la conformité des Cérémonies de l'initiation ancienne avec les épreuves que pratiquent encore aujourd'hui les Francs-maçons dans l'admission d'un Récipiendaire.

ÉPREUVES PAR LES QUATRE ÉLÉMENS,
Qui se Pratiquoient dans la Réception des inities a Memphi

Fig. 41 Jean-Michel Moreau le jeune, *Test by the Four Elements, as Administered during the Reception of Initiates in Memphis,* **1791, engraving, 19.8 × 34.6 cm. From Alexandre Lenoir,** *La Franche-Maçonnerie rendue à sa véritable origine,* **1814. Paris, Bibliothèque Nationale de France, Réserve.**

spiraling downwards one hundred and fifty feet. Finally, at the bottom of the well, he will have to pursue another passage for one mile and a quarter, always alone and in silence, and without other light than the weak glow of his lamp. It is this experience that shall make him say that the truth is at the bottom of the well.[116]

Behind this underground exploration in search of Isis beaconed the experience of the Sophisian well of Truth and the difficulties involved in entering it. Interestingly, however, the Sophisians often dropped earth and air from their list of elements and replaced them with bread, as in the formula "every Sophisian owes his fellowman bread, fire, and water."[117]

The substitution of bread for earth and air must be interpreted in the context of the Sophisian philanthropic agenda, behind which lurked bigger plans for a radical and utopian change of human society as a whole. If Cuvelier says that every Sophisian owes his fellowman bread, fire, and water, he alludes to a nonnegotiable moral obligation that members incur upon

initiation to provide food, drink, shelter, and warmth to any destitute individual.[118] Of course, a strong charitable commitment is common coin for any Masonic organization; what is out of the ordinary, however, is the uncompromising fervor and the structures of mutual surveillance marshaled for its enforcement. Cuvelier de Trie managed to invest the Sophisians' charitable mission with a unique intellectual superstructure aimed at radical social change, which, for lack of a better term, might best be called "coerced philanthropy."

Poignant examples of these practices come from the description of both levels of the Scholar of Hieroglyphics degree. After the rituals of class-one initiation, the newly admitted adept was asked to "put the maxim of charity into practice" and to bestow largesse upon "the poor assembled to this end in the vestibule of the temple."[119] The commitment becomes even more specific for class-two initiates to the Scholar of Hieroglyphics: "In this class the Sophisian must put into action part of his vow by selecting and adopting a poor person, whom he relieves every month according to the recipient's needs and his means, and whom he will keep as long as the poor person is alive. As soon as the latter is dead, the Sophisian will take on a new one. This prodigious act of charity is subject to the inspection of the Agathos, who is accountable to the Grand Patriarch [Cuvelier de Trie] concerning the enforcement of this law. Other than assistance in the form of money and goods, the Sophisian owes to his poor person friendship, consolation, counsel, and protection."[120] That this structure of mutual surveillance was more than just rhetoric can be learned from the *nomenclature* of Sophisian officers printed on the occasion of the order's installation in 1801. In this text, published as an addendum to the *Règlement*, the Sosis officers are described as an internal police force and as "conservators of the Order. They form amongst themselves a secret council, whose mission is to reinforce the rules, to police, and to supervise the Sophisians, both in- and outside of the Pyramid."[121] The Sosis, offspring of the sun god Helios according to the ancient Egyptian historian Manetho, reported their observations directly to the Sophisian Supreme Council but had no executive rights of their own ("by themselves, they can only observe but cannot act"). Although in 1801 their most important obligation was to protect the secrecy of the mysteries, definitions of tasks were sufficiently broad to imagine their being used as a fifth column to reinforce the charity obligations of individual members.

Of course, mutual surveillance regimes are nothing unusual in Masonic organizations; however, under Cuvelier de Trie's leadership, a distinctly Orwellian drive defined the rules of the game. This aspect of Sophisian activities came into sharper focus at the time of the restoration of the order in 1818. In the following year Cuvelier launched a competition for proposals outlining how members of all Masonic bodies could be compelled to subscribe to a single charitable institution, loosely based on the model of chivalric orders during the Crusades.[122] To finance this idea, he even proposed a compulsory annual Masonic charity tax. The ultimate goal of the competition projects was to leave such a lasting impression on regular Masons and non-Masons alike that everyone would rally to Cuvelier's cause and support the installation of the system of coerced philanthropy by society at large. The announcement was also peppered with some surprisingly snide remarks about its being time "to finally dissipate this cloud of good-for-nothing bums who make it a profession to assail our outer sanctuaries and who strip orphans and widows of our aid by force of intimidation." But other than Guerrier de Dumast's initiative to sponsor a manufactory established to employ

"poor apprentices and orphans," the archives are mute about eventual entries or the outcome of the competition.[123] This silence is hardly surprising, since Cuvelier de Trie himself had already outlined the social agenda for acceptable submissions in such detail as to make the competition itself superfluous. If the initiative was launched as a covert public relations coup for the Sophisians, Cuvelier certainly did not hold back on his global pretensions. The call for entries was to be mailed to "all regular French and foreign lodges," and the submitted proposals could be written in either French, Latin, Italian, German, or English.

PROFESSORSHIP OF THE GRAND MYSTERIES

The intellectual emphasis of the Sophisian rituals shifts again for the third and final degree, the Professorship of Grand Mysteries, which mimics academic or university structures and conventions observed in learned societies. The Professorship offered two specializations: the class-one degree in hieroglyphics, leading to the rank of Hierogrammatist, and the class-two degree in arts and sciences, which conferred the title Mystagogue. Admission was conditional upon the fulfillment of three criteria:

> 1st To have constantly preserved the purest morals and rendered all obligations towards *Patrie*, family, and order.
> 2nd To know in depth the mysteries and hieroglyphics of the first and second degrees; and finally to know how to explain them with clarity.
> 3rd To have studied, in part or comprehensively: Natural History in its Three Ages, Morals, Philosophy, History, Geology, Geography, Mathematics, Physics, Medicine, Anatomy, Philology, Astronomy; but while overflowing with human knowledge, [the initiate] will attach himself to one of the Sciences following his taste and deepen it enough eventually to become a professor.[124]

No doubt a Sophisian candidate to the Professorship of the Grand Mysteries faced an ambitious educational program. Compared to the previous degrees, however, the study manual for the Professorship uses illustrations very sparingly. The core of the Grand Mysteries' visual program consisted of two Egyptian landscape illustrations marked as "Alpha" and "Omega" (pls. 13–14). This time, no corresponding solutions manual exists, since "to explain [the hieroglyphics of the Grand Mysteries] is not necessary to the one who understands them, and it is dangerous to do so to the one who does not understand them."[125]

Egyptian landscape "Alpha" features a by-now fa-miliar Sophisian iconography (pl. 13). There are pyra-mids in the background, and the composition is divided by a meandering Nile. Symbolic animals populate the foreground: a Gallic cock on a mastaba, a sleeping lion associated with the sun and with Isis, a hawk, symbol of Horus, holding the hooked cross of Isis as goddess of generation in its beak, a Scarabeaus beetle in flight, and a crocodile. At the far right, a symbolic entrance to the Sophisian underground chambers is included. The Latin inscription below the composition points out that both silence and justice are the attributes of God. The choice of symbols with their insistence on Egyptian content was judicious, since the rank of hierogram-matist, associated with the drawing, referred to the *hi-erogrammateis*, or scribe-priests in ancient Egyptian temples.[126]

The pendant "Omega" illustration, on the other hand, is a novelty in the Golden Book (pl. 14). It de-picts a furnace hooked up to the flask of a distillation device that is filled with a gold-colored liquid. The flask is mounted on a metal cauldron richly adorned with sculptural fishes, a relief with the head of the Apis bull, and a faucet in the form of a sphinx. The final brew flows liberally into a head-shaped receptacle and fertil-izes the flowers blossoming in its vicinity. In the back-ground there is the inevitable group of three pyramids.

To all intents and purposes, one can interpret this composition as an allegory of alchemical manipula-tions aimed at transmuting base materials into gold with the help of the philosopher's stone. But as sug-gested by the head receptacle and the blooming flowers on the right, the gold refined by Ponce-Camus's ap-paratus was of intellectual rather than physical nature. In pondering this simile, one should keep in mind that throughout the eighteenth century Freemasonry and alchemy were alter egos, as can easily be verified in the biographies of famous adventurers like Casanova or Cagliostro.[127] In the premodern era, alchemy, like Free-masonry, would sometimes be used by its practitioners as a means for fraudulent manipulations and fast-track social advancement among the rich and influential. But while these abuses certainly occurred, it also holds true that alchemists not only developed deeply felt philosophical and spiritual insights about their place in the universe, but also laid the foundation for modern chemistry. It is hardly surprising, therefore, to find an illustration of alchemical paraphernalia in the section of the Golden Book where the perfection of knowledge in the arts and sciences is celebrated. Unfortunately, however, the descriptive texts of the manuscript have nothing to say about the drawing, so that one is obliged to look for explanations outside of what the Sophisians themselves can offer.

The caption which associates the furnace illus-tration with the Greek letter omega refers the astute reader back to the body of Hermetic literature. At the turn of the fourth century A.D., Zosimus of Panopo-lis, the ur-father of all modern-day chemists, wrote a treatise entitled *On Apparatus and Furnaces: Authen-tic Commentaries on the Letter Omega*, which would eventually find its way into the *Corpus Hermeticum*.[128] Zosimus presumably originated from Panopolis (Akh-mim) in Upper Egypt, where he is said to have in-spected a furnace kept in a temple at Memphis in his early youth. Later, he settled in Alexandria, where he was exposed to a syncretistic milieu absorbing the spiritual cross-currents of Platonism, Gnosticism, and Judaism, as well as the "oriental" wisdom of Hermes and Zoroaster. The details of the alchemistic operations outlined in this first chemistry book need not concern us here. What matters is that Zosimus was first to as-sociate the type of experimental setup depicted in the Golden Book, which had uncounted successors in late classical and Renaissance handbooks on alchemy and chemistry (fig. 42), with "the great and wonderful let-ter omega [that] heads the section on apparatuses for the liquid of sulphur, furnaces of all sorts, mechanical and simple alike, and all matters in general."[129]

Significantly, modern scholars of Hermetic litera-ture distinguish between "philosophical" and "techni-cal" Hermetica. In this dichotomy, the first term refers to the type of spiritually guided interest in knowl-edge, or *gnōsis*, that allows the individual to see the divine world and to attain the final bliss of the soul by overcoming the materiality of physical existence. By contrast with the intellectualism of this approach, technical Hermetica take a more practical stance:

In the first place, it is clear that many of the technical texts associated with or attributed to Hermes were writ-ten and used by people who did not pretend to be anything other than working magicians, casters of horoscopes and so on—in short, straightforward technicians. They were practical men, close to the rhythm of everyday life and to the native culture of the Nile valley—hence the re-semblance of much that they wrote to the products of the Egyptian tradition, whether as straight translation or, in varying degrees, interpretation. At the same time, though, there were strong influences at work from the broader Hel-lenistic world, especially . . . in the field of astrology.[130]

Intuitively at least, the Sophisians seem to have under-stood this distinction, since they divided the Profes-sorship of the Grand Mysteries into two branches. The

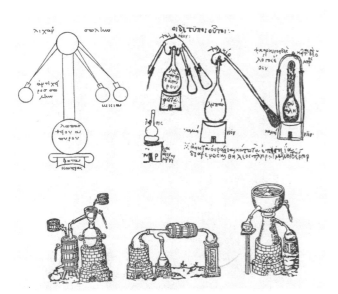

Fig. 42 Examples of Furnaces and Distillation Apparatuses from Late Classical Antiquity (upper register) to the Renaissance (lower register). From Hermann Schelenz, *Zur Geschichte der pharmazeutisch-chemischen Destilliergeräte*, 1911.

more scholarly branch of the Hierogrammatist can be roughly compared to the philosophical strain of hermetic thought, while the Mystagogue's works were closer to those of the pragmatic magicians and casters of horoscopes in Ptolemaic and Roman Egypt, who are lurking behind Zosimus's treatise on the letter omega.

Fortunately, the Golden Book contains descriptions of the ceremonies that accompanied the discerning of the Professorship of Grand Mysteries, also known in Sophisian terminology as "Triumph." A gouache drawing in the solutions manual shows a dramatic shift from lugubrious underground caves to a sun-drenched Egyptian outdoor setting (pl. 15). An idealized Sophisian community has assembled alongside of a pyramid for the final examination of the candidate. Seated on a stool in the center, the examinee is facing the five Isiarques, dressed in black and red and equipped with augural staffs. A mixed group of male and female Sophisian officers, seated on curving benches, observes the spectacle. The only underground prop preserved for the outdoor setting is the veiled and sphinx-hooded Ark in the foreground. Led by banner-carrying officials, an even larger cortege of adepts advances from the background behind the pyramid. In the far distance, obelisks, pyramids, and tombs glisten on a desert plain. The only hint of vegetation comes in the form of the palm tree in the middle ground, near the areas where the Sophisians have congregated.

The composition has an immediate precedent in Moreau le jeune's previously mentioned engraving of

the *Procession in Honor of Isis* (fig. 37), which was explained by Lenoir in his *La Franche-Maçonnerie rendue à sa véritable origine* as follows:

The Egyptians of Memphis, Bubastis, Canopus, and surrounding cities came together once a year in Thebes, in the temple of Isis, to render homage to the grand goddess, mother of Nature. After the celebration of the mysteries, participants formed, as if in a pilgrimage, an immense procession composed of the idols of the Egyptian gods, of priests, of female priests, and of the people. The cortege left the temple, crossed city and countryside, all the while chanting hymns in Her honor. . . . The scene [in the engraving] takes place in the vast plain crossed by the Nile. The tombs of the Pharaohs occupy the foreground of the picture, and one perceives in the background the celebrated city of the Hundred Gates [Thebes], whose principal entry was defended by several fortresses, which in themselves were preceded by an alley seven and a half miles in length, lined by colossal statues arranged in two parallel rows, representing sphinxes with a woman's head and with the head of a ram. . . . As the cortege leaves the city, the benevolent mountains of Abyssinia, whose peaks scrape the sky, are faintly visible in the distance. . . . There are dances and fight shows, which stand in opposition to the gravity of the priestly cortege, still far out of sight. The sea limits the horizon. Isis, in the guise of a bear and sitting on a throne placed on a litter carried by four men, opens the ceremonial march. The statue of the goddess is preceded by a group of warriors and gladiators armed with spears and javelins, who, furious in their holy enthusiasm, pretend to fight each other, beat each other, and seem to kill each other. The priests, armed with clubs, following the custom, roam the city with the golden chapel enclosing the image of the god of war, therein revered. Upon the arrival of the procession at the gate of the temple, armed men assume the pose of blocking the entry of the statue that the priests wanted to bring in. The latter, seized by religious enthusiasm, hit their opponents over the head with great blows of their clubs until they become masters of the place; they manage to introduce the divinity to the sanctuary. However, there is assurance that this kind of combat was only simulated, and if the blood flowed in rivers from one end to the other, it was only a simple trick, like the ones used in our theaters today.[131]

Indulgence in Egyptian pageantry also informed the textual description of the Sophisian initiation to the Professorship. This time, however, the violent aspect of Lenoir's spectacle was edited out by Cuvelier and his company. In contrast to the lower degrees, access to the Grand Mysteries was gained through intellectual exercises only. There is no more talk of physical hardship or intimidation, but the reader witnesses an elegantly choreographed, celebratory event, with a priestly procession issuing from a temple, the singing of hymns, and the joining of "the people" (a term for the Sophisian community at large) with the temple college to celebrate the candidate:

> After the Patriarch has established the date [for the Triumph], the order convenes by class in the halls equipped for the diverse receptions. The class-two initiates of both sexes are in the Temple of Wisdom. It is underneath the temple's peristyle that the Grand Procession takes shape under the supervision of the Diactoros, the Hermorus, and the Cerices. The procession starts to move the moment the people are placed in the enclosure arranged for this purpose in the countryside behind the Great Pyramid. Following the customs since time immemorial, the cortege issues forth from the pyramid by the avenue of the Sphinx, complying with the ordinary marching order; but the Patriarch, preceded by the two large banners of the order, is carried by the Mystophores on his seat. If he is absent, the Patriarchal seat shall be carried as described above, but shall be empty and embellished with the golden cross. The march is accompanied by music from the Sacred Trumpets. The Sophisians appear in the procession according to the body and the class to which they belong. Thus the Isiades follow the Isiarques, the matrons the Sosis, etc. . . . and female aspirants follow male aspirants; all are with costumes and the signs and decorations according to their degree and titles. After the Ark is put down and the Isiarques take their seats at the foot of the pyramid, the Patriarch gives the signal to the Nomarque to start the opening of the mysteries. After this announcement, according to the rule, one sings the Hymn to Orpheus. The Patriarch gives the order to bring in the initiate; he appears in silence escorted by the Mystophores; he is wearing the costume of the second-class Aspirant (black tunic). The Isiarque, charged with bringing speech to the solemnities, makes known to the people the virtues and talents of the initiate that opened the entry to the sanctuary: but no matter how vigilant a society, it can go wrong. The Isiarque, before conferring the Triumph, asks in the name of the order if anyone has a reproach to make of the initiate. Silence equals consent; he is proclaimed worthy of the Triumph. The Sophisians play harmonious music. They dance around the Triumpher, spreading flowers in his way; incense billows all around him from the burners: during this time he is clothed in the blue dalmatic and the insignias of initiation. [From] the initiate's place in the outer sanctuary, he is led by ladies to a throne on the left of the tribunal, beneath the Harpocrates facing the Ark. The Patriarch sends him the Pastophores and banners as a sign of honor; he shows the initiate to the people, saying: "Thus shall be honored the mortal who practices the wisdom of Nature." The initiate thanks the order and explains before the people some of the principles he has learned. At this

Fig. 43 Marie-Nicolas Ponce-Camus, *Golden Book of the Sophisian Order, Rebus for the Class-Two Professorship of the Grand Mysteries Degree: 'Avenue of the Sphinx'* (?), ca. 1819–21, pen, ink, and gouache on paper, 5.9 × 17.5 cm (illustration). Paris, Bibliothèque Nationale de France, MSS FM 4.15, fol. 49r.

point the discourse in prose and in verse is pronounced. Thereafter the hymn of good deeds is sung, while the purse of the Agathos circulates to collect contributions. Finally, in the name of the Patriarch and the tribunal, the Nomarque announces the end of the mysteries.[132]

Since Cuvelier had spent most of his professional life as a playwright, for good reasons the description of the Triumph initiation reads like a liturgy of stage directions. Clearly, the reader no longer visualizes an idealized, hypothetical assembly in ancient Egypt like the one depicted in the accompanying drawing, but an actual event that took place inside a closed building. The reality may not have been quite as glorious as the text implies: the "Avenue of the Sphinx" possibly designated a simple flight of stairs flanked by sphinxes and animal figurines, as illustrated in the Golden Book's study manual for the third degree (fig. 43). As far as the procession was concerned, Cuvelier de Trie needed to be carried in his "Patriarchal seat," because, by the time these lines were written, he was almost certainly paralyzed. The "discourse" mentioned in the text refers to the dissertation a candidate for the Professorship was expected to write and present before the congregation. The Golden Book proposes two topics or "hypotheses-to-be-developed" for this exercise, one dealing with the problem of whether Nature is imperfect, the other with the question of why the soul is immortal.[133] Both dissertation topics are written in a form that suggests a deep-seated pessimism about the physical aspect of human existence, ideas prevalent in Gnostic and Hermetic teaching. Although these dissertation topics had no predetermined solutions or outcome, the Golden Book clearly defined the parameters within which the candidate's individuality and creativity could develop.

Another observation that can be extracted from this description is the suffocating importance of hierarchies and ranks within the order, which were carefully clothed in Egyptian terminology. For all intents and purposes, Cuvelier de Trie was the center of the Sophisian universe, and he appears under a dizzying array of aliases, including Grand Isiarque, Grand Hierophant, Great Patriarch, and Great Conservator. Despite their sometimes Byzantine convolutions, Sophisian hierarchies were a painstakingly organized affair, created on the model of the colleges formed by ancient Egyptian temple priests. Above the Grand Isiarque, there was a council of Seven Invisible Sages.[134] One may envision this body of "ghost governors" as being composed of honorary members and great dignitaries, such as for example the Comte de Lacépède, member of the same lodge as Voltaire, Chancellor of the Legion of Honor, and Napoleon's appointed overseer in the world of societies with secrets. Although the Sophisians themselves are silent on its derivation, the concept of the Seven Sages was plagiarized from Platonic teachings. Plato's Seven Sages appear in his *Protagoras*, where they offer "short, memorable sayings" as fruits of their wisdom to Apollo at his Temple in Delphi.[135] Mottos like "Know thyself" and "Nothing in excess," which they had inscribed on the temple walls, were "on every tongue" in ancient Greece. According to Plato, the Seven Sages became the epitome of the style of ancient philosophy, characterized, as it were, by "laconic brevity," the same literary quality celebrated in the Sophisian *Apophthegm.*

Below the Seven Invisible Sages, there was the Supreme Tribunal, consisting of five Isiarques, with Cuvelier de Trie at its head, which organized all regular activities of the order. A corresponding body for female members comprised an equivalent number of Isiades. Beyond doubt, the Isiarques were permanent members with colorful careers whose names the surviving documents are sometimes not shy to reveal. There was Baron Joseph Fauchet, Robespierre's ambassador to the United States during the Terror, a collaborator in Bonaparte's coup d'état, and the prefect of Florence during the Napoleonic occupation of Italy.[136] After 1824 Fauchet succeeded Cuvelier, but apparently he made it his priority to channel his support and energy into the *Frères Artistes*, rather than the Sophisians. Another identifiable Isiarque, Jean Laurès, was a high-ranking financial administrator in Napoleon's regime who, like Fauchet and other Sophisians, remained unemployed after the Restoration. On exceptional occasions the Seven Invisible Sages and the Supreme Tribunal would meet to form the Secret Conclave, which was convoked, for instance, after the death of the Grand Isiarque to designate a new leader. Below the Supreme Tribunal there would have been a plethora of "grand officers" with Greco-Egyptian names, such as, among others, the Sosis or advisers and internal police force, the Harpocrates maintaining the rule of silence, the Hermorus directing the tests of the initiate, the Diactoros or king of arms, and the Trophador, charged with distributing the "mystical bread."[137]

A curious document bound with the *Mélanges Lerouge* in The Hague attests to the complexity of the Sophisans' spiritual bureaucracy. Pasted on the inside of the manuscript's cover, one finds a leaf with samples of stamps associated with Sophisian high officers (fig. 44). In the upper left corner there is a triangular stamp with a pyramid, which stood for the order as a whole. Imprinted to the right of the pyramid stamp is a large, round sun-stamp with a human face in the center of radiant beams of light, which belonged to the Great Patriarch. Below are five smaller round seals, which corresponded to the five Isiarques, each with his own distinct emblem: a heart (finances—charity/Fourth Isiarque), an eye (surveillance/First Isiarque), a mouth (eloquence/Second Isiarque), a rising thunder-bird/Phoenix (Hyper-Nomarque—administration of provincial "pyramids"/Third Isiarque), and a pointing hand (writing—secretarial work/Fifth Isiarque).

Beyond the spectacle, what could an adept reasonably hope to obtain spiritually from the highest degree of initiation? The answer may have varied individually, but what can be gleaned from the last entries in the Golden Book leaves a rather sobering afterglow. Abandoning logical context completely, the concluding discourse of the Mystagogue breaks down into magic gibberish:

Fig. 44 Seals of the Sophisian Order, the Grand Isiarque, and the Five Isiarque, ca. 1820, ink stamps, diameter variable from 2.9 to 4.2 cm. The Hague, Cultureel Maçonniek Centrum "Prins Frederik," Kloss Collection, Ms. 240.B.74 ("Mélanges Lerouge").

Tripsare Copsem.

Glorious degree where the veil of Isis is lifted, where the adept of Osiris accomplishes the work *par excellence!* . . . but what if the watering was insufficient, if the sweat has not fecundated the philosophical earth, if the matrix has guarded the fetus, if finally *Caligo* [dimsightedness] remains on the eyes of comprehension? . . . Hosannah (shouts Hermes with the choir of his disciples) that Zeus may be blessed! . . . He bestows or refuses according to his powerful will . . . Let it be fulfilled in the eternal circle and that glory may transmit itself to the most worthy hands!! The sky has been shining on the moral work, no obstacle, perfection is here . . .

CHESELVASSEZGUSINE.

Without decoration, without distinction, deprived of this language more or less brilliant, standards of the cohorts of servitude, whose shreds woven as substitute retain captive liberty in her generous movements, man no longer recognizes the paternal force of the Grand Mada, he can thus buy free all his bothers from death; his index finger points towards heaven, unique goal, his mouth repeats with respect the two sacred words *Zeons Erutan*; he receives in quantities: plenitude of virtues from the second, noble gifts from the first, and their unbreakable consequence, *bonheur de l'âge d'or*, all of which inundate with joy his soul with certainty of a second life. Three times happy thus! The admirer of truth, the lover of Isis, and the sage of the lantern [Diogenes] spreads his good deeds and remains insensible to the vain sounds of eulogy.

If life is an end, may he nobly fulfill his destiny? . . .
If it is a beginning, what can he not expect? . . .
End of the Grand Mysteries and the Studies
of the Sacred Order of the Sophisians.[138]

One might reasonably be tempted to doubt the mental stability of the author. If these were Cuvelier's words, they speak of radical self-doubt as to whether there was any value in his accomplishment as a charity worker or spiritual leader. Cuvelier may have felt his end approaching, and he realized that there would be no posterity for his organization beyond his own lifetime. There is also the issue of the disenfranchisement of the defrocked Napoleonic leadership class—"without decoration, without distinction"—and its status during the Restoration, which sullenly reverberates in this conclusion torn between pessimism for the here-and-now and optimism for the beyond. Cuvelier and other Sophisians may also have felt a bitter sting of nostalgia for the Napoleonic age—the *bonheur de l'âge d'or*—which left the only hope for an undefined rebirth. Most importantly, however, the Grand Isiarque may have experienced sneaking self-doubts whether in the modern, scientific world there could be any place for the mysteries of Isis. As the demise of

the Sophisians after 1824 demonstrated, all of these concerns were justified.

SOPHISIAN SYNCRETISM

It is now time to step back and look at the larger picture of the diverse cultural currents that made the Sophisian phenomenon possible. By this point, it will have become sufficiently clear that the materials contained in the Golden Book are woven out of a nearly inextricable maze of mythological, philosophical, religious, semiotic, and historical references, ranging chronologically from Ptolemaic Egypt to the most recent events of the French Revolution and the Napoleonic campaigns in the Near East. As far as the Sophisians were concerned, there can be no doubt that the imposing complexity of their syncretism was deliberate, since the Golden Book makes a point of summarizing the order's intellectual genesis as follows:

The Mysteries were created in Egypt by King Osiris,
In Thrace by Orpheus,
In Persia by Zoroaster,
In Cyprus by Cyniras,
In Athens by Erechtheus.
From thence they passed to Rome,
then to Lutecia [Roman settlement of Paris].
They came back directly from Egypt after the Glorious Expedition of
the French army, but they could not fully establish themselves until the
savants of the order had exploited documents in the ancient Greek and Roman traditions.[139]

Despite its mythical overtones, this genealogy reveals a clear understanding on the part of the Sophisians that the sources for their mysteries were based mainly on Greco-Egyptian and Roman materials. Bonaparte's Egyptian campaign may figure prominently on the list, but its impact was probably confined to visual impressions without much affecting the intellectual content. This is not surprising, since true Egyptian hieroglyphics remained inaccessible even to scholars on the eve of Champollion's breakthrough discovery, an event which in itself raised more questions about ancient Egypt than it actually answered.[140] Depictions of newly discovered Egyptian temples, monuments, inscriptions, and artifacts, by contrast, were widely imitated in European fine and applied arts during the 1810s and 1820s, courtesy of the prototypes provided by the monumental plates published by Napoleonic fiat in the twenty volumes of the *Description de l'Égypte*.

It also needs to be borne in mind that the Greco-Egyptian and Roman literary sources that inspired the Sophisians were the common intellectual currency of the most educated members in Napoleon's administration, as the numerous references to Plutarch, Herodotus, Diodorus of Sicily, and their likes in Denon's *Voyage dans la Basse et la Haute Égypte* or Guerrier de Dumast's *La Maçonnerie* make apparent.

The question remains whether it is possible to isolate a limited group of distinct themes, traditions, and sources that will help make better sense out of the extant documents related to the order. The foundations of the Sophisians' intellectual edifice were provided by Hermetic literature and the Isis cult, two phenomena that share common cultural and religious roots in Hellenistic antiquity. Much like the Sophisian order, Hellenistic Greece and, to some extent, imperial Rome looked to ancient Egypt as a land of wisdom and fountainhead of spiritual revelations.[141] Greek philosophers on the "Grand Tour" penetrated deep into the Nile valley to visit Egyptian temples and to question their priests, an effort frequently thwarted by language barriers. Their goal was to partake in the prestige of a land regarded as intrinsically holy and a culture that was believed to have produced the first religious cults. Alexandria in particular evolved into the clearinghouse for Greco-Egyptian cultural and intellectual exchanges of any kind. It was from this idiosyncratic historical and cultural situation that Hermetic writings and their legends emerged.

Despite the sometimes festive and theatrical superficiality of Sophisian rituals, one should not dismiss an essential structural similarity between the mind-set of the Greco-Egyptian Hermetists and that of the Sophisians. In both Hermetic and Sophisian initiation, spiritual perfection and self-knowledge were at the center of the neophyte's quest.[142] This objective could only be attained by successively mastering more sophisticated contents and hierarchically organized levels of knowledge, to which a student might gain access through study manuals and personal exchanges with a mentor. Initiation itself, by contrast, was strictly a group experience that was often enacted with dramatic overtones. After initiation, social bonds and group identity were regularly reaffirmed by the sharing of food in *agapes* or banquets. There is also a good deal of shared ground as far as the urge to overcome bodily confines and the shackles of earthly materiality are concerned, because these restraints hold back the mind from attaining a higher level of spirituality. Hermetic and Sophisian teachings are pseudo-secret disciplines that embrace purification and offer the dual promises of spiritual illumination and rebirth

as ultimate goals. One might argue that the same could be said, with some tolerance for variations, of any Masonic or pseudo-Masonic organization from the eighteenth century to the present day. But the Sophisians were exceptional in that they consciously culled their ideas from Hermetic texts. For this reason similarities with Hermeticism were not coincidental, but were deliberately integrated into the Sophisian canon. Cuvelier's adepts transcended mainstream Masonic interests not only because of their (however fragmentary) insider knowledge of Greco-Egyptian culture and religion, but also because their rituals amounted to a true *Gesamtkunstwerk*, where painting, theater, and music merged into a holistic experience.[143]

In one respect, however—the question of whether Isis could be unveiled—the Sophisians diverged from classical thought models. Cuvelier's admission that Isis's—Nature's—veil can finally be lifted under certain circumstances by human intellectual effort is in itself strong evidence for a modern, rational approach to the mysteries of the Egyptian goddess. Early modern natural sciences of the seventeenth and eighteenth centuries may have evolved from the legacy of magic, but their practitioners saw their mission as wrenching from Nature her secrets, an idea expressed in the allegory of the unveiling of Isis. Pierre Hadot, it may be recalled, characterized this violent and scientific attitude to nature as "Promethean," in opposition to the "Orphic" approach of the Hellenistic world, defined by agnosticism and peaceful symbiosis. The Sophisian view of Nature inserts itself in the Promethean paradigm, because Cuvelier's all-too-human followers, by virtue of their initiation to the Grand Mysteries, claimed to know Nature and to understand her secrets. Contemporaries of Heraclitus and Diogenes Laertius, on the other hand, would have vehemently denied even the possibility of lifting Isis's veil, since Nature remained, in the Hellenistic worldview at least, inscrutable.

One may reasonably wonder how the Sophisians had obtained access to Hermetic literature. The eighteenth and early nineteenth centuries were notoriously barren in recent reeditions of Hermetic texts. One has to go back to the Renaissance, and especially to the plethora of Latin translations, reeditions, and commentaries issuing forth from the Neoplatonic academy in Florence, where Marsilio Ficino had assembled the first *Corpus Hermeticum* by 1471, to find Hermetic sources available to early nineteenth-century readers.[144] Ficino's work was sponsored by Cosimo de' Medici, who had arranged for an eleventh-century Byzantine copy of the Corpus, once owned as a badly truncated manuscript by Michael Psellus, to be brought to Italy by a

Bulgarian monk. True, there was published a French translation of the Corpus as early as 1557 by Gabriel du Préau, which would have been accessible in Parisian libraries, but this effort had little or no scholarly posterity in France.[145] In retrospect, there can be no doubt that the golden age of Hermetic literature was the late fifteenth through the seventeenth century. In fact, the author Hermes Trismegistus himself was an invention of the Neoplatonic editors and had only very tenuous roots in the culture that actually produced the texts grouped together under his name. Although first doubts about the identity of the semidivine sage and his writings surfaced as early as 1614 with the publication of Isaac Casaubon's *De rebus sacris et ecclesiasticis exercitationes XVI*, belief in the legendary author lingered on even as Hermes fell into renewed obscurity over the next three centuries.[146] Likewise the Sophisians may have been victims of the delusion first established by the Ficino edition; at least there is no indication that they took Hermes Trismegistus's revelations for anything other than a genuine testimony written by the patron saint of magic himself. In fact, the Sophisians revered Hermes Trismegistus as the most ancient of all sages, who lived more than fifteen thousand years ago. Again, they erred drastically, since the Hermetica date from somewhere between the late first to the late third century A.D. Following the lead of Italian Renaissance scholars, the Sophisians mistook esoteric convolution as a guarantee of antediluvian derivation.

Despite its complex intellectual ancestry, the order's mixture of scholarly and spiritual urges was not an isolated phenomenon in early nineteenth-century France. Far from it, one has to understand the order as part of a larger Egyptophile milieu, which ranged from Champollion's linguistic objectivity to Alexandre Lenoir's speculative syncretism.[147] It is clear that within this bandwidth, the Sophisians occupied a place much closer to Lenoir. Indeed, the role of his book *La Franche-Maçonnerie rendue à sa véritable origine* deserves closer analysis as a blueprint for Sophisan activities after 1818. As far as Lenoir's background was concerned, he would have blended in perfectly with Cuvelier's order. Born in 1761, he was a painter by training, a passionate supporter of Enlightenment ideas, and an ardent participant in the French Revolution.[148] In 1795 he had established, in the secularized convent of the Petits Augustins, the *Musée des monuments français*, which became the central repository for medieval religious art and architectural fragments "orphaned" in the aftermath of anticlerical vandalism. Like most of the Sophisians, Lenoir experienced the Restoration under Louis XVIII as a destruction of both his career and his life's labor, since his museum was forcibly closed in 1816 and many of its objects returned to their original ecclesiastic settings.

Although Lenoir's authority rested on his expertise in medieval art, his private passion concerned Egyptian culture. His book on the alleged origins of Freemasonry was based on the premise that Egypt was the cradle not only of all Masonic rituals, but also of religion in general. In fact, Lenoir seriously pondered the revival of "ancient and mysterious institutions . . . under different forms in modern times" as a means to purge the world of "religious fanaticism."[149] For him, Freemasonry was a true *Über-Religion*, "whose principal and moral ends comprise all the others." One can easily conceive how the Sophisians would fit into the promises of this scheme. In contrast to Cuvelier's group, however, Lenoir had no qualms about introducing Cagliostro in the context of his discussion of alchemy. For today's reader the museum director's writings may discredit themselves because of his unfortunate tendency to conflate the alleged mystery religions of Egypt, Persia, Israel, India, and Japan indiscriminately. Moreover, he was probably familiar with Terrasson's novel *Séthos* and may have used some of the abbé's misguided ideas on Egyptian initiation as a source for his writing. Still, even the most obscure Hermetic sources were not beyond the ken of his eclectic knowledge, so that one may find, alongside of standard references to Plutarch, technical Hermetists like Iamblichus of Apamea claiming their place in his account.[150]

Lenoir's book was published at a critical juncture in Sophisian history. In 1814 Ponce-Camus had just joined the order, but the work of the Parisian Grand Pyramid was interrupted because of the impending collapse of the Napoleonic empire. When the Sophisians revived their activities in 1818, several new elements appear in their rituals. These innovations strongly suggest a familiarity with Lenoir's book. Previously alien to Sophisian initiation, the emphasis on visual information as a base for hermeneutics figured foremost among these novelties. The visual dimension was epitomized by Ponce-Camus's freshly conceived gouache illustrations for the Golden Book. There is a strong correlation in the formal presentation of the materials covered in *La Franche-Maçonnerie rendue à sa véritable origine* and the Sophisian manuscript. Lenoir's publication is constructed around the various engravings of Egyptian sculptures, deities, and fantasy scenes, many in vignette format, which the museum director had obtained from the fashionable printmaker Moreau le jeune. Moreau had engraved the plates in the early 1790s for F. H. Stanislas Delaulnaye's monumental twelve-volume study *Histoire générale et particulière des religions et du culte de tous les peuples du monde tant anciens que modernes,* of which only a single volume ever saw the light of day in 1791.[151] In an ironic twist of fate, Delaulnaye had intended to use the engravings to adorn an openly anti-Masonic study. Moreau, eager to dispose of his work after the failure of the publication project, then sold the completed Egyptian plates to Lenoir. The museum director recycled the prints with great ingenuity, as large portions of his book are dedicated to iconological exegeses and speculations based on Moreau's imagery. This emphasis on iconology as base for pseudo-Egyptian hermeneutics may have provided Ponce-Camus with a model for organizing his Golden Book.

The parallels do not stop here. All the standard Sophisian heroes, themes, and symbols receive their credit in Lenoir's treatise. The protagonists Isis and Osiris, Typhon, Harpocrates, and Hermes appear next to the extras Apis, Ptah, Kneph, Neith, the world egg, the Hierophant, and the Sosis. Phallic worship and the quest for Nature's secrets underneath Isis's veil were also for Lenoir issues inextricably linked to the Egyptian mysteries.[152] A remarkable similarity also ruled the selection of décor, including such details as the columns of Thoth-Hermes, the moon and the sun, canopic jars, serpents, palm trees, sistrums, and golden Orphic lyres. The pyramid of the Sophisian siglum (fig. 44), "emblematic figure for the religion of the Egyptians," and the Ark also played critical roles in his spiritual peregrinations.[153] Lenoir's idiosyncratic terminology, which referred to the Egyptian deities jumbled together in Moreau's plates as "hieroglyphic paintings" or simply as "hieroglyphics," presented a semantic nuance eagerly followed by the Sophisians. Time and again, he indulges in flowery elaborations to situate the tests through the four elements in their original Egyptian context. He takes his readers on protracted underground trips to initiation ceremonies below the foundations of the pyramids. At long last, he reemerges for the festivities celebrated in honor of Isis at equinox and solstice with banquets, song, and dance.[154] Lenoir's treatise by itself does not suffice to explain the iconography of Ponce-Camus's Golden Book or the choreography of Sophisian rituals, but it may have provided valuable inspiration for Cuvelier and Ponce-Camus when they reconceptualized the ritual contents of the order after 1818.

Finally, the life experiences of the Sophisians must also be given their due credit when explaining the form and contents of the rituals. Born typically between

Fig. 45 Marie-Nicolas Ponce-Camus, *Golden Book of the Sophisian Order, Apophthegms: The Giving Tree Alma,* ca. 1819–21, pen, ink, and gouache on paper, 11.8 × 6.9 cm (illustration). Paris, Bibliothèque Nationale de France, MSS FM 4.15, fol. 15v.

1750 and 1780, most members had not only consciously observed, but also deliberately promoted the molding of eighteenth-century Enlightenment ideals into Revolutionary actions. The texts of the Golden Book still bristle with the vocabulary of the early 1790s—words like *patrie, liberté,* and, inevitably, *lumière.* One of the *Apophthegms* even features a tree of liberty, freshly reincarnated as the Sophisian giving tree Alma (fig. 45). Cuvelier de Trie was intimately familiar with this iconography and its connotations. At the height of Robespierre's Terror he had written a Jacobin play, *mêlée de chants, pantomimes et danses,* entitled *La Fête de l'Être Suprême,* in which he praised the worship of the tree of liberty. The performance opened with the following scenes:

Scene I.
At the rising of the curtain, daylight has not come on entirely. The peasants come out of their houses. Soft and rustic music announces the arrival of dawn. The peasants work on building an altar.

Scene II.
Female peasants arrive and adorn the altar with festoons, and the Tree of Liberty with ribbons in three colors. The male and female peasants bring in the Statue of Liberty,

which they put up in the foreground on a platform so that she dominates the countryside.

Scene III.
One hears a march in the distance: the National Guard, its commander in advance, and the *Sans-culottes*, armed with pikes, patrol the scene to the sound of the drum and arrange themselves in battle formation.[155]

The play, written when Cuvelier was still in his early twenties, was dedicated to the author's father, who taught him to "love the Supreme Being." The scenario was one of Cuvelier's very first attempts as a playwright, but despite all its uncouthness, it reveals the full extent to which the Revolution's break with Old Regime religious institutions informed Sophisian thought.

The cult of the Supreme Being was the end product of the episode of Revolutionary history that had started out with the persecution of Catholic clergy, proceeded with the sack of churches and convents, and culminated in the wholesale abolition of Christianity. Inspired by Rousseau's celebration of natural religion, the patriotic substitute cults of Reason and, later on, of the Supreme Being defined the spiritual climate of the 1790s.[156] The latter was Robespierre's brain child, but it fell upon Jacques-Louis David to translate and choreograph its contents for public consumption, much like Ponce-Camus would give visual and ceremonial form to Cuvelier de Trie's flights of fantasy.

As Jurgis Baltrušaitis and Erik Hornung have shown, the cult of the Supreme Being did have a Napoleonic aftermath, when a naturalized French Isis received official sanction in the early nineteenth century.[157] Historians during the Empire were eager to uncover medieval and Renaissance sources allegedly proving that the Egyptian goddess had not only lent her name to the city of Paris (*ParIsis, Parisius, Paria Isis*) in the distant past, but that she also had been worshipped in the shrine at the foundation of Notre Dame cathedral. Physical remains of her adjacent cult center at Melun, near Paris, were said to continue to exist. The currency of these speculations was such that in 1811 Napoleon approved the introduction of an Isis figure, copied straight from the Bembine Tablet, on the prow of the ship of state in the Parisian coat of arms. The new design made Isis, to all intents and purposes, the central deity of the French capital and the patron saint of the Napoleonic empire (fig. 46). For Guerrier de Dumast, the central role of Isis worship in the foundation of the city of Paris remained incontrovertible as late as 1820.[158] In light of this wider cultural context some of the Sophisians' claims and ritual practices

Fig. 46 Design for the Coat of Arms of the City of Paris with an Isis Figure at the Prow of the Ship of State, color-lithograph after a drawing from 1811, 15.3 × 13.4 cm. From Anatole de Coëtlogon and L.-M. Tisserand, *Les Armoiries de la ville de Paris*, Vol. I, 1874.

would have been much less anachronistic than they may seem today.

A perhaps even more remarkable aspect of the early nineteenth-century Isis revival is the reinforcement of its vitality during the Restoration. Peace had brought downtime for Napoleon's aging warriors, whose acquiescence was often bought with pensions, which could not, however, prevent Napoleonic nostalgia from flourishing clandestinely in their circles. It also brought prosperity for French society in general, thereby laying the material foundations for a phenomenon that Guerrier de Dumast described in 1820 as a "fever for secret societies" gripping the country, a fashionable movement in which the Sophisians ultimately played but a small part.[159] The most interesting question, perhaps, concerns the psychological needs that the Sophisians and other such esoteric societies addressed during the late 1810s and 1820s. The shattering of the political order after 1789 had cast spiritual certainties—and most particularly the position of the Catholic Church—into disarray, thereby multiplying the quandaries of human existence, identity, and belonging. Concurrently, there opened up a new universe of increasingly polymor-phous forms of spiritual self-expressions whose range of topics kept expanding with colonial conquests of non-European countries, improved means of mass com-munication, and a heightened sense of individualism in post-Revolutionary society. When approached from this perspective, the contradictions and paradoxes inherent in the teachings of the Sophisians have ultimately very little to do with ancient Egypt, but all the more with the birth throes of modernity.

4

The Sophisians on Stage: Boulevard Theaters and the Spell of Egyptomania

Nulla res multitudinem efficacius regit quam superstitio.
(Nothing governs the multitude more efficiently than superstition.)
—Quintus Curtius Rufus, *Historiae Alexandri*, as quoted by
Cuvelier de Trie in *L'Enchanteur Morto-Vivo*[1]

THE SOPHISIANS' DELIBERATE HERMETICISM SUGGESTS A private world jealously shielded from the curiosity of outsiders and the general public. Surprisingly, there was an openly accessible and distinctly populist component to the order's Egypticizing mysticism. Like any other secret society, the Sophisians faced the dilemma of attracting new members, ideally of outstanding social pedigree, while keeping their own existence and ritual practices under wraps. Cuvelier de Trie and his associates came up with an ingenious formula to address this challenge by exploiting the so-called secondary theaters with which they were professionally associated as yet another recruiting ground, besides the military and Masonic circles. Indeed, part of the Sophisians' membership list reads like a roll call of the leading proprietors, producers, playwrights, composers, and actors of the Parisian popular stages clustered around the boulevard du Temple. As will emerge from the analysis of some of Cuvelier de Trie's plays later in this chapter, the dividing line between themes from Sophisian initiation and the performances offered for public consumption in such raucous establishments as the Théâtre de l'Ambigu-Comique and the Cirque Olympique was very fluid. For Cuvelier and his colleagues the stage was just another venue from which to broadcast the Sophisian moral and social worldview to the widest possible audience. Yet, the Sophisian roots in boulevard theater were not just confined to philosophical matters. Sometimes even the props, scenography, and special effects prescribed for Sophisian rituals in the *Livre d'or* are nothing but fanciful reincarnations of materials first conceived for Cuvelier's boulevard plays. To fully appreciate the importance of the theatrical context of Sophisian activities, however, one has to understand the genesis of French popular theater at the turn of the nineteenth century and, more specifically, the impact of the French Revolution and its aftermath on the subcultures of the Parisian stages.

Prior to 1789 privately operated theaters in France existed in a highly regulated and culturally stratified environment. The ancien régime had put in place a number of rules to protect the three state-subsidized Grand Theaters—the Comédie-Française, the Comédie Italienne, and the Opéra—from competition.[2] These so-called theater privileges denied the *petits théâtres* the right to stage fully dialogued plays, banned their establishment in the vicinity of any existing Grand Theater, and required prior approval from the privileged theaters for any newly composed script. Moreover, the Opéra demanded monetary compensation for any staged performance that involved musicians, singers, or dancers. For the better part of the eighteenth century, the *petits théâtres* had dealt with these challenges by divising ingenious strategies of evasion. The prohibition against staging dialogued plays, for instance, was avoided by the introduction of pantomime pieces. As time went by, dialogues continued to slip in with ever greater frequency, but lip service still had to be paid to the pantomime classification by introducing mute characters or individuals forced by some ever-so-artificial twist of destiny to communicate in sign language.[3] Remnants of this tradition are still evident in the many pantomimes Cuvelier de Trie composed well into the early nineteenth century, some of which featured such self-defeating oddities as a "mute troubadour."[4] Pantomimes presumably also appealed to Cuvelier because they allowed for the introduction of a Sophisian subtext, namely the idea of silence, to the plays.

Despite their limited opportunities for growth under the scheme of royal protectionism, the *petits théâtres* did manage to carve out a well-defined niche for themselves in the intellectual and cultural life of the ancien régime. Very few of these establishments were housed in permanent structures. In fact, their original homes were the wooden shacks erected on the fairgrounds of Saint Germain, Saint Laurent, or Saint Ovide, with their diverse attractions of tightrope walkers, jugglers, puppet players, street performers, sideshows, or cafes, as well as their clandestine activities of gambling and prostitution. This original context of semi-legality and impermanence, daily testing the boundaries of censorship and official toleration, offered sensations and entertainment for spectators from all classes of society, including the occasional noble who delighted in "slumming it."[5] Fashionable Rococo painters like Antoine Watteau relished the fairground subculture, which provided them with models for a type of theatrical iconography that was highly appreciated by their aristocratic clientele.[6] When the *forains* (fairground people) moved during the second half of the eighteenth century to either the old city ramparts that had become the boulevard du Temple at the northern fringes of Paris or, later, to the arcades of the Palais Royal, they brought along their shadowy reputation as members of the Parisian demimonde.

The French Revolution changed the status of the small theaters for good. On January 19, 1790, the National Assembly declared the abolition of theater privileges, thereby establishing the legal basis for an unprecedented boom period for boulevard theaters. Subject to a simple declaration to the municipal authorities, every French citizen now enjoyed the right to open a theater, to select its location without interference from competitors, and to stage plays of any genre. One of the trailblazers for the freedom of theaters was a future member of the Sophisians, Millin de Grandmaison, who had published the treatise *Sur la liberté du théâtre* in 1790.[7] This essay deserves close consideration because of the basic philosophical ideas underpinning its arguments. Millin went to great lengths in distinguishing "theater in a free state" from "theater in a despotic state," branding theater privileges as just one specific, if critical, aspect of the Old Regime's generalized political despotism and tyranny. Interestingly, in defending his arguments, Millin relied on the Declaration of Human Rights, and specifically the article on the freedom of the press, of which the "liberty of the theaters is a very essential part."[8] By extension, Millin defended the abolition of all forms of censorship, affecting, besides the press, theaters and other types of creative expression, since "the liberty of theaters cannot be compromised without attacking freedom of thought."[9] Implicit in these arguments is the observation that theaters became a battleground over the freedom of opinion, suggesting that much broader issues of political and social control were at stake in the 1790 discussion.

Millin's treatise was also a plea for economic liberalism in the theater world. He predicted that the abolition of the privileges would entail a commensurate increase in the number of stages, but that ultimately the self-regulating mechanisms of the market would establish natural limits for growth. These predictions proved to be correct in that the number of stages on the boulevard du Temple increased dramatically after 1791, but many theaters could not sustain themselves in the long run.[10] Nevertheless, the entertainment boom afforded opportunities for personal, social, and, occasionally, financial advancement for an increasing number of young men and women. The drive to take to the stage was met with skepticism, especially by the bourgeoisie. As any cursory reader of Casanova's *History of My Life* will know, eighteenth-century European societies considered association with the world of the stage a social stigma. Under the ancien régime, some priests in the Catholic Church denied actors the sacraments, turning any marriage or funeral into a potential challenge for the allegedly "unchristian" outcasts.[11] Even after the widespread secularization of French society in the aftermath of the Revolution, biases against the *comédiens* lingered on, since theaters were now perceived as a corrupting influence on impressionable youths.[12]

CUVELIER DE TRIE AND REVOLUTIONARY THEATER

It was in this climate that Cuvelier de Trie arrived in Paris in the summer of 1790. As a member of the National Guard, he was supposed to represent the "armed citizens" of his local town of Boulogne-sur-mer during the pompous Revolutionary *Fête de la Fédération* held on July 14 at the Champ de Mars.[13] Cuvelier was no stranger to the city. He had previously studied law at the Parisian Collège des Grassins, where he had also absorbed a heavy dose of teaching in classical literature. After he passed the bar in October 1785, Cuvelier returned to the Calais region, but kept in touch with his former fellow students in the capital. Subsequent to his participation in the *Fête de la Fédération*, "the ideas of liberty and the spirit of equality, generally adopted by the Nation, completely changed Cuvelier's destiny, as they promised the improvement of conditions in accordance with philosophy's spreading of enlightenment across all classes of society."[14] Although Cuvelier never detached himself entirely from the military during these years, the focus of his interest shifted to the world of the Parisian popular theaters.

Twenty-four years of age, a law degree in his pocket, and distinguished by a new appointment as General Lafayette's aide-de-camp, Cuvelier certainly did not fit the stereotype of an impressionable youth at risk from the allure of the stage. Nevertheless, during the same period he associated himself with Mlle Montansier's theater, also known as the Théâtre du Palais Royal in reference to its fashionable location in the architectural complex that the Duc d'Orléans had built north of the Louvre.[15] One of the leading theater entrepreneurs of the late eighteenth century, Mlle Montansier had shrewdly managed to assemble an entertainment empire during the ancien régime that included five provincial venues in addition to her headquarters at Versailles.[16] A decisive factor for this unprecedented accumulation of theater privileges was Mlle Montansier's close personal relationship with Marie-Antoinette, who appointed her, unofficially at least, "entrepreneur-general of pleasures to the court," and charged her with entertaining the queen not only at Versailles, but also at the royal residences of Saint-Cloud, Marly, Fontainebleau, and Compiègne. Given the intensity of Revolutionary rage vented against Marie-Antoinette after 1789, Mlle Montansier inevitably faced suspicions of royalist sympathies owing to the favors she had previously enjoyed. To make up lost ground, she decided to transfer her theater from Versailles to Paris in October 1789, a move which followed the pattern of royal concessions to the demands of the Parisian population. The new location close to the Palais Royal put her business squarely in the center of political agitation as Revolutionary events radicalized. By 1792 Mlle Montansier had begun to fear for her life. To keep her persecutors in check, she financed and organized, as a token of her devotion to the Revolution, a *Compagnie franche des Artistes Dramatiques*. The term described a "free company" of volunteers for the Revolutionary Wars recruited mostly from the employees of her theater.[17] The timing of this gesture was certainly appropriate, since it came in the aftermath of the Brunswick Proclamation of July 25, 1792, in which the Austrian and Prussian monarchies threatened ruin to French soldiers and civilians alike, should the Revolutionaries injure Louis XVI and his family.

Revolutionary France responded by declaring a state of emergency and a general mobilization that depended heavily on the enrollment of "volunteers" from all walks of life. Because of his prior military experience, Cuvelier was made a captain of Mlle Montansier's *compagnie franche*, which also included theater people from other Parisian stages.[18] The unit must have been quite small—some eighty or two hundred men depending on the source[19]—but references or allusions to service in the *compagnie franche* appear with notable frequency in a number of Sophisian biographies.

Cuvelier's playwright-colleague and fellow Sophisian Alexandre Duval, for instance, recalled his contribution as "orator and troubadour" to the unit.[20] Comments such as Duval's raise questions concerning the military value of the free company. While there are some reports about bravery on the battlefield shown by members of the Montansier unit, their most important task appears to have been that of bringing theatrical performances to the site of battle so as to uplift the morale of the troops. At least once, Mlle Montansier participated directly in these activities:

> At the news of the victory at Jemappes [in Flanders] and an altercation to which her company had contributed, Mlle Montansier, ever skillful, looked for an advantage she could derive. From Paris, she sent a stagecoach filled with costumes [to the front], and called for Mlle Rivière, who accompanied her in the *chaise* that carried them up to Cuesmes. There, Mlle Montansier's plan won the approval of General Dumouriez, and after a few hours one could see a theater rising from the plain of Jemappes whose construction, due to the heartiness and the imagination of the French soldier, left but little to be desired. There was really a French *fête nationale* at Jemappes from which nothing was lacking.[21]

The passage shows that the most important task of the Montansier unit under Cuvelier's command was the production of war propaganda. Such strong links between the theater, the military, and the manipulation of public opinion during the radical phase of the French Revolution are less incongruous than they may seem at first glance. Under Robespierre's regime, the French ministry of war was teeming with formerly unemployed actors and playwrights, whose only qualification for their jobs was their staunch antiroyalism paired with a zealous devotion to the Republican cause.[22] Almost inadvertently, Cuvelier himself had joined the ranks of those theater people who gained their livelihood from political propaganda. Before long, this engagement would evolve into a permanent professional vocation.

Cuvelier's records in the French military archives at Vincennes show that between 1792 and 1793 he reported to one of the most infamous generals of the Revolution, Antoine-Joseph Santerre.[23] Although no longer a household name, Santerre played a crucial role during many of the landmark events between 1789 and the fall of Robespierre in 1794. At the outbreak of the Revolution, Santerre was a well-to-do brewer who lived in the popular and soon-to-be seditious Faubourg Saint-Antoine. When rumors circulated that the cannons of the Bastille pointed at his neighborhood, Santerre organized the resistance of the local population, which resulted in the siege of the fortress-prison, whose final surrender he negotiated. Santerre's reputation as fearless hero of the Bastille earned him not only a promotion to the rank of general but also great popularity with the Parisian lower classes, especially after word spread that he opened his home to the hapless prisoners he had personally liberated. After the storming of the Tuileries on August 10, 1792, Santerre arrested the royal family and transferred them to their prison in the tower of the Temple enclosure. The allegedly too compassionate treatment of the royals under Santerre's supervision earned him some misgivings among the Parisian population. Later, the ambiguity of his role in revolutionary events further deepened, when, at Louis XVI's execution on January 21, 1793, Santerre ordered the infamous drum roll to suffocate the king's voice as he attempted to address the spectators one last time.

While the nature of Cuvelier's relationship with Santerre remains undefined with respect to his engagement in Mlle Montansier's free company, it moves into clearer focus in 1793, when the Committee of Public Safety sent both men to fight the insurgents in the Vendée.[24] Compared to the struggle with the Austrian and the Prussian armies around Jemappes, the Vendée assignment turned out to be a strategic and moral challenge. The military mission in 1792 had been of the utmost clarity: to save the *patrie* and the newly established republican order from foreign royalist aggressors. The altercations in the Vendée, on the other hand, involved the Revolutionary armies in a demoralizing theater of civil warfare, in which Frenchmen fought Frenchmen over issues of religion, mass conscription, and the form of government. The guerrilla tactics of the Vendée insurgents succeeded in drawing out a conflict that left no hope for a decisive outcome, but claimed a rising toll of human lives. Santerre's short-lived command in the Vendée ended in October 1793, when he was recalled to Paris, arrested by Robespierre on trumped-up charges of royalist sympathies, and sent to jail for the remaining months of the Terror. Cuvelier's misadventure in the Vendée, however, only ended in May 1795, when he received a severe gunshot wound in the breast, which he barely survived. As sketchy as these early episodes from Cuvelier's biography are, they nevertheless confirm his personal implication in the momentous upheavals of the Revolution—circumstances that colored his view of the world in general and of human nature in particular. These experiences also kindled Cuvelier's search for fulfillment in the conflicting longings for esoteric introspection and a messianic drive to improve human conditions. Both tendencies found their natural outlet in Cuvelier's work as a playwright and as an organizer of secret societies.

Censorship of theatrical performances in France at the turn of the nineteenth century typically followed a cyclical pattern, where "with each revolution censorship was abolished, and in each case was reestablished within a few years."[25] Thus, the Directory government that replaced Robespierre's terror regime gradually tightened and institutionalized the grip of control on what was written in the newspapers or shown on stage.[26] Returning to his theatrical vocation, Cuvelier now played an important role in implementing the guidelines for theatrical censorship. After his recovery in 1795, he obtained a new position as one of the *commissaires de l'instruction publique* in the ministry responsible for education, censorship, and propaganda. In this capacity he was "charged with overseeing libraries [i.e., privately operated reading rooms], museums, theaters, and public festivities [*fêtes publiques*]."[27] Almost certainly, he and his colleague Millin de Grandmaison were assigned the task of reviewing plays submitted for approval by theater companies. When appropriate, they would also compose pieces at the government's request. At about this time, Cuvelier celebrated a breakthrough success as author and playwright with his *Le Damoisel et la bergerette*, a fifteenth-century short story published with accompanying musical scores that continued to be performed on Parisian stages for the next twenty years.[28] The combination of censor and author was neither thought of as objectionable, nor did it present a conflict of interests. Rather, the government considered it a concession to the writers' guild that censors, if proven reliable and ready to collaborate, were picked from among the insiders of the theater world. For Cuvelier, the appointment to the position of *commissaire de l'instruction publique* meant that he had regular dealings with theater professionals, including proprietors, directors, writers, and actors, from a wide variety of stages. This network allowed him to establish personal connections, which he used not only for the advancement of his own literary career, but also for the foundation of the *Frères Artistes*, chartered in 1796/97 as a confraternal organization for theater people. In May 1796 Cuvelier left his "position and right" in the censorship bureau "to an employee who had no other financial resources," while continuing "to work as an *homme de lettres* and dramatic author on works of the imagination."[29] Apparently, an appointment to a position as a theater censor could also carry connotations of governmental charity towards dramatic artists who faced difficult times.

NAPOLEON AND THE PARISIAN STAGES

How Cuvelier managed to juggle producing plays for the popular stages while also fighting in wars across Europe during the early years of the Napoleonic age remains difficult to determine. In any case, one can observe a dramatic increase in the number of pieces Cuvelier published after 1799.[30] This date coincided with Napoleon's return from Egypt and his ascent to political power, both of which were events of epic dimensions for the Parisian popular stages. They affected theatrical productions in two ways. Public fascination with the Egyptian campaign triggered a boom in performances dabbling in any kind of Orientalist theme, whether in historical guise or as re-creations of contemporary military events. While demand for public entertainment kept increasing, Napoleon's idiosyncratic views on theatrical representations led to a further tightening of institutional constraints for boulevard stages. These developments culminated in the theater decree of 1807, which closed down all but four of the secondary theaters.

Napoleon's unexpected return from Egypt in October 1799 immediately attracted attention from the literary milieu and the world of the stage.[31] The one-month period between Bonaparte's arrival on French soil at Fréjus and his coup d'état on November 9 was punctuated with well-calculated public appearances of the future first consul at various theaters. As the stage historian Charles-Maurice Descombes later recalled, the pattern emerged even prior to Bonaparte's arrival in Paris, when pleas to attend an impromptu play given in his honor tied up the general for an extra day at Lyons.[32] The performance itself was miserable, as the actors had insufficient time to study the text and were intimidated by the crowds and their distinguished spectator alike. Nevertheless, Napoleon appeared to enjoy himself. The *Moniteur universel* reported that Bonaparte's first appearance in Paris caused "a delirium" and added that not long ago "the death of this extraordinary man seemed so certain that one could not doubt it without being considered a Jacobin."[33] Pro-Napoleonic poems filled with inevitable Egyptian lore were eagerly snapped up and printed by the press, while newspaper editors wondered aloud why "the authors of vaudeville, so skilled at impromptus, have not announced anything so far on the 'Return of Napoleon.' This subject holds at least as much interest as the *Retour d'une comète* or a *Voyage astronomique dans les airs*."[34] The query was answered by the letter of an anonymous (and possibly invented) playwright, who thought "like you do, Citizen, that the return of Bonaparte attracts greater interest than the passage of

a comet or a voyage in a hot air balloon. That is why I have been busying myself for some days in celebrating this return in a piece I titled *La Taverne*."[35]

Meanwhile, Napoleon's every step in public was watched carefully, and his appearances in the theaters especially were always worth a headline. On October 24, Napoleon attempted to attend a performance of *Le Rêve* and *Ariodant* incognito, but was promptly spotted: "He hid himself in a loge of the rez-de-chaussée. Some persons, having recognized him, informed their neighbors, and calls of *Vive Bonaparte!* resounded. The hero, always modest, noticing that he was discovered, left after the first act of *Ariodant*."[36] Just four days prior to the 18th of Brumaire (November 9), a notice inserted in the *Moniteur universel* reported as follows on the first performance directly referencing Napoleon's Near Eastern military adventure:

> The new management of the Opéra has opened this theater on the 10th of Brumaire with a presentation of *La Caravane du Caire*. The crowd that the play attracted proves that the public is well disposed to rendering justice to the zeal and the efforts of our administrators. A young Mameluke, brought along by Bonaparte, attended the presentation. He attracted all the glances, but his attention was fixed on the stage, where he seemed greatly amazed to see the customs and costumes of his country. At every turn, this play contains allusions to the expedition of the French in Egypt. Each time they appeared, they were greatly applauded.[37]

The Mameluke's amazement (or, better still, incomprehension) can only too easily be understood if one takes into consideration that the play, *La Caravane du Caire*, was originally written in 1783 for the court theater of Louis XVI at Fontainebleau.[38] Its libretto was coauthored by none other than the Comte de Provence, the future king Louis XVIII, who would oust Bonaparte from power on two occasions. Although the Opéra management had obviously taken pains to adapt the piece to current events, the situation was anachronistic in the extreme. Here, an exotic narrative filled with Orientalist stereotypes and perpetuating in its basic structure the bucolic and naïve views on Egypt held by the Enlightenment, was offered for consumption to a native of the country, vanquished by Napoleon's army and displaced to Paris. From a political point of view, the event was no less bizarre, as the play was meant to apotheosize Napoleon with a narrative written by one of his greatest political adversaries. Cultural and political inconsistencies notwithstanding, the success of the performance at the Opéra proved beyond doubt that there was a demand for a new type of mise en scène of the Orient, one that acknowledged the need for both rectification and re-enchantment following the Egyptian campaign. By 1799, no dramaturgical conventions yet existed for satisfying this demand. As time passed, however, the vacuum was filled by the boulevard theaters, which molded Orientalist themes culled from all periods of history to fit the dramaturgy of one of its most successful genres, melodrama.

Boulevard theaters and their staff were among the first to rush to Napoleon's support after the 18th of Brumaire. As Maurice Albert pointed out, pro-Napoleonic enthusiasm in the theatrical milieu of the capital knew no bounds, especially at the beginning of Bonaparte's rule:

> Nowhere did the First Consul find more hot-blooded and valuable apologists. There were the chansonniers of Vaudeville, the Troubadours of the rue de Louvois and the Marais, the mimes of the Ambigu-Comique, and the acrobats of the late M. Nicolet, who were the first to consecrate the grand attempt at liberty. . . . The military pantomimes, the exhibition of uniforms and flags, the sounding of the clarion and bellicose fanfares, the gunshots and battle simulacra—all these buoyant pieces lavished by the directors on the Parisians, who showed themselves only too gullible, seconded the future projects of the emperor as efficiently as the impromptus of Brumaire had served the General's political moves. The plays kindled the taste for matters of war; it was a school of soldiery in miniature: maneuvers to make one laugh, while waiting for the real ones.[39]

Napoleon himself took advantage of the popular theaters as long as they were useful to him in the pursuit of his objectives. But beyond this purely utilitarian point, his attitude was marked by condescension. Culture, including theater culture, had to contribute to the glory of France and to the moral improvement of the population.[40] If it did not, it could not claim a right to be tolerated. Bonaparte was especially taken aback by what he perceived as the lower-class origins and intrinsic vulgarity expressed in the spectacles of the popular theaters, which for him were "tragedies for chambermaids."[41] The eighteenth-century stereotype that minor theaters were the exclusive haunts of "wig dressers, domestics killing time while their masters attend the Opéra (lest they engage in more serious debaucheries), or the unemployed," was hopelessly outdated (if it had ever held true) by the early nineteenth century.[42] In fact, one of the most striking features of the secondary theaters as social venues was that the divisions between the working classes, the bourgeoisie, and the aristocracy became permeable. Josephine herself was an acknowledged aficionado of the boulevard theaters, which earned her the emperor's reprimands on more than one occasion, when she took advantage of Napoleon's absences to indulge in her habit. In a letter written from Osterode on March 17, 1807, Bonaparte advised her "not to attend the *petits spectacles* in a small loge; that is inappropriate for your rank: you should only go to the four Grand Theaters, always taking a large loge."[43] When the empress still remained recalcitrant one week later, the tone became harsher: "To be agreeable to me, it is absolutely necessary to live as if I were in Paris. Thus, you will not go to the *petits spectacles*, or other places. . . . This, my friend, is the only way to earn my approval. Grandeur has its inconveniences: an empress cannot go where a private person goes."[44]

The letters to Josephine were written at a moment when Bonaparte was about to deal a lethal blow to the cottage industry of boulevard theaters. On August 8, 1807, Napoleon signed the theater decree, which prohibited all but eight theaters in the capital.[45] Included in this number were the four nationally subsidized Grand Theaters of the Comédie-Française or Théâtre de l'Empereur, the Odéon or Théâtre de l'Impératrice, the Opéra, and the Opéra-Comique. Only four privately owned, "secondary" theaters were allowed to continue operations under the decree: the Théâtre de l'Ambigu-Comique, the Théâtre de la Gaîté, the Théâtre du Vaudeville, and the Théâtre des Variétés. Scores of other popular theaters excluded from the list had to close within a week's notice. The decree conformed to Napoleon's notions of socially stratified cultural consumption, and to his obsession with administrative control. Indeed, Bonaparte was initially inclined to do away with the minor theaters altogether, but was swayed by the argument that these establishments provided diversion for the masses, which could help diffuse problems with dissent and civil unrest.[46] During the deliberations that led to the theater decree, Napoleon had as his closest adviser another Sophisian, Regnaud de Saint-Jean-d'Angély, coauthor of the *Code civil*, member of the French Academy, and, since 1804, Attorney-General at the Imperial High Court (*procureur général de la Haute Cour imprériale*).[47] Régnaud may actually have been the one who phrased the wording of the decree and gave Napoleon's decision the legal stamp of approval.

THE AMBIGU-COMIQUE THEATER AND THE CIRQUE OLYMPIQUE

The upheavals of the Napoleonic theater decree left Cuvelier de Trie's literary career all but unaffected, since he mostly worked for two establishments that for different reasons escaped the rigors of Bonapartist censorship. These two theaters were the Théâtre de l'Ambigu-Comique and the Cirque Olympique. Circumstantial evidence strongly suggests that the activities of the Sophisians in the early nineteenth century were tied to their stages.

The Théâtre de l'Ambigu-Comique ranked first on the list of minor theaters exempted from the 1807 decree. It was founded in 1769 by Nicolas-Médard Audinot, a *comédien* from the Foire Saint Germain with deep roots in eighteenth-century fairground culture.[48] Audinot started out his business as a puppet theater featuring characters modeled on those of the *Comédie Italienne*, but later switched to child actors. In 1770 he moved to the boulevard du Temple, where he built a permanent theater with a neoclassical façade after plans by the architect Jacques Cellerier. By this time, the troupe consisted mostly of adult performers. Over the following years, the *pantomime-dialoguée*, a precursor of the type of melodrama pioneered by Cuvelier de Trie, became a specialty of the Ambigu-Comique. In 1795 Audinot retired from business and handed over the management of the theater to a collective of employees. This experiment was short-lived and drove the theater into financial difficulties. Three years later, the Ambigu-Comique was bought by one Marquis de Puisaye, whom Brazier describes as "a rich capitalist."[49] Puisaye invested heavily in remodeling the premises of the theater and hired a new director named Corse, who was formerly employed by Mlle Montansier's theater. In the wake of these reorganizations, the Ambigu-Comique experienced a long period of prosperity, remarkable for celebrated performances that distinguished the theater as one of the foremost stages on the boulevard du Temple. After Corse's death in 1816, Mme de Puisaye, who was now running her late husband's theater, asked Audinot's son, Nicolas-Théodore Audinot-D'Aussy, to become her business partner and to manage operations. With the help of the owners of the Cirque Olympique and a third business partner, Audinot-D'Aussy bought Mme de Puisaye's shares and continued to run the Ambigu-Comique until his death in 1826.

Louis-Léopold Boilly's 1819 genre painting *The Entrance to the Théâtre de l'Ambigu-Comique before a Free Performance* (pl. 16), preserved in the Louvre, is an interesting historical document with respect to theatrical life during Audinot-D'Aussy's directorship.[50] The viewer's attention is immediately drawn to the undisciplined behavior of the working-class crowd in the right foreground, as they compete to gain admission to the free performance through the narrow entryway of the theater. The scuffle is about to get out of control, as a gentleman has already been pushed to the ground. The rowdy crowd features a cross-section of those lower-class stage enthusiasts who earned the boulevard theaters the epithet "popular": domestics, blue-collar workers, and craftsmen. Clearly, the prospect of a free ticket was enticing for spectators living on small incomes. One may assume that it was precisely the type of boisterous and uncouth behavior captured by Boilly that inspired Napoleon's horror for boulevard theaters. The artist, however, made sure to counterbalance the scuffle on the right by making a concession to class diversity in the left foreground, where a bourgeois family, complete with nursemaid and domestics, watches the altercations with a mixture of fascination and disgust. Yet, their presence can only be explained by the fact that they, too, hope to gain admission to the free performance.[51] Significantly, the bourgeois onlookers are depicted in the company of uniformed police that may have been called in to control the brewing riot.[52] Class distinction is further underscored by the barefoot beggar boy who approaches the head of the bourgeois family. Such spatial divisions along class lines were not uncommon in early nineteenth-century French art.[53] What makes Boilly's painting so interesting from a sociological point of view, however, is the fact that the artist selected the setting of the Ambigu-Comique to show that, while all classes enjoyed boulevard theaters, class distinctions were by no means abolished.

The background of Boilly's painting features a segment of the whitewashed neoclassical façade of the Ambigu-Comique, on which is posted a broadside announcing Cuvelier de Trie's play *Les Machabées, ou la prise de Jérusalem*, a "sacred drama for grand spectacle," which is apparently the reason for the commotion.[54] The *Machabées*, first performed in 1817, was coauthored by another Sophisian playwright, Léopold-François-Hugues Chandezon. An Orientalist melodrama modeled on themes from the biblical Apocrypha, the spectacle apotheosized the Jewish martyrs of the persecutions of the Syrian king Antiochus IV Epiphanes in 165 B.C. The performance was rich in Sophisian overtones, not only because another initiate, Amédée, set the play to music, but also because the scenography prominently featured the stage prop of the Sophisian "Sacred Ark" (fig. 29), this time inserted in the historical context of the profanation of the Temple of Solomon in Jerusalem.[55]

Sophisians occupied positions at almost all levels of management and staff of the Ambigu-Comique. Both the Marquis de Puisaye's widow and their son Louis-Antoine were members of the order, as was Audinot-D'Aussy, who also appeared on the annual *tableaux* of the *Frères Artistes* by 1809.[56] Cuvelier himself wrote many of the most successful plays in the Ambigu-Comique's repertoire, such as *C'est le diable, ou la Bohémienne* (1797/98), which featured (nomen est omen?) an ethereal sorceress named Sophaia, *Les hommes de la nature et des hommes policés* (1800/1801), and *Les Machabées, ou la prise de Jérusalem.*[57] One of Cuvelier's Sophisian coauthors, Philippe-Jacques de Laroche, is known to have collaborated in the writing of scripts for the same establishment. Another Sophisian playwright and a founding member of the *Frères Artistes*, Hector Chaussier, managed the theater as its director at one point. Ponce-Camus was in demand as a set designer and special effects engineer at popular theaters throughout Paris, and it would be surprising if he had not worked for the Ambigu-Comique. Between 1818 and 1832, the Sophisian composer Amédée, an illegitimate son of the founder Nicolas-Médard Audinot and half brother of Nicolas-Théodore Audinot-D'Aussy, set more than fifty plays to music for the Ambigu-Comique. Finally, the theater's *régisseur général* of many years, François Varez, was also a member of the Sophisians.[58] This unusual concentration of dramaturgical talent with links to Cuvelier's order marked the Ambigu-Comique as one of the hot spots of Sophisian activity.

Cuvelier's other professional mainstay was the Cirque Olympique, the first permanent circus-amphitheater established in Paris.[59] As the name implies, the Cirque Olympique was a mixture between a circus and a theater, which specialized in animal performances, including a standard repertoire of equestrian exercises. Typically, the quadruped actors were either integrated into the dramaturgical plot, a task at which Cuvelier excelled, or featured in separate programs as introductions or interludes. The Cirque Olympique's foundation dated back to 1783, when a British entrepreneur called Philip Astley opened the precursor of the establishment near the entry to the Faubourg du Temple. With respect to the contents of the performances, the Cirque Olympique, like the Ambigu-Comique, could trace its lineage back to the eighteenth-century *forains* and street performers:

> At its origin, [the Cirque Olympique] contented itself with receiving the least precious remains of the abandoned heritage of the old fairground people, when the mountebanks' booths, transported from the Faubourg Saint-Germain to the boulevards, became true theaters.

As in times past, canaries were trained to dance on the tightrope, deer played cards or set off cannons, rats formed a quadrillion, seals played music, and monkeys, like Turco, may he rest in peace, could not be found at Nicolet or Audinot, but with the Franconis [at the Cirque Olympique]. And while the naturally peace-loving animals—the dog Moreau, Marbot's Lisette, or the donkey Bidassoa—distinguished themselves on the battlefield or in military memoirs, all of Paris was drawn to the boulevard du Temple to see the surprising exploits of savage and ferocious animals tamed behind the scenes. There was Kiouni, the most graceful of all elephants, dancing the Gavotte, and Coco, the most gallant deer, who distributed flowers to the ladies while threatening their husbands with his antlers. There was the bear Martin, a retired hunter, and the acrobatic goat, more gracious than the Taglioni, tigers sweet as pussycats, which licked the cheeks of small children, . . . and horses, above all, horses.[60]

The original Astley arena, which consisted of a ring twenty meters in diameter, surrounded by two tiers of boxes and illuminated by some two hundred lamps, was well equipped to handle such extravaganzas. Astley relied from the start on an Italian expatriate animal dresser named Antonio Franconi to develop the repertoire of his circus. In 1793 Franconi, who had fled his native Udine following a duel and subsequently earned his living as an itinerant juggler, soothsayer, and equestrian performer in France, managed to lease the amphitheater, whose name he changed to Cirque Franconi. Together with his sons Laurent and Minette, Antonio Franconi established a legendary Parisian circus dynasty that continued to exist until the theater mile on the boulevard du Temple was demolished in the wake of Baron Haussmann's urban renewal program for Paris.

The year 1807 was an important turning point for the circus, because it changed location and moved to another part of town near the Palais Royal, where, on the grounds of a former Capuchin convent on the rue du Mont-Thabor, the Franconis built a new arena seating twelve hundred spectators. In the wake of this relocation, the business changed its name again and became the Cirque Olympique. The timing of this expansion may surprise, because it roughly coincided with the repressive regime of Napoleon's theater decree. There have been numerous speculations about why the Franconi circus escaped these upheavals untouched. Of course, the simplest explanation is that, by virtue of being a circus and not a theater, the Cirque Olympique fell outside the classifications of the 1807 decree.[61] Such formalities, however, could not have fooled Napoleon's administration, intimately familiar with the popular theaters' strategies to evade censorship by deliberately confusing genres. The Cirque Olympique had permission to stage acts in which horses and other animals played important roles, and it used this privilege as a license to stage "pantomimes." Official boundaries, however, were habitually further transgressed, since the Franconis' mimes "conversed fluently by the fall of the Empire."[62]

The Cirque Olympique and its artists may have owed their toleration first and foremost to Cuvelier's skill at flattery. For the occasion of the grand opening of the Cirque Olympique at the Mont-Thabor site in December 1807, he composed *La Lanterne de Diogène*, an "equestrian pantomime" featuring "four small tableaux of four great centuries."[63] In this performance, the famous Greek philosopher, following a revelation he received from the oracle at the temple of Delphi, explores Western history in search of the VIR, the greatest man and hero of all times. He meets Alexander the Great, Augustus, and Charlemagne, but each time, after consulting the Book of Destiny presented to him by a temple priest, refuses the candidate upon reading about his shortcomings. When he arrives at Napoleon's equestrian statue, Diogenes blows out his lantern, the prearranged sign that he has found the VIR. In the final scene Bonaparte receives the crown of immortality amidst thundering background noise and a great mêlée of French infantry, cavalry, and "allegorical personages."[64] Napoleon always enjoyed such flatteries, provided they accommodated his taste. With his *Diogène* and equestrian dramas, Cuvelier hit Bonaparte's nerve so that, in the future, the emperor considered the Cirque Olympique a "healthy establishment leading to the development of martial skills and horsemanship," a judgment tantamount to a license to prosperity.[65]

Whether genuine pro-Napoleonic enthusiasm or an opportunistic drive to stay in business motivated such attempts at the cultural deification of the emperor remains an unresolved question. In his more private writings, Cuvelier professed to abhor flattery, since "extreme politeness is nothing but lies in action."[66] Nevertheless, after the return of the Bourbons, Cuvelier jumped at any occasion to compose a *pièce de circonstance*, such as *La Gloire et la Paix* of 1823, a prose poem for stage in the form of a dialogue between Glory (the Napoleonic age) and Peace (the Restoration).[67] The work, written in honor of the Duc d'Angoulême's recent success in reinstalling the Bourbon king Ferdinand VII on the Spanish throne, concluded with a conciliatory call on Royalists and Bonapartists alike to unite for the sake of national unity.

Compared to Napoleon's rule, the Restoration certainly proved to be a golden age for minor theaters. Censorship rules, if not lifted entirely, were enforced with greater leniency, stages proscribed by the 1807 decree were allowed to reopen, and the general prosperity of peacetime drew spectators to the entertainment districts in unprecedented numbers.[68] Military spectacles and mystery passion plays remained hits at the box office, but direct references to the Napoleonic age or representations of the deposed emperor on stage fell outside the boundaries of official toleration. The fashionable aspects of Restoration theatrical life at the Cirque Olympique are illustrated in an engraving depicting the interior of the Mont-Thabor site (fig. 47). The arena, in the center, consisted of a circular manège, to which a regular theatrical proscenium was attached to the right. Spectators were accommodated in loges of varying sizes on three levels. The interior decoration was sumptuous in every respect. Fluted columns supported an expansive ceiling, which featured putti playing with horses. In the central ring, a number of equestrian exercises took place concurrently, while illumination was provided by large candelabras suspended from the canopy above. The demeanor of the audience in the foreground stands in striking contrast to the riotous crowd depicted in Boilly's painting of the entrance to the Ambigu-Comique. The spectators of the Cirque-Olympique seem to be mostly well-kempt, upwardly mobile members of the bourgeoisie, an observation confirmed by the circumstance that after 1815 the restored aristocracy discovered the Cirque Olympique as one of its preferred social venues.

In this positive economic and cultural climate, the Cirque Olympique returned to its original site on the boulevard du Temple. The move was imposed by the planned installation of the French treasury at the Mont-Thabor site, but fortunately the old amphitheater in the Temple district stood empty ever since Philip Astley's death in 1814.[69] The Franconis managed to acquire the site, restore the premises, and reopen the circus on the boulevards by February 8, 1817. A fire triggered by one of the pyrotechnical effects that customarily concluded performances destroyed the Cirque Olympique in 1826.

Sophisian following among the collaborators of the Cirque Olympique was substantial, but did not include the establishment's management as was the case at the Ambigu-Comique. Neither Astley nor the Franconis, for instance, were members of the order. Nevertheless, Sophisian membership at the Cirque was commensurate with Cuvelier's prolific output of plays written for the Franconis between 1807 and 1824. Typically, Cuvelier wrote one to three plays per year for the Cirque,

Fig. 47 Interior View of the First *Cirque Olympique*, engraving, 10.4 × 15.5 cm. From Mme B***, *Les animaux savants*, 1816. Paris, Bibliothèque Nationale de France.

which translated into a literary production much larger than that for the Ambigu-Comique. The Sophisian composer Jacques Foignet, for example, coauthored the musical scores for one of Cuvelier's most successful *pièces historiques* given at the Cirque Olympique, the *Bataille d'Aboukir, ou Les Arabes du desert*, of 1808. He also conceived the accompaniment for Cuvelier's equestrian spectacle *Cavalo-Dios, ou Le Cheval génie bienfaisant*, which premiered in the same year at the Cirque.[70]

Ponce-Camus, whose important contributions were frequently omitted from the imprints of theater pieces, received credit at least once as choreographer and special effects coordinator for Cuvelier's *Le volcan, ou L'Anchorète du val des laves*, a "magical pantomime" in three acts situated on Mt. Etna near Catania (Sicily), which was performed for the first time at the Cirque in March 1812.[71] The scenography is a textbook example

of what Angela C. Pao has described as the "powerful assault on the senses" that audiences expected from better boulevard performances.[72] In this case, it required the creation of a complete "interior of a volcanic grotto," home of the anchorite, which featured a "double arcade formed by lava." To create the right kind of atmosphere, flames shot up from the crater, while the Faustian story line of one Marquis Castelfieri signing over his soul to the evil genie Inferno unfolded. Subsequent pyrotechnical tricks included a blue flame that, conjured by Inferno, "shot up from the ground all the way to the skies," "rings of fire," and an "iron altar illuminated by a mysterious conflagration." One of the Franconi daughters played the female lead character Angelina, an innocent young girl whose body, bewitched by Inferno's spell, decomposed on stage to assume a state of putrefaction similar to the painting of a female cadaver in the Sophisian "cabinet of retreat" (fig. 36). Restored to her original form, she was later abducted by her suitor, the Duke Delmonte, who had sold his soul to Inferno. The kidnapping scene required a movable chariot on an inclined slope, which a *machiniste* like Ponce-Camus would have known how to operate on tracks invisible to the theater audience.[73] According to the Sophisians' Golden Book, similar "abductions" on movable chariots were integral features of the order's initiation ceremonies. During theatrical performances, the most spectacular special effects were typically reserved for the climactic finale of a melodrama. In the case of *Le volcan, ou L'Anchorète du val des laves*, the closing scene required that Inferno and his black minions be swallowed by a stream of hot lava in the wake of a timely eruption of Mt. Etna. Remarkably, the play featured yet another Sophisian, the seasoned actor Luc-Vincent Thierry the elder, in the role of Delmonte's domestic and partner in crime.

The social network of the Sophisians in the Parisian theater world extended well beyond the confines of the Ambigu-Comique and the Cirque Olympique to include many theater directors, musicians, and actors associated with the type of stages that Napoleon's 1807 decree sought to eradicate. One individual who stands paradigmatically for this wider context of the order was the theater entrepreneur Louis-Christian-Emmanuel-Apollinaire Comte, nicknamed "physicien du roi" in reference to his skills as a magician, which earned him the patronage of the restored Bourbon court.[74] Comte came from a background similar to those of Nicolas-Médard Audinot or Antonio Franconi. The runaway son of a Swiss watchmaker, he began his theatrical career as an itinerant ventriloquist and sorcerer. In 1814 he established himself in Paris, assumed the title "physicien du roi," and rented a small stage in the basement of the Hôtel des Fermes to open a childrens' theater. In 1817, Comte took over the recently abandoned Cirque Olympique arena on the Mont-Thabor site, where he opened his Théâtre de jeunes comédiens (later, Théâtre de jeunes élèves), which featured a troupe of child actors performing for an audience of youths. Between acts, Comte himself would typically perform magic tricks, which were advertised as experiments in physics. Commercially, the Théâtre de jeunes comédiens could not sustain itself and had to close soon after its opening. The failure of the enterprise was partially due to licensing restrictions that required Comte's actors to perform behind a gauze curtain separating them from the audience. Moreover, some of the child actors allegedly caused Comte some "vexations" with the police. Under the lenient censorship rules of the 1820s, Comte continued to operate theaters in the newly es-

tablished covered passages with shops and cafes, such as the *Passage des Panoramas*, where he set up shop in 1820, or the *Passage Choiseul*, where he opened his *Théâtre Comte* in 1827. In the same year Comte's royal privilege was affirmed, when he was asked by the court to organize the birthday party for the Duc de Bordeaux, grandson of Charles X, who turned seven. As revealed by the records of the *menus plaisirs du roi*, administered partly by another Sophisian, Fauchon d'Henneville, the young duke and his guests were entertained by a *spectacle de marionettes de M. Comte, phisicien*.[75] Comte is also known to have entertained Sophisian reunions with his magical tricks. At the *Fête Sophisienne* in 1821, for example, he showed a *Magie blanche, suivie d'expériences de physique*.

FREEMASONRY AND THEATER LIFE

Many aspects of Sophisian social life retained the characteristics of a theatrical confraternity, a legacy inherited from the *Frères Artistes* lodge, which appears to have been the critical link between the Sophisians and the world of Parisian popular theater. Indeed, theatrical confraternities and pseudo-Masonic organizations had deep roots in eighteenth-century stagecraft. According to Victor Couailhac, such forms of social organization spread across the theatrical profession in an attempt to deal with the challenges imposed by the itinerant lifestyle of many actors: "One could see actors—and sometimes actors of a certain merit at that—traveling with great difficulty and covering distances as great as 250 miles, while living on vegetables that they dug from the fields. The best salvation is the following, which is still practiced today: dramaturgic Freemasonry. While traveling through a town where the theater is full of activity, the out-of-luck traveler addresses himself to his brothers, and a collection is made."[76] A distant echo of this tradition subsisted even in the writings of Cuvelier, who concluded his 1808 collection of short stories and anecdotes with a note to the reader that "the town of Calais possesses a superb lodge, held with great regularity . . . by [Sophisian] Pigault-Maubaillarcq, . . . where Master Masons, while traveling, are well received and find love of the arts and humanity, along with the broadest range of knowledge, and a modesty matched only by [the host's] talents."[77]

During the Empire, ties between the Parisian secondary theaters and Freemasonry were particularly strong. In 1791, Alexandre Lenoir, one of the principal tastemakers of the Egyptian rites at the turn of the nineteenth century, designed and built the Théâtre de la Cité, which staged, for example, Cuvelier's *L'Empire de la folie, ou La Mort et l'apothéose de Don Quichotte* (1798/99), a "buffoon pantomime," or his *Les Tentations, ou Tous les diables* (1798/99), an "allegorical pantomime" in three acts.[78] Shortly thereafter Lenoir erected the Petit Panthéon dancehall, which subsequently became the Théâtre du Vaudeville. In the aftermath of the forced closures mandated by the 1807 theater decree, many stages were converted to Masonic temples. This was the fate, for example, of the Théâtre Molière and the Théâtre de la Cité, where Marshal Lannes and General Poniatowski organized a reception for an adoption (female) lodge, which was attended by Napoleon and Josephine as guests of honor.[79] The visit came after the Grand Orient de France established some of its branches in the abandoned foyer of the Cité theater in 1808.

Freemasonry could also provide for the contents of plays, as in the case of Cuvelier's *La Fille sauvage, ou L'Inconnu des Ardennes*, a melodrama in three acts first performed at the Théâtre de la Gaîté on March 31, 1812.[80] At the center of the plot is a girl named Lilia, found abandoned by her parents in the German part of the Ardennes forest in 1542. The disenfranchised heir of a vast estate, she grew up to develop the "character of a being born in the forest, removed from society, . . . who searches for food in the trees and in flowing waters [and who] wears the base skin of beasts," all of which amounts to a thinly disguised celebration of Rousseau's notion of the *homme de la nature*.[81] The villains in the play are one Countess d'Argonne, Lilia's aunt, and her associate Romaldy, who killed Lilia's mother and helped the Countess to appropriate the Argonne estate illicitly. Sixteen years later, the Countess learns that her niece, once abducted by Romaldy and left to die in the forest, is still alive. Fearing that her misdeed will be revealed, she decides to gain control of Lilia. Fortunately, however, Lilia is protected by the "Companions of the Forest, a type of secret society united by an unbreakable oath," who "make it their job to save the oppressed."[82] The Companions are described as a confraternal organization of woodcutters and hunters permanently roaming the forest.

Nineteenth-century French Freemasons would have interpreted this description without difficulty as an allegory of the *Fendeurs-Charbonniers*, a para-Masonic organization founded in Paris around 1743 by a certain Chevalier Beauchaine that claimed to descend from confraternities of woodcutters and charcoal burners in heavily wooded areas, such as the French Alps, the Jura region, or the Black Forest.[83] Lacking this specialized knowledge, the general audience would have interpreted the play as a romantic idealization of brigands hiding in the woods. Far from being Robin Hoods, however, Cuvelier's Companions work towards maintaining the social status quo and restoring property to an unjustly persecuted aristocracy. Secrecy and anonymity are imperative conditions for the Companions' "doing good deeds"; the only reward they hope to receive is "peace of conscience." The apparent purpose of the play, written and presented with a general audience in mind, was to make an apology for secret societies, while carefully avoiding the terms "Charbonnerie" or "Freemasonry." The Companions are under the command of an "obscure and mysterious" man, the "Unknown," an escapee from Romaldy's vast system of underground prisons, where he was held as a madman. In due course, the "Unknown" turns out to be Lilia's long lost father. Skepticism towards the honorable objectives of the Companions is expressed mainly from the side of the villains. Thus, an encounter between Romaldy and a representative of the Companions, a woodcutter called Faustin, culminates in threatened persecution of the secret society:

Romaldy

Such an association must be very dangerous; I will engage the Countess to have it put under surveillance.

Faustin

Monseigneur's always the master . . . but I've got to let him observe that the King of France has given us permission to carry this small distinction.
(He shows an ax drawn on his dress above the left breast.)

Romaldy, *interrupting*

That was when the woodcutters were formed into a company to wage war against Charles V . . . This country has since returned to order. This distinctive mark no longer has a right to exist. The King will know it.

Faustin

But if we are united only to wage war on ferocious beasts that ravage the forest, or on the bandits who imitate them . . . the King couldn't find it bad, could'e?[84]

Multiple readings of the dialogue are possible. For Cuvelier, an obvious figure for positive self-identification would have been the "Unknown," since, as he pointed out on a different occasion, "the one who gives with the intention of receiving tributes of gratitude deserves to be bankrupted."[85] On the same autobiographical level, the "company to wage war against Charles V" could stand for Mlle Montansier's *Compagnie franche des Artistes Dramatiques*. By extension, the Companions of the Forest would have been a simile for Cuvelier's own *Frères Artistes*, who emerged out of another "disorderly period" of French history, the Revolution. In both play and Revolutionary reality, the country was threatened from the East—by the Habsburg empire in the sixteenth century and the Prussian and Austrian armies in 1792. The king's legitimizing of the Companions of the Forest, which ultimately permits the restoration of Lilia's birthright while triggering Romaldy's downfall, may have been intended as a nod to Napoleon's tolerance and patronage of Freemasonry.

If references to the genesis of the *Frères Artistes* inform the unfolding of the plot, Sophisian overtones determine its symbolism and props. Lilia, herself deaf-mute owing to her upbringing in the forest, is courted by Gabriel, a mute young man from a bourgeois family, who can communicate with her in sign language. This narrative twist provides a pretext for Gabriel to give the command of silence, associated in Sophisian rituals with Harpocrates (figs. 27, 34), in order to enhance the mysterious pitch of the play. The gesture is later repeated by other actors as well. The scenography of *La Fille sauvage* featured a cross-section of Romantic stereotypes, including wild forests, ruined castles, rock-cut entryways, hidden trapdoors, grottoes, and an underground prison maze reminiscent of Piranesi's prints. Amidst such paraphernalia, the spectator encounters, at the beginning of Act II, a Well of Truth designated with a signboard pointing out directions to "THE FOUR WAYS." According to the Egyptosophic literary tradition, including Terrasson, Lantier, Lenoir, or the Sophisian Golden Book, candidates for Egyptian-rite initiation had to enter first the Well of Truth in order to submit to the test by the four elements. From this interpretation it follows that the marker of the four ways could be a hidden allusion to the tests by earth, air, fire, and water, understood in their symbolic significance by insiders, but concealed in their meaning from the ignorant multitude. Within Cuvelier's plot, the Well of Truth is devoid of any narrative function, but simply exists as an independent prop amidst the convoluted battle between good and evil unfolding on stage.

Cuvelier's fascination with eulogizing secret societies took on an eerie twist with his play *Le Tribunal invisible, ou Le Fils criminel* of 1802, which recounts the tragic outcome of a father-son conflict in Saxony.[86] Rixhem, Count of Heidelberg, is the head of an "invisible tribunal," which brings to justice the "powerful oppressors that ordinary tribunals could not touch,

or condemns villains so cunning that they find impunity in the silence or the disorder of the law."[87] Aided by Schwarz, the leader of a group of miners, Rixhem convenes an "invisible tribunal" in the basement and maze-like fortification system of an abandoned part of his own castle. Unfolding events force Rixhem to use the power of his vigilance committee against his own son, Baron Evrard, currently governing the family estate, who had killed his sister Anna for carrying on a love affair with the Landgraf of Westerborg and who harbors patricidal feelings against Rixhem. Since, however, "it is not sufficient to punish the guilty, but, above all, to save the innocent," the activities of the "invisible tribunal" focus on hiding Anna's son Astolphe from Evrard's wrath.[88] An intriguingly Egyptianizing detail in the stage directions reveals that the access to the underground setting from which the resistance was organized could be gained through the pedestal of an old obelisk in the courtyard of the otherwise medieval castle; unfortunately the author failed to explain how such a monument came to be erected in this remote part of Germany. The message of *Le Tribunal invisible* and *La Fille sauvage* is essentially identical, namely that secrecy and silence are necessary preconditions for collectively doing good deeds.

Both plays are also typical examples of Cuvelier's vast production of melodramas from the Napoleonic era and the Restoration. Of the four genres that minor theaters were licensed to perform—vaudeville, pantomime, *féerie*, and melodrama—none defined the cultural identity of the boulevard stages as strongly as the last one.[89] In fact, modern melodrama was the end point of a literary evolution that gradually merged pantomimes and *féeries* into a new genre. Like no other type of performance, melodrama arrested the attention of audiences with splendid stage designs, frequent changes in décor, and a never-ending spectacle of special effects, including pyrotechnical rains of fire, flash illuminations, characters miraculously emerging from the floor through trapdoors, chariots moving across the proscenium, and airborne dragons. Such trickery made spectators overlook the frequent inconsistencies found in melodramatic plots, which eventually became a hallmark of the genre itself.

MELODRAMA AND THE EMPOWERMENT OF IMAGINATION

The term melodrama was a creation of Jean-Jacques Rousseau, who understood by this neologism a type of spectacle in which dialogue and music alternated.

By the early nineteenth century, however, the modern definition of melodrama, grounded in the cultural context of the rise of Romanticism in art and literature, had taken root. Henceforth, the term designated a form of popular prose tragedy, frequently written with naïve overtones, that drew inspiration from picturesque themes culled more or less arbitrarily from across historical time and space: "[Melodrama] liked to borrow its subjects from the chivalry of the Middle Ages, Italy before the Renaissance, Spain before the expulsion of the Moors—countries and ages which the *école classique* would have admitted only exceptionally to the stage. In crenellated castles or Venetian palaces, across secret corridors, in underground dungeons, and behind trap doors that could lead either to homicide or liberation, a somber and often silly intrigue took place, often interrupted by moral discourse, apostrophes to Providence, and invariably crowned by the triumph of oppressed innocence and underestimated virtue."[90] The type of modern melodrama described here was the joint literary invention of Cuvelier de Trie and another renowned boulevard playwright, René-Charles Guilbert de Pixérécourt.[91] Because Pixérécourt's life and activities are much better documented than Cuvelier's, posterity has bestowed upon Pixérécourt the title of "father" of melodrama. Some contemporaries, however, like the theater critic Armand Charlemagne, perceived melodrama primarily as Cuvelier's invention.[92] Whereas Pixérécourt was a member of the nobility who, during the Terror, emigrated to Koblenz in Germany, Cuvelier, who actively supported the Revolution, came from the same social class that most eagerly gobbled up his melodramatic concoctions, namely the lower bourgeoisie. The differences in approach of the two authors are also evident in their attitudes towards their audiences. Pixérécourt's condescending tone is obvious, for example, in his statement that he wrote for those who could not read.[93] Cuvelier, as the epigraph to this chapter shows, understood that melodrama was both a means of manipulating the masses and an opportunity to insinuate subtle philosophical messages acquainting the world at large with hermetic Sophisian ideas.

A distinct subset of melodramatic performances concerned representations of the Orient on stage. Such plays typically fall into two categories: on the one hand, the *genre historique*, comprising exotic passion plays with tenuous roots in a remote (and frequently apocryphal) historical past; on the other, *à-propos* or *pièces de circonstance*, a type of melodramatic news reporting which recreated current events, most notably Napoleonic battles, in a condensed and dramaturgically heightened form.[94] Early nineteenth-century playwrights inherited a complex legacy of conventions from the Enlightenment for dealing with the Orient. Many of these received notions did not stand the test of reality of the Egyptian campaign and the closer contacts between Europe and the Near East at the turn of the century. Voltaire's principal Orientalist plays, *Zaïre* (1732), *Alzire* (1736), *Mahomet* (1742), and *Tancrède* (1760), for instance, followed the literary structure of classical French tragedy, but integrated Enlightenment discourse on Oriental despotism into the content of the plots.[95] Since Voltaire refrained from attacking Christianity directly for political reasons, Oriental tyranny became a substitute term synonymous with everything reprehensible about the religious intolerance of absolutism. By attacking the East, Voltaire intended to criticize conditions at home, but inadvertently planted the seed for dreams of Western colonial grandeur.

Voltaire's comparatively balanced view of religions in East and West could no more function as a role model for boulevard playwrights than the wholesome utopias of an Orient, bucolic and prosperous once disabused of native despotism, that were disseminated as late as 1798 in the French press.[96] Instead, melodramas presented a strictly dualistic worldview that thrived on the epic conflict between Westerners and their Oriental adversaries.

In Cuvelier's plays, this conflict could reach back as far as the Old Testament in *Les Machabées*, which pitted the Jewish family rising in revolt against the pagan Syrian king Antiochus IV Epiphanes. The conflict centers on the threatened profanation of the Temple of Solomon housing the Ark of the Covenant by Antiochus, who wants to replace Jewish religion with worship of the Hellenistic deity Jupiter-Olympus at the holy site.[97] The spectators' sympathies rest from the beginning with the Jews as they prepare their final stand in the siege of Jerusalem rather than sacrifice before Jupiter-Olympus's altar. A complex plot of hostage-taking and self-sacrifice culminates in the inevitable defeat of the Jewish heroes. Yet, justice is served in the end by the wrath of the "omnipotent being," who sends earthquakes and thunder to quell Antiochus and to destroy the statue of Jupiter-Olympus erected on the rubble of the Temple of Solomon. The obligatory *tableau général* that concluded any melodrama featured the coronation of the Jewish martyrs in heaven. As far as stagecraft was concerned, *Les Machabées* offered a rich selection of typically Sophisian props. Not only did the play feature the Sophisian "Sacred Ark" (fig. 29) in its original cultural and historical context of the Temple of Solomon, but it also included such elements as the Sophisian cinerary urn (fig. 48). The

Fig. 48 Marie-Nicolas Ponce-Camus, *Golden Book of the Sophisian Order, Cinerary Urn Raised on Pedestal as Emblem of Death*, ca. 1819–21, pen, ink, and gouache on paper, 6.8 × 8.3 cm (illustration). Paris, Bibliothèque Nationale de France, MSS FM 4.15, fol. 33v.

latter prop was described in Cuvelier's script as an "emblem of death . . . raised on a pedestal," in which Salmonée was to collect the ashes of her martyred son Mizaël.[98] Other set directions describe the celebrations organized in the Syrian military camp by Antiochus. The leader of paganism was supposed to preside over his fête on a "triumphal seat" not unlike that of the Sophisian Grand Isiarque. "Sacred trumpets" were to announce the festivities, which begin with Heliodorus distributing largesse among his soldiers and culminate in a "warrior dance." Cuvelier was apparently afraid

that such an accumulation of historical details pushed the boundaries of what was acceptable for melodrama, since he disparaged his play in the introduction with self-effacing modesty as a "theater piece of a very secondary genre."

Besides the biblical tradition, the Crusades provided a wealth of materials that lent themselves to melodramatic reinterpretation. Cuvelier's *Le Renégat, ou La Belle Géorgienne*, for instance, a "chivalresque pantomime . . . drawn from the chronicles of the Crusades," debuted at the Cirque Olympique in 1812.[99] The plot takes place in Acre after the capture of the city by the Christian army in 1191, when the English crusader Humphrey betrays his French companion in arms to the Sultan of Egypt, Saladin. Fortunately, the French hero St. Amand can count on the support of a beautiful Georgian woman, Aldina, kept in the Caliph's harem, to avert the betrayal. In the closing scene, the traitor Humphrey is torn apart by wild animals in a Roman amphitheater, while the crusader king Conrad of Jerusalem and his army manage to save St. Amand and Aldina from a similar fate at the last minute. Of course, the interior of the Cirque Olympique and its menagerie of wild animals would have been perfectly equipped to handle the staging of the drama. Cuvelier's script for *Le Renégat* is remarkable for the inclusion of terminology associated with Napoleon's Egyptian campaign. Humphrey's ragtag army of Muslim fighters, for instance, includes "Ethiopians and Circassian Mamelukes," i.e., classifications of Oriental types with which the French public would have been familiar from the Napoleonic Egyptian campaign. Moreover, even less educated spectators could have made connections between the Crusader episode presented on stage and the Knights Templars' eviction from Jerusalem a century later, which led to the installation of the order in the Temple enclosure adjacent to the theater district.

Oriental villains populate a great number of Cuvelier's plays. In his *Le Vieux de la montagne, ou Les Arabes du Liban*, a thirteenth-century melodrama written in 1815 for the Théâtre de la Porte Saint-Martin, the beleaguered Crusaders are aided by the Druses of Lebanon in their struggle against Arabic despots.[100] A mute boy of Christian faith, but raised in a sheikh's harem, makes possible the final victory, which is announced by the noisy disintegration of an obelisk on stage. Similarly, Cuvelier's adaptation of *Le More de Vénise, ou Othello* in 1818 uses the Shakespearian theme of the Ottoman threat to the Venetian republic to introduce a treacherous Egyptian fortune-teller who, trained "in the deepest undergrounds of the pyramids of Egypt," operates an alchemical tripod sustaining a blue flame.[101] In an odd deviation from the Shakespearian original, the sorcerer uses this device to bewitch Othello's handkerchief. Cuvelier also prescribed the use of insinuating voices from the background that were supposed to manipulate the behavior of lead characters, a dramaturgical device that also appeared in the context of Sophisian female initiation.[102]

Orientalist subtexts sometimes appear in the most unlikely of narrative frameworks. In Cuvelier's version of Puss in Boots, *Le Chat botté, ou Les 24 heures d'Arléquin* of 1802, Harlequin is drafted into war against the Ottoman Turks.[103] Only when his wife and their two children are kidnapped by the enemy does he take matters into his own hands. Tired of the dangers of the profession of war, he finally moves on to become a professor. The *pantomime-féerie* ends in a typically Sophisian manner, with Harlequin—really an average man of the people whom the Puss in Boots enables to live out his private fantasies of grandeur—enthroned amidst his family in a neoclassical peristyle temple. The description of the stage set for this final scene evokes strong associations with the "Temple of Wisdom" featured in the Golden Book as prescribed setting for the initiation to the degree of Scholar of Hieroglyphics (pl. 11).

Another *pantomime-féerie*, entitled *L'Enfant du Malheur, ou Les Amans muets*, originally written for the Ambigu-Comique in 1797/98, featured a Persian setting as pretext for an eclectic parade of fairy-tale characters, including a scale-covered warrior defending a bridge, a child abducted into the sky by fire-spitting dragons, and a mean-spirited fairy swallowed by flames in an act of divine punishment.[104] Even Cuvelier's equestrian dramas could fall victim to the temptation of "orientalizing" the plot, as was the case with *Cavalo-Dios, ou Le Cheval génie bienfaisant*, conceived for the Cirque Olympique in 1808.[105] The "lead actor" in this "equestrian fairy-tale mêlée," unfolding during the Moorish occupation of Granada in the Middle Ages, is the horse Zephir in the role of Cavalo-Dios. The horse's timely snatching of a magic wand helps break the spell of the evil sorcerer Alquimagos, which enables the young Spanish chevalier Almanzor to liberate his love Rosabella, held captive by a Moorish suitor named Zegrino.

In contrast to these outpourings of pure literary fantasy, there existed a small number of *pièces de circonstances* that recreated Napoleonic battles, as known through press reports and book publications, for the amusement of Parisian audiences. Cuvelier begun experimenting with the genre in 1809, when he created *La Belle Espagnole, ou L'Entrée triomphale des Français à Madrid* for the Cirque Olympique in an attempt to adapt current military events in Spain to the theatrical conventions of melodrama.[106] One year later, inspired by the successful launch of *La Belle Espagnole*, Cuvelier presented *La Bataille d'Aboukir, ou Les Arabes du desert*, a "pantomime military action" that derived its inspiration from the land battle of Aboukir in early August 1799.[107] Aboukir was synonymous not only with the loss of the French navy, but also with the last victory of Napoleon on Egyptian soil, when an alliance of British and Turkish forces failed to dislodge the French troops. There is no dearth of Oriental traitors and misdeeds in *La Bataille d'Aboukir*, but the true villain is Sir Tiger-Bold, an Englishman who holds the wife and young son of a French chasseur named Derville hostage. The play ends happily with a victory on the battlefield and the liberation of Tiger-Bold's victims, while the British officer puts an end to his own life. The *Bataille d'Aboukir* relinquished melodrama's typical lore of magic, mystery, and special effects, deriving its visual appeal from the equestrian performances required to stage scaled-down battle scenes against a décor consisting of a desert scene with pyramids.

It took Cuvelier almost a decade to mount another historical episode from the Egyptian campaign in *La Mort de Kléber, ou Les Français en Égypte*, performed for the first time at the Cirque Olympique in 1819.[108] The spectacle presents an anomaly in that it escaped the restrictions of Restoration censorship on the theatrical representation of Napoleonic themes. Possibly it was deemed harmless because of its "factual" presentation of a decidedly unheroic episode of the Egyptian campaign, the assassination of Napoleon's successor, General Kléber, by Islamic fundamentalists. Cuvelier used the occasion to express his personal regret over the loss of the Napoleonic conquest, because it "deprived Egypt of the honor of becoming a French colony." Although biased in the extreme, the plot does make an attempt to situate the killing in the context of the previous revolt of Cairo and the greater liberties granted to native women under French rule. It recounts Kléber's assassination from the perspectives of both the French occupiers and the assassins in parallel story lines, but assigns the final responsibility for his death to an Ottoman conspiracy. Allegedly, Cuvelier's commemoration of Kléber's fate in 1819 was occasioned by the erection of a funerary monument in the General's home town of Strasbourg. One may speculate, however, to what extent Cuvelier's Sophisian contacts with Egyptian campaign veterans may have influenced his presentation of events from the past. In any case, the pattern of hybridizing historical facts with esoteric fiction that emerges from the analysis of Cuvelier's Orientalist theater pieces holds the key to understanding Sophisian rituals and the order's intellectual objectives.

To summarize how the diversity of Sophisian themes integrates into the narrative structure of Cuvelier's plays, one can cite a *féerie melodramatique* from 1806 entitled *L'Enchanteur Morto-Vivo, prologue cabalistique, suivi de L'Ile de Silence, ou l'Arléquin malgré lui*.[109] The performance derived its tension from the development of two parallel story lines. The first story line takes place in the supernatural realm, where the "Enchanter" Morto-Vivo, or the good principle, battles Vechia, "an old sorceress, ugly and mean." The second story line concerns mortals in the earthly realm, who are, by manipulation of Vechia, transported from Bologna to the Island of Silence. The prologue of the play opens with a scene in Vechia's study, which the stage directions describe as follows: "The theater represents the interior of a tower, whose walls are covered with hieroglyphic characters. One sees to the right and to the left cabalistic books and instruments of physics. Reflections of moonlight illuminate the set and the objects with a bluish sheen. To the right of the actress is a tomb."[110] The walls inscribed with "hieroglyphic characters" and the "bluish sheen" of the moonlight evoke associations with the "Syringe" illustration from the Sophisians' Golden Book (pl. 6). At the rising of the curtain, Vechia is seen supporting herself on a coffin, in which she keeps Morto-Vivo. She recounts how she subdued and captured the Enchanter, whose "severe virtues constantly sabotaged the magic operations that a villainous genie has given me the power to execute by initiating me into all cabalistic studies."[111] Yet, Morto-Vivo's powers have not been extinguished entirely, since he challenges Vechia from his tomb to a competition by means of fiery letters that flash up on his coffin. (Cuvelier, by contrast with Pixérécourt, wrote for audiences that were literate!) Vechia accepts the challenge. In order to find a test case by which to measure their magical strengths, Vechia conjures up a "Golden Book," dropped "from the vault of the theater by a winged chimera." While the set directions call it a *Livre d'or*, Vechia refers to the document as the "Book of Destinies," in which one may find "truth beyond the clouds that hide the future from the eyes of the vulgar ignorant." Both Vechia and Morto-Vivo agree on an intrigue that involves a triangular love story in Italy: Columbina, daughter of a rich Venetian patrician, loves Amato, a poor but good-hearted Bolognese fisherman. Columbina's father Fabricio, however, wants to marry her to an elderly Bolognese gentleman of his own social standing named Pandolfo. As the story unfolds, Morto-Vivo champions the liaison between Columbina and Amato, while Vechia tries to undermine his efforts by promoting the union between Columbina and Pandolfo. Before the sorceress and the Enchanter disappear into the ether, Vechia transports the players to the Island of Silence, where the mortals can only communicate by sign language. The prologue concludes with Vechia's being spirited away in a dragon-drawn chariot.

Subsequently, disguises and identities multiply. Vechia assumes the body of a beautiful young woman to seduce Amato, who resists her advances. By this time Amato has metamorphosed into Harlequin, which required a change of appearance. He now sports a black cloak and mask similar to the outfit prescribed for Sophisian initiation (pl. 4) in order to prepare his clandestine escape with Columbina. Vechia's revenge for being spurned by Amato consists in making his black disguise permanent. Confusion becomes complete after Columbina, too, disguises herself as a man and her father's male domestic, Josco, as a woman. Fabricio's and Pandolfo's attempt to arrest the young lovers, both now dressed as men, ends in failure, when Amato/Harlequin jumps into the waters of a lake. While Josco is chained and whipped in Amato/Harlequin's place, the latter changes into a barrel found by fishermen, who bring it ashore as a treasure. Harlequin/Amato emerges from the barrel amidst flames and pursued by six small devils. Fortunately, Morto-Vivo comes to his rescue with a magic golden ring that allows Harlequin/Amato to take on any disguise he desires. Morto-Vivo also guides him to Columbina, who has fallen under the spell of Vechia disguised as a young warrior. Upon finding Vechia in Columbina's company, Harlequin/Amato challenges the sorceress to a duel in full armor. Again, the battle between good and evil remains inconclusive.

The resolution of the plot is outlined in the third act, which featured a set design consisting of "a garden with two small temples to the left and to the right, closed with elegant curtains. In the center, there is a kiosk closed by sky-blue curtains and embellished in rose and silver. On the first temple, to the right, one reads: TO FRIENDSHIP; on the second, to the left: TO LOVE; and on the kiosk: TO VOLUPTUOUSNESS."[112] Similar temples with inscriptions also dot the Sophisian iconography in the Golden Book, as seen for instance in the illustration of the "Temple of Wisdom" (pl. 11). Against this picturesque backdrop, Amato, who by now has shed the disguise of Harlequin, searches for Vechia's magic golden violet, a hidden symbol for Napoleon's rule, attached to the bridle of her horses.[113] He raises the curtains of the two temples, but only the lifting of the kiosk's curtain sets in motion a ballet of Vechia and her rose-festooned nymphs. When Amato still remains unswayed and insists on rescuing Columbina from Pandolfo, he is thrown into a dungeon and tortured by demons "in a thousand different ways." Fortunately, Amato has managed to secure Vechia's golden violet so that he can escape the torture chamber. At the last moment, Amato, Morto-Vivo, and their army of "underground warriors" can prevent the forced marriage between Columbina and Pandolfo. Vechia and her minions are defeated in a violent battle; finally the sorceress, tied to the back of a dragon, is spirited away. The performance closes with the union between Columbina and Amato before the relabeled "TEMPLE OF FELICITY" surrounded by altars inscribed with the words "LOVE," "MARRIAGE," and "HAPPINESS."

As naïve as some of the clichés of these eclectic pageantries may appear today, they addressed the psychological needs of early nineteenth-century audiences. Behind the trite Orientalist stereotypes, Egyptosophic reveries, and hidden Masonic subtexts of melodramatic performances, there lurked informed commentaries about the social and political upheavals of the time. Cuvelier's career as a dramaturge seems to confirm Peter Brooks's assessment that

> the origins of melodrama can be accurately located within the context of the French Revolution and its aftermath. This is the epistemological moment which it illustrates and to which it contributes: the moment that symbolically, and really, marks the final liquidation of the traditional Sacred and its representative institutions (Church and Monarch), the shattering of the myth of Christendom, the dissolution of an organic and hierarchically cohesive society, and the invalidation of the literary forms—tragedy, comedy of manners—that depended on such a society. Melodrama does not simply represent a "fall" from tragedy, but a response to the loss of the tragic vision.[114]

Beyond this, melodrama presented a meaningful tool for the empowerment of audiences. Cuvelier and his colleagues enabled their anonymous spectators to make moral choices and thereby to become passive participants in the plays—an opportunity for involvement that was rarely granted even to the socially and culturally privileged audiences of the ancien régime.

Cuvelier's *Les Hommes de la nature, et les hommes policés* (1800/1801) presents an example of how this empowerment of audiences could be accomplished.[115] The play takes Jean-Jacques Rousseau's dichotomy between society and human nature as a starting point.

The dramaturgical structure follows the pattern of the *Enchanteur Morto-Vivo* in that the author introduces the plot through two heavenly beings, a male Sylph and a female Syphide, who argue in the prologue over whether the *hommes de la nature* (society in its primordial state) or the *hommes policés* (civilized society) yield a superior form of social organization. They agree to put their ideas to test, almost as in a scientific observatory, by following from above the evolution of an island population of native American "savages" after the arrival of British colonizers. The comparatively simple plot features two native Indian lovers, Ohi and Hea, whose courtship is interrupted by the arrival of the British governor Badman, who ventures to gain Hea's heart by showering her with trinkets from civilized society. The conflict of cultures escalates when Badman tries to rape Hea, who is rescued by Ohi. The governor has Ohi arrested, but Hea, disguised as a man, takes his place in prison. When Hea is about to be executed in Ohi's place, the Sylph and the Sylphide intervene to strike Badman with thunder. The outcome of the contest, as the Sylph concedes, is inconclusive, since "one cannot establish a general rule from a specific event."[116] Ultimately, it remains up to the individual spectator to provide an answer to the philosophical question that the play purports to investigate.

Another dramaturgical device to engage audiences in melodrama was the introduction of groups of extras, generically referred to as "the people" in Cuvelier's stage directions, who may express feelings of fear or joy, but whose role is mostly confined to celebrating the triumphant heroes of the final scene.[117] Never is there an explanation of who "the people" are or what exactly their function is. The most likely explanation would be that they are meant to represent a link between the audience and the actors on stage. They are participants in the play on one level, yet their activity remains confined to passive adulation. By contrast with the "the people" in Sophisian rituals, where the term referred to the entire Sophisian community of initiates, the on-stage populace in public theater performances provided the anonymous spectator with an anchor for self-identification in the plot.

In the final analysis, there is more common ground between popular theater performances and Sophisian initiation than one might have expected. Although Sophisian rituals demanded from initiates an incomparably broader educational background and greater cultural sophistication than melodrama, both institutions catered to the same psychological needs. The Enlightenment had invested every human being with the same right to pursue happiness.[118] Mass entertainment and individualized modes of spiritual fulfillment superseding a singular, monolithic religious superstructure were but two expressions of the same quest. The events of the Revolution further accelerated the translation of abstract philosophical ideas into political and social practice. Henceforth, the place of an individual in society was no longer determined by privileges of birth, but by merit and ambition. Greater social mobility, however, was dependent on an individual's ability to transcend the fixed coordinates of "knowing one's place" in the social fabric in order to imagine what he or she *could* be. Fantasy therefore became a means of social and political empowerment. It is for this reason that both melodrama and Sophisian rituals should be interpreted as cultural phenomena in the formation process of an early modern consciousness.

Conclusion:
Egyptosophy versus Anti-Egyptosophy

In fact, only man can put himself in communication with Nature. He studies Her, he understands Her.
Without him, earth would not even have a name, and God would be for Her as if He did not exist.
—A. L. A. Fée, *Le Darwinisme*[1]

AT THE TURN OF THE NINETEENTH CENTURY, EGYPT HAD become for a surprisingly large number of educated individuals a code word for a mentality at the border-line between politics and philosophy, one that is liable, from today's perspective at least, to get all too easily eclipsed by a smoke screen of talk about mysteries. The importance of staking out the intellectual parameters of this mentality goes beyond a mere discussion of the Sophisian order and embraces some of the fundamental epistemological questions confronted by early modern society. While acknowledging the testimonials of the Sophisians and the wider milieu of their sympathizers goes a long way towards deciphering this politico-philosophical code, oftentimes one can learn even more from the polemics of Egyptosophy's dissenters, which might, for lack of a better term, be called Anti-Egyptosophy.

A convenient starting point for a discussion of these anti-Egyptosophic tendencies is the year 1739, when the French clergyman Abbé Antoine Pluche published the first edition of his *Histoire du ciel*. Pluche's treatise is a curious hybrid account of religious and scientific history with a heavy fixation on ancient Egypt as the root of the twin evils of idolatry and superstition.[2] His objective in writing the thousand-page book was to align Christian teachings with selected aspects of Enlightenment rationalism and scientific discoveries, from which "religion had nothing to fear" as long as the more recent doctrines followed "three or four very simple laws."[3] If they did not, however, there was a problem.

The main targets of Pluche's rhetorical diatribes were theories on the origins of life that failed to recognize the "special will of the Creator."[4] In particular, he took exception to those "poets and philosophers," like Spinoza, Descartes, or Newton, who conceived of creation in terms of inanimate primordial matter from

which life evolved through arbitrary "movement." Pluche's struggle was with ideas that, with hindsight, can best be described as evolutionist:

All philosophers agree on the idea of a chaos made up of indifferent corpuscles that have combined in the formation of every kind of [living] body, although they each call it by a different name. It is a vague material, undetermined and universal, which they claim is self-creating or could have created itself under the influence of movement. Indeed, from this indifferent conglomerate of corpuscles everything imaginable is supposed to have emerged. On account of the possibility of forming a world from corpuscles by means of a simple introduction of general movement, I feel obliged to counter the fabricators of systems. . . . Since a clump of earth, no matter how it is moved and how violently it is agitated, cannot become anything other than earth, it thus follows that matter, in whatever form one may imagine it, whether it be moved in one direction or in circles, will not produce a world, but only chaos.[5]

The abbé apparently considered himself something of a modern-day church father, preaching the book of Genesis and the "Physics of Moses" in the name of rationality fighting against the aberrations of a pagan revival under the false guise of the Enlightenment. Since the birth of idolatry, fostered by the invention of "symbolic writing" (i.e., hieroglyphics), coincided with the first inquiries into secularized explanations for life, nature, and human existence in ancient Egypt, Pluche felt compelled to assert "the infinite superiority of Christianity's *lumières* over those of humanist philosophers," whether they be past or present.[6]

In keeping with the logic of these arguments, the strategy of pounding the reader with cross-references to ancient Egypt defined most of the contents of the

130

Histoire du ciel. For Pluche, there was no doubt that the antecedents of the secularized worldview held by Enlightenment atheists and deists issued from the colleges of temple priests in ancient Egypt, who "suffocated all religion with the principle of philosophy." The sacerdotal class also misrepresented "gods as just different parts of nature," an affirmation extending beyond the well-established association of Isis with nature and fertility. Religious life in Pluche's Egypt was rife with deception and hypocrisy. The rules of secret rituals and silence were upheld in the temples not only to obscure the scientific ambition and vainglorious erudition of the priests unraveling laws of nature and the universe otherwise meant "to stay absolutely hidden," but also to abet "sexual license [*libertinage*], abominable infamies, and cruel superstitions."[7]

Pluche's moral thundering cannot, however, conceal that he was utterly consumed by his obsession with Egypt. Published just eight years after Abbé Terrasson's *Séthos*, the *Histoire du ciel* represented the very antithesis of the best-selling Egyptosophic novel. Rather than cementing Egypt's reputation as a wellspring of the most profound mysteries, Pluche tried to unravel the evolution of Egyptian civilization and its imagery by rational explanation. To this end, he reproduced and analyzed hundreds of engravings with Egyptian sculptures and artifacts, ordered strictly by iconographic content and culled mostly from antiquarian tomes published since the Renaissance. These visual trappings offered the additional advantage of introducing a pedigree of scholarly learnedness typically associated with the works of antiquarians like Boissard, Montfaucon, Winckelmann, or de Caylus, which Pluche undoubtedly hoped would help him beat the philosophes at their own game. But the plates also fulfilled a secondary function as evidence for the deplorable penchant for idolatry and materialism that Egypt bequeathed first to Greece and later to the whole of Western civilization. Rather than expressing the profundity of Egyptian mysteries, Pluche argued that the origins of art derived from the astronomical observations that informed the contents of Egyptian religion and spawned the invention of hieroglyphics and writing, which then evolved into an "excessive love of worldly goods," such as painting and sculpture.[8] Under this scheme, Egyptian iconography could be demystified easily by utilitarian explanations. Thus, the dog-headed Anubis (pl. 3, fig. 31), for instance, was simply a messenger associated with the appearance on the heavenly canopy of the dog-star Canicula (Sirius), which customarily announced the arrival and passing of the Nile's annual inundations to the populace.[9] The

initial usefulness of such symbolism was subsequently corrupted by the caste of temple priests, who appropriated pictorial representations as tools for exploiting the superstition of the common people. Owing to Pluche's preconceived ideological agenda, the protagonists of the Egyptian pantheon, such as Isis, Osiris, and Horus, come across as static and isolated deities rather than as interactive agents woven into the narrative fabric of the Egyptosophic tradition.

Whereas the first volume of the *Histoire du ciel* focuses on Egyptian history, religion, art, and cosmogony, the second volume takes a more philosophical approach and deals mostly with the history of the sciences. Again ancient Egypt provides the backdrop for a discussion from which Hermes Trismegistus emerges as a manipulative sorcerer and arch-villain of alchemy, whose successors arrogate the divine prerogative for creation in a mock self-proclamation:

> All obeys our laws. We are the true kings of the earth, because all is subservient to our desires. And if, to prove our powers, we limit ourselves to some known experiments, it is because we would be extremely imprudent to profane the mysteries of our art by communicating them to the people or exposing them to the ridicule of spirits guided by unbelief. . . . The doctrine of our father Hermes Trismegistus is contained in the metamorphoses of Prometheus, admirable summary for what we call primary matter. There is but one universal nature, indifferent to the forms it assumes, capable of retaining all, and which becomes, at one time or another, sulphur or phlogiston, salt, mercury, pewter, silver, gold, or anything we would like to prescribe. . . . With three principles which will carry us hardly beyond primary matter, we will build the entire universe. To diversify the parts or to form species, it suffices to prudently alter the matrices upon which these principal agents are received.[10]

Pluche might as well have paraphrased the cornerstone of the Sophisian nature-centered theory of creation, expressed in the "numerical triangle" of the BN Golden Book, which answered the primordial mystery of the "moral triangle"—"What is Nature? Wisdom, Truth?"—with the basic unity of three principles: "1. Generating Force, 2. Matrix required for Generation, 3. Engendered word . . . *Trinitas unitas*; because 3. without 1. and 2. would not be engendered; 1. without 2. would not be generator; 2. and 3. without 1. would only be a mechanic without a motor. *Sol generat, terra recipit, natura vivit* [The sun causes reproduction, the earth receives the fertile seed, nature prospers]."[11] The riddle is clarified by the illustration of the facing page featuring the hidden phallus flanked by the sun, the goat, and the hooked cross (pls. 8–9). This idiosyncratic combination of textual and visual information allows for an interpretation in which the sun stands for the male principle or generating force; earth for the female principle, since she is the matrix required for generation, otherwise also associated with wisdom; and the engendered word for nature and truth (their offspring). Aristotle's theory of life appears to have informed this instance of Sophisian vitalist speculation, since the Greek philosopher, in particular in his treatise *De generatione animalium*, maintained that in the reproductive process the male supplies the "principle of the form," whereas the female contributes merely the "matter" of the "generated offspring."[12] He concludes that this division is the reason "why in cosmology they speak of the nature of the Earth as something female and call it 'mother,' while they give to the heaven and the sun and anything else of that kind the title of 'generator,' and 'father.'" In contrast to Aristotle, however, the "generated offspring" of the Sophisians is not of biological, but of intellectual nature.

To complicate matters, the Latin inscription "Sol generat, terra recipit, natura vivit" in the BN manuscript is followed by a violently struck-out postscript that remains all but illegible. Based on a reprint of the complete triangle texts inserted in a collection of Cuvelier's literary fragments published as *Nouvelles, contes, historiettes, anecdotes et mélanges* in 1808, the postscript can be reconstructed to read: "inde Deus genitor, Virgo genetrix, et Jesus caro de carne [God is begetter, the Virgin is birth-giver, and Jesus is flesh out of flesh]."[13] The expression that Jesus "is flesh out of flesh" is obviously adapted from the book of Genesis (2:33), where Eve is described by Adam as "flesh of my flesh [caro de carne mea]." How is this statement supposed to be interpreted and why was it crossed out with such insistence? The context and location of the postscript suggests that the biblical trinity occupies a subservient position with respect to the allegedly more ancient, nature-centered trinity of the Sophisians. Perhaps the postscript was inserted as a nod to Christianity, admitted only as the latest embodiment of a principle that had more ancient and immutable roots— a historical worldview entirely consistent with Sophisian teachings.[14] The act of eliminating the postscript, however, confirms that introducing a Christian subtext into Sophisian teaching could provide the grounds for contentions within the group, a danger that was neutralized by getting rid of the passage entirely. It should also be remembered that politics and religion, as Guerrier de Dumast reminded his readers, were topics officially prohibited from Masonic discourse.[15]

In light of such intricacies, Pluche's fears about the merger of Egyptosophy with Enlightenment ideas seem far less delusional than his writings initially suggest. When the controversies over Comte de Cagliostro's questionable Egyptian rite agitated Europe during the last two decades of the eighteenth century, the type of anti-Egyptosophic rhetoric pioneered by Pluche again set the tone of the discussion. Nevertheless, important shifts had occurred. Egyptosophy and the philosophical positions associated with it were no longer a nebulous specter, but now had a face attached to them. In the process, they also became closely linked with the spread of Freemasonry across Europe—a circumstance that Egyptosophy's critics, rightly or wrongly, exploited in their attacks, stressing aspects of atheism and political conspiracy with ever greater urgency. A good example of these tendencies is the fake "will" of Cagliostro, published anonymously at the height of the French Revolution in 1791. Taking the literary form of a confession allegedly written by Cagliostro while imprisoned by the Vatican, the pamphlet purported to reveal the inner political workings of the Egyptian rite:

It is not Heaven that is promised to the Initiates, but Earth. They consider it as their domain, and the kings as usurpers.... Their lodges are venues for terrible tests, which precede the sermons themselves, encouraging the realization of the bloody fairy tales of the atheists and covering the earth with a sect of assassins. This sect has circles, that is to say committees composed of a certain number of persons initiated in the same sect, who suffered the same tests and are bound by the same oaths, and who correspond by means of unknown hieroglyphics.... These circles have their *frères voyageurs*. These are ordinary men of a simple and modest outer appearance, who seem educated and pretend to practice philanthropy. In fact, they are spying out the secrets of the courts, offices, tribunals, academies, schools, and families before returning to their circles equipped with a pile of notes, of observations, and intelligence of all kinds concerning the character and intentions of the people locally encountered, the foibles of princes, and the occupations of philosophers.[16]

At least as far as the rituals were concerned, the author of the "will" reveals himself as a well-versed insider, given the many surprisingly detailed parallels with Sophisian Egyptian-rite initiations outlined in the BN Golden Book:

The candidates [of Cagliostro's Egyptian rite] take an oath to observe the commandments and to keep eternal silence concerning the mysteries. After this, they are sent on symbolic travels; the first underneath a sky-blue vault, the second amidst lighting and thunder; during the third, one draws blood. . . . They are shown the two columns engraved by Thot, and one explains to them the mystical meaning of the symbolic characters there incised. Upon re-entering the temple . . . they are led to the triple statute of Isis, Osiris, and Horus, which had but one eye. This statue was covered with a veil and carried the inscription "I am all there was, all there is, and all there will be—no mortal till now lifts my veil." The Initiate was then permitted to lift the veil up to the breast, where another inscription carried these words: "I am all there is, all there was, and all there will be." The ceremony concludes with an admonition.[17]

Cagliostro's faked "will" is a fascinating document, because it casts light on the perception of Egyptosophy at the critical juncture of the French Revolution. Almost thirty years later Guerrier de Dumast still struggled with this difficult legacy, when, to refute the hypothesis that a Masonic conspiracy triggered the overthrow of the ancien régime, he denounced Cagliostro's activities as "convulsive follies."[18] Indeed, 1789 was a turning point not only because Egyptian esoteric teachings were now assumed to have political connotations, but also because political positions and philosophical attitudes appeared henceforth as inextricably linked.

A case in point is Sylvain Maréchal's *Dictionnaire des athées anciens et modernes*, first published in 1799. Maréchal was associated with the extremist Society of Equals, a proto-Socialist group led by Gracchus Babeuf that promoted a return to radical Jacobin politics and the redistribution of property during the Directory. But while Babeuf and his coconspirators were guillotined in 1797 for trying to overthrow the government, Maréchal was allowed to continue his career as a writer, which culminated in the publication of his dictionary of atheists throughout history. Although mostly forgotten today, Maréchal's compendium triggered a major public scandal at the turn of the nineteenth century. Indexed instantly by the Vatican, the dictionary unleashed an avalanche of "pamphlets, libels, refutations, and writings of all kinds," condemning the work in the strongest terms.[19]

From the point of view of the Egyptosophic debate, the *Dictionnaire des athées* was remarkable for the attention given to ancient Egypt and its sacerdotal class. Under the entry "Egyptians," Maréchal collectively labeled all inhabitants of the country, past and present, as atheists. In support of this argument, he cited the church father Eusebius as well as the eighteenth-century theologian Pawel Ernest Jabłonski.[20] A second entry, discussing the term "Isiaques," is even more revealing. It is easy to perceive in this neologism the

antecedent of the Sophisian "Isiarques," who formed the board of supervisors of the order. Both Maréchal's and Cuvelier's terms derived from Isis and were meant to designate the temple priests committed to the worship of the goddess. Maréchal is more inclusive in that he also counts temple priests in Rome as "Isiaques." These priests defined themselves as atheists by their fondness for materialism, documented in Macrobius's statement that Isis was but "the nature of things." Her pictorial representation, "symbol of Nature, virgin, mother, and nurse, is self-sufficient and contains in itself the faculty for creation and for sustaining what she has produced."[21] By the same token, the Egyptian Orpheus also found himself in the gallery of Maréchal's atheists, since he was the first to "assign divinity to nature" and otherwise "kept a profound silence concerning a [higher] intelligent being."[22] Admittedly, Maréchal often lacked selective rigor with regard to those whom he admitted to his illustrious circle. The Egyptians shared their fate for instance with the Druids, Chaldeans, Chinese, and Indians; the "Isiaques" were joined by the Encyclopedists, Freemasons, and all Academicians. For single individuals the selection criteria were at least as stunning, since Confucius, Diogenes, Herodotus, and Cicero found themselves in the company of Voltaire, Descartes, Diderot, Benjamin de Laborde, the Sophisian General Brune, and, inevitably, Napoleon Bonaparte. The value of Maréchal's dictionary entries resides mainly in the fact that they show how strongly the mental link between ancient Egypt and atheism had become ingrained in French intellectual life by the turn of the nineteenth century.

At this time, according to Guerrier de Dumast, such attitudes could be encountered in particular amongst members of the military as well as other "thoughtless persons" who "suffered the misfortune of believing in nothing and disdaining all that is religious, [and who] came to the Lodge with the unique intention of finding diversion. . . . Touched by moral lessons that their estrangement from anything that resembles a cult had rendered foreign to them, . . . they started to think about themselves, about human society, about the creative causes of the world. They became more serious, more sensible, and bettered themselves; but while they could not return to religion, they at least made one [for themselves] out of Freemasonry."[23] At least among some members of the *Frères Artistes* and the Sophisians, the atheist legacy of the Revolution thus appeared to linger on until the 1820s. Although Guerrier de Dumast's statement mostly concerned the situation during the 1790s through the Empire period, when militarism ran high in French society, it may

Trouvé dans les Tombeaux des Rois de Thebes,
Et réimptimé par Cox, Fils, et Baylis, Great Queen Street, Paroisse de Saint-Oiles, à Londres.

Fig. 49 Vignette of Jean-Gabriel Peltier's Anti-Bonapartiste Newspaper *L'Ambigu* (Nos. I to V), 1802, newsprint, 9.5 × 12.3 cm. Brussels, Musée Royal de l'Armée et d'Histoire militaire, Fonds Brouwet.

likewise serve as a general portrait of the Revolutionary generation from which so many Sophisians were recruited. Yet, many members, including Guerrier de Dumast and Cuvelier de Trie, adamantly avowed their Catholicism, but their adherence was not without twists and turns. Cuvelier, for instance, consider it his "glory to profess [this] cult," but couched the admission in a strange pornographic short story slandering the libertine behavior of the clergy in countryside.[24] Guerrier de Dumast arrived in 1825 at the conclusion to renounce Freemasonry completely in favor of liberal Catholicism. Henceforth he amused himself with tearing up copies of his poem *La Maçonnerie*, bought at great costs from antiquarian book sellers across France, with pincers so as to be able to burn the pages of his book individually.[25]

The events of the Napoleonic conquest of Egypt were certainly instrumental in pushing the eighteenth-century Egyptosophic debates ever more firmly into a political corner. In the years after 1798, any mention of Egypt evoked instantaneous associations with Bonaparte, a circumstance that invited satirical exploitation by Napoleon's enemies. Jean-Gabriel Peltier, for instance, was a French journalist in British exile who held strong anti-Bonapartist and reactionary pro-Catholic views, which he regularly voiced through his newspaper *L'Ambigu: Variétés atroces et amusantes, journal dans le genre égyptien*, renamed beginning with issue number ten from June 1803, *L'Ambigu, ou Les Mystères d'Isis*.[26] The most unusual aspect of this newspaper was its vignette on the front page of the first nine issues featuring Bonaparte's crowned head mounted on the body of a sphinx (fig. 49). The sphinx's body as well as most of its attendant hieroglyphics and symbols were copied from the plates illustrating Vivant Denon's *Voyage dans la Basse et la Haute Égypte*. Prominent examples of Denon's iconography include the flying hawk in the upper right corner as well as the dog and cat flanking the pedestal's pseudo-hieroglyphic inscription.

After the Peace of Amiens in March 1802 Napoleon requested British legal assistance in persecuting his slanderer, which was granted without the customary delays that had marred previous such attempts. Peltier's trial aroused considerable public attention and culminated in the defendant's furnishing the following interpretation of the vignette:

> I do wish neither to deny that the vignette represents the head of Bonaparte, nor that my intention was to depict him in the Egyptian form of a Sphinx: the lion body is the symbol of his power; the tail between his legs that of his duplicity; and the paws stretched out forward that of his ambition to jump at anything in his reach. A hieroglyphic crown, half sliding from his Brutus head, suggests the anti-republican intrigues that took place at his court in order to appoint him King, Emperor, or Consul with term limit or for life; to empower a hereditary rule or to let him select his successor. An Egyptian genie, one wing turned towards his head, another pointing down to his tail, I envisioned as a symbol of prudence that all commentators needed to exercise in their plans and means of execution, whether they be open or hidden. A mass of Egyptian hieroglyphics, accumulated on the pedestal of the Sphinx, had a no less poignant significance. A crown surrounded by eyes marked the center—it is not difficult to recognize in it the object that attracts the Sphinx's glance: two sparrow-hawks or *Chouans* were placed to the right and to the left of the crown, like immovable guardians of day and night. A ladder and a suspended ax express the punishments that attend regicides, rebels, and thieves. Finally, a dog and a cat, placed at the extremities, were markers for the concord and union that rule far away from the crown.[27]

Peltier reacted to the lawsuit brought against him with a telling gesture of self-censorship by eliminating Napoleon's head and the right wing of the "Egyptian genie" in the upper right corner of the vignette for issues number six through nine. With renewed hostilities between France and Britain in spring 1803, the cancellation of Peltier's permit to publish *L'Ambigu*, pronounced after issue nine, was revoked. Numbers ten through eighteen featured a new vignette of a Pharaoh (i.e., Napoleon) slaying his enemies, followed by yet another design for numbers nineteen through thirty,

which derived from a ceiling painting with astronomical symbols found in the temple at Hermonthis. Both of the latter designs were also pastiches after Denon. It is noteworthy that Peltier's political satire took aim specifically at the "mysterious" aspect of Egypt, which was also underscored by the choice for the new subtitle of *L'Ambigu*. Of course, long before Denon or Peltier, the figure of the Sphinx itself had acquired the status of an iconic symbol of all unresolved riddles concerning human civilization. In the light of recent events, however, Napoleon had indelibly imprinted his name on the Egyptosophic tradition, a fait accompli that even his most ardent detractors had to acknowledge.

Egyptosophic controversies sprang up in the most unlikely venues during the early years of the nineteenth century. The Caribbean island of Saint Lucia was one such place. Between 1802 and 1804 the French military doctor Jean-François Pugnet was stationed on this piece of volcanic rock just south of Martinique. Pugnet was an Egyptian campaign veteran with a strongly developed instinct for the connection between Egyptosophy and proto-evolutionism, but he had no apparent connection with the Sophisians. To make his philosophical point more forcefully, he had brought along some souvenirs, including papyrus fragments covered with hieroglyphics and figurative drawings that he interpreted to be Isis processions, as well as a copy of his book on the outbreak of the plague during the Napoleonic campaigns in the Near East.[28] The frontispiece of his medical treatise was a source of great pride for Pugnet, since it reproduced a drawing he had personally copied from the decorations of the temple at Denderah (pl. 17). To overcome the boredom that apparently characterized life on his Caribbean outpost, Pugnet busied himself with developing an exegesis of the Denderah frieze, which for him explained nothing less than the origins of the human species. He apparently shared these speculations liberally with other French colonial administrators, including one Fabien Richelme from the neighboring island of Martinique, who was offended enough to summarize the gist of Pugnet's theories for posterity:

> Several adult black men present themselves in a pose such that their torsos, bent over in reverse at the pubis, form a right angle with their lower extremities. Their heads extend the horizontal line of their torsos, and their upper extremities remain wedged in between symbols off to the sides. Thus, every one of them stands in relation, from above, with a very large fiery globe that overcasts most of his body and, from below, with a rather large and very black scarabaeus beetle that makes spring forth from the earth a red fluid at the upper end, as well as a red human

embryo sprayed by a jet of sperm at the lower end. Does this hieroglyphic language not express the thought of the ancients? Namely, that the heat of the sun and the humidity of the soil were the true procreators of the earth? The first men, those from whom the Egyptians themselves received life, issued forth from the earth closest to that star [the sun]; or, more literally, the red man was born to the black man and the latter to the soil. The black man is certainly an Ethiopian, and the Egyptian is identified by the red skin that he retains to the present day. . . . Earth, fertilized by the sun, engendered the first man. Man, instructed by need, gave his first attention to the cultivation of the soil. This is the description that M. Pugnet gave of the art work in question. This is the explanation he provided.[29]

The frieze thus interpreted by Pugnet was apparently well known to the Sophisians, who considered the artifact important enough to be discussed in the BN Golden Book under the heading "diverse hieroglyphics of the order." Cuvelier's text indeed offers a reading of its iconography that, although apparently developed independently from Pugnet's, reveals a basic consensus as to how the wisdom of ancient Egypt could help elucidate philosophical truth about the origins of life:

> The scarabaeus beetle has both sexes; it drags behind it a bag with eggs with which it fecundates itself. The following hieroglyphic has been found in the hypogea (ruined underground tombs of the kings of Thebes): a nude man with a well-formed body *mittens semen suum* [amidst ejaculation]; the ellipsis that forms the jet is retraced by small red balls; the product is a small figure of a man who moves over the earth. But one also has to note that the line of the small red balls starts with a scarbaeus beetle inscribed by disc-shapes, and then attains the mouth of the man—[Symbolic meaning:] *creator* who is not present but as an agent of Transmission.[30]

It is not surprising that such opinions were regarded by many outsiders as so contentious that they warranted the strictest secrecy. Richelme's reaction to Pugnet's revelations provides an example of the type of objections to anticipate. By his own admission, Richelme claimed to have kept a polite silence in his personal dealings with Pugnet on Saint Lucia. Nevertheless, by 1807, after a British invasion had ousted his interlocutor from the neighboring islet, Richelme no longer felt such inhibitions and published in St.-Pierre Martinique a *Mémoire relatif aux Monumens de l'Égypte*, in which he strongly condemned Pugnet's teachings in the name of both public morality and what he took for common sense: "I do not know whether [his explana-

tion] has the approval of scholars in Europe. But I can give assurance that, as for myself, it has humiliated me greatly in my capacity as a man created by God, and even more so in my capacity as a white man. . . . 'What!,' did I say to myself, 'the earth sprouted like a mushroom? What! We, the others, the white men, so enlightened, so advanced in civilization, should have descended from African negroes, so stupid, so brutish, so vicious! . . . Ah! Let us dismiss an opinion so distressing!'"[31] As Richelme's reaction reveals, Egypotosophy held so strong a transgressive charge precisely because, despite all affirmations to the contrary, it dealt not with ancient Egypt, but with some of the most contentious issues that the early modern age faced with a growing sense of urgency: questions of whether religion and myth could still claim a place in a rational world order, of how the relationship between colonizers and colonized was to be defined, or of what explanations science offered for racial difference and the origins of mankind. The Egyptosophic position assumed a radically progressive stance in which religion was reduced to Deism and Naturalism, colonization could lead to cultural hybridization, and the principle of equality (as interpreted by the 1789 *Déclaration des Droits de l'Homme*) derived its philosophical superstructure from evolutionary theories.

Indeed, the dabbling in vaguely proto-evolutionist models of natural history and the controversies they spawned provided a background for philosophical inquiries within the Sophisian group. This observation becomes particularly obvious when taking into account the writings of three prominent natural scientists—Geoffroy Saint-Hilaire, Comte de Lacépède, and Antoine-Laurent-Apollinaire Fée—who were members of the order. Of the three, both Geoffroy and Lacépède were part of the scientific élite attached as faculty to the Parisian natural history museum in the Jardin des Plantes, one of the premier biological research institutes of early nineteenth-century Europe. Fée, by contrast, was an upwardly mobile army pharmacist who finished his days as a professor of medicine and natural history at the University of Strasbourg.

Among the three, Lacépède was probably the most superficial proponent of evolutionary theory. Within a decade he published two works with encyclopedic ambitions, the *Histoire naturelle de l'homme* (1821) and *Les Âges de la nature* (1830), that are of particular interest for this discussion.[32] In both instances, Lacépède showed an unfortunate gusto for sweepingly combining observations from unrelated disciplines and selling the resulting academic concoction as a mark of his scientific genius. In his earlier publication, for instance, he drew attention to the alleged analogy between the stages of human development, especially the years from birth through puberty but also including middle and old age, and the evolution of world history. In this biologically determined model, ancient Egypt occupied a privileged position as the place of origin for human history, corresponding roughly to the stage when an infant starts to acquire his first intellectual faculties. Later developments, such as the civilizations of ancient Greece and Rome or the discoveries of America, Africa, and Asia, pushed human society to maturity, but remained indebted to the structures laid out in the earliest developmental stages.

The later *Âges de la nature* makes an attempt to "tie the history of man to that of the terrestrial globe" in order to describe a continuum between geological and historical time.[33] Under this scheme, ancient Egypt occupied an even more pivotal position than previously, since it now linked geo-biological metamorphosis to the evolution of human civilization and the onset of history. Lacépède conceived of the origins of the universe as a kind of "big bang" (conveniently explained with mathematical formulas), but argued against theories of accidental creation. Whereas he relied mostly on Alexander von Humboldt for his account of the earth's geological formation, his explanation for the emergence of life is spottier. The cooling process of the earth's surface supposedly awakened the forces of magnetism (which he also calls "galvanism") that incited the "vital movement" giving rise to plant and animal life.[34] Evolutionary details are henceforth of little concern for Lacépède, who contented himself with recording how certain species are "observed" at a certain point in geological time and how, in what he calls the "twelfth age," man "appears" on the surface of the earth. Almost in passing he assures his baffled readers that his theories conform to the teachings of Moses and the book of Genesis, which, in any event, relied on the "geological opinions of ancient Egyptian priests."[35]

The civilizational processes began, according to Lacépède, in antediluvian times, when hunter-gatherers discovered fire, learned how to withstand the elements, started to cultivate land, and domesticated animals. Pantomime evolved into language, and the idea of the divine formed in response to human terror in the face of the untamed powers of nature. Tools were invented; dance and music encouraged first attempts at hieroglyphic writing, which in turn spawned the advent of painting and sculpture.[36]

A cataclysmic event, which Lacépède prided himself in identifying with the legendary Atlantis, put a sudden end to these early experiments at civilization.

Connections between the upheavals and the biblical deluge he quickly dismissed, as it was "not becoming" to speak on these matters except for "bishops and doctors of the Church." In the wake of the global inundation, humankind withdrew to mountainous regions to survive and later to repopulate the earth. As an example he cites central Africa, from whence descended the Ethiopians and the earliest Egyptians, who, on their way north, mixed with the race that had survived in the Caucasus. Citing Champollion and Pastoret, Lacépède then retold the Egyptian creation story, in which inanimate chaos, Athor or Athir, was stirred into action by Kneph or Phtos, the fiery spirit who breathed life into inert matter and hence became the "supreme organizer" of the world. From his seeds sprang Osiris, who gave fertility to earth, and Isis, his sister and wife, who, in her form as "fecundated nature," became the mother of all beings.[37] Later developments in ancient Egyptian history met with Lacépède's stringent criticism, since he found government reduced to a "theocracy in disguise," where hypocritical temple priests organized in colleges used rituals and religious mysteries to exercise power over a superstitious population and to prop up a political system based on tyranny. It was they who, because of their knowledge of how to read and write hieroglyphics, interpreted the laws of Hermes and perpetuated their despotic rule through hereditary dynasties. All other world civilizations, including India's and China's, closest in spirit and chronology to the Egyptian according to Lacépède, followed and modified patterns first developed on the fertile shores of the Nile.

Such facile conflations of natural sciences with pre-Christian history were not frowned upon for lack of rigor in the early nineteenth century—as they would certainly be today—but were typical products of the infancy of the "late" discipline of geography.[38] Posterity has been kinder to the accomplishments of Lacépède's fellow Sophisian and colleague at the *Muséum d'histoire naturelle*, Étienne Geoffroy Saint-Hilaire, whose work as a zoologist qualifies him, along with Bacon, Pascal, Lamarck, or Goethe, as a harbinger of Darwin's theories on the evolution of species.[39] This eminent place in the history of science, however, did not preclude engagement in scholarly controversies or wanderings into esotericism, of which there was plenty in Geoffroy's career. Venturing into comparative anatomy, he advanced his views on natural philosophy with particular brio in 1830, when he published his *Principes de philosophie zoologique*, a collection of essays and documents intended as a refutation of his colleague and (former) friend Georges Cuvier, who also taught at the *Muséum*.[40] The two cornerstones of his argument, originally presented to the Royal Academy of Sciences, were his "theory of analogy," admitting the scientific validity of comparative studies between human and animal anatomy, and the idea of the "unity of composition" to which it gave rise. The latter concept, also called "unity of plan," suggested that all vertebrates share a basic blueprint when it comes to the arrangement of organs that defines the bodily composition of an organism. With these theories Geoffroy departed from time-honored Aristotelian principles, defended by Cuvier in the controversy, which considered the function of organs and not their place in anatomy as the basis of zoology.

All the while, Geoffroy carefully avoided giving his imprimatur to evolutionary natural history, as understood prior to Darwin's groundbreaking publications. According to him, species did not mutate or adjust to their natural environment, eliminating the explanatory need for a natural selection process. As maintained in his 1831 essay *Le Degré de l'influence du monde ambiant pour modifier les formes animales*, there was only one origin of species, all of which came into being at once and henceforth perpetuated themselves basically unchanged over time. Geoffroy contrasted his philosophical model, aptly labeled the "indefinite in-boxing" of the development of beings, with the views of the "partisans of the system of evolution," who "gave themselves over to the feelings of theologians, because they could only find support in a living faith centered on a sort of pre-ordained incarnation, and on a mystery that requires no greater intellectual effort than to be believed."[41]

Some four years later Geoffroy set out to attack the doctrine of vitalism, which maintains on its most basic level that life cannot be explained in mechanistic terms, but requires a "divine spark," "energy," or the Aristotelian "superior and more divine" element.[42] Geoffroy's essay on the *Loi universelle (Attraction de soi pour soi)* was indirectly pitched against his colleagues at the Muséum d'histoire naturelle, Lamarck, Lacépède, and Cuvier, whose support of vitalism singled them out as conservative proponents of the Aristotelian theory of life, expressed in particular in the classical philosopher's treatises *De anima* and *De generatione animalium*. As vitalism shared common ground not only with Aristotle, but also with the alchemical tradition of the "four humors" that had informed Western medical theory from antiquity through the eighteenth century, Geoffroy taunted vitalists for "taking refuge, as a means of explanation, in occult forces, the principle of animation [of matter], and the assumption that

there exists a chemistry of life."[43] Proposing a machinist counter-model to vitalism, he liked to compare the workings of living beings to those of a watch. To prove his theories right, Geoffroy envisioned applying Newtonian physics to biology in order to arrive at a universal law of "mutual attraction" (*attraction de soi pour soi*), the only one capable of satisfactorily explaining the mysteries of the origins of life and confirming the infallibility of nature.

The controversy between the vitalists and machinists had a much broader scientific base than the narrow confines of the Muséum d'histoire naturelle or the Sophisian order. Most of the arguments advanced by Lacépède and Geoffroy had intellectual antecedents in eighteenth-century thinkers ranging from Kant to Lavoisier, while their contemporary echoes in the early nineteenth century are too numerous to count.[44] What set the Sophisian scientists apart, however, were their recurrent references to Egypt. On this account, the autobiographical passages in Geoffroy's research publications are particularly revealing. Both his concept of the "unity of composition" and his theory of "mutual attraction" (*attraction de soi pour soi*) were the results of a scientific epiphany that he experienced during the British siege of Alexandria in 1801.[45] While the French army made its last military stand against the advancing British and Turkish troops, Geoffroy, risking his life amidst exploding shells, was busily comparing different species of electric fish. He described the event as a moment of both feverish scientific activity and great intellectual acuteness, one that changed the course of his life and inspired him to ask larger questions about the principles of life and nature. Only one other moment in his career could compare with it. In 1827 new insights into teratology inspired Geoffroy to study naturally occurring monstrosities and deformations in organisms, the findings of which confirmed his machinist theory of "mutual attraction" (*attraction de soi pour soi*) originally formulated on Egyptian soil.

Lacépède died in 1825. Geoffroy followed him in 1844, fifteen years prior to Darwin's publication *On the Origins of Species* in 1859. Given the chronological distance to the heyday of Cuvelier de Trie's order, it seems a fortunate circumstance that there exists a Sophisian commentary on Darwin's theories, written in 1864 by Antoine-Laurent-Apollinaire Fée, then a seventy-five-year-old professor of botany and natural history at the University of Strasbourg. Fée had served in his youth as an army pharmacist during the Napoleonic wars in Spain and was perfectly conversant with the scientific theories professed by the faculty of the Muséum, most particularly with Lamarck's and Geoffroy's musings.

Following Geoffroy's lead, Fée argued for the immutability of species, which precluded Darwin's process of natural selection.[46] He also rejected the Darwinian hypothesis that chance (or chance mutation) was the engine of evolution, since the workings of chance as a modifying force on organisms could not be empirically observed. Most importantly, Darwinism violated the universal principle that "nature does not jump [*natura non facit saltus*]," a saying originally derived from Leibniz and Kant, which Fée considered the cornerstone of his rational and scientific world order. In the final analysis, Fée rejected Darwinism in the name of rationality, since the theory "dismembers the miracle [of life or of nature] and thus pretends, by simplifying it, to satisfy the demands of reason, while in reality adding to the difficulties by furthering marvelous fact that escapes rational explanation."[47]

Whereas Fée found Geoffroy's arguments useful to refute Darwinism and to show that many of its tenets were "not something absolutely new,"[48] he revealed himself to be a supporter of vitalism as he further developed his arguments on the origins of life: "The force of the agents to which the earth owes what one might call its vitality cannot be fathomed. Light might shine more or less brightly, caloric [flux of heat] might have greater or lesser levels, electricity and magnetism might have more or less intensity; yet they do not cease to be caloric, electricity, or magnetism, each with similar properties and a single unified way of acting."[49] A good understanding of the origin and context of vitalist theories of life, even if short of offering comprehensive explanations, provides at least an intellectual backdrop for some of the existentialist questions raised during Sophisian ceremonies for advanced degrees. For instance, to qualify for the class-two degree in arts and sciences of the Professorship of the Grand Mysteries, the candidate was asked to provide a solution to the following problems soliciting evolutionary speculation:

> 1st hypothesis to be developed. From the hyssop [herb used in Mosaic rites of purification] to the oak, from the ant to the elephant, Nature seems to strive to march from perfection to perfection. Is not the single stem of the polyp the first sketch, the primordial type of the marvelous interior of man, at once the most complex and the most perfect being? Why did perfection stop at this point? Was the creator incapable? That would be impossible, if man is the last echelon of the sublunary beings. Does the ladder end with man? Why does it not lead step by step from the good to the better by rendering matter diaphanous and striving towards aerial intelligence, up to the level of pure spirit, the perfect point of its immersion in the source of life, of mixing and aggregation of

divine essence, of the reunion of the soul of all things with nature? Man always hopes: this vague hope, is it not the word for the enigma of death?[50]

Unfortunately, no samples of solutions presented before the Sophisian examination committees have survived. However, one could conceive of the following passage from Fée's refutation of Darwinism as a response liable to have won the approval of the examiners during his own initiation: "Given the well-known specificities of the cell, could one not deduce the impossibility of the metamorphosis of one plant into another plant, of one animal into another animal? Otherwise, not only would the form have changed, but also the profound nature of elementary organs. That would mean admitting a true metamorphosis. One form would be destroyed to create another, like a Phoenix rising from the ashes, always younger and always more beautiful. It does not seem like nature operates this way. She may be subject to movement, but this movement is limited in its scope: this is a law."[51] Fée shared with Cuvelier (and presumably most other Sophisians) an essentially vitalist outlook on the origins of life, which had much larger social and ontological ramifications than simply being an account of natural history. Vitalism emerges as a phenomenon of modernity and a moment of empowerment for the self from Fée's commentaries, once he starts describing his own place in the universe: "I am nothing more than an atom, but this atom is endowed with the faculty for thought and free will."[52] Understood more broadly, vitalism thus offered the promise of self-fulfillment and the discovery of the potentiality of the individual in a new world order based on the liberation of intellectual powers, whereas evolutionism reduced the individual to the passive victim of chance and Nature's moods.

In my introduction and in chapter 2, I described how the Sophisian phenomenon challenged established notions of historical linearity and normative expectations of colonialism and the Enlightenment. The paradoxes that emerged from this discussion form a subset of problems within a more epic struggle between traditionalism and modernity that drove Sophisian activities. The Sophisians sought to find answers to the large questions of human existence—What is nature? What is religion? What is life?—but all too often found themselves entangled in a web of contradictions forced on them by historical circumstances.

Their attitude towards science is paradigmatic in this respect. The development of scientific knowledge in the modern world depended on open forms of communication, public discussion of new ideas, and the dissemination of discoveries in print.[53] These concepts stand in contrast to the medieval or alchemical tradition of science, in which knowledge about the physical aspects of human existence and its environment was understood to be a secret that could only be shared with other initiates, but that remained closed off from the curiosity of outsiders and the ignorant masses. Clearly, the Sophisians shared the point of view of the medieval/alchemical tradition in that the Egyptian "wisdom" in their custodianship was the preserve of the few. Guerrier de Dumast, for instance, reinforced this point by distinguishing an "esoteric" principle of knowledge, typical of the "infancy of societies," when a "protection of the sciences against barbarism, envy, and prejudice" was required "amongst the ancients, and especially the Orientals," from an "exoteric" principle, prevalent in "more advanced societies," that left the sciences "vulnerable to attack from all sides."[54] The elitism implied by the esoteric approach was alloyed by the fact that the Sophisians prided themselves on transcending class barriers and recruiting members from diverse social and professional backgrounds.[55]

Moreover, distinctions between science and religion were kept deliberately vague, since the Sophisians defined themselves as both a college of Egyptian temple priests and a shadow academy of modern scientists. The Aristotelian and vitalist theories of life they embraced proved to be a perfect fit for the Janus-faced identity of the order. Nonetheless, the choice of Isis as a tutelary deity evoked, as Jurgis Baltrušaitis has pointed out, memories of the "French Revolution battling the Church by re-animating Egyptian divinities. . . . Egyptian theogony became an instrument of atheism, and, at the same time, a temptation and a secret belief structure."[56] By the early nineteenth century, Isis, her associated deities, and her body of pseudoscientific wisdom, far from being neutral tropes, had acquired not only connotations of anticlericalism, but also a heavy political charge that was the direct outgrowth of the Egyptian campaign. During the Restoration, when overt references to the Empire period were no longer permissible, Napoleonic associations with Isis had to be outwardly denied, while her symbolism continued to rally the partisans of Bonaparte and the supporters of the anti-Bourbon liberal camp.

Attitudes towards sexuality and the role of women in the order were also full of ambiguities. Jonathan Israel's rule of thumb that, during the Enlightenment, "the more radical the philosophical standpoint, the more emphatic [the] impulse not just towards the emancipa-

tion of woman but of the human libido itself," holds true with some reservations for the Sophisians as well.[57] Cuvelier de Trie's short stories published in 1808, for example, describe a rose-colored world filled with voyeuristic priests stalking female penitents exposing themselves, incestuous cousins, mass rape scenes among American Indian tribes, or cross-dressing Greek shepherd youths.[58] The eighteenth-century tradition of libertine texts and imagery certainly also cleared the way for acceptance of the Isis cult and the phallic worship associated with the goddess. By the same token, Cuvelier's writings, including the Sophisian texts, are brimming with celebrations of (mostly female) virtue, chastity, and innocence—values held in high regard by Enlightenment thought, which maintained that "girls must be taught from an early age to love virtue for its own sake, rather than having chastity imposed on them, and must learn proper, safe and uplifting ideas."[59] Consistent with the Enlightenment's ideal that women should be allowed to partake fully in intellectual activities, Cuvelier's groups admitted female initiates on the basis of equality with men. But although some Sophisiennes can be identified as performers in the Fête Sophisienne (Hommage aux Dames) of 1821, none of them ever signed the tableaux of either the Frères Artistes or the order. In the absence of other documents attesting to female Sophisian activity, one has to assume that the rule of an "unequal androgynity" that Gisèle and Yves Hivert-Messeca observed with respect to early nineteenth-century female Freemasonry in France, also applied to the Sophisians.[60]

Caught in the maze of the paradoxes outlined above, the Sophisians thought that reviving ancient Egypt as a model for reconciling mysticism with reason, science with vitalism, and religion with nature offered a solution to the manifold dilemmas of their times. More recent phenomena, such as the colonization of Egypt or the conventions of popular theater, provided a structure for situating this quest in a modern framework, but failed ultimately at addressing the contradictions inherent in the teachings of the order. The fortunes of the Sophisians were strongly linked to the public interest in the figure of Isis as a harbinger of civilization and life, which had precedents in the Hellenistic age and the Renaissance, but attracted a particularly strong following from the eighteenth century through the Napoleonic age. Subsequently, the activities of groups like the Sophisians may have paved the way for the ongoing fascination with Isis later in the century, as epitomized by literary figures such as Gérard de Nerval, Auguste Villiers de L'Isle-Adam, or Madame

Blavatsky. Even though this interest lessened somewhat in the course of the twentieth century, it never subsided completely, as the writings of André Breton or Umberto Eco show.[61] For centuries prior to the Sophisians, Isis had already proved her ability to adapt to changing cultural circumstances. Her revival in early nineteenth-century France continues to fascinate from a historical perspective precisely because now she also became a symbol for the trials and tribulations of the Revolutionary and Napoleonic periods, as well as for their afterglow during the Bourbon Restoration.

Appendix:
Members of the Sacred Order of the Sophisians

Establishing a definitive list of Sophisian members can be a tricky undertaking. Some adepts may appear as full-fledged members in the Golden Book, while their real role was perhaps purely ornamental or honorary. Other Sophisians, who may have assumed significant and active parts in the rituals, did not sign the annual rolls because, as grand dignitaries, they were exempt from this requirement. Omissions may have occurred by pure chance or documents may have been lost. In the final analysis, the best indicator for gauging the importance of any given member within Cuvelier's groups is his or her biography. This appendix represents an attempt to reconstruct Sophisian biographies on the basis of information found in the BN Golden Book, in the annual *tableaux* of the lodge and the chapter of the *Frères Artistes*, and in standard bibliographical sources.[1] Occasionally, specialized biographical references are given in footnotes.

Information compiled in this manner was then divided into three parts. Part 1 discusses Sophisian members who, according to the BN Golden Book, had joined the order before 1821, including initiates inactive or deceased by this date.[2] Despite evident inconsistencies, like Cuvelier de Trie's surprisingly late forty-fourth position, members appear to have been listed on this *tableau* roughly according to the period of their joining the Sophisians. This circumstance motivated the decision to include the members' numerical rank in the BN Golden Book roster; this rank, however, should not be construed as a descriptor of a member's position within the hierarchy of the group.

Part 2 contains new adepts joining the order after 1821, whose names figure on a separate list inserted as an addendum to the BN Golden Book.[3] As opposed to the *tableau* in part 1, this list consists exclusively of original signatures, but does not contain any additional identifying information, such as profession. Again, information in the BN Golden Book was correlated with the contents of the archives of the *Frères Artistes* to help establish the identity of the members. For the signatories Pierre Baparin, Beraud-Frost, Coquardou, Eggly, L. Hontain, Leslange, and J. M. Raoul no additional biographical information could be extracted. They are therefore omitted from part 2.

Finally, part 3 includes members and associates attested by sources outside the BN Golden Book. Some of these individuals were mentioned as initiates in the invitation to the *Fête Sophisienne* (*Hommage aux Dames*) from 1821, preserved in the *Mélanges Lerouge* in The Hague. This invitation is particularly precious because it is the only document to reveal the names of female members, the Sophisiennes, who otherwise did not appear on the rolls of the Golden Book or the archives of the *Frères Artistes*. Again, several male members mentioned in the invitation—Aumassip, Grand, Passemare, Marquis de Verteillac—could not be further identified and were therefore omitted from part 3 of the appendix.

Sophisian Members Before 1821 According to the BN Golden Book (Fols. 2v–3r)

François **Amédée** (1784-1833), 110th member of the Sophisians, achieved distinction as a musician (viola), composer, and playwright who frequently published under the pseudonyms Amédée-Adrien or simply Adrien. His real name was François-Amédée Lanneau. Amédée was the illegitimate son of Nicolas-Médard Audinot, the founder of the Théâtre de l'Ambigu-Comique, for which he set to music more than fifty plays between 1818 and 1832, including Cuvelier de Trie's Old Testament melodrama *Les Machabées, ou La Prise de Jérusalem* (1817). Half brother of fellow Sophisian Nicolas-Théodore Audinot-D'Aussy, Amédée was a founding member and secretary of the Société des concerts du Conservatoire in Paris in 1828/29.

Claude-Charles Comte **Aubry de la Boucharderie** (1773–1813) is listed as the 43rd member of the Sophisians. He obtained his first military appointments during the Revolutionary Wars and was made a captain of artillery during the French occupation of Italy in 1799. In 1802 he was a member of the ill-fated military expedition sent to Saint-Domingue (Haiti) to assert control over the island and to restore slavery by Napoleonic order. Severely wounded, he returned to France in 1803, was promoted to colonel of the eighth artillery regiment, and participated in Napoleon's campaigns in Germany and Russia. In 1812 he obtained the rank of division general. His name is inscribed on the east side of the Arc de Triomphe.

Nicolas-Théodore **Audinot-D'Aussy** (1778–1826), 88th member of the Sophisians, held the rank of a *Hermorus* in the order by 1821; he was active in the lodge of the *Frères Artistes* between 1809 and 1824. A playwright and violin teacher, Audinot-D'Aussy became co-owner and director of the Théâtre de l'Ambigu-Comique on the boulevard du Temple in 1816. Initially, he managed the theater as the business partner of Mme de Puisaye, a *Sophisienne* and widow of the theater entrepreneur Marquis de Puisaye. Later, Audinot-D'Aussy bought Mme de Puisaye's shares and became one of the coproprietors of the establishment, thereby restoring to his own family the theater founded in 1769 by his father, Nicolas-Médard Audinot.

Joseph-Marie **Audin-Rouvière** (1764–1832), 123rd member of the Sophisians, was active in the lodge of the *Frères Artistes* between 1807 and 1831. When twenty years of age Audin-Rouvière left the clergy to study medicine in Montpellier, but the turmoil of the

Revolution prevented him from completing his doctoral degree in Paris. During the 1790s he became a proponent of inoculation and published on the subjects of urbanism and hygiene. Between 1794 and 1798 the French military administration sent him to Italy as the head physician of the army hospital in Milan. When he finally returned to Paris in 1800, he was in possession of a secret recipe that would earn him a fortune. For the next twenty years Audin-Rouvière relentlessly promoted his invention, the *grains de vie*, a quack all-purpose medicine in the form of silvery pills. To this end, in 1820 he even published an amateur medical handbook entitled *Médecine sans médecine*, which circulated widely. His fortunes thus established, he devoted the last years of his life to culinary pleasures and contributed regularly to the *Almanach des gourmands*, a gastronomical guidebook. He fell victim to the cholera epidemic in Paris during April 1832.

David **Baillot** (b. 1776), 85th member of the Sophisians, participated in the activities of the *Frères Artistes* in 1819, when he was responsible for organizing the banquets of the lodge as *Maître des Fêtes*. He is described as an *homme de lettres* in the archives of the lodge, a term frequently suggesting links with the world of the stage in the Sophisian context.

Jacques **Balluet** (b. 1775) is listed as 77th member of the Sophisians. He served under Cuvelier de Trie's command as second lieutenant of the *guides interprètes* in Rostock and was wounded in Danzig on May 19, 1807.

Jean-Martin **Barouillet** (b. ca.1757), 51st member of the Sophisians, is documented as active in the *Frères Artistes* lodge between 1796 and 1813. Barouillet was employed between 1807 and 1813 as deputy section head in the Legion of Honor, and apparently retired by the time of the Restoration. He also moonlighted as a playwright for the Parisian boulevard theaters, writing under the pen name Jean Martin.[4] Between 1803 and 1814, Barouillet coauthored at least four plays with Cuvelier de Trie, including *Le Faux ami* (1810).

Alexandre-Henry-Joseph **Bérenger** (b. 1784), 28th member of the order, held the Sophisian rank of a *Hermophile* by 1821. He was active in the Lodge of the *Frères Artistes* between 1808 and 1813 and earned his living as a businessman.

Jean-Baptiste **Bessières, Duc d'Istrie** (1768–1813), 73rd member of the Sophisians, was one of Napoleon's closest advisers. His military career began in 1792, when he served together with Joachim Murat, Bonaparte's future brother-in-law, in the Constitutional Guard, then assigned to protect Louis XVI and his household in the midst of popular uprisings. In 1795 he encountered Napoleon for the first time, while serving in a detachment of the *Guides de l'Armée d'Italie*. Three years later he left with Bonaparte for Egypt, where he rose to become a member of his inner circle. As a token of the general's favor, he was selected to accompany Bonaparte during his secret escape from Egypt in 1799. A commander of the consular and later the imperial guard, he was promoted in 1804 to one of Napoleon's fourteen Marshals. He participated in all of the Napoleonic Wars and was killed in Saxony in 1813, leaving his wife and son in debt from the expenses incurred by his lifestyle. His name is inscribed on the east side of the Arc de Triomphe.

Jean-Baptiste-Jean-Antoine-Marie-Jérôme **Brouilhony** (1783–1841), 98th member of the Sophisians, was a noncommissioned officer in the 8th Cuirassier Regiment. He served during the Napoleonic Wars in Italy (1805–6), Prussia (1807), and Spain (1808–10), where he was wounded and lost the use of his right arm. After 1810 he was employed as a military supplier to the French armies in Germany, but lost all of his modest fortune with the collapse of the Empire in 1814.

Guillaume-Marie-Anne Comte **Brune** (1763–1815), 68th member of the Sophisians, was, besides Bessières, the only Napoleonic Marshal in the order. Brune participated as an honorary member in the activities of the *Frères Artistes* between 1808 and 1813. Disinherited by his parents, he arrived in Paris at the onset of the Revolution to study law, but instead became an apprentice to a typographer. He soon developed literary ambitions of his own as a journalist and critic, while associating himself politically with Danton and the Cordeliers club. He participated in the Revolutionary Wars as a volunteer and supported Robespierre until his fall. In 1797 he was promoted to the rank of general during the campaign in Italy. Early in 1798 the Directory sent him to Bern in Switzerland to impound the municipal treasury—some twenty-two carriages of coin—to finance Napoleon's Egyptian campaign. He was rewarded with succeeding Napoleon as high commander of Italy, but soon found himself administering the French armies in Holland. Although Brune rallied to Napoleon after the 18th of Brumaire, Bonaparte's trust in his military skills eroded quickly, and Brune obtained mostly diplomatic assignments. Thus, in 1802 he was sent to Constantinople to mend diplomatic ties with the Ottoman empire, disrupted since the Napoleonic invasion of Egypt. By 1807 Brune had fallen completely into Napoleonic disfavor for accepting a bribe from the Senate of the city of Hamburg and for treating Napoleon with insufficient reverence while negotiating the terms of Sweden's capitulation. Nevertheless, Brune received a new military appointment as commander of Southern France during the *cent jours*, which would be his undoing. In August 1815 his carriage was assailed by stone-throwing Royalists in Avignon. Seeking refuge in the city's Palais Royal, he was shot and killed. His body was then dragged through the town and finally thrown into the Rhône river. The Sophisians seem to have regarded Brune as a martyr, as is evident from some of the poems read at the funerary ceremonies for Paul-Louis Mariton in 1819. His name is inscribed on the south side of the Arc de Triomphe.

Louis-Marie-Joseph-Maximilien **Caffarelli du Falga** (1756–99), 64th member of the Sophisians, was a trained military engineer and fortification specialist. A descendant of an old noble family from Languedoc, Caffarelli made no secret of his sympathies for Louis XVI in his military unit, which earned him a fourteen-month prison term during the Terror. While serving under General Kléber in Germany in 1795, he lost a leg in battle and was promoted to general. Despite his wooden prosthesis, he volunteered to accompany Napoleon to Egypt, where he was responsible for improving the fortifications of Cairo and the construction of windmills, previously unknown in the country. Caffarelli also played an important role in the scientific exploration of Egypt. A scholar at the Institut de France, he was the head of the Commission for Sciences and Arts, from which the Institut d'Égypte evolved. While the campaign was prepared, he selected the titles for the library and the scientific equipment for the planned learned society of Cairo. As presiding member of the section for Political Economy of the Institut d'Égypte, he was not only a prolific lecturer, but also one of the most controversial, on one occasion affirming that property was theft. During the revolt of Cairo in the fall of 1798, a group of French engineers was massacred in Caffarelli's house, and all the scientific equipment from the Institut in his custody was vandalized. Since he was killed in action while laying siege to the fortress of Acre in 1799, Caffarelli's admission to Sophisian membership lends credibility to Cuvelier's account of how the group was founded "on the soil of the most ancient mysteries." His name is inscribed on the south side of the Arc de Triomphe.

Carrera or **Carrère**, 124th member of the Sophisians, was a surgeon. He came from a family of physicians of Catalan origin, which had strong ties to both Spain and France during the eighteenth and nineteenth centuries.

François-Alexandre **Cassabois** (1773–1834), 30th member of the Sophisians, was active in the lodge of the *Frères Artistes* between 1819 and 1831. Cassabois was a commissioned officer in the Garde du Corps législative and worked as an army supplier.

Castagniez, listed as 13th member of the Sophisians, was a rear admiral.

Jean-François De **Caze** (1781-1851), 86th member of the Sophisian, was active in the lodge of the *Frères Artistes* in 1819, at which time he had already had a colorful political past. Caze was born in the French town of Montauban, but left in 1808 to settle in Spain, where he worked as a spy for Napoleonic France. He engineered the accession of Joseph Bonaparte to the Spanish throne, which allowed him to rise from paymaster of the French army to the positions of treasurer to the Spanish crown and governor of the region of Castilla y León. By 1812 he also held the title of secretary general of the government of Northern Spain. Forced to return to France under the Restoration, he began publishing on his recent experiences in Spain. Since his accounts were written from an unrepentantly pro-Napoleonic perspective, he irked the Bourbon government. The July Monarchy afforded Caze the possibility of a political comeback, and, for a few months in 1830, he became secretary general of the newly installed French colonial government of Algeria. He then returned to Spain, where he died in Madrid in 1830.

Léopold-François-Hugues **Chandezon** (b. 1788), 24th member of the Sophisians, was active in the Lodge of the *Frères Artistes* between 1819 and 1827. A prolific playwright working for the boulevard theaters, Chandezon coauthored more than a dozen pieces in collaboration with Cuvelier de Trie between 1816 and 1824, including the popular Near Eastern melodrama *Les Machabées, ou La Prise de Jérusalem* (1817).

George-François **Chatelanat** (b. 1794), 121st member of the Sophisians, was a Swiss national active in the lodge of the *Frères Artistes* in 1822. He is described in both the archives of the lodge and the Sophisians' Golden Book as engaged in business.

Bernard-François Hector **Chaussier** (1769–ca.1838), 47th member of the Sophisians, engaged in the activities of the *Frères Artistes* between 1797 and 1807. Chaussier's father François, a noted Dijon physician, chemist, and anatomist, convinced him to study medicine. While he obtained his medical degree only in 1818, Chaussier's contribution to Parisian boulevard theater won him fame. His first political play, with the timely title *Les Jacobins aux Enfers*, was given in 1795 and followed by some thirty more

pieces over the next decade. Since their writing styles, contents, client theaters, and targeted audiences were identical, Cuvelier de Trie and Chaussier became occasional collaborators. Chaussier also made appearances as an actor at the Théâtre des Jeunes Artistes, and, for a short period of time, he was the director of the Théâtre de l'Ambigu-Comique. By the late 1810s his vaudeville plays, *comédies parades*, and *hilarodies* were performed less frequently, and Chaussier concentrated instead on the publication of "medical miracles," such as counter-poisons, living dead, or immaculate conceptions. The *Livre d'or* notes that he was forced to abandon his practice as an eye doctor, and the archives of the *Frères Artistes* lodge add that he was employed with the French revenue service by 1807.

Augustin-Amable **Chuppin** (b. 1751), 19th member of the Sophisians, participated in the activities of the *Frères Artistes* between 1807 and 1812. According to both the archives of the lodge and those of the Sophisian order, he was a deputy division head in the ministry of the interior.

Cobb, listed as 56th member of the Sophisians, is described in the *Livre d'or* as a lieutenant colonel and a *Cipaye*, French for the Anglo-Indian term *Sepoy*, or mercenary Hindu soldier enlisted in the service of a Western power, most typically Great Britain.[5] The French army maintained a small infantry unit of *Cipayes* to protect the minor colonial outposts in India, particularly at Pondicherry, throughout the eighteenth and early nineteenth centuries. *Cipayes* also figured in Cuvelier de Trie's plays, but in this context the expression referred to Westernized American Indian mercenaries from the New World.[6] If anything, the term needs to be interpreted broadly. Perhaps the Sophisian initiate Cobb was identical with James Cobb (1756–1818), secretary of the East India Company, who attained this position after forty-three years of service in 1814. Parallel to this official career he wrote numerous plays for Drury Lane, the London equivalent of the boulevard du Temple. Cobb was in every sense Cuvelier's British homologue, with his penchant for melodramatic exaggerations. He is known to have translated and adapted several plays from the Parisian popular stages for consumption by London theater audiences, including a work by the Sophisian author Alexandre Duval (*A House to Be Sold*, 1802).

Edouard-Pierre-David Baron de **Colbert** (1774–1853) is listed as the 78th Sophisian member. The scion of a wealthy, aristocratic family, he avoided charges of royalist sympathies by enrolling as a volunteer in the army at the outbreak of the Revolution. Together with his brothers, Auguste and Alphonse, he participated in the Egyptian campaign. After Napoleon left for France in 1799, Colbert negotiated the surrender of Murad-bey, leader of Mameluke resistance and Bonaparte's erstwhile archenemy in Egypt. Colbert's diplomatic skills and facility with the Arabic language convinced Mourad-bey to become a staunch military ally of the French administration during the last phase of the campaign. His association with general Reynier's insubordinate anticolonialist camp in 1801 led to Colbert's temporary arrest in Alexandria by Menou's orders, and disgraced him in Napoleon's eyes. Rehabilitated in August 1802, he was promoted to *Capitaine Adjudant Major de Mamelucks de la garde de Bonaparte*, commanding those Mameluke soldiers who elected to evacuate Egypt with the French army and who were now at Bonaparte's personal disposal. Colbert participated in the major Napoleonic Wars, including the Russian campaign, and was promoted to division general in November

1813. He kept his position and esteem initially under Louis XVIII's rule, but his open support for Bonaparte, published in a newspaper anecdote during the *cent jours*, earned him a two-month prison term and four months of exile in 1816. During the July Monarchy Colbert's lost honor was restored, when he was asked to participate in a colonial expedition to Constantine in Algeria and was appointed aide-de-camp to Louis-Philippe's second son, the Duc de Nemours. While exercising this function in 1835 he narrowly survived the Fieschi attempt at Louis-Philippe's life, during which Colbert was wounded by an explosive device fired from a building on the boulevard du Temple. His name is inscribed on the west side of the Arc de Triomphe.

Louis-Christian-Emmanuel-Apollinaire **Comte** (1788–1859), 120th member of the Sophisians, assumed the title "physicien du roi," as noted in the *Livre d'or*, after he settled permanently in Paris in 1814. The term physician needs to be interpreted in a strictly theatrical context, referring to a professional sorcerer with a repertoire of physics tricks. Comte was the son of a watchmaker from Geneva, who ran away from home when he was fifteen. He started out as a ventriloquist, but soon discovered his true calling as a magician. In 1809 he was apprenticed to a master of this discipline, the sorcerer David in Bordeaux. Once he arrived in Paris, Comte would become a theater entrepreneur. He first rented a small stage in the basement of the Hôtel des Fermes, but in 1817 took over the Salle du Mont-Thabor, previously occupied by the Cirque Olympique, where he founded the Théâtre des Jeunes Comédiens. Both actors and audience consisted of children; performances were interspersed with magical tricks or puppet theater. Over the next decade, Comte's youth theater would change venues and names frequently. His royal privilege was affirmed in 1827, when, at a birthday party, the seven-year-old Duc de Bordeaux, grandson of Charles X, and his guests were entertained by a *spectacle de marionettes de M. Comte, phisicien*. Comte also performed during Sophisian reunions. On the occasion of the *Fête Sophisienne* in 1821, he contributed a show consisting of "white magic, followed by physical experiments."

Stanislow-Marie **Cousin**, 27th member of the Sophisians, was a medical doctor practicing in Paris.

Jean-Guillaume-Augustin **Cuvelier de Trie** (1766–1824), 44th member of the Sophisians and founder of the order in Paris, presided over the lodge of the *Frères Artistes* since its inception in 1796/97 until his death in 1824. The Sophisians referred to him as *Grand Isiarque* or *Souverain Patriarche*. From the time of the French Revolution until the mid-1820s, Cuvelier sought to find a formula for merging his interests in theater, mysticism, militarism, Egyptosophy, and Freemasonry. He first arrived in Paris to study law at the Collège des Grassins and was admitted to the bar in 1785. Cuvelier returned to his hometown of Boulogne-sur-mer, but was sent back to the capital as the local representative for the *Fête de la Fédération* on July 14, 1790. Over the next couple of months he discovered his vocation for the Parisian stage and started to write plays. In 1792 Cuvelier became the captain of the *Compagnie des Artistes Dramatiques*, an all-volunteer corps of actors, playwrights, and stage workers organized by the Théâtre Montansier in the Palais Royal. But instead of defending the newly declared republic against monarchist hostility from Prussia and Austria, Cuvelier was sent to fight in the demoralizing civil war in the Vendée region under the command of the Sans-Culotte General Santerre, which left him severely wounded. Between 1795

and 1796 he held a position as division head in the Commission de l'instruction publique, the ministry for education, censorship, and propaganda of the Directory period, which also controlled the theaters. By 1800 he enrolled again in the army, participated in the campaign in Graubünden (Switzerland), and fought with the Armée du Rhin. On account of his English language skills he was appointed commander of the *guides interprètes*, an élite troop assembled at the camp de Boulogne in anticipation of a French invasion of Great Britain. During the campaigns in Prussia and Poland, Cuvelier, now directly under the command of Bonaparte's minister of war, General Berthier, continued serving as a captain in the same unit of interpreter-scouts. Due to his ill health, he was sent back from Warsaw to Paris in 1807, ending his military career. Despite these commitments in the course of almost three decades, Cuvelier managed to write some 150 theater pieces for the Parisian boulevard theaters, where some of his works remained part of the repertoire over many years. Most of his plays were written for Audinot-D'Aussy's Théâtre de l'Ambigu-Comique and the Théâtre du Cirque Olympique, owned by the Franconi family. Cuvelier was the mind and soul behind the Egypticizing rituals of the Sacred Order of the Sophisians. He is buried in the Père Lachaise cemetery in Paris.

Joseph-François **Dalmas de Pracontal** (1749–1825), 36th member of the Sophisians, held the rank of an *Isiarque* by 1812. He was a founding member of the lodge of the *Frères Artistes*, in which he was active until 1813. As a veteran of the American War of Independence, Dalmas had participated in the Battle of the Bermudas and the siege of Yorktown (1780–83). Appointed captain in 1785, he continued to receive promotions during the early phase of the Revolution: in 1789 he supervised the artillery installations in Brest; in 1791 he was made captain-commander and admitted to the chivalric order of Saint-Louis. One year later, with the purging of nobles from the French army in full swing, he decided to emigrate. As the archives of the *Frères Artistes* document, Dalmas was back in Paris during the Directory and Empire, but worked this time for the revenue service in charge of collecting consumption taxes (*contributions indirectes*, 1807–12). On account of his nobility, he managed to start a second naval career during the Restoration. In 1815 he obtained ad hoc the rank of colonel and took command of the marine installations, first in Toulon, and later in Brest.

Joseph **Dantan** (d. 1813), 76th member of the Sophisians, served as an interpreter of Oriental languages at the French embassy to the Ottoman court in Constantinople at the turn of the nineteenth century.[7] As a *dragoman*, he not only possessed a profound knowledge of Islamic law, but also spoke and wrote Arabic and Turkish fluently. While serving under the French *chargé d'affaires* Pierre-Jean-Marie Ruffin in 1798, he and a third French diplomat were arrested by order of the Reis-Effendi (foreign minister) during an official audience scheduled to discuss Napoleon's invasion of Egypt, then formally part of the Ottoman empire. The arrest of the three diplomats was a prelude to the systematic persecution of French citizens in Turkish territory. During the entire three years of the Egyptian campaign Dantan and his companions were kept as Ottoman hostages in the infamous Castle of Seven Towers near Constantinople, returning to their regular diplomatic posts only after the French evacuation of Egypt. It seems that Dantan still worked as diplomatic interpreter under General Brune, another Sophisian, who was appointed French ambassador to the Ottoman court in September 1802. Dantan died in Constantinople on June 2, 1813.

Aimé-Louis-Charles **Delaberge, Sr.** (1787–1835), 116th member of the Sophisians, was active in the lodge of the *Frères Artistes* in 1819 and held the Sophisian rank of an *Agathos* by 1821. Trained at the École militaire at Fontainebleau in 1805, he became the aide-de-camp of General Ornano in 1811 and a commodore in 1813. He also participated in the campaigns in Prussia and Poland (1806/7), Spain and Portugal (1808–11), and France (1814).

Charles-Edme **Delaunoy** (b. 1787) is listed as 31st member of the Sophisians. His participation in the *Frères Artistes* lodge is documented between 1818 and 1819. He was employed as the head of an office for the collection of consumption taxes, the *contributions indirectes*.

Antoine-Guillaume Maurailhac **Delmas de la Coste** (1766–1813), 79th member of the Sophisians, came from an impoverished noble family. His military career was punctuated by incidences of insubordination and disciplinary measures. While still a lieutenant in 1788, he was dismissed for insubordination, but reinstated during the Revolution. In 1793, after the successful defense of Landau in Germany, he was promoted to division general, only to be arrested as a royalist sympathizer a few days later. A second arrest followed in 1794 for the same reasons, but again the charges were dismissed after a month spent in prison. In 1797 Delmas joined the Armée d'Italie, which he even commanded on an interim basis for a few days in 1799. He publicly criticized Napoleon for rehabilitating Christianity during the rededication ceremonies of Notre-Dame ("a beautiful *Capucinade* not worth the million men it had cost"), for which he was temporarily exiled from Paris. His involvement in 1804 with an alleged royalist plot, orchestrated by General Moreau, disgraced him even more profoundly with the administration and resulted in his being exiled to Switzerland until 1813. Called back to active duty after the disastrous Russian campaign, Delmas was killed in action during the Battle of Leipzig in October 1813. His name is inscribed on the east side of the Arc de Triomphe.

Jacques **Dervaux** (1790–1822), 87th member of the Sophisians, actively participated in the lodge of the *Frères Artistes* between 1819 and the year of his death in 1822. He worked as a dental surgeon in Paris.

Jacques-Zacharie **Destaing** (1764–1802), 42nd member of the Sophisians, began his military career as a volunteer during the Revolution. In 1796 he participated in the Italian campaign and was selected to accompany Bonaparte on the Egyptian expedition. After the Battle of the Pyramids, Destaing was named brigadier general and later received appointments as commander of Cairo and the Bahireh province (August 1799). He was a protégé of General Menou, who promoted him to division general and chief of staff. Following Menou's orders, in May 1801 Destaing arrested a dissident group of generals who had rallied to General Reynier, another Sophisian member who was then stationed in Alexandria. While in Egypt, Destaing married a sixteen-year-old girl from the Greek ethnic minority named Anne Nazo, whose father served in the Légion Grecque of the French armed forces. In 1802, after the Egyptian campaign had ended, Reynier challenged Destaing to a duel in the Bois de Boulogne, in the course of which Destaing was killed. Destaing's name is inscribed on the south side of the Arc de Triomphe.

Auguste-François **Dondey-Dupré** (b. 1763), 12th member of the Sophisians, was active in the Lodge of the *Frères Artistes* be-

tween 1811 and 1818. A writer, editor, and printer, Dupré-Dondey owned, together with his son Prosper, a publishing house in Paris that specialized in scientific publications dealing with the Orient, French translations from English, and Masonic texts. The company controlled the only printing presses for Oriental languages in private hands at the time.

Prosper **Dondey-Dupré** (1794-1834), 89th member of the Sophisians, participated in the activities of the lodge of the *Frères Artistes* from 1819 to 1827 and held the Sophisian rank of *Nomarque* by 1821. Prosper was the son of Auguste-François Dondey-Dupré and co-owner of the family's publishing business. Towards the end of the Empire he also appears to have worked for the army administration. Dondey-Dupré, jr. not only composed Masonic poems and *éloges funèbres*, but also edited and contributed to fashionable periodicals of the 1820s, such as the *Revue Britannique*, a monthly journal with excerpts from the British press in French translation, or the *Étoile*. The emphasis of his literary ambitions, however, was on Eastern languages (including modern Greek), which inspired him to join the Société asiatique and to translate Hindi dramas into French. Upon the death of Cuvelier de Trie in 1824, Prosper delivered his funerary oration at the Père Lachaise cemetery, which was subsequently published as an obituary by the Dondey-Dupré presses.

Mathieu **Dudon** (b. 1773), 22nd member of the Sophisians, engaged in the activities of the *Frères Artistes* lodge between 1811 and 1818 and practiced medicine in Paris.

Claude-Jean **Dufour** (b. 1798), 102nd member of the Sophisians, was associated with the lodge of the *Frères Artistes* between 1819 and 1824 and served as an army doctor in Paris.

Michel **Dumolard** (1763–1818), listed as 67th member of the Sophisians, was one of Napoleon's colonels. He had joined the military as a lieutenant in 1791, when he became the aide-de-camp of General Lapoype. Together they joined the Rhine Army in 1792. In the same role Dumolard later participated in the Italian campaign (1798/99). After another stint in Germany, he was appointed in 1801 commander of the citadel of Turin, where he had to put out a brewing revolt that left him wounded. Dumolard sustained injuries in the battles of Caldiero (1805) and Roveredo (1809), and served during the French occupation of Catalonia between 1810 and 1812. He obtained another position as military commander during the *cent jours*, but was decommissioned after the second Restoration.

Jean-Georges-Edouard **Dupas** (b. 1734), 66th member of the Sophisians, participated in the activities of the lodge of the *Frères Artistes* between 1812 and 1819. As a director in the army administration during the Empire, he was responsible for the food supply of Napoleon's troops, but during the Restoration he switched to a civilian position as inspector general for the provisioning of Paris.

Jean-Léopold **Duplan** (b. 1777), 26th member of the Sophisians, was active in the *Frères Artistes* lodge between 1809 and 1831 and practiced medicine in Paris.

Antoine-Louis-Germain Collard **Dutilleul** (b. 1779), 21st member of the Sophisians, is documented as an active member of *Frères Artistes* between 1809 and 1818. Another employee of the army administration, he started out as paymaster of the first military division. Replacing fellow Sophisian de Caze after the latter's appointment as treasurer to the newly installed King of Spain, Joseph Bonaparte, Dutilleul became paymaster general of the French armies in Spain in 1811. One year later he was appointed receiver-general of military contributions. During the Restoration he held a civilian job as inspector for property and income taxes (*contributions directes*) in the city of Melun.

Alexandre-Vincent Pineu **Duval** (1767–1842), 112th member of the Sophisians, participated in the activities of the *Frères Artistes* as an honorary member in 1819. Duval stands out within the order as a polymath engaged in a wide range of intellectual pursuits; however, his greatest achievement is that he managed to be elected to the French Academy in 1812, despite being an author of boulevard theater pieces. While barely fourteen years old, Duval had left France to fight in the American War of Independence. Upon his return he became an engineer in the Corps des ponts et chaussées, and helped to build the Dieppe canal. Previously, he had studied architecture at the Academy, during which time he developed a nascent interest in theater. After 1789 he lost his employment as architect in the royal household. Next, he joined the studio of the engraver Massard, for whom he drew portraits of the deputies in the Constitutional Assembly. He also took to the stage in 1791 at the Théâtre Montansier near the Palais Royal. As a staff member of this establishment, in 1792 he was forced to enroll in the volunteer corps of the *Compagnie des artistes dramatiques* under Cuvelier de Trie's command, in which he became the "orator and troubadour." His patriotism notwithstanding, Duval was arrested during the Terror and remained in jail until early 1794. Thereafter, he devoted his undivided attention to his theatrical career, first as an actor, later as a playwright and director at the Odéon, also known as the Théâtre de l'Impératrice, attached to Napoleon's court (1808–16). When one of his scripts inadvertently incited Napoleon's ire in the spring of 1802, Duval elected voluntary exile in Russia until 1803. For the most part, the style and content of his pieces were no different from Cuvelier's literary output. In the 1830s Duval added novels and works of literary criticism to his oeuvre, as well as a history of French theater. He finished his career as a librarian of the Bibliothèque de l'Arsenal during the July Monarchy.

Esenhart, 59th member of the Sophisians, was a Prussian merchant resident in Berlin.

Jean-Antoine-Joseph **Fauchet** (1761–1834), 20th member of the Sophisians, held the rank of *Isiarque* in the order. He was a founding member of the *Frères Artistes* in 1796/97 and succeeded Cuvelier de Trie as the lodge's *Vénérable* in 1824, a position he still maintained under the July Monarchy. Fauchet was a politician who became one of the most highly decorated dignitaries of the Empire period. Trained as a lawyer during the ancien régime, Fauchet embraced the ideals of the French Revolution instantaneously. After the declaration of the republic in September 1792, Fauchet became a senior staff officer in the Ministry of War, followed by an appointment as secretary-general of the government's Executive Council. One year later Robespierre appointed Fauchet to the position of French ambassador to the United States. He arrived in Philadelphia in 1794. After his return to France he published a treatise entitled *Coup d'oeil rapide sur l'état actuel de nos rapports politiques avec les États Unis de l'Amérique septentrionale* (1797), disabusing the French public of any lingering idealism concerning fraternal Franco-American relations. The Directory government asked Fauchet to participate in the expedition against the slave revolt on Saint-Domingue (Haiti), but he refused on account of his marriage plans with Marie-Élisabeth-Joséphine Holtz, presumably a relative of the Sophisian member Charles Holtz. Fauchet supported Napoleon's coup d'état, which earned him successive appointments as prefect of the Var department (March 1800), prefect of the Gironde (December 1805), and prefect of the Arno in Florence (March 1809). As prefect of the Var department installed in Toulon, Fauchet would have organized the disembarkation of the returning troops of Napoleon's Egyptian army in 1800/1801. Dismissed by the Restoration government in 1814, he was reconfirmed in his previous political positions during the *cent jours*, only to be removed again in 1815.

Jean-Baptiste Roger le Chevalier **Fauchon d'Henneville** (1780–1856), 97th member of the Sophisians, held the rank of a *Cérice*, or messenger of *Hermorus*, during the *Fête Sophisienne* of 1821; he associated himself with the *Frères Artistes* between 1822 and 1824. Under the Bourbons, Fauchon d'Henneville was promoted in April 1816 to chief of staff of the National Guard in Paris.[8] In the early 1820s he was the secretary of the *menus plaisirs du roi*, organizing the entertainment program (theater, opera, music) and official ceremonies at the court of Louis XVIII.

Antoine-Laurent-Apollinaire **Fée** (1789–1874), 119th member of the Sophisians, was associated with the *Frères Artistes* lodge between 1819 and 1822. A colorful intellectual, Fée managed to reconcile the profession of pharmacist with a career as a writer. In 1809 he participated in the French occupation of Spain as an army pharmacist. After the collapse of the Napoleonic empire he opened a pharmacy in Paris at 19 rue du Bac, which he operated between 1815 and 1825. In 1819 he founded the Société des pharmaciens de la Seine, and published his first and only theater piece, entitled *Pélage*, which he had written a decade earlier while stationed in Spain. He was also active as a poet, composing melancholic Masonic odes and funerary elegies. In 1823 Fée was elected an associate of the Academy of Medicine in Paris, which qualified him as a lecturer in the military hospital of Lille and the training hospital of Strasbourg. A decade later he finally earned his doctoral degree in medicine in order to become a professor at the University of Strasbourg. He officially retired from this position in 1852, but continued to teach botany and natural history in the same faculty until the Prussian invasion of 1870, when he sought refuge in Geneva. Fée died in Paris in 1874. Besides his pharmaceutical handbooks and scientific writings on plants, he published a life of Linnaeus (1832), a treatise on the instincts and intelligence of animals (1853), a commentary on Darwin (1864), a travel description of Switzerland (1835), and his *Souvenirs* of the Napoleonic War in Spain (1856).

Charles-Gabriel Foignet, called Jacques **Foignet père** (1753–1823), 109th member of the Sophisians, is inscribed in the registers of the *Frères Artistes* between 1809 and 1813. He arrived in Paris in 1779 as an instructor of harpsichord, harp, solfeggio, and singing. Presumably his position was tied to the royal household. The events of the French Revolution opened new career opportunities for Foignet, who now worked mostly as a composer for the popular stages of Paris. His first such position was with the Théâtre Montansier near the Palais Royal, where he may have encountered Cuvelier de Trie for the first time. Between 1808 and 1811 Foignet set at least six plays by Cuvelier to music, including the immensely popular *Bataille d'Aboukir, ou Les Arabes du désert* (1808), inspired by historical events of the Egyptian campaign. Foignet was also concerned with the administration of theaters. In 1798 he became the director of the Théâtre Montansier. He managed the Théâtre des Jeunes Artistes with its staff of child actors between 1801 and 1805, as well as the Théâtre des Victoires nationales until 1805. Along with Piccinni, Foignet was the composer of choice for the Sophisians. He set to music Cuvelier's *Hymne sacré des Anciens Mystères*, which was customarily performed at the culmination of the order's Egyptian-rite initiation ceremonies.

Foularde, 15th member of the Sophisians, was a lawyer in Antwerp.

Honoré-Joseph-Antoine Comte de **Ganteaume** (1755–1818), 60th member of the Sophisians, joined the French merchant fleet as a sailor at age fourteen. He participated in the American War of Independence, serving under fellow Sophisian General Destaing in the Battle of Granada and the siege of Savannah. His most extensive experience as a naval officer, however, was acquired in the Eastern Mediterranean. Because of this expertise, Napoleon appointed him chief of staff to the French navy during the Egyptian campaign. Ganteaume barely survived the sea battle of Aboukir on August 1, 1798, and thereafter replaced Admiral Breuys, who was killed in action, as commander-in-chief of the French navy in Egypt. In this capacity he participated in the Syrian campaign, but the hour of his greatest fame came in August 1799, when he organized Bonaparte's secret escape from Egypt. Ganteaume was the captain of the *Murion*, the vessel that safely disembarked Napoleon in Southern France after a six-week odyssey across the Mediterranean. Napoleon's initial fondness for Ganteaume proved ephemeral. Now a rear admiral, Ganteaume was charged in 1801 with the task of sending supplies to sustain the French troops that remained in Egypt. The expedition, consisting of seven vessels with five thousand soldiers, ended in failure, and Napoleon lost confidence in Ganteaume. Nevertheless, he was asked to organize another expedition to the Antilles and Saint-Domingue (Haiti) in 1804. Four years later his ships broke the British blockade of Corfu. During the *cent jours* he remained mostly neutral, but convinced Marshal Brune to surrender Southern France to the Bourbons in 1815. Besides being a military leader, Ganteaume was also a preeminent figure in French Masonry and a driving force for the reestablishment of the Grand Orient de France during the Consulate. His name is inscribed on the south side of the Arc de Triomphe.

Étienne **Geoffroy Saint-Hilaire** (1772–1844), 45th member of the Sophisians, was one of Europe's leading natural scientists at the turn of the nineteenth century. When barely out of his teens Geoffroy Saint-Hilaire was named assistant keeper and lecturer at the cabinet of natural history in the Jardin royal des plantes in Paris. In 1793, while only twenty-one years of age, he became the first professor of zoology in France, teaching in the Muséum d'histoire naturelle along with the famous botanist Lamarck. The faculty was later expanded to include the future Sophisian member Comte de Lacépède, who specialized in serpents and fish. Geoffroy Saint-Hilaire was one of the most prominent scientists to join the Egyptian campaign in 1798. A founding member of the Institut d'Égypte, he maintained a lively correspondence with Lacépède in Paris throughout the Egyptian sojourn, during which time he also became close friends with other Sophisians, such as

General Reynier and architect Charles Norry.[9] Prior to his return to France, he managed to pass a large consignment of biological specimen, live animals, ancient Egyptian mummies, and other curiosities through British controls. Back in Paris, these spoils were celebrated as symbols of the advancement of scientific knowledge in the wake of Napoleon's campaign. After another scientific expedition to French-occupied Spain and Portugal in 1807, he was offered the newly created chair for zoology in the faculty of sciences at the University of Paris, which he retained until his death. In many respects, the insights Geoffroy Saint-Hilaire gained from his studies in embryology, teratology, and paleontology anticipate Darwin's theory on the origin of species.

Etienne-François **Girard** (b. 1766) is listed as the 62nd member of the Sophisians. According to both the records of the *Frères Artistes* for 1801 and the French military archives at Vincennes, he was employed at the prefecture of Toulon in the Var department when Napoleon's troops returned from Egypt. In this position he would have worked under another Sophisian, Var prefect Joseph Fauchet. Girard may have played an important role in the foundation stages of the order in France, since his inscription on the funerary column of the Sophisian "pyramid" lists him as a *Grand Isiarque*, a position otherwise reserved for Cuvelier de Trie. For most of his life, Girard seems to have been a career soldier. In 1793 he had assisted Bonaparte in laying siege to Toulon, then a fervently royalist port town that received British support. The success of this operation was an important milestone in Napoleon's career, earning him a promotion to brigadier general. Girard later helped to put down the Vendée uprising (1798–1800) and participated in the Napoleonic campaigns in Italy (1796–98) and Spain (1805–8). He was the mayor of Toulon between 1819 and 1822, and again between 1830 and 1836. Sophisian records, which claim that he died "as a hero" while commanding the siege of Girona in Spain, are inconsistent with the French military archives, which show that Girard was alive and well in 1819, when he claimed his military pension from the South of France. Girard never appears to have lived in Paris and hence was not a regular participant in Sophisian reunions.

Lewis **Goldsmith** (1763/64?–1846), 34th member of the Sophisians, was a British newspaper editor and political demagogue of Portuguese Jewish descent who lived mostly in Paris and London during the nineteenth century. One of the last great adventurers of the age of the Enlightenment, Goldsmith was involved with British radical politics in the late 1780s and became an instant convert to the ideals of the French Revolution after 1789. By 1792 he had established contact with Masonic circles and the Illuminati in Frankfurt. During the Revolutionary Wars he traveled across Germany, Poland, and Holland. By 1797 he was back in London, where he started publishing his first pro-French newspaper, *Albion*, in 1799. The journal's sexually laced polemics and violent slanders against Europe's monarchies discredited Goldsmith with British authorities. Between 1801 and 1802 he traveled frequently between London and Paris, where, apparently with the backing of the Consulate government, he launched the rabidly pro-Napoleonic newspaper *Argus, ou Londres vu de Paris* in October 1802. Pressured by Talleyrand to moderate the tone of the newspaper, Goldsmith fell out with the French government and turned to the British ambassador for help in the spring of 1803. The French secret services readily detected his betrayal and turned him into a double agent. Now a spy in Napoleon's service, he was sent to Germany and Poland to intercept British diplomatic correspondence by bribing post office officials. His activities were detected and he was sent back to Paris, where he worked as an interpreter and translator between 1805 and 1809. In May of 1809 he and his family boarded a ship in Dunkirk to emigrate to America, but instead they were put ashore in England, where Goldsmith was imprisoned. Switching allegiances one more time, he bought his freedom by writing and publishing anti-Bonapartiste propaganda in the service of the British government and the exiled Louis XVIII (*Anti-Gallican Monitor*, 1811–14; *Anti-Corsican Monitor*, 1814–18). By 1816 his newspaper turned against the Restoration government and his former benefactor Louis XVIII, whom he accused of liberalism and nepotism. Nevertheless, Goldsmith was back in Paris for extended sojourns in May 1818 and November 1819, during which time he most likely came in contact with the Sophisians. During his second trip he ran afoul of the French government again and had to leave the country for Britain. Despite these setbacks, he was back to France for good in 1825 and, after another stint as newspaper editor, secured a minor post with the British embassy in Paris, where he died in the rue de la Paix on January 6, 1846. Besides Goldsmith's work as a polemicist, he was also a great theater enthusiast and critic.

Pierre-Guillaume **Gratien** (1764–1814), 58th member of the Sophisians, entered the military as a volunteer in the Parisian section of the *Enfants-Rouges* in 1790. In 1793, now a brigadier general, he was arrested for a short period of time based on accusations of incompetence. His military career resumed only in 1795, when he helped to put down the Vendée uprising. By 1807 he was serving as lieutenant-general under General Brune in the Dutch army of Louis Bonaparte, King of the Netherlands. Between 1810 and 1814 he was frequently transferred among the Napoleonic armies in Portugal, Spain, Germany, Russia, Austria, and Italy. He died of natural causes at Plaisance, France, on April 24, 1814.

Grenier de la Croix, 39th member of the Sophisians, was a retired lawyer.

Auguste-Prosper-François **Guerrier de Dumast** (1796–1883), 104th member of the Sophisians, participated in the activities of the *Frères Artistes* between 1819 and 1822 and was renowned internationally as one of the leading Orientalists of the nineteenth century. His life and career can be divided into two distinct periods. Prior to 1825, Guerrier de Dumast, who was trained as a lawyer, worked an *intendant militaire* (senior army administrator on the quartermaster-general's staff) for the Restoration government. He was a fixture in Parisian Masonic circles around 1820 and published extensively on Masonic subjects; his essays and poems frequently advocated the derivation of the Masonic craft from ancient cultures, particularly ancient Egypt and India—a claim allegedly founded on archeology and the sciences (*La Maçonnerie*, 1820). Together with fellow Sophisian Prosper Dondey-Dupré, he was a member of the Société asiatique by 1822, an engagement which foreshadowed his academic interest in Oriental languages. These involvements led to Guerrier de Dumast's embracing of the philhellenic cause, dedicated to the liberation of Greece from Ottoman political repression (*Chios, la Grèce et l'Europe*, 1822; *A mon ami Piccolos*, 1861). It was he who, in about 1819, introduced a group of exiled Greek professors, headed by linguist Nicolos Sava Piccolos from the defunct Princely Academy in Bucharest, to the Sophisians. The year 1825 marked a turning point in Guerrier de Dumast's life: he settled in Nancy, married a woman from a family of local notables, renounced all Masonic teachings, and converted to liberal Catholicism, which acknowledged the intellectual and moral values of the Enlightenment. Cultural and academic occupations in Nancy now took center stage in his life. In 1841 he helped found the local historical museum, and in 1854 he became a leader in reestablishing the University of Nancy; he also played an active role in the local Académie de Stanislas. Until the German occupation of the town between 1870 and 1873, Guerrier de Dumast held the chair for Sanskrit and Arabic languages at the university. In keeping with the Sophisian worldview on the evolution of civilization, his teachings on Orientalism were steeped in classical overtones (*L'Orientalisme rendu classique*, 1853). Guerrier de Dumast was the author of 189 books and monographs.

Jean-Pierre **Guillemet** (1774–1816), 50th member of the Sophisians, was associated with the *Frères Artistes* lodge between 1807 and 1813. Like other Sophisians, Guillemet began his military career as a volunteer during the Revolutionary Wars. In November 1796 he was appointed aide-de-camp to General Brune, to whom he remained personally attached throughout the Napoleonic era. He served under Brune during the wars in the Vendée, in Holland, and in Italy between 1798 and 1801. When Brune was sent to Constantinople in the fall of 1802 to mend diplomatic relations with the Ottoman empire, Guillemet accompanied him. By 1805 both men were back in France; Guillemet subsequently served in the Napoleonic war in Spain from 1806 until 1813, when he was promoted to the rank of brigadier general. During the *cent jours*, Guillemet was reappointed Brune's chief-of-staff in Southern France, stationed in the Var department. By contrast with Brune, Guillemet survived this last episode of the Napoleonic era unharmed, but died only one year later of natural causes.

Guillet, Jr., 106th member of the Sophisians, is described as a professor in the Golden Book.

Guillet, Sr., 105th member of the Sophisians, is described as a schoolteacher in the Golden Book. Most likely he was the author of *Lectographie, méthode de lecture et d'écriture*, a learning aid for reading and writing published in 1846.

Guerle, listed as the 54th member of the Sophisians and described in the records of the order as a Prussian artist from Silesia, can presumably be identified as the German composer and musician Joseph Augustin Gürlich (1761–1817). Gürlich had attended the Jesuit school in Breslau, Silesia, and subsequently studied theology, before discovering his talent for music in Berlin, where, by 1790, he joined the royal Prussian chapel as a player of the contrabass. He influenced the musical scene in Berlin not only because of his numerous compositions, but also because of his teaching activities focusing on musical theory. In 1816, one year before his death, he was appointed director of the Prussian royal chapel.

Joseph **Hélitas de Meun**, 100th member of the Sophisians, was a retired military officer, former colonist, and the coauthor of Cuvelier de Trie's plays *Le Roi et le pâtre* (1820) and *La Mort du Tasse* (1821).

Charles-Henri-Alexis-François **Holtz** (1777–1814) appears twice on the Sophisian membership list of the Golden Book (No. 3 and No. 46); he participated with interruptions in the activities of the *Frères Artistes* lodge between 1807 and 1809.[10] Entering the French navy at twelve years of age, Holtz participated in the expedition to put down the slave revolt in Saint Domingue (Haiti) in 1792 and joined the Egyptian campaign as ensign officer. A survivor of the sea battle of Aboukir, where he served on board the *Franklin*, he was integrated into the land army's Légion nautique, a division formed exclusively from the remains of the French navy, in which he rose to the rank of a lieutenant. While in Egypt, he was appointed aide-de-camp of General Friant. After his return to France, Holtz served in the Garde impériale, an élite corps of Napoleon's personal bodyguards. He participated in the Napoleonic Wars in Italy (1802/3), Spain (1808–9), Germany (1809, 1813), and Russia (1812), still serving mostly under Friant. Holtz fought in the Battle of Austerlitz, but died from wounds sustained during the siege of Hamburg in January 1814, by which time he held the rank of colonel.

August Wilhelm **Iffland** (1759–1814), 37th member of the Sophisians, was a celebrated German actor, playwright, and theater director who maintained strong ties to European Masonic circles. A native of Hanover, he celebrated his debut in Gotha in 1777. Around 1790 he started writing anti-Revolutionary plays for the theater of Mannheim, where he had been working since 1779. The French invasion of this city initially made him flee to the theater in Weimar, but in 1796 he received an appointment as director of the National Theater in Berlin, followed by a call to become director-general of the Prussian Royal Theater in 1811. Iffland died in Berlin in 1814. His interest in Freemasonry is attested by a Masonic play entitled *Der Magnetismus*, which he wrote in 1787. The award for the best German actor, the *Iffland-Ring*, conferred continuously since the late nineteenth century, is named after him.

Jean-Baptiste-François **Jacqueminot** (1781–1861), 70th member of the Sophisians, was associated with the lodge of the *Frères Artistes* between 1808 and 1813. His father was Jean-Jacques-Ignace Jacqueminot, Comte de Ham, a deputy of the Conseil des Cinq-Cents during the Directory, who supported Napoleon's coup d'état in 1799, which subsequently earned him a seat as a senator during the Empire. Like Guerrier de Dumast, Jean-Baptiste-François Jacqueminot worked as an *intendant militaire*, or army commissioner, and in this capacity he accompanied the French military to Spain, Germany, Poland, and Russia. Because of his loyalty to Napoleon, he was retired during the first Restoration, but reactivated during the *cent jours* and managed to hold on to minor military positions until 1819. At the beginning of the July Monarchy, he briefly became a Counselor of State, after which time he served as an administrator in the National Guard.

Bernard-Germain-Étienne de la Ville-sur-Illion Comte de **Lacépède** (1756–1825), 35th member of the Sophisians, presided over the six *Sosis*, or council of conservators of the order. He was also an honorary member of the *Frères Artistes* between 1808 and 1818, which distinguished him as one of the most powerful individuals in either organization. Indeed, Lacépède was one of the most highly decorated dignitaries of the Napoleonic age. A multitalented academician, he was a distinguished natural scientist with numerous works on biology and physics to his credit. Yet Lacépède's intellectual interests were remarkably diverse, as he also wrote poems, composed operas, and commented on historical events. He began his career during the ancien régime as keeper of the cabinets in the Royal Gardens of Paris, from which the Muséum d'histoire naturelle would evolve, and he later taught at the Muséum together with Geoffroy Saint-Hilaire. During the moderate phase of the Revolution he presided over the Séction du Jardin des Plantes and was elected to the Legislative Assembly in 1791. During the Terror, however, Lacépède retired from the Parisian

political scene to the countryside, which helped him, despite his noble origins, to survive this period unharmed. In 1795 he was elected to membership in the section of anatomy and zoology of the Institut, and in 1799 Napoleon appointed him to the French Senate, whose president he became in 1801. After Lacépède was made Grand Chancellor of the Legion of Honor at its inception in 1803, he emerged as the most easily recognizable figurehead of the Empire regime besides Napoleon himself, since he was always the first to speak on formal occasions. Lacépède's untimely appointment to headmaster of the University of Paris during the *cent jours* earned him disgrace under the Restoration government. An important part of Lacépède's job during the Empire consisted of controlling the activities of Masonic lodges for the Emperor, first as *second grand surveillant* (1803) and later as *grand admininstrateur général* (1804) of the reorganized Grand Orient. Undoubtedly, the circumstance that since 1783 he had frequented the same lodge of the *Neuf Soeurs* that initiated Voltaire in 1778 qualified him for these posts in Napoleon's eyes. Lacépède's documented personal involvement with the *Frères Artistes* and the Sophisians possibly emboldened Cuvelier de Trie to present his organizations as descendants of the *Neuf Soeurs*.

Jean-Baptiste-Raymond Baron de **Lacrosse** (1760–1829) is listed as 17th member of the Sophisians and was mentioned as an honorary member of the lodge of the *Frères Artistes* in 1822. He served as rear admiral in the French navy and during the ancien régime completed numerous tours of duty to French overseas colonies, including the Antilles, Guadeloupe, Martinique, and the Indian Ocean. In 1792 he even became interim colonial governor of Guadeloupe, but was arrested upon his return to France on account of his noble descent. Rehabilitated in 1795, he was sent to Ireland in 1796 to organize an insurrection against Great Britain. Following a breakneck chase by the British navy, Lacrosse's Irish mission ended in a dramatic shipwreck off the French coast. Next, he obtained a short diplomatic assignment in Spain; yet by 1801 the Directory government sent Lacrosse back to Guadeloupe to put down a revolt. He was supposed to take charge of the island as colonial prefect, but violent opposition from the native population forced him to flee almost instantly to neighboring Dominica. Only after reinforcements arrived in 1802 was he able to accomplish his mission. By 1803 Lacrosse's health had deteriorated so badly that he had to leave for France, but later in the year he was charged again with the inspection of the ports at Le Havre and Boulogne, narrowly repelling a British attempt at landing in 1804. Between 1811 and 1812 he held his last position as prefect of the port of Rochefort.

Auguste **Lambert**, 118th member of the Sophisians, was a popular playwright. Between 1807 and 1832 he published about half a dozen plays, several of which were written under the pseudonym César-Auguste.

Michel-Ange **Lancret** (1774–1807), 75th member of the Sophisians, was an engineer and mathematician who participated in the Egyptian campaign as a scientist. Upon arrival in Cairo he was put in charge of requisitioning the possessions—real estate and furniture—abandoned by the former Mameluke rulers. He was instrumental in the topographical exploration of the Nile delta, refurbished a canal linking Alexandria to the Nile, and investigated the system for the collection of real estate taxes under the Mamelukes, the French reform of which triggered the first revolt against the new rulers. As a member of the mathematics section in the Institut d'Égypte (presided over by none other than Napoleon himself), Lancret made history when he became the first scholar to present the newly discovered Rosetta stone before a learned society. Another one of his lectures concerned the cult of serpents in Said. Lancret joined Fourier's scientific mission to explore Upper Egypt down to Philae before returning to France in 1801. In 1805, following the death of Conté, he became the general editor of the *Description de l'Égypte* and in this capacity helped to define what constituted the "scientific" exploration of Egypt. Many of the topographical descriptions and maps in the *Description* can be traced back to Lancret.

Philippe-Jacques de **Laroche** (b. 1765), 25th member of the Sophisians, frequently wrote under the pseudonym Létoile Hubert. He was active in the lodge of the *Frères Artistes* between 1818 and 1827. Like Cuvelier, Delaroche was a prolific author of melodramatic plays written mostly for the Théâtre de la Gaîté and the Théâtre de l'Ambigu-Comique between 1806 and 1825. He coauthered with Cuvelier two theater pieces, *Bélisaire* (1815), inspired by a novel of Mme de Genlis, and *L'Homicide, ou Les Amis du Mogol* (1817). Laroche also wrote a poem delivered at the funerary service for fellow Sophisian Paul-Louis Mariton in 1819.

Lartigue, 125th member of the Sophisians, worked as a cashier in a bank.

Antoine-Charles-Louis Comte de **Lasalle** (1775–1809), 52nd member of the Sophisians, met Bonaparte during the conquest of Italy in 1796 and joined the Egyptian campaign two years later. Lasalle's saying that the "waters of the Nile are not champagne" summarized the sentiment of deception widely shared across the French troops upon arriving in Northern Africa. After the Battle of the Pyramids, he was promoted to the rank of colonel of the hussars. Lasalle also followed General Desaix's expedition down the Nile to Aswan, but returned to France in early 1800. Subsequently, he participated in the Napoleonic Wars in Germany, Poland, and Spain, where he served under another Sophisian, Jean-Baptiste Bessière. His military career culminated in a promotion to division general on December 30, 1806. Lasalle was killed in action during the Battle of Wagram in July 1809; his name is inscribed on the east side of the Arc de Triomphe.

Jean **Laurès** (b. 1750), 69th member of the Sophisians, was active in the lodge of the *Frères Artistes* between 1801 and 1824. He appeared among the five *Isiarques* of the order by 1821, attesting to his high standing in the group. Laurès's professional life seems to have been uneventful: he held changing administrative positions in the ministry of finance and custom offices during the Consulate and Empire, but was retired by the time of the Restoration.

Nicolas-Eloi **Lemaire** (1767–1832), 65th member of the Sophisians, participated in the activities of the *Frères Artistes* between 1818 and 1819. By 1821, Lemaire held the Sophisian rank of *Harpocrate*, responsible for the maintenance of silence during the rituals. Outside the Sophisian "Pyramid," Lemaire was a professor of Latin, rhetoric, and classical poetry at the University of Paris. When the Revolution broke out, he had just finished his education at the Collège de Sainte-Barbe and the Collège Duplessis-Sorbonne, and was about to start his teaching career. During the Terror, equipped with his *certificat du civisme* issued by the same section over which Lacépède presided, he and Geoffroy Saint-Hilaire managed to free their imprisoned professor-colleagues from the Jardin royal des Plantes, suspect only on account of the name of their institution. Lemaire reemerged in a nonacademic context only in 1798/99, when he was named commissioner of the government to the Parisian central bureau of police. In this function he closed down the Société du Manège, a neo-Jacobin society, which earned him the hatred of many unrepentant Revolutionaries. Lemaire was about to be appointed minister of the interior by the Directory when Napoleon's coup d'état put an end to his political ambitions. He returned to his academic career, but managed to retain a minor post in the ministry of the interior, reporting to Lucien Bonaparte. By 1803 Lemaire's personal situation had become so unstable that he decided to leave for Italy, where he enchanted audiences in Milan, Parma, and Turin with his skills at improvisation in Latin verse. At the same time he began work on his Latin edition of Pliny, which would amount to more than thirty volumes. Upon his return from Italy, he was elected to the Institut and published a Latin poem in the style of Virgil on the occasion of the first birthday of Napoleon's son, the King of Rome (*Virgile expliqué par le siècle de Napoléon*, 1812). In 1820 it was Lemaire who formally introduced Guerrier de Dumast's prose poem *La Maçonnerie* before the assembled *Frères Artistes*.

Jean-Frédéric-Auguste **Lemière de Corvey** (1771-1832), 71st member of the Sophisians, was associated with the *Frères Artistes* between 1797 and 1813. Like Cuvelier de Trie, he was both a soldier and an author of melodramatic plays who also concerned himself with the writing of musical scores for opera and theater. At the outbreak of the Revolution, Lemière worked as a composer and playwright for the Théâtre Montansier, which he left in 1792 to serve as a volunteer during the Revolutionary Wars, possibly in the *Compagnie des artistes dramatiques* along with Cuvelier de Trie and Alexandre Duval. Lemière's commitment to the ideals of the Revolution is further attested by his participating as a lieutenant in the storming of the Tuileries in August 1792. By 1794 he collaborated with fellow Sophisian Alexandre Duval, whose plays for the Opéra-Comique he coauthored and set to music. During the Napoleonic Wars, Lemière was called to arms again and fought in Holland, Italy, Germany, Poland, Dalmatia, and Spain. After capturing an Austrian general in Italy, he received a promotion to division commander. Although he had to fight again in the Battle of Waterloo in 1815, Lemière longed to return to his vocation as a composer, which he was able to pursue full-time only during the Restoration. All in all, he wrote about twenty plays, sixty musical scores, and a military treatise about the alleged superiority of irregular armed forces over a disciplined army (*Des partisans et des corps irréguliers*, 1823).

Pierre-Joseph **Lion** (b. 1737), 81st member of the Sophisians and associated with the *Frères Artistes* between 1801 and 1813, was born at Point-à-Pitre, Guadeloupe.[11] He sat in the Convention and later the Conseil des Cinq-Cents (1795–97) as a deputy of the French colony where he originated. During the Empire he also worked in the paymaster general's office of the French army. He was initiated into the lodge *La Tendre Fraternité* at Saint-Pierre Martinique in 1774.

Jean-Thomas-Guillaume **Lorge** (1768–1826), 63rd member of the Sophisians, was associated with the *Frères Artistes* lodge between 1818 and 1822. A career soldier of humble origins, Lorge joined the military under the ancien régime. In September 1793 he was promoted to brigadier general and served in the Rhine army under General Kléber by 1795. Between 1798 and 1800 he fought with the French army in Switzerland and Italy, and was promoted to division general in April 1799. Subsequently, he participated in the Napoleonic Wars in Germany, Spain, Poland, and Russia. After the collapse of the Empire, Louis XVIII made Lorge his commissioner to arrange the return of the remaining prisoners of war from Spain and Portugal, for which he was rewarded with the title *chevalier de Saint Louis* in July 1814. Lorge's name is inscribed on the north side of the Arc de Triomphe.

Charles-René **Magon de Médine** (1763–1805), 32nd member of the Sophisians, was a captain in the navy. He completed numerous tours of duty to protect French trade and colonial interests in the Indian Ocean between 1786 and 1798. Among his greatest accomplishments was the reclaiming of the island of Diego Garcia from the British in late 1786. When Magon finally returned to France in 1798, he discovered that he had fallen into disfavor with the Directory government because of Sans-culotte accusations dating from the Revolution. Magon's name was cleared, and in 1801 he was sent on a new mission to Saint-Domingue (Haiti), where he destroyed the Fort Dauphin. By 1802 he was confirmed a rear admiral. Magon died at the Battle of Trafalgar in 1805. His name is inscribed on the south side of the Arc de Triomphe.

Étienne-Louis **Malus de Mitry** (1775–1812), 83rd member of the Sophisians, was a distinguished physicist and engineer.[12] While still a young man, he made breakthrough discoveries in optics, especially in the polarization of light and refractions on curved surfaces. In 1793 he was called up by the army and developed an expertise in the building of fortresses, acquired while working on the reinforcement of the harbor at Dunkirk. He subsequently became one of the very first students at the newly founded École Polytechnique, established by another Sophisian, Gaspar Monge. Malus participated in the Egyptian campaign as both a scientist and a soldier. He fought in the Battle of the Pyramids, fortified the port of Damietta, and was named a founding member of the mathematics section in the Institut d'Égypte, presided over by Napoleon. Malus was one of the few Sophisians who participated in the Syrian campaign, where he organized the makeshift military hospital of Jaffa, rendered famous through Antoine-Jean Gros's painting in the Louvre. Although Malus contracted the plague during his stay in Jaffa, he survived and remained in Egypt until the end of the campaign in 1801. After his return to Europe, he settled in the German town of Giessen, where he married the daughter of the local university's chancellor. He dedicated the rest of his life completely to his scientific research in physics. However, the events of the Egyptian campaign had seriously compromised his health, a circumstance that contributed to Malus's premature death in 1812.

Pierre-Thomas **Malvezin**, 93rd member of the Sophisians, was a notary from Bordeaux who practiced in this city between 1820 and 1834.[13]

Paul Louis **Mariton, Sr.** (1760–1819), 57th member of the Sophisians, figured among the order's five *Philisiarque* officers. He is documented as an active member of the *Frères Artistes* between 1807 and 1813. Mariton was a Parisian banker who may have supported the group financially. His death in 1819 was universally mourned by Cuvelier de Trie's adepts, as attested by their funerary rituals, poems, and speeches published in the Masonic periodical *Hermès, ou Archives Maçonniques*.

Abdallah Jacques de **Menou** (1750–1810), 33rd member of the Sophisians, played a preeminent role in French Revolutionary politics and the Egyptian campaign. During the ancien régime he already had obtained the rank of field marshal when the Revolution broke out. A member of the nobility, he was elected deputy of the Estates General in 1789. Subsequently, he figured amongst the small minority of nobles who switched sides and supported the Third Estate in its struggle against the clergy and the aristocracy. As the events of the Revolution unfolded, Menou became one of the principal proponents of a conscription army. Although he had just been promoted to the rank of division general, he shrank from putting down the uprising of the seditious Faubourg Saint-Antoine in 1795, as ordered by the Directory. His assignment was finally accomplished by Bonaparte, who called Menou back to active duty for the Egyptian campaign in 1798. During the expedition, in March 1799, he married a native wife, converted to Islam, and adopted the name of Abdallah. After the assassination of Napoleon's successor, General Kléber, by Muslim radicals (June 1800), Menou became the last French commander-in-chief in Egypt, but had to surrender the colony to the British in August 1801. It was Menou who had fellow Sophisian General Reynier arrested by Destaing in Alexandria to quell the growing discontent with his style of leadership during the last phase of French rule over Egypt. Despite Menou's incompetence, Napoleon continued to support him and would not allow any criticism of his decisions. Menou was subsequently made governor of the Piedmont region in Italy and died, severely in debt, as governor of Venice on August 13, 1810. His name is inscribed on the south side of the Arc de Triomphe.

Mercier, 7th member of the Sophisians, became a Parisian police officer (*Inspecteur officier de paix*) in 1815.[14]

Mical, 5th member of Sophisians, was a *sous-préfet* in Limoges.

Michel, 94th member of the Sophisians, was a banker in Paris.

Louis **Milfort** (1752–1820), 41st member of the Sophisians, was born under the name of Jean-Antoine Leclerc. He adopted a number of aliases during his lifetime, including Jean Leclerc Milfort, Louis Le Clerc Milfort, and, most importantly, Tastanegy, or Grand Chief of War of the Creek Indian Confederacy. Milfort's life as an adventurer began after he allegedly killed a servant in the king's household during a duel. A soldier of fortune, he fled to North America in 1775, where he became the Creek nation's Tastanegy, a charge he obtained because of his friendship with Alexander McGillivray, the Scottish Indian Head Chief of the nation. Milfort stayed with the Creeks for at least ten years, adopted the lifestyle of the Indians, and married McGillivray's sister. Allegedly, he refused to let President George Washington bribe him with a general's commission and commensurate pay in exchange for betraying the interests of his tribe. His tenure as Grand Chief of War came to an end around 1795, when he began to make arrangements for a return to his home country in order to broker a Franco-Creek military alliance. Before Milfort left America, he had to obtain a passport from the French ambassador to the U.S. government in Philadelphia, Jean-Antoine Fauchet, another future Sophisian. Upon his arrival in Paris, he immediately began lobbying for the acquisition of Creek territory and the repossession of Louisiana by France. To this end, with the help of a ghostwriter, Milfort published a romanticized account of his life with the Creek Indians (*Mémoire, ou Coup-d'oeil rapide sur* *mes différents voyages et mon séjour dans la nation crĕck*, 1802). Milfort's book was apparently inspired by the prospect of riches to be gained from a French expedition to Louisiana under his command, the planning of which was supported by the foreign ministers Delacroix and Talleyrand-Périgord. The French political agenda for the Louisiana territory shifted during the Consulate. Napoleon, who considered the possession a political and financial liability, finalized the sale of Louisiana to the United States in 1803. Not only were Milfort's hopes dashed, but he also acquired a reputation with France's military administration as troublemaker. To quiet his constant demands, he was promoted to general, but sent instantly into retirement, cushioned by a generous pension.

August-Aubin **Millin de Grandmaison** (1759–1818), 48th member of the Sophisians, was one of France's premier natural scientists, publicists, and antiquarians at the turn of the nineteenth century. Independently wealthy, he developed an early interest in botany and languages, both classical and modern, during the 1780s. He attended courses taught at the Muséum d'histoire naturelle, helped found the French chapter of the Société Linnéenne, and worked in the Bibliothèque du Roi. During the Revolution, he lost most of his personal fortunes. Nevertheless, his pro-Revolutionary fervor was unwavering, as attested by his editorial work for the *Chronique de Paris*. Among his many writings from these years, Millin composed a treatise advocating the abolition of theater privileges, a condition for the rise of boulevard theaters during the 1790s (*Sur la liberté du théâtre*, 1790). Arrested during the Terror, he subsequently became one of the division heads in the Commission de l'instruction publique, together with Cuvelier de Trie. The year 1794 was a watershed in Millin's intellectual development, because he accepted a position as curator of antiquities and medals in the Bibliothèque Nationale, which shifted his interests to classical art; the same year he also became the editor of the *Magazine encyclopédique*. As a consequence, his interest in the natural sciences waned; he sold his ornithological collection and began acquiring Egyptian, Greek, Roman, and Gothic antiquities, along with large numbers of books and engravings, for his private cabinet. Of great interest to Millin were medals and coins. An extended trip to Italy in 1811/12 yielded a particularly rich harvest of more than seven hundred artifacts. During the Restoration, either Millin's or Denon's *cabinet de curiosité* was a required stop on any trip to Paris for Europe's educated elites. In the course of his lifetime Millin published more than 250 books and monographs, most of which deal with the natural sciences and the history of art in classical antiquity.

Gaspar **Monge** (1746–1818), 38th member of the Sophisians, was another scientist of international reputation, best known for his work as a geometrician and his invention of "descriptive geometry," which revolutionized the drawing of engineering plans for architecture, masonry, and stonecutting. Because his method was introduced to improve fortress design, it was kept secret for many years by the French army's corps of engineers. After the storming of the Tuileries on August 10, 1792, Monge entered the political scene and became interim minister of the navy in Danton's cabinet, in which capacity he figured among the signatories on the death warrant of Louis XVI in January 1793. Arrested by Robespierre, he was set free because his engineering skills were needed for the production of cannon and gunpowder. Subsequently, he became one of the founders of the École Polytechnique. Monge came to Napoleon's attention during the 1796 campaign in Italy, when he organized the shipping and restoration of works of art plun-

dered by the French occupiers. He helped prepare the Egyptian campaign by confiscating Arabic typeface from the presses of the Vatican. Immediately after embarkation, he joined Bonaparte's inner circle on board the *Orient* as a sign of the commander's special favor. Upon arrival in Cairo, he was appointed first president of the Institut d'Égypte; Napoleon, like Monge a member of the mathematics section, reserved for himself the vice-presidency. Together with Berthollet, Monge supervised all scientific and archeological missions by the French scholars in Egypt. During the revolt of Cairo, it was he who organized the defense of the Institut. Monge also wrote numerous archeological descriptions of ancient Egyptian monuments, and participated in the disastrous Syrian campaign, in the course of which he narrowly survived the plague epidemic. When the time came for Napoleon to leave Egypt in 1799, Monge was again with him on board the *Murion*. Upon his return to France, he was made president of the Commission des sciences et des arts, which supervised and edited the publication of the official *Description de l'Égypte*. Highly decorated, he returned to his professorship at the École Polytechnique and participated in the Russian campaign, but was stripped of all honors and positions during the Restoration.

Nezot, 74th member of the Sophisians, is described in the Golden Book as a Greek living and working on the Ionian Islands (Corfu, Paxos, Lefkas, Cephalonia, Ithaca, Zante, and Cerigo, comprising the Septinsular Republic between 1800 and 1807) as an interpreter of Oriental languages. The Ionian Islands were in French possession from 1807 through 1814, and French cultural influence remained strong even after the end of Bonaparte's rule in matters such as education, scientific knowledge, and language.[15]

Claude-Etienne **Niodet** (b. 1797), 117th member of the Sophisians, was associated with the *Frères Artistes* between 1819 and 1822. By 1821, he held the Sophisian rank of *Pastophore*, or carrier of the Ark during the order's ceremonies. The lodge's archives describe him initially as a student of law in Dijon, later as an attorney in the provinces.

Jean-Baptiste-André **Noiseux** (b. 1760), 9th member of the Sophisians, participated in the activities of the *Frères Artistes* between 1807 and 1813. He was a naval commissioner responsible for the transport of chain-ganged prisoners to the marine base at Rochefort (*commissaire de la conduite des chaînes*), where they would be subject to forced labor in the ship yards. In April 1792 Noiseux himself was detained for excessive cruelty used against a group of prisoners he brought from Orléans to Rochefort. Nevertheless, he was soon released and continued to work as prison officer at least until the end of the Napoleonic era.

Charles **Norry** (1756–1832), 8th member of the Sophisians, was active in the lodge of the *Frères Artistes* between 1807 and 1813. Norry had joined the Egyptian campaign as an architect, charged with the task of building barracks, army hospitals, and a gunpowder factory. He was a student of Charles de Wailly, builder of the original Odéon theater in Paris, whom he had accompanied during Wailly's travels to Russia, Switzerland, and Italy. Norry was a founding member of the literature and arts section of the Institut d'Égypte, where he presented his archeological measurements of the "Pompey's Pillar" in Alexandria, undertaken during the month of August 1798. Homesick and disillusioned, Norry narrowly avoided the revolt of Cairo, which was described to him in a letter by fellow Sophisian Geoffroy Saint-Hilaire.[16] Following the uprising, he resigned from the Institut in the fall of 1798 to leave for France. Norry's attitude towards the events of the Egyptian campaign changed significantly after his return. He began to glorify his experiences, first in a short travel description (*Relation de l'expédition d'Égypte*, 1802), later in a play following the model of Cuvelier de Trie's melodramas that he claimed to have written in 1801, while being quarantined in Ancona (*L'Entrée des Français au Kaire*, 1830). During the Empire, Norry was employed by the ministry of the interior as inspector general of civilian buildings and contributed to the *Description de l'Égypte*; after 1815 he continued to serve on the advisory board for royal buildings.

Palleman, 92nd member of the Sophisians, was a pharmacist in the Périgord.

Joseph **Pariset** (1770–1835), 10th member of the Sophisians, participated as a sergeant major in the Egyptian and Syrian campaigns. Pariset served as a quartermaster during the Revolutionary Wars in 1792/93. For his military accomplishments in Egypt he was promoted to the ranks of lieutenant (1799) and captain (1801). Together with Cuvelier de Trie he was stationed at the camp de Boulogne in anticipation of an invasion of Great Britain in 1805/6, and participated in the Napoleonic campaign in Germany, where he was wounded in the Battle of Jena in October 1806.

Parrot-Laboissière, 91st member of the Sophisians, was a lawyer in the Périgord.

François-Pierre **Petitbeau** (b. 1786), 103rd member of the Sophisians, is documented as active in the *Frères Artistes* lodge between 1822 and 1828. By 1821 he held the Sophisian office of *Agathophile*, and earned his living as a pharmacist in Paris.

Demetrios N. **Photilas** (b. 1787), 114th member of the Sophisians, was part of a group of Greeks who joined the *Frères Artistes* around the time of the outbreak of the Greek War of Independence in 1821. He signed the lodge's membership roll only once, in 1822. Like the leader of the group of exiles, Nicolos Sava Piccolos, Photilas was a professor at the Princely Academy (Academy of Saint-Sava) in Bucharest, where he taught Greek between 1816 and 1821. The Princely Academy was a hotbed of Greek resistance to Ottoman domination, linked to the *Philiki Hetairia*, a para-Masonic secret society that organized the national uprising against the Turks from Western Europe. Both of Cuvelier de Trie's societies were adamantly philhellenic, embracing the cause of Greek national liberation as their own. Photilas's presence in Bucharest is still attested in 1820, when he played as a lay actor in a modern-Greek adaptation of Plutarch's *Phocion*. Apparently, he settled in Paris at about the time of the closing of the Princely Academy in 1821 and was still actively engaged in militant French and German philhellenic societies by 1829.

Louis-Alexandre **Piccinni** (1779–1850), 29th member of the Sophisians, engaged in the activities of the *Frères Artistes* between 1813 and 1822. Louis-Alexandre was the grandson of the famous Italian composer of operas Niccolò Piccinni, who celebrated his greatest triumphs in Paris, where he frequented Voltaire's lodge of the *Neuf Soeurs*. Louis-Alexandre was trained to become a musician and composer from his earliest childhood. But whereas his grandfather performed at the Royal Academy of Music, Louis-Alexandre's world was initially that of the boulevard theaters. He received some brief training from Niccolò in 1799 before starting his career at

the Théâtre Freydeau (1802) and the Théâtre des Arts (formerly Théâtre Montansier, 1804). Thereafter, he worked intermittently for the Théâtre de la Porte Saint-Martin (1803–7, 1810–16) while holding the official position of second accompanist to the emperor's chapel (1804). Louis-Alexandre's fortunes rose after the return of the Bourbons. In 1814 he was appointed chief accompanist of the royal chapel and accompanist of the dauphine's private music. By 1816 he was *Maître de chant* at the Royal Academy. In addition, he held positions with the Parisian Opéra, climbing from third chorus master to first, and overseeing stage designs in the 1820s. From the latter position he was dismissed without cause in 1826, in protest of which he published a pamphlet. Besides these official commitments, Piccinni composed many musical scores for the ceremonies of the *Frères Artistes* and the Sophisians. In 1811 he set to music Cuvelier de Trie's *Conseils de Mentor dans l'asile du silence*, a play with strong Sophisian overtones. Eight years later, he is mentioned as the lodge's *maître de l'Harmonie*. In this role he performed during the funerary ceremonies for the deceased Sophisian Mariton in 1819 and at *Fête de la Sophisienne* in 1821.

Nicolos Sava **Piccolos** (1792–1866), 115th member of the Sophisians, was the leader of the exiled group of philhellenic professors from the defunct Princely Academy of Bucharest (Academy of Saint-Sava), who were admitted to Cuvelier de Trie's groups between 1819 and 1821. Despite Piccolos's fervent Greek patriotism, he was of Bulgarian descent. His real name was Nicolas Savov Hadžiiliev, but he assumed the name Piccolos—derived from the Italian "piccolo" in reference to his short height—during his studies in Padua. As a scholar, Piccolos made a name for himself in Balkan intellectual circles for his translations into modern Greek of texts by French Enlightenment authors such as Descartes, Rousseau, and Bernardin de Saint-Pierre. Himself a graduate of the Princely Academy, he returned to teach French at his alma mater between 1810 and 1816. Piccolos left Bucharest long before the closing of the Academy in 1821 and settled with his former teacher, Konstantinos Vardalachos, on the Greek island of Chios, where he continued his teaching activity between 1816 and 1817. By 1818 he had followed Vardalachos to Odessa, where he adapted Sophocles' tragedy *Philoctetes* to modern Greek. Political activities and association with the *Philiki Hetairia* now played a central role in his life. In October 1818 he traveled to Paris to study medicine and to muster support for the Greek battle of independence. While in France, he collaborated closely with Adamantios Korais, another linguist and the public figurehead of the Greek battle for political liberation, who used Piccolos as a liaison with philhellenic supporters in London in 1821. Concurrently, Piccolos became acquainted with the Sophisian Guerrier de Dumast, who translated one of his patriotic poems into French (*Chios, la Grèce et l'Europe*, 1822), and who arranged for the introduction of the Greek faction to Cuvelier de Trie. In 1822 Piccolos left Paris to fight in Greece. Before long, however, he decided to accept a teaching position in philosophy at Lord Guilford's newly founded Ionian Academy at Corfu. He only stayed on the British-controlled island until 1825, when he settled in Bologna to complete his doctorate degree in medicine, which was finally conferred by the Academy of Pisa in 1829. He returned to Bucharest to practice medicine during the 1830s, but moved back permanently to Paris in 1840, where he died in 1865.

Pigault-Maubaillarcq, 2nd member of the Sophisians, was a merchant from Calais who attempted to build a literary career by following the example of his brother, Pigault-Lebrun, a celebrated writer of theater plays and adventure novels during the Empire and the Restoration. He was also a commander in the National Guard of Cuvelier de Trie's native region of Pas-de-Calais. Pigault-Maubaillarcq's two principal narratives, *La Famille Wieland, ou Les Prodigues* (1808) and *Isaure d'Aubigné* (1812), an epistolary novel, purport to be translations from the English language.

Marie-Nicolas **Ponce-Camus** (1775–1839), 96th member of the Sophisians, participated in the activities of the *Frères Artistes* between 1813 and 1824 and, in his roles as *garde des sceaux et des archives* and *maître des fêtes* (1819–22), created the Sophisians' *Livre d'or* of the Bibliothèque Nationale. Presumably, it was also he who conceived the special effects that were part of Sophisian initiation ceremonies. A student of Jacques-Louis David, Ponce-Camus began exhibiting history paintings and portraits in the Salon of 1802; he also worked as a miniature painter and stage engineer for the popular theaters on the boulevard du Temple. To prepare him for a career as a notary, Ponce-Camus received his early education at the Collège des Quatre-Nations. Objecting to his parents' wish for him to pursue a career in the legal profession, he began frequenting David's studio in the 1790s, but was called to fight during the Revolutionary Wars and later to serve as an officer in the National Guard during the Directory. Through the first three decades of the nineteenth century Ponce-Camus appears to have made a living by arranging the special effects for the Théâtre de la Gaîté and the Cirque Olympique, frequently collaborating with Cuvelier de Trie. His greatest success as a history painter was the exhibition of *Napoleon Meditating before the Coffin of Frederick II of Prussia* in the Salon of 1808, which pleased the emperor so much that he acquired it for his country retreat at Versailles. Ponce-Camus secured a number of commissions during the Empire, mostly of subjects celebrating Napoleonic grandeur (*Napoleon at Osterode*, 1810; *Meeting of His Majesty the Emperor and His Royal Highness Prince Charles*, 1812). His devotion to David and his reputation as a painter of Napoleonic themes brought Ponce-Camus into conflict with the Bourbon arts administration, and his composition *Alexander Visiting the Studio of Apelles* was banned from the Salon of 1819 on account of its being a thinly disguised allegory of Bonaparte's patronage of David. Although he confined himself to privately commissioned portrait painting thereafter, Ponce-Camus continued to show regularly in the Salon until 1831.

Florimond-Benjamin-Joseph **Prissette** (1777–1839), 99th member of the Sophisians, was a director of the revenue offices at Aachen (1804) and Maastricht (1808) under the Napoleonic occupation of Germany and the Netherlands. During the Restoration he was the financial controller responsible for Cuvelier de Trie's native region Pas-de-Calais (1815), from whence he moved on to become the head administrator of several French arrondissements and départements, including Le Havre (1819) and Beauvais (1831).

Louis-Charles-Antoine le Marquis de **Puisaye** (1779–1824), 84th member of the Sophisians, was associated with the *Frères Artistes* between 1819 and 1822 and held the Sophisian rank of *Hermophile* by 1821. In his *Chroniques des petits théâtres*, Brazier described de Puisaye's father a "rich capitalist" who bought the Théâtre de l'Ambigu-Comique in 1798, when the establishment was in financial difficulties. He invested heavily in the remodeling of the premises, which earned him such great returns on his investment that he abandoned all other forms of financial speculation to become

a theater entrepreneur. Louis-Antoine's mother, who directed the theater for a while after her husband's death, was one of the most prominent Sophisiennes. The Puisaye family was known for its monarchist and pro-Bourbon sympathies.

Michel-Louis-Étienne **Regnaud de Saint-Jean-d'Angély** (1760–1819), 72nd member of the Sophisians, was a politician and lawyer often nicknamed Napoleon's "gray eminence" because he partly authored (2,281 articles) and edited the *Code civil* in 1804.[17] A childhood friend of the first "martyr" of the Revolution, the regicide Lepeletier de Saint-Fargeau, Regnaud was a deputy of the Estates General in 1789, in which role he drafted legal documents for the Third Estate. Later on he also sat in the Convention. Regnaud was put in prison as an alleged Girondin sympathizer under Robespierre, but managed to survive the Terror unharmed. During the Italian campaign he served as an administrator of army hospitals, which gave him the opportunity to meet Napoleon. He embarked with the French troops destined for Egypt in 1798, but fell sick during the passage so that he was forced to stay behind on Malta, conquered by Napoleon en route to North Africa. Regnaud was appointed government commissioner of the island during the French occupation. On the 18th of Brumaire he immediately rallied to Bonaparte, who subsequently showered him with honors and appointments, such as Councilor of State, Attorney-General at the Imperial High Court (*procureur général de la Haute Cour impériale*, 1804), Secretary of State to the Imperial Family (1807), and member of the French Academy (1803). A deputy in the Chambre des cent jours of 1815, he convinced Napoleon during the last phase of his rule to resign in favor of his son. The Bourbons treated Regnaud harshly. He was added to the list of the thirty-three exiles from Paris, which resulted in an Odyssey between 1816 and 1817 that included stops in New York, Holland, Aachen, and Brussels. Regnaud was only allowed to return to France when he was dying in 1819. Regnaud had been an active participant in French Masonic life since 1789, and in 1807 he became Honorary Grand Orator of the Grand Orient.

Jean-Louis-Ébénézer **Reynier** (1771–1814), 1st member of the Sophisians, may have been the original founder of the order during the Egyptian campaign. Reynier was a Swiss from Lausanne who first served as a volunteer in the French armies of the Revolutionary Wars from 1792 to 1794. During the Directory he held several military appointments in Holland and Germany. In 1797/98 he was charged with the preparation of the Egyptian campaign, to which end he was promoted to the rank of division general. Once in Egypt, he fought in the Battle of the Pyramids, helped repress the revolt of Cairo, participated in the Syrian campaign, was elected a member of the Institut d'Égypte (section for political economy), and became governor of the province of Charkieh. After General Kléber's assassination, Reynier chaired the judicial proceedings against the radical Islamists who perpetrated the killing. An open opponent of the new commander-in-chief of Egypt, he was arrested on Menou's order by General Destaing in May 1801 and shipped back to France. In Paris he lost no time publishing a treatise revealing Menou's incompetence (*De l'Égypte après la bataille d'Héliopolis*, 1802), which was censored by Napoleon, who ordered the destruction of all available copies. On May 5, 1802, Reynier challenged Destaing to a duel, in which the latter was killed. In response to these events, Reynier was temporarily banned from Paris, but later participated in the Napoleonic wars in Italy, Spain, Portugal, Germany, Poland, and Russia. His name is inscribed on the south side of the Arc de Triomphe.

Jacques **Richard** (b. 1757), 82nd member of the Sophisians, was associated with the *Frères Artistes* between 1796 and 1822. A member of the Academy of Music, Richard was a ballet master at the Parisian Opéra and held an additional appointment at the Théâtre des Arts in the early 1800s.

Simon Alexandre **Rotrou** (1769/70–1819), 11th member of the Sophisians, was associated with the *Frères Artistes* between 1807 and 1819. Rotrou was employed in the paymaster-general's office of the French navy between 1784 and 1789, before being appointed colonial deputy commissioner of the Ile de France (Mauritius) in the Indian Ocean, where he stayed from 1790 to 1799. On account of his bad health, he returned to France via Boston, New York, and Hamburg in 1799. During the French occupation of Holland, he served as commissioner of the marine in charge of supplies in Antwerp (1807–12) and Rotterdam (1812–13), where he was severely injured during an uprising.

Joquin **Roussel**, 111th member of the Sophisians, is described in the Golden Book as an *homme de lettres*.

Hector **Rouxelles** (b. 1794), 55th member of the Sophisians, appears in the archives of the *Frères Artistes* in 1824. He is described as a proprietor and *homme de lettres*.

Henry **Royanez** (b. 1754 or 1755), 40th member of the Sophisians, was engaged in the activities of the *Frères Artistes* between 1808 and 1819. Previously, he had been an employee in the customs house of Alexandria during the Egyptian campaign. General Kléber charged Royanez in December 1799 to find a marble block for the sculptor Jean-Jacques Castex, whom he had commissioned to produce a replica of the zodiac discovered in the temple complex at Denderah.[18] Royanez was a lawyer by training who later worked as a secretary in the prefecture of Mezière.

Saint-Brice, Jr., 80th member of the Sophisians, was associated with the *Frères Artistes* between 1808 and 1813. He was a commissioner of the navy stationed in Boulogne, Trieste, and Antwerp during the Empire.

Constantin and Christopher **Sakellarios**, 107th and 108th members of the Sophisians, were brothers of Greek descent associated with the Princely Academies of Bucharest and Jassy. Their presence in Paris by February 1820 is attested in the context of their overseeing a Franco-Greek edition of Fénélon's *Télémaque* translated by Demetre Govdelas, a professor at the Princely Academy in Jassy. The publication, sponsored by a wealthy Moldavian boyar named Nicolas Rosetti-Roznovanu, was printed in one thousand copies and features many engravings. Concurrent with this project, Constantin Sakellarios corresponded with Piccolos, which suggests a shared interest in the cause for Greek national and cultural revival.

Jean-François-Auguste **Sarraire** (1772–1810), 14th member of the Sophisians, may have met Cuvelier de Trie while serving as first lieutenant of the *guides interprètes* of Napoleon's army assembled at the camp de Boulogne (1804/5).[19] He participated in the siege of Genoa in 1800 and the campaigns against Prussia (1806), Poland (1807), and Austria (1809). By the time of his death in the Balkans in 1810, he was a colonel in the Eighth Light Infantry Regiment.

Pierre **Selme** (b. 1774), 122nd member of the Sophisians, was a businessman and lawyer who participated in the activities of the *Frères Artistes* between 1811 and 1825.

Göran Magnus Baron **Sprengporten** (1740–1819), 53rd member of the Sophisians and a native of Swedish-Finland, emerged on the European political scene in 1772, when, as a general in the Swedish army, he helped king Gustavus III overturn the old Swedish constitution and quashed resistance to restored royal power in the Stockholm Senate. For this maneuver, he used loyal troops from the Finnish province that he governed. After a dispute with Gustavus III, he traveled to Holland and Russia, where he held a position as chamberlain and lieutenant-general under Catherine the Great in St. Petersburg. He helped defend Russian interests against incursions from the Ottoman empire in the south, when Gustavus III declared his intentions to attack St. Petersburg in 1788. Again, Sprengporten used his connections in the Finnish province to thwart the plans of his former master by kindling Finnish nationalist sentiments. Later, as a diplomat in the service of Czar Paul I, he negotiated the peace treaty and subsequent alliance between France and Russia. To this end he traveled to Paris in 1800, an experience that made him a great admirer of Napoleon and Napoleonic France.[20] In 1809 he helped Czar Alexander I engineer a successful revolution against Gustavus III, for which he was rewarded with the post of governor-general of the Finnish province.

Albert-Louis-Valentin **Taviel** (1767–1831), 18th member of the Sophisians, was associated with the *Frères Artistes* between 1819 and 1822 and held the Sophisian rank of *Agthos* by 1821. A career soldier, Taviel participated in the Revolutionary Wars in Corsica and Northern France between 1792 and 1795. Promoted to division general in 1811, he continued to serve during the Napoleonic campaigns in Germany, Switzerland, Austria, Italy, Spain, Portugal, and Russia. Taviel retained his position with the military during the Restoration, when he was employed as inspector of artillery in the Alpes region and on Corsica. His name is inscribed on the west side of the Arc de Triomphe.

Jean-Antoine **Tempié** (1758–1800), 6th member of the Sophisians, actively participated in the *Frères Artistes* lodge in 1797. A lieutenant in the French navy, he died under tragic circumstances in 1800 during the sea battle of Curaçao against the British fleet. Tempié had started his career in the navy as a sailor in 1778 and became a navigator one year later; by 1781 he was a captain stationed in Nantes. On November 6, 1796, Tempié was named navigation supervisor for one of the ports on the island of Guadeloupe (*chef de mouvements d'un port de l'île de Guadeloupe*). Illness, financial troubles, disputes with the military administration, and missed transport vessels, among other misfortunes, endlessly delayed his departure from France. Letters in the archives of the French navy from this period complain that Tempié's "behavior . . . is as miserable as his reputation." When he finally arrived at his destination at the end of December 1798, he learned that the local representative of the Directory government, General Desfourneaux, had already filled his position. Subsequently, Tempié was sent to supervise the fort of the remote island of St. Martin, from which he embarked with the ill-fated expedition against Curaçao. In spring 1801 Tempié's wife and daughter set sail for Guadeloupe to claim their inheritance, only to remain stranded in penury on the island. The Sophisians, however, believed Tempié to be alive and well in Louisiana for many years. Their acquaintance with him may have dated from the preparatory phase of the Egyptian campaign, which coincided with Tempié's drawn-out efforts to secure a passage to Guadeloupe from various French seaports. Predicated on his early joining of the *Frères Artistes* in 1797, Tempié's Sophisian membership must be regarded as honorary.

Luc-Vincent **Thierry, Sr.** (b. 1734), 16th member of the Sophisians, engaged in the activities of the *Frères Artistes* between 1808 and 1813. He was an actor in melodrama who performed on several occasions in Cuvelier de Trie's plays, as for example in the role of Cassandro in *Le Gnôme, ou Harlequin tigre et bienfaisant* (Théâtre des Jeunes Artistes, 1805); as Raymond, an "old (mute) French troubadour," in *L'Entrée des chevaliers français dans Sérica* (Jeux Gymniques, 1811); and as a chamberlain in *Le Volcan, ou L'Anachorète du val des laves* (Cirque Olympique, 1812). Thierry's son was first dancer and instructor of dance at the Ambigu-Comique theater.

Tiron, 95th member of the Sophisians, was a Parisian banker.

Bernard-Jean-Baptiste **Trichon Saint-Paul** (1785–1854), 23rd member of the Sophisians, participated in the activities of the *Frères Artistes* between 1809 and 1819 and worked as paymaster general of the French armies in Spain under Marshals Ney and Bessière, another Sophisian member. In 1809 he was stationed in Portugal and later took part in the battle of Waterloo. After the collapse of Napoleon's empire, he worked for the administration in charge of settling the French foreign debt (*rédacteur à la commission de liquidation des créances étrangères*, 1817–19). During the Second Republic he became the mayor of Bar-le-Duc.

François **Varez** (b. 1780), 90th member of the Sophisians, was associated with the *Frères Artistes* between 1819 and 1822. Besides being a playwright, he also worked as *régisseur général*, first at the Théâtre de la Rue de Chaume (also known as Théâtre du Boudoir des Muses), from which he was lured away to the Théâtre de l'Ambigu-Comique by fellow Sophisian Marquis de Puisaye. By 1827 he left the Ambigu-Comique to work as stage director for the Théâtre de la Gaîté.

Jean-Antoine Comte de **Verdier** (1767–1839), 4th member of the Sophisians, was a career soldier who had already served under the ancien régime as a deputy lieutenant. He participated in the Revolutionary Wars and the Italian campaign, during which he was promoted to brigadier general, before joining Napoleon's expedition to Egypt. Verdier took part in the Battle of the Pyramids and the Syrian campaign. He was commander of the Damietta province and later of Cairo (March 1800), where he was taken prisoner after the capitulation of the capital (September 1800). Together with Reynier, he was part of the internal opposition movement again Menou's rule. Subsequently, he fought in the Napoleonic Wars in Italy, Austria, Spain, and Russia. During the *cent jours* Verdier helped Marshal Brune organize Napoleon's last military stand at Marseilles and later at Toulon. He was sent into retirement during the Restoration. The Sophisian records assign to him, among other posts, that of a "commander of Paris," yet he never seems to have held such a charge officially. His name is inscribed on the south side of the Arc de Triomphe.

Joseph-Marie **Vermant Mariton** (b. 1773), 61st member of the Sophisians, was associated with the *Frères Artistes* between 1801 and 1819. He was a writer (*homme de lettres*), possibly of theatrical plays, and a captain of cavalry. Between 1808 and 1809 he also worked for the French revenue service. During the Restoration he obtained a new charge as captain in the Gendarmerie, guarding chain gangs of prisoners.

Vigeac, 101st member of the Sophisians, was a medical doctor in Paris.

Guillaume-André **Villoteau** (1759–1839), 49th member of the Sophisians, was a musician and musicologist. An ordained priest, Villoteau studied music under Le Sueur in the *Maîtrise* of Le Mans Cathedral and attended classes in Oriental languages at the Sorbonne. During the Revolution he joined the Opéra chorus, soon gaining the post of chorus leader, and appeared as a performer in Cuvelier de Trie's Jacobin play *La Fête de l'Être Suprême* in about 1792. Villoteau participated in the Egyptian campaign as an *artiste musicien*, or musical entertainer, but refused to sing for Bonaparte on account of the scientific nature of his appointment. However, Villoteau was not an academician and never was elected to the Institut d'Égypte. During the campaign, he built a large collection of native musical instruments, which he learned how to play. This collection was later featured in the plates of the *Description de l'Égypte* along with Villoteau's essay on Egyptian music and its history. Villoteau's initial passion concerned the music of the Greek minority in Egypt, but he also learned to appreciate Arabic tunes. After Kléber's assassination, Villoteau became General Menou's secretary during the last phase of the Egyptian campaign. In keeping with the principles of Masonry, Villoteau held a moralizing view on music, believing that its goal was the advancement of civilization as opposed to being pleasurable.

Athanasias **Vogorides** (ca.1785 or 1791–1826), 113th member of the Sophisians, was another former professor at the Princely Academy in Bucharest and a militant supporter of the cause of Greek liberation. Of Bulgarian descent, Vogorides's real name was Athanas Bogoridi of Kotel. He attended the Princely Academy of Bucharest as a student from 1798 to 1805 and returned as a teacher of Latin, German, French, English, and Greek poetry and epistolography (literary composition), as well as of natural sciences, starting in 1810. In 1811 or 1812 Vogorides resigned from this teaching position in Bucharest to study medicine in Vienna. Before long he came to the attention of the Austrian secret services, which prompted him to leave Vienna and to complete his medical studies in Würzburg, where he earned his doctorate degree in 1816. Like Piccolos, Vogorides was a founding member of the Graeco-Dacian Literary Society, promoting modern Greek as a means to shape national identity, a contributing editor to the first modern Greek literary periodical, *Logios Hermes*, a member of the *Philiki Hetairia*, and a close associate of Adamantios Korais, all of which put him squarely at the center of philhellenic political activism. In August 1819 Vogorides settled in Paris, allegedly to practice medicine, but the real reason may have been to assist Korais logistically in organizing the struggle for Greek independence. Over the next three years Vogorides constantly traveled between Paris, Vienna, London, and Walachia. From the dossiers on Vogorides maintained by the Austrian and French secret services in 1821, it emerges that he was mainly concerned with recruiting volunteer soldiers in Western Europe, coordinating their transport to Greece, and collecting and distributing funds donated for the Greek cause. Little is known about Vogorides after 1822, when he was mentioned for the only time in the archives of the *Frères Artistes*. At about this moment, apparently, he became estranged from both Piccolos and Korais, with whom he had even shared an apartment; nonetheless, he was short-listed as a possible candidate to serve as representative of the Greek government to France in 1825. The following year, Vogorides died in Paris. Rumor had it that he was poisoned.

SOPHISIAN MEMBERS AFTER 1821 ACCORDING TO THE BN GOLDEN BOOK (FOL. 27R)

Pierre-Auguste **Adet** (1763–1832) was a medical doctor, chemist, politician, and diplomat. France's revolutionary government sent Adet to Saint-Domingue (Haiti) in 1791 to help put down a slave revolt. He stayed on the island as colonial administrator until after the fall of Robespierre, when he was asked to supervise mines and later to serve as a diplomat in Geneva. In 1795 he was sent to Philadelphia as the new French minister plenipotentiary to the United States, replacing in this position Jean-Antoine-Joseph Fauchet, another future Sophisian. Like Fauchet and Milfort, Adet favored a French repossession of Louisiana. Because of this stance, Franco-American relations deteriorated rapidly so that he could no longer fulfill his functions by November 1796. When he left the United States in April 1797, there was an official state of war with France that did not end until 1800. In 1799 Adet was invited to return to Saint-Domingue as colonial commissioner, which he refused. During the Consulate he became a government adviser on issues dealing with the navy and the colonies. By 1803 he was serving as the prefect of Nièvre. Adet was elected to the French Senate in 1809 and, as a master-counselor at the Court of Accounts (*conseiller-maître à la Cour des comptes*), signed in 1814 the note that sealed Napoleon's fall from power. Nonetheless, during the *cent jours* he rallied again to the Napoleonic cause, which did not prevent him from retaining his position at the Court of Accounts during the second Restoration. Parallel to his activities as a politician, Adet published extensively on chemistry and developed an alternative periodic table, which, however, never gained acceptance.

Charles-François Baron **Desbureaux** (1755–1835) appears as an honorary member on the rolls of the *Frères Artistes* between 1807 and 1828. During the ancien régime Desbureaux was sent as a naval officer to America. He also fought during the Revolutionary Wars in northern France, Belgium, and Germany, and was appointed brigadier and division general, both in 1793. In 1800 a long-forgotten embezzlement scandal over money that Desbureaux had illegally removed from the treasury for invalid soldiers during the siege of Nantes in 1793 attracted renewed attention from the military administration. The investigation does not appear to have affected Desbureaux's military career unduly. In 1801 he commanded the second French expedition against a slave revolt on Saint-Domingue (Haiti), where, upon arrival in 1802, he held the rank of inspector general of the army. However, because of an illness, within a year he returned to France, where he continued to hold leadership positions in Napoleon's army administration. During the first Restoration he was decorated with the title *chevalier de Saint-Louis* (October 1814), but was forced to retire from his military career after the second return of the Bourbons, who would not forgive his renewed support for Napoleon during the *cent jours*.

Jean-Nicolas **Dufour** (b. 1784) was a manufacturer of head scarfs. He is also recorded as an active member of the *Frères Artistes* in the late 1820s.

Pierre **Dumay** (b. 1788), who signed the rolls of the *Frères Artistes* in 1822, was a landscape painter who exhibited two views of Normandy in the Salon of 1837.

Denis-Jean-Joseph **Dufilho** (b. 1799), who is frequently mentioned in the archives of the *Frères Artistes* between 1825 and 1835, was described as a proprietor and an elector.

Francisque-Martin-François **Grenier de Saint-Martin** (1793–1867) was a painter who showed in the Parisian Salon from 1810, when he presented his version of *Atala*, until his death in the 1860s. A student of Jacques-Louis David and Pierre-Narcisse Guérin, Grenier de Saint-Martin started his career with Napoleonic subject matter but after the Restoration concentrated mainly on genre and peasant scenes. Numerous reproductive lithographs, such as the *Mauvais sujet et sa famille*, popularized his art over the course of the nineteenth century.

L. **Grenier de Saint-Martin** was an actor who performed in Cuvelier's plays *Cavallo Dios* (1808) and *Martial et Angélique, ou Le Temoin irrecusable* (1810). Presumably he was the father of the painter Francisque-Martin-François Grenier de Saint-Martin.

Jean-Etienne **Houssement** (b. 1775) was a button manufacturer associated with the *Frères Artistes* between 1809 and 1827.

Jean **Hutz** (b. 1784), member of the *Frères Artistes* in 1824, was associated with the French navy.

Antoine-Edme-Nazère **Jacquotôt** (b. 1758) frequented the *Frères Artistes* lodge between 1825 and 1827. He was an attorney at the royal court during the Restoration.

Alexandre **Jallot** (b. 1794) was listed as a member of the *Frères Artistes* in 1824 and worked as a pharmacist at a hospital.

Louis-Henry **Leroi** (b. 1799) was a trained lawyer and active as a member of the *Frères Artistes* in 1822.

Salomon **Levy** (1773–1829) was a professional soldier with a long career that lasted from 1792 until the end of the Empire. He came from a Jewish background and participated in the Revolutionary Wars. The Directory government sent Levy to fight in Germany and Switzerland. Together with Cuvelier and many other Sophisians, he passed through the camp de Boulogne in 1805/6 and later participated in the campaigns of Spain, Portugal (1808–11), and France (1814). He was promoted to the rank of lieutenant and captain, both in the same year, 1813.

Joseph **Nebel** (b. 1783), a commissioner of war, was listed as a member of the *Frères Artistes* in 1822, when he resided in Britain.

Pierre-Lambert-Florian **Rouma** (b. 1790), an entrepreneur, was active as a member of the *Frères Artistes* between 1822 and 1831.

B. **Vendryes** may have been identical with the director of the Société de Brésil who was the defendant in a case brought against this company which specialized in the import of tropical wood, in the late 1830s.[21]

SOPHISIAN MEMBERS AND ASSOCIATES ATTESTED BY OTHER SOURCES

The Sophisienne **Audinot-D'Aussy** was the wife of the director and co-owner of the Théâtre de l'Ambigu-Comique, Nicolas-Théodore Audinot-D'Aussy. After her husband's death in 1826, she managed the theater in times of financial difficulties.

Jean-Baptiste-Patrice **Beaufils** (1775–1836) was a military doctor who practiced at the army hospital of La Flèche (1795–99), joined the Rhine Army (1799–1801), and accompanied Napoleon's troops to Austria (1806–9), Russia (1812), and Germany (1813). He continued to treat wounded soldiers during the 1814 campaign in France. Documented as a member of the *Frères Artistes* between 1818 and 1824, Beaufils participated as a member of the Sophisian order in the *Fête Sophisienne* of 1821.

The Sophisienne **Berlot** performed as a pianist during the 1821 *Fête Sophisienne*, playing a "fantasy" that she had apparently composed herself.

Frédéric-Charles Vicomte **Bois d'Enemetz** was the father of Edouard-Louis-Maxime-Daniel Comte Bois d'Enemetz, who had the barricades at the Faubourg du Temple, Faubourg St. Antoine, and Belleville demolished during the 1848 revolution. The invitation to the 1821 *Fête Sophisienne* mentions him as a member of the order.

Mme **Camus** was the wife of the painter Marie-Nicolas Ponce-Camus. She performed as a singer and actress in many of Cuvelier's plays, such as the *Conseils de Mentor dans l'Asile du Silence* (1811) and *L'Entrée des cavaliers français dans Serica* (1811).

The Sophisienne **Dengremont** sang the "air of initiation," composed by Louis-Alexandre Piccinni, during the 1821 *Fête Sophisienne*. She may have been the wife of the actor Dengremont, engaged at the Théâtre du Palais-Royal in 1831.[22]

Vivant **Denon** (1747–1825) is often cited in Masonic literature as a member of the Sophisians. A travel writer, art collector, diplomat, archeologist, and museum director, Denon knew Cagliostro first-hand from his tenure at the French embassy in Naples during the 1780s. He subsequently accompanied Napoleon on the Egyptian campaign, which resulted in the publication of an illustrated travel description, the *Voyage dans la Basse et la Haute Égypte* (1802), a book that kindled the taste of Egyptomania during the Consulate and Empire. The literary success of the *Voyage* helped Denon secure the directorship of the Louvre museum under Napoleon's rule. Removed from his position during the Restoration, he remained a fixture of several Masonic lodges, including the adoption (female) lodge *Belle et Bonne*, which maintained ties with Cuvelier's *Frères Artistes*. Denon constitutes a historically unique link between Cagliostro's Egyptian rite and Freemasonry during the Restoration.

Mme **Dondey-Dupré** was the wife of the publisher and Sophisian initiate Auguste-François Dondey-Dupré. She is mentioned in the invitation to the 1821 *Fête Sophisienne* as one of the *Isiades* of the order.

Edmont **Grandmanche** was a medical doctor mentioned in the invitation to the 1821 *Fête Sophisienne* as a Sophisian; he is also listed in 1827 as a member of the *Frères Artistes*.

Louis-Léon Baron **Langlois de Septenville** (1754–1844) came from an old family of ancien régime nobility. In 1768, aged fourteen, he joined the royal musketeers and became a quartermaster in the king's army. Langlois survived the Revolution unharmed and supported Napoleon's coup d'état. A member of the legislative body during the Empire, he remained in the good graces of the Restoration government and subsequently served as a mayor of the town of Montdidier (1823–30).

Montainville's name is mentioned in the Sophisians' *Livre d'or* preserved at the Grand Orient of France. He was apparently spearheading the effort to establish a second Sophisian "pyramid" (temple) in the southern port city of Toulon, for which he was granted charter rights by the order in the early 1810s.

Mme de **Puisaye mère** became the director of the Théâtre de l'Ambigu-Comique in 1816 until she turned it over to another Sophisian, Nicolas-Théodore Audinot-D'Aussy. A Sophisienne, she is mentioned in the invitation to the 1821 *Fête Sophisienne* as one of the *Isiades* of the order.

Pierre **Vignes** (b. 1778) was a medical doctor mentioned in the 1821 invitation to the *Fête Sophisienne* as a member of the order; he was active in the *Frères Artistes* lodge between 1819 and 1827.

Notes

INTRODUCTION

All translations from French sources by author, unless noted otherwise.

1. Grégoire Kolpaktchy, "Introduction," in *Livre des morts des anciens Égyptiens* (Paris: Ominum littéraire, 1954), 35.

2. The scope of existing literature on the Egyptian campaign is monumental. A fairly complete bibliography of printed primary sources has been published by Philippe de Meulenaere, *Bibliographie raisonnée des témoignages oculaires imprimés de l'expédition d'Égypte (1798–1801)* (Paris: Chamonal, 1993). Another extensive bibliography that also includes the most important archival and secondary sources pertaining to the campaign can be found as an appendix to Yves Laissus's *L'Égypte, une aventure savante avec Bonaparte, Kléber, Menou, 1798-1801* (Paris: Fayard, 1998), 555–84. The most detailed military history of the campaign remains Clément de La Jonquière, *L'Expédition d'Égypte 1798–1801*, 5 vols. (Paris: Charles-Lavauzelle, 1899–1907). La Jonquière's account contains a very extensive selection of reprinted primary sources but unfortunately stops with Bonaparte's departure from Egypt in August 1799. To supplement La Jonquière for the period between August 1799 and October 1801, Antoine Galland's *Tableau de l'Égypte, pendant le séjour de l'armée française*, 2 vols. (Paris: Galland, 1804), can be consulted. A member of the Commission des Sciences et des Arts, Galland participated in the expedition as editor and printer of the official proclamations and newspapers released by the Armée de l'Orient and the Institut d'Égypte. Among the more recent literature on the campaign, Henry Laurens's *L'Expédition d'Égypte, 1798–1801* (Paris: Colin, 1989), remains the standard reference.

3. The Egyptian campaign was the direct offspring of both the Enlightenment and the French Revolution, whose anticlerical attitudes were counterbalanced, respectively, by a recourse to reason or to the "cult of the Supreme Being." For Edward Said, *Orientalism* (New York: Vintage, 1979), 42, 80, "the Napoleonic invasion of Egypt in 1798 . . . was in many ways the very model of a truly scientific appropriation of one culture by another, apparently the stronger one. [Napoleon's] plans for Egypt therefore became the first in a long series of European encounters with the Orient in which the Orientalist's special expertise was put directly to functional colonial use. . . . With Napoleon's occupation of Egypt processes were set in motion between East and West that still dominate our contemporary cultural and political perspectives."

4. For an extensive account on the outbreak of the plague, as well as its treatment and its impact on the aborted campaign into Syria, see René-Nicolas Dufriche Desgenettes, *Histoire médicale de l'armée d'Orient par le médecin en chef R. Desgenettes*, 2 vols. (Paris: Croullebois et Bossange, 1802). Bonaparte's chief medical officer, Desgenettes had poignantly refused to administer the poison to the plague-stricken soldiers, a charge that fell on a phar-

macist named Royer. See Darcy Grimaldo Grigsby, *Extremities: Painting Empire in Post-Revolutionary France* (New Haven and London: Yale University Press, 2002), 89–96, for a discussion of native resistance and especially the poisoning of soldiers by Napoleon's order (notes 96–98 provide an extensive survey of primary sources detailing the accusation of poisoning).

5. For the manpower of the invasion force, see Commandant de Villebois-Mareuil, "Le Centenaire de l'expédition de l'Égypte: Comment se préparait une campagne coloniale en 1798," *Le Correspondant* 192, no. 860 (July 25, 1898): 228. Others have placed the total invasion force somewhat higher, at between thirty-five thousand and thirty-six thousand. See Meulenaere, *Bibliographie raisonnée*, 249, 253. Desgenettes counted a total of 8,915 deaths as of September 1800. About half of the deceased had been killed in action or died from injuries sustained in battle (4,468); the other half succumbed to diseases and accidents (4,447). Desgenettes, *Histoire médicale*, 1:177–8. There are no statistics available for the last year of the French occupation, but it is reasonable to assume that more than ten thousand members of the expedition force died over the three-year period of the campaign.

6. Laissus, *L'Égypte*, 557. The author cites a letter by Bourrienne, Napoleon's secretary, from June 17, 1802, to Baron Fain requesting that "all the papers on Egypt that could exist in the archives of the government" be rendered directly to the First Consul, Napoleon (AN, AF IV/1687). The transfer of the documents took place on June 26 and September 20, 1802. A note by Fain indeed affirms that all these papers "have been burned, by order of Her Majesty, in September 1807." Laissus verified that the holdings of the Archives Nationales in Paris have enormous gaps when it comes to documents relating to the Egyptian campaign.

7. Jurgis Baltrušaitis, *La Quête d'Isis: Essai sur la légende d'un mythe* (1967; repr., Paris: Flammarion, 1985), 8. On Egyptomania in general, see, for instance, *Egyptomania: Egypt in Western Art, 1730–1930*, exh. cat. (Paris, Ottawa, and Vienna: National Gallery of Canada and Réunion des Musées Nationaux, 1994). It is a noteworthy circumstance that the prodigious outpouring of autobiographical travel descriptions from the Egyptian campaign was heralded by Vivant Denon's vastly popular *Voyage dans la Basse et la Haute Égypte*, 2 vols. (Paris: Didot, 1802), whose author frequented Sophisian circles. By 1852 even the food supplier to the Armée de l'Orient, one Alexandre Lacorre, had published his diary, entitled *Journal inédit d'un commis aux vivres pendant l'expédition d'Égypte: Voyage à Malte et en Égypte, expédition de Syrie* (Bordeaux: Crugy, 1852). On the impact of the Egyptian campaign on French nineteenth-century painting, see Todd Porterfield, *The Allure of Empire: Art in the Service of French Imperialism, 1798–1836* (Princeton: Princeton University Press, 1998). Porterfield summarizes the phenomenon on pages 78–79: "The first time the Egyptian campaign was played out, in Egypt and Syria, it was a quick defeat. The second time the Egyptian

campaign was conducted—on the walls of the Napoleonic Salons—it looked like a triumph of French civilization." For the impact of the Egyptian campaign on the decorative arts, see James Stevens Curl, *The Egyptian Revival: An Introductory Study of a Recurring Theme in the History of Taste* (London and Boston: Allen & Unwin, 1982), 107–52. On the bringing of the Egyptian Campaign to the Parisian stage, see Angela C. Pao, *The Orient of the Boulevards: Exoticism, Empire, and Nineteenth-Century French Theater* (Philadelphia: University of Pennsylvania Press, 1998), 107–79. As we shall see in chapter 4, a great number of the producers, playwrights, and composers associated with Egyptianizing plays were members of the Sophisian order.

8. On the revival of Egyptian-rite Masonry after 1798, see Gérard Galtier, *Maçonnerie égyptienne, Rose-Croix et néo-chevalerie: Les Fils de Cagliostro* (Monaco: Rocher, 1994), 40–41.

9. The term *hauts grades* implies in this context that only Master Masons were eligible to join the Sophisians. Arthur Dinaux in his *Les Sociétés badines, bachiques, littéraires et chantantes, leur histoire et leurs travaux* (Paris: Bachelin-Deflorenne, 1867), 224–25, referred to the Sophisians as a "secret society of the army."

10. *Livre d'or: Institution de l'Ordre Sacré des Sophisiens dans la France*, BN-MSS, FM 4.15; hereafter *Livre d'or* [BN]. Pages in the BN copy are cited by the stamped numbers on the verso. The only twentieth-century scholar aware of the Golden Book's existence at the BN was Jean Bossu, who discussed it in his article "La Petite histoire maçonnique: Au Temps du mélodrama le F∴ Cuvier [sic] de Trie fut le 'Crébillon des Boulevards,'" *Les Lettres mensuelles: Revue de libre discussion philosophique et sociale*, new series 6, no. 4 (August/September 1958): 7–8. Bossu's notice was mainly intended to inspire future research into the Sophisians and remains superficial; he was unaware of the existence of the other documents related to the order.

11. *Livre d'or, ou Institution de l'Ordre Sacré des Sophisiens dans la République française*, GODF, Ms. AR. Coll. Meyer, pièce 20; hereafter *Livre d'or* [GODF].

12. *Livre d'or* [BN], fols. 25r–26r, "Charte Constitutionelle," Section 3, Articles 1–11.

13. Auguste-Prosper-François Guerrier de Dumast, "Un Chapitre de l'histoire littéraire française: Renaissance de la rime riche," *Mémoire de l'Académie de Stanislas*, 4th ser., 12 (1880), 19.

14. *Mélanges Lerouge*, CMC, Kloss Collection, Ms. 240.B.74. On the 1835 sale of the document, see the *Catalogue de livres manuscrits et imprimés sur la franc-maçonnerie et les sociétés secrètes provenant du cabinet de feu M. Lerouge . . . dont la vente aura lieu . . . le 7 janvier 1835 . . . rue des Beaux-Arts, no. 6* (Paris: Leblanc, 1834), 64, lot no. 494: "Mélanges concerning the Order of the Sophisians, established in the Pyramids of the French Republic, part manuscript, part letter print." A copy of the sales catalog can be found in the BN-MSS, FM Baylot impr. 2412.

15. Ordre Sacré des Sophisians, *Règlement de l'A-*[spirance]/*Nomenclature des officiers* (Paris: Year IX—1800/1801). I was able to locate three extant copies of the pamphlet: BN-MSS, FM Baylot impr. 349; BVP, *Frag[ments] pop[ulaires]*, Cote 705.801, no. 4; a final copy is bound with the *Mélanges Lerouge* in The Hague, CMC.

16. L∴ & Ch∴ Frères Artistes: *Tableaux* [1797–1840], BN-MSS, FM 2.78; *Livre d'or* [BN], fols. 2v–3r (tableau for all members up to 1819/1820), 27r (tableau for 1821 and after).

17. August-Prosper-François Guerrier de Dumast, *La Maçonnerie, poème en trois chants avec des notes historiques, étymologiques et critiques* (Paris: Arthus Bertrand, 1820). One copy at the BN-RDJ, RÉS. H 2309. On Guerrier de Dumast, see Jean

Bossu, "Francs-Maçons d'autrefois—XXIII: Guerrier de Dumast, Catholique libéral," *Renaissance traditionelle* 62-63 (April–July 1985): 227-29; Y. Le Moigne, article "Guerrier de Dumast (Auguste-Prosper-François)," in *Dictionnaire de biographie française*, ed. Michel Prevost and Roman d'Amat, 19 vols. to date (Paris: Letouzey et Ané, 1933–), 17:5–7; Claude Rétat, "Initiations, initiatives: Prosper Guerrier de Dumast dans les 'mines de l'Orient,'" *Chroniques d'histoire maçonnique lorraine* 10 (May 2000): 8–54.

18. Guerrier de Dumast, *La Maçonnerie*, ix–x, xiv, 134, 161, 275, 262–63, 293–97, 320–21. Augustin Barruel's *Mémoires pour servir à l'histoire du jacobinisme* (London: Le Boussonier, 1797/98) started the legend that the French Revolution was a Masonic conspiracy.

19. Rétat, "Initiations, initiatives," 17.

20. The *Frères Artistes*'s sanction for *La Maçonnerie* is obvious from the contents of two brochures, bound with the BN copy of Guerrier de Dumast's book (RÉS. H 2309), that summarize the deliberations of the lodge from May 5 and May 31, 1820. They discuss the decision to award a gold medal to Guerrier de Dumast for his publication and to consider the poem as a "classical" text, which was to be given to members "who brought merit to the lodge by their zeal, their diligence, or their works." The poem's contents and intentions were summarized by a Sorbonne professor of Latin poetry, the Sophisian Nicolas-Eloi Lemaire. The decision to adopt his proposals was approved by the Sophisians Cuvelier de Trie, Jean-Antoine-Joseph Fauchet, Jean Laurès, Jean-François de Caze, Louis-Alexandre Piccinni, Antoine-Louis Collard Dutilleul, Jacques Dervaux, Alexandre-Henry-Joseph Bérenger, Marie-Nicolas Ponce-Camus, Jean-Léopold Duplan, and Philippe-Jacques Hubert Delaroche. See the *Scéance du Conseil des Conservateurs, du 5 mai 1820 (ère vulg∴)* and the *Rapport fait à la R∴ L∴ des FF∴ Artistes, dans sa scéance du 31 mai 1820 (ère vulg∴), par le F∴ Orateur Lemaire, professeur de poésie latine à la Faculté des Lettres de Paris, Chevalier de la Légion d'honneur.*

21. Louis Amiable, *Une Loge maçonnique d'avant 1789: La R∴ L∴ Les Neuf Soeurs* (Paris: Alcan, 1897), 65–68, 145–46, 293–95, 345; Guerrier de Dumast, "Un Chapitre," 19.

22. François-Timoléon Bègue Clavel, *Histoire pittoresque de la franc-maçonnerie et des sociétés secrètes anciennes et modernes*, 3rd ed. (1844; repr., Paris: Veyrier, 1989), 34–35; Jean-Claude Bésuchet de Saunois, *Précis historique de l'ordre de la franc-maçonnerie, depuis son introduction en France jusqu'en 1829*, 2 vols. (Paris: Rapilly, 1829), 2:299–301; English translation quoted from Dudley Wright, *Women and Freemasonry* (London: Rider, 1922), 82. It is important to underline the difference of this ceremony from the type of receptions organized by adoption lodges (female lodges that were "adopted" by a male lodge, but whose members were excluded from parts of the male rituals), which had existed in France since 1774. Mme de Xaintrailles was admitted to the *Frères Artistes* as if she were a man.

23. *Dossier "Xaintrailles,"* SHD-DAT, Xr 49; *Amazons to Fighter Pilots: A Biographical Dictionary of Military Women*, ed. Reina Pennington and Robin Higham, 2 vols. (Westport and London: Greenwood Press, 2003), 1:493–94; Gisèle and Yves Hivert-Messeca, *Comment la Franc-Maçonnerie vint aux femmes: Deux siècles de Franc-Maçonnerie d'adoption feminine et mixte en France, 1740–1940* (Paris: Dervy, 1997), 177–78. Mme de Xaintrailles's Parisian address was boulevard du Temple No. 30, located in the immediate vicinity of the boulevard theaters presumably used by Cuvelier's groups for receptions and initiations.

24. *Livre d'or* [BN], fol. 26r, "Charte Constitutionelle," Section 4, Articles 3: "Women are admitted to initiation."

25. Plutarch, *De Iside et Osiride* 2, 351e, ed. and tr. John Gwyn Griffith (Cardiff: University of Wales Press, 1970), 118–21; Manly P. Hall, *The Secret Teachings of all Ages: An Encyclopedic Outline of Masonic, Hermetic, Quabbalistic, and Rosicrucian Symbolic Philosophy* (1928; repr., New York: Tarcher/Penguin, 2003), 121, 132; Guerrier de Dumast, *La Maçonnerie*, 70.

26. Clavel, *Histoire pittoresque*, 407; Jean-Marie Ragon, *Orthodoxie maçonnique, suivie de la maçonnerie occulte et de l'initiation hermétique* (Paris: Dentu, 1853), 181–84; Dinaux, *Les sociétés badines*, 224–25; Georg Franz Burkhard Kloss, *Geschichte der Freimaurerei in Frankreich aus ächten Urkunden dargestellt (1725–1830)*, 2 vols. (1852–53; repr., Graz: Akademische Druck- und Verlagsanstalt, 1971), 1:406. Georg Schuster, in his *Die geheimen Gesellschaften, Verbindungen und Orden* (1906; repr., Wicsbaden: Fourier, 1995), 2:262, repeats the earlier entry by Kloss. The standard reference in modern literature is the *Dictionnaire de la franc-maçonnerie*, ed. Daniel Ligou, new ed. (Paris: Quadrige, Presses universitaires de France, 2004), 892: "Sacred Order of the Sophisians. Created in 1801 within the Parisian lodge *Les Frères Artistes* by former members of the Egyptian campaign. It comprises three degrees: 1) Aspirants, 2) Initiates, 3) Members of the Grand Mysteries."

27. *Livre d'or* [BN], fols. 2r–3v, 27v.

28. Louis Milfort, *Mémoire, ou Coup-d'oeil rapide sur mes différents voyages et mon séjour dans la nation crěck* (Paris: Giguet et Michaud, Year XI—1802). A French reprint is available under the title *Chef de guerre chez les Creeks*, ed. Christian Buchet (Paris: France-Empire, 1994). See also the English translations and introductions to Milfort's treatise, *Memoirs, or a Quick Glance at My Various Travels and My Sojourn in the Creek Nation*, ed. and tr. Ben C. McCary (Kennsaw: Continental Book Company, 1959); *Milford's Memoirs, or a Cursory Glance at My Different Travels and My Sojourn in the Creek Nation*, tr. Geraldine De Courcy, ed. John Francis McDermott (Santa Barbara: The Narrative Press, 2000).

29. Besides Piccolos, this group included: Demetrios N. Photilas, the brothers Constantin and Christopher Sakellarios, and Athanasias Vogorides. With the exception of the Sakellarios brothers, they all had taught at the Princely Academy of Bucharest in the 1810s, which evolved at this time into a hotbed of Greek patriotism and cultural resistance against Turkish domination. The teaching of the Greek language in particular served as a catalyst for this development. See Ariadna Camariano-Cioran, *Les Académies princières de Bucarest et de Jassy et leurs professeurs* (Thessaloniki: Institute for Balkan Studies, 1974), 58–59, 134–135, 160, 172, 174, 254, 360, 485–92, 525. On Piccolos, see Tatjana E. Kirkova, "Nicolas S. Piccolos—Sa vie, son oeuvre," *Bulgarian Historical Review* 5, no. 3 (1977): 18–37; Roxane D. Argyropoulos, "Nicolas Piccolos et la philosophie néohellénique," *Balkan Studies* 25, no. 2 (1984): 235–42; on the Sakellarios brothers, see Nicolae Isar, "Deux correspondants de N. Rosetti-Roznovanu: Coray et Guilford. Une Lettre de Piccolo," *Revue des études sud-est européennes* 8 (1970): 365–72. See also in particular, Camariano-Cioran, *Les Academies princières*, 491, note 572, and 647–48. Together with Champollion and Korais, one of the brothers was a member of the Ionian Academy at Corfu; Stamati Théodore Lascaris, "L'Académie Ionienne: Un Institut littéraire à Corfou sous la domination napoléonienne," *Revue des études napoléonienne* 25 (July–December 1925): 215–16. On Vogorides, see Dorothea Kadach, "Ein Aufklärer des Balkan: Dr. Atanas

Bogoridi," *Südost-Forschungen* 34 (1975): 125–65; Athanassis E. Karathanassis, "Αθανάσιος Βογορίδης: Βιογραφικά και εργογραφικά ενός εκπροδώπου τού Νεοελληνικού Διαφωτισμού," *Παρουσία* 7 (1991): 125–68. The Greek faction in the Sophisian order maintained strong ties with the *Philiki Hetairia*, a para-Masonic secret society that organized the national uprising against the Turks from Western Europe. Its primary ideological supporter in Paris was Adamantios Korais, a close friend of Piccolos and his associates. On Korais, see Stephen George Chaconas, *Adamantios Korais: A Study in Greek Nationalism* (New York: Columbia University Press, 1942).

30. Guerrier de Dumast, "Un Chapitre," 21–22, note 1. See also Guerrier de Dumast's *Chios, la Grèce et l'Europe, poème lyrique, accompagné de notes explicatives, suivi de la traduction, avec le texte en regard, d'une épitre grecque-moderne, adressée, en 1820, par N. S. Piccolos à G. Glaracés* (Paris: Schlesinger, 1822) and his poem *A mon ami Piccolo, quarante vers sur deux rimes (rêne et li)* (Nancy: Vagner, 1861). Philhellenic sentiments ran especially high in a treatise published as *Proposition faite à la scéance du quatorzième jour du premier mois de l'an D∴ L∴ V∴ L∴ 5826 (14 Mars 1826) par le F∴ E∴ J∴ Thayer, troisième Or∴, et imprimée par ordre de la ⊡ des FF Artistes à l'Or∴ de Paris* (Paris: Dondey-Dupré, 1826). One copy in Paris, BN-MSS, FM 2 Baylot 41, no. 5. The author, Edouard James Thayer, was a lawyer and a prominent member of the *Frères Artistes* in the late 1820s. In this document he steered a political course in clear opposition to the French government's pro-Ottoman stance on the Greek question (3–5): "The conduct of our Brothers has always shown that egoism was far from their mind and that the most ardent philanthropy ruled their soul. We have seen a thousand proofs for this; last year, whilst responding to a call made in the name of religion and humanity, all the lodges of France merged their tribute to children and to the widows in need with the nation's philhellenic contribution. They showed that, in the heart of Masons, there is always a rope for a bell to sound all that is noble and generous! But if one year ago we empathized with the misfortunes of a people battling against the most terrible of tyrannies, can we now remain insensible to its unhappiness? . . . Vain talk is not sufficient; what is needed is action. It is necessary that the one who abhors the crimes of these renegades [i.e., the Ottomans], contributes to furnish to the Greeks the means to defend themselves against the attacks launched by this filth. If the rifles used by the Turks carry the brand of a French manufacturer, it is necessary that these same manufactories furnish arms to the Greek. If some of our compatriots see themselves amongst the ranks of the Barbarians, there must be even more who see themselves siding with the Hellenes." On the cultural and historical context of philhellenism in general, see for example Eugène Asse, *Les Petits Romantiques: Antoine Fontaney, Jean Polonius, l'indépendance de la Grèce et les poètes de la Restauration, Jules de Rességuier, Edouard d'Anglemont* (Geneva: Slatkine, 1968), 89–120; Nina Athanassoglou-Kallmyer, *French Images from the Greek War of Independence, 1821–1830: Art and Politics under the Restoration* (New Haven and London: Yale University Press, 1989).

31. William Francis Patrick Napier, *The Life and Opinions of General Sir Charles Napier, G.C.B.*, 4 vols. (London: Murray, 1857), 1:285–86. On Lord Guilford, see also Z. Duckett Ferriman, *Some English Philhellenes: VI. Lord Guilford* (London: The Anglo-Hellenic League, 1919), 94. On the history of the Ionian Academy on Corfu in the early nineteenth century, see also Lascaris, "L'Académie Ionienne," 203–16.

32. The bases for all biographical research on Cuvelier de Trie are his autograph curriculum vitae, written on October 27, 1810,

contained in *Dossier personnel "Cuvelier, Jean-Guillaume-Augustin,"* SHD-DAT, 2 Yf 4852, and P.[rosper] Dondey-Dupré fils's *Paroles funèbres prononcées à la tombe de notre ami J.-G.-A. Cuvelier de Trie, capitaine de cavalerie en retraite, chevalier de l'ordre royal de la légion d'honneur, cons∴ ad vitam de la R∴ L∴ des Artistes O∴ de Paris* (Paris: Dondey-Dupré, 1824). Additional archival sources can be found at the Archives Nationales, which preserve Cuvelier's documents from the Légion d'honneur (AN, LH 642/93) and the files that his widow submitted to the Beaux-Arts administration (AN, F 21/1008). The latter dossier contains an interesting missive that Cuvelier signed on August 7, 1822, in which he tried to persuade the arts administration of his fervent admiration for the Bourbons, as well as letters from the 1830s in support of Cuvelier's widow that were signed by the poet Alphonse de Lamartine along with two other members of the *Chambre des députés* and the writer Casimir Delavigne. These sources are not always consistent, so that, in case of doubt, I followed the information provided by Cuvelier himself in his dossier from the military archives. Additional biographical information was gleaned from Pierre-Jean-Baptiste Bertrand, *Précis de l'histoire physique, civile et politique de la ville de Boulogne-sur-mer et de ses environs, depuis les Morins jusqu'en 1814,* 2 vols. (1828; reprint, Marseille: Lafitte, 1975), 2:596–98; François Morand, *L'Année historique de Boulogne-sur-mer: Recueil de faits et des événements intéressant l'histoire de cette ville, et rangés selon leurs jours anniversaires* (Boulogne-sur-mer: Déligny, 1859), 10–11; Adolphe de Cardevacque, *Dictionnaire biographique du département du Pas-de-Calais* (Arras: Sueur-Charruey, 1879), 114–15; and J. Decoster, article "Cuvelier de Trie (Jean-Guillaume-Auguste)," *Dictionnaire de biographie française,* 9:434.

33. See chapter 4 for a more detailed analysis of Cuvelier's theatrical career. A chronological list of his plays from 1793 to 1824 can be found in Alphonse Mahul, *Annuaire nécrologique, ou Complement annuel et continuation de toutes les biographies, ou Dictionnaires historiques,* 7 vols. (Paris: Baudouin, 1821–26), 5:68–76. Mahul counted a total of one hundred and ten plays, but the real number may have been closer to 150, judging from the holdings of the Bibliothèque Nationale and other French libraries. Twenty-six of the plays cataloged by Mahul were written before the turn of the nineteenth century and performed at a variety of theaters, such as the Théâtre Montansier, the Théâtre de la Cité, L'Ambigu-Comique, and the Théâtre des Jeunes-Artistes. One of the earliest mentioned pieces, with the suggestive title *La Fête de l'Être-Suprême,* consisted of six *scènes patriotiques* and dated from 1794.

34. Bossu, "La Petite histoire maçonnique," 7; Pao, *The Orient of the Boulevards,* 142–43.

35. See the explanation of the term mimodrama in Cuvelier de Trie, *La Mort de Kléber, ou Les Français en Égypte: Mimodrame historique et militaire en deux actes* (Paris: Fages, 1819), 4.

36. Among the wealth of studies on Cagliostro and his life, a few stand out: Marc Haven, *Le Maître inconnu Cagliostro: Étude historique et critique sur la haute magie,* 4th ed. (1964; repr., Paris: Dervy, 1996); Denyse Dalbian, *Le Comte de Cagliostro* (Paris: Laffont, 1983); *Cagliostro: Dokumente zu Aufklärung und Okkultismus,* ed. Klaus H. Kiefer (Munich, Leipzig, and Weimar: Beck, 1991); Philippe Brunet, *Cagliostro: Biographie* (Paris: Bourin, 1992); and Iain McCalman, *The Last Alchemist: Count Cagliostro, Master of Magic in the Age of Reason* (New York: Harper Collins, 2003). On Cagliostro's Egyptian rite, see specifically *Rituel de la franc-maçonnerie égyptienne,* ed. Marc Haven (1948; repr., Paris: Télètes, 2003); and Robert Amadou, *Cagliostro et le rituel de la maçonnerie égyptienne* (Paris: Sepp, 1996).

37. François-Charles Roux, *Les Origines de l'expédition d'Égypte* (Paris: Plon-Nourrit, 1910); Trandafir G. Djuvara, *Cent projets du partage de la Turquie (1281–1913)* (Paris: Alcan, 1914); Shafik Ghorbal, *The Beginnings of the Egyptian Question and the Rise of Mehmet Ali: A Study in the Diplomacy of the Napoleonic Era Based on Researches in the British and French Archives* (London: Routledge, 1928), 1–4; Henry Laurens, *Les Origines intellectuelles de l'expédition d'Égypte: L'Orientalisme islamisant en France, 1868–1798* (Istanbul and Paris: Éditions Isis, 1987).

38. Said, *Orientalism,* 83.

39. Jean-Edouard Goby, "La Composition du premier Institut d'Égypte," *Bulletin de l'Institut d'Égypte* 29 (1948): 345–67, and 30 (1949): 81–99; Laissus, *L'Égypte,* 523–26; Robert Solé, *Les Savants de Bonaparte* (Paris: Seuil, 1998); *Il y a 200 ans: Les Savants en Égypte,* ed. Marie-Noëlle Bourguet and Yves Laissus, exh. cat. (Paris: Nathan, 1998).

40. See the *Convention pour l'évacuation de l'Égypte,* art. XI., reprinted in Galland, *Tableau,* 2:73–74. This gentlemen's agreement notwithstanding, Britain confiscated a limited number of outstanding artifacts from the withdrawing French scholars, including the famous Rosetta stone and the sarcophagus of Nectanebo II, which popular belief associated with Alexander the Great. See Jean-Marie Carré, *Voyageurs et écrivains français en Égypte,* 2 vols. (1956; repr., Cairo: IFAO, 1988), 1:157.

41. François Collaveri, *Napoléon franc-maçon?,* rev. ed. (Paris: Tallandier, 2003), 16.

42. Ibid., 76–77.

43. *Installation de la loge impériale des Ch∴ de St-Jean-d'Acre, à l'Or∴ du XIIe régiment d'infanterie légère par le G∴ O∴ de France-Honneur-Patrie, le VIIe jour du 6e mois de l'an de la V∴ L∴ 5806* (Paris, 1806). Cited after Collaveri, *Napoléon franc-maçon?,* 132–33. On the Napoleonic savior legend in general, see Jean Tulard, *Napoléon, ou Le Mythe du sauveur* (Paris: Fayard, 1977).

44. Thomas Crow, *Emulation: Making Artists for Revolutionary France* (New Haven and London: Yale University Press, 1995), 244. The tradition of reading the painting as an apotheosis of Napoleon's miraculous healing touch goes back to François-René de Chateaubriand, "De Buonaparte et des Bourbons," in *Oeuvres complètes,* 22 vols. (Paris: Pourrat, 1833–1835), 19:20, and has become an accepted art historical interpretation since the publication of Walter Friedlaender's article, "Napoleon as 'Roi Thaumaturge,'" *Journal of the Warburg and Courtauld Institutes* 4 (1940–41): 139–41. Grigsby, *Extremities,* 73, has recently questioned this established interpretation of Napoleon as *roi thaumaturge* in the painting. She stresses the supremely rational motivation behind the touch, meant to disprove the contagious nature of the plague and to assert that fear promoted its spread. In either case, it is evident that Gros assigned to Bonaparte the role of a superhuman savior endowed with the ability to prevent the disease from running its course.

45. Galtier, *Maçonnerie égyptienne,* 41; Collaveri, *Napoléon franc-maçon?,* 76.

46. Galland, *Tableau,* 1:82.

47. Ibid., 1:120–21, and Antoine-Clair Thibaudeau, *Histoire générale de Napoléon Bonaparte, de sa vie privée et publique, de sa carrière politique et militaire, de son administration et de son gouvernement,* 6 vols. (Paris and Stuttgart: Ponthieu & Cotta, 1827–28), 5:105. Thibaudeau apparently only summarized Galland's story. An earlier version of Galland's account appeared in the

Courier [sic] de l'Égypte 25 (Pluviôse 3, year VII—January 22, 1799): 3–4. Reprinted in volume 4 of *The Journals of Bonaparte in Egypt, 1798–1801*, ed. Salah al-Din al-Bustani, 10 vols. (Cairo: Al-Arab Bookstore, 1971). A detailed description of the arrival of the same caravan from Nubia can also be found in Vivant Denon's *Voyage*, 1:103–4. As opposed to Galland, he described the head of the caravan as a Nubian prince "who was lively, gay, impetuous, and clever, all of which were shewn in his physiognomy: his color was deeper than bronze, his eyes very fine and well set, his nose somewhat turned up and small, his mouth very wide, but not flat, and his legs, like those of all Africans, bowed and lank." Cited after Vivant Denon, *Travels in Upper and Lower Egypt*, tr. Arthur Aikin, 2 vols. (London: Longman, Rees, and Phillips, 1803), 1:264.

48. Darius Spieth, "Michel Rigo and Bonaparte's Egyptian Campaign (1798–1801): Portraits of the Divan in Cairo," *1650–1850: Ideas, Aesthetics, and Inquiries in the Early Modern Age* 13 (2006): 133–63; Laissus, *L'Égypte*, 148–49. As Napoleon's personal property, this portrait series found a new home after the Egyptian campaign in the general's Malmaison residence in France, where it is still located today.

49. Homi K. Bhabha, *The Location of Culture* (London and New York: Routledge, 1994), 2.

50. *Livre d'or* [BN], fol. 83v.

1. SOME SOPHISIAN PRECURSORS

1. Cited after *Rituel*, ed. Haven, 16.

2. Giuliana Toso Rodinis, *La commedia degli intrighi e degli amori: Le più belle lettere da Napoli di Dominique Vivant Denon (1782–1785)* (Florence: Olschki, 1977), 144.

3. *Correspondance politique, Naples*, AAE, vol. 109, fol. 320.

4. Rodinis, *La commedia*, 147.

5. Dalbian, *Le Comte de Cagliostro*, 110–14; Haven, *Le Maître inconnu*, 115–44.

6. The necklace contained 540 diamonds, which amounted to 2,800 carats. It was originally commissioned by Louis XV for his favorite, Mme du Barry, but was never delivered. Böhmer and Bassange had made several unsuccessful attempts to interest Marie-Antoinette in the necklace but were turned down by the queen. Brunet, *Cagliostro*, 204–05.

7. The literature on Vivant Denon's life and work is far too extensive to be listed comprehensively. Among the basic biographies, a few stand out: Pierre Lelièvre, *Vivant Denon, homme des Lumières, 'ministre des arts' de Napoléon* (Paris: Picard, 1993); Giuliana Toso Rodinis, *Dominique Vivant Denon, i fiordalisi, il berretto frigio, la sfinge* (Florence: Olschki, 1977); Ibrahim Amin Ghali, *Vivant Denon, ou La Conquête du bonheur* (Cairo and Paris: IFAO, 1986). Although somewhat dated, the standard reference in English on Denon remains Judith Nowinski's *Baron Dominique Vivant Denon (1747–1825): Hedonist and Scholar in a Period of Transition* (Rutherford: Fairleigh Dickinson University Press, 1970). Of great importance for any study of Denon's activities in the arts is also the catalog accompanying the large retrospective exhibition at the Louvre, *Dominique Vivant Denon: L'Oeil de Napoléon*, exh. cat. (Paris: Réunion des Musées Nationaux, 1999). For Vivant Denon's work as a graphic artist, see Petra ten-Doesschate Chu, *The Illustrated Bartsch: French Masters of the Nineteenth Century, Vivant Denon*, 2 vols. (New York: Abaris, 1985–88). On his role as Louvre director, see Jean Chatelain, *Vivant Denon et le Louvre de Napoléon* (Paris: Perrin,

1973), and particularly his published official correspondence in *Vivant Denon, directeur des musées sous le Consulat et l'Empire: Correspondance, 1802–1815*, ed. Marie-Anne Dupuy and Isabelle Le Masne de Chermont, 2 vols. (Paris: Réunion des Musées Nationaux, 1999).

8. Mathieu Couty, *Jean-Benjamin de Laborde, ou Le Bonheur d'être fermier-général* (Paris: Michel de Maule, 2001), 199–201; Dalbian, *Le Comte de Cagliostro*, 24–25.

9. Jean-Benjamin de Laborde, *Lettres sur la Suisse adressées à Mme M.*** par un voyageur françois en 1781*, 2 vols. (Geneva and Paris: Jombert, 1783), 1:5–7 (Letter II, dated June 15, 1781).

10. Ibid., 1:48–49.

11. Couty, *Jean-Benjamin de Laborde*, 230–32; Dalbian, *Le Comte de Cagliostro*, 130, 274.

12. Pierre-André Coupin, "Notice nécrologique sur M. le baron Denon," *Revue encyclopédique* 28 (July 1825): 31. A slightly altered version of the anecdote can be found in Amédée-David de Pastoret, *Éloge historique sur la vie et les ouvrages de M. le B.on Denon* (Paris: Firmin-Didot, 1851), 3–5: "[Louis XV] approached him and inquired what he desired.—'Nothing,' answered Denon.—'But what are you doing here every morning?' — 'I come to see His Majesty; I like to watch Him.'—'Very well,' replied the king; but you come every day.'—'Yes, Sir; I am fortunate. I love the arts, I draw. The face of His Majesty is an excellent model. I would like to record it faithfully, and I am looking for an occasion to do so."

13. Brunet, *Cagliostro*, 187.

14. Roger Portalis and Henri Beraldi, *Les Graveurs du dix-huitième siècle*, 3 vols. (Paris: Morgand et Fatout, 1880–82), 1:731; Francesca Fedi, "Diplomatie et franc-maçonnerie dans la seconde moitié du XVIIIe siècle," in *Les Vies de Vivant Denon*, 2 vols. (Paris: La Documentation française, Musée du Louvre, 2001), 1:196, 210, note 10.

15. Nowinski, *Baron Dominique Vivant Denon*, 27–30.

16. Albert de LaFizelière, *L'Oeuvre originale de Vivant Denon*, 2 vols. (Paris: Barraud, 1873), 1:5: "A friend of Denon, M. de Norvins, who knew his most intimate thoughts, described in the following terms the type of emotions that the king experienced in the presence of this charming child [Denon]. 'This old, blasé libertine [Louis XV],' he said, 'tired by the monotony of etiquette, of customary flattery produced on demand, fatigued by his official entourage and his intimate schemers, found a frequent savior in the wide and open friendliness, in the joyful and independent ideas of this young man [Denon], who won the day amidst the fastidious speech of the court with all sincere gayness; all the vigor of the base Burgundy spirit.' Whenever a pasty and pompous storyteller tried to amuse the king with some scandalous anecdote, sluggishly retold, Louis XV would interrupt him immediately, saying: 'Tell this to Denon; he will recount it to me this evening.' In fact, since his earliest youth Denon possessed the outstanding ability to add value to the simplest story and to spice it up with an extraordinary flavor."

17. Ghali, *Vivant Denon*, 27–42.

18. Jean-Benjamin de Laborde, *Choix de chansons mises en musique*, 2nd ed., 4 vols. (Rouen: Lemonnyer, 1881). To enhance the bibliophile appeal of his publication, Laborde commissioned the most highly esteemed book illustrator of the day, the engraver Moreau le jeune, to embellish the volumes with one hundred of his prints. However, due to Laborde's chronic shortage of funds, Moreau only delivered twenty-five prints, and the author had to content himself with other, less famous printmakers to complete the publication. Couty, *Jean-Benjamin de Laborde*, 124, 157.

19. Pierre Laujon, *Oeuvres choisies, contenant ses pieces . . . , ses fêtes . . . , ses chansons et autres opuscules, avec des anecdotes, remarques et notices relatives à ces divers genres*, 4 vols. (Paris: Patris, 1811), 4:225–37. On the *Caveau*, see also Paul Chaponnière, *Piron, sa vie et son oeuvre* (Paris: Jullien, 1910), 53–56; Maurice Dutrait, *Étude sur la vie et le théâtre de Crébillon (1674–1762)* (1895; repr., Geneva: Slatkine, 1970), 51–56. For Laborde's role in the *Caveau*, see Couty, *Jean-Benjamin de Laborde*, 51–52.

20. Jean-François Marmontel, *Mémoires*, ed. John Renwick, 2 vols. (Clermont-Ferrand: Bussac, 1972), 1:159.

21. Ibid., 1:169; Pastoret, *Éloge*, 3; Laujon, *Oeuvres choisies*, 4:232.

22. Guerrier de Dumast, *La Maçonnerie*, 39–40; Roger Richard, *Dictionnaire maçonnique: Le Sens caché des rituels et de la symbolique maçonnique* (Paris: Dervy, 1999), 266.

23. On this print, see Anatole Marquis de Granges de Surgères and Gustave Bourcard, *Les Françaises du XVIIIe siècle: Portraits gravés* (Paris: Dentu, 1887), 132–33. The authors include biographical references about the Laborde couple and comment on the great rarity of the print in the nineteenth century.

24. Denon enclosed Laborde's letter of recommendation with a thank-you note of July 7, 1775, mailed to the philosopher from Geneva three days after the visit took place. The note was published in *Monuments des arts du dessin chez les peuples tant anciens que modernes, recueillis par le baron Vivant Denon . . .* , ed. Pineu Amaury-Duval and Jacques-Charles Brunet, 4 vols. (Paris: Brunet Denon, 1829), 1:16–17: "I am sending you back my letters of recommendation [*mes passeports*], whose effect has been pre-empted by my haste and your accommodating nature." Denon annotated his copy of the letter with a reminder about the *passeports* in the margin: "These were the letters by M. de Laborde that only arrived in Geneva after my return from Ferney." Laborde's acquaintance with Voltaire dated back to the fall of 1765, when he completed a composition left unfinished after the death of the harpsichordist Pancrate Royer, to whom the philosopher had entrusted the musical score for his *Pandore*. Couty, *Jean-Benjamin de Laborde*, 59.

25. Letter from Denon to Voltaire, Geneva, July 3, 1775, in *Voltaire's Correspondence*, ed. Theodore Besterman, 107 vols. (Geneva, 1953–65), 91:96–97, no. 18423.

26. Letter from Denon to Voltaire, December 31, 1775, in ibid., 92:206, no. 18700: "In truth, I am saddened by the impression that my work left on you. I am not trying to make excuses: I failed in my goal, because it did not give you the kind of pleasure that I intended. But I can assure you of the sensation it has caused here: people find it full of expression. Everybody clamors for it, and those who have the honor to know you, assure everyone that this work is of the utmost fidelity."

27. Letter from Voltaire to Denon, December 20, 1775, in ibid., 92:179, no. 18675: "I cannot fathom why you depicted me as an emaciated monkey [*singe estropié*], with a drooping head and one shoulder four times higher than the other."

28. All the protagonists from Voltaire's household were fully identified in a description of the print that appeared in *Les Annonces, affiches, faits divers* (January 3, 1776), 4. A follow-up notice on January 12, 1776, informed readers of Laborde's identity.

29. See the prospectus inserted in the first volume of Beatus Fidelis Anton Johann Dominik Baron de Latour-Chatillon de Zur-Lauben's *Tableaux topographiques, pittoresques, physiques, historiques, moraux, politiques, littéraires de la Suisse*, 2 vols. (Paris: Clousier, 1780–86), at BN-RDJ, M16.

30. Louis Guimbaud, *Saint-Non et Fragonard d'après des documents inédits* (Paris: Le Goupy, 1928), 13–26. On the business dealings between Laborde and Saint-Non, see Couty, *Jean-Benjamin de Laborde*, 166–74.

31. Coupin, "Notice nécrologique," 33. On Fragonard's original *Satyre et chèvre* etching, see Georges Wildenstein, *Fragonard aquafortiste* (Paris: Les Beaux-Arts, 1956), 11–14, nos. iii–vi; and 47–48, no. xxxiii. An even more spectacular discovery was made in Pompeii during the 1760s, when a naturalistic marble sculpture of a satyr in sexual intercourse with an apparently undaunted goat was unearthed. The work was hastily locked away by personal order of King Charles of Spain. Walter Kendrick, *The Secret Museum: Pornography in Modern Culture* (New York: Viking, 1987), 6. Upon completion of his studies at the French Academy in Rome in 1761, Fragonard also executed a suite of four etchings depicting *Bacchanales* and a *Jeu de satires* (both 1763) after reliefs found in the Mattei palace in Rome, which anticipate the *Satyre et chèvre* Denon later copied.

32. Couty, *Jean-Benjamin de Laborde*, 177–80.

33. Richard Abbé de Saint-Non, *Voyage pittoresque dans les royaumes de Naples et de Sicile*, 5 vols. (Paris: Clousier, 1780–86).

34. Salvatore Russo, *Il viaggiatore curioso: Lettere di Denon e Houel a Landolina* (Palermo: Lombardi, 1993), 12; Marie-Anne Dupuy, "Chronologie," in *L'Oeil de Napoléon*, 495. The exact date of Denon's appointment as the *sécretaire de l'ambassade* in Naples remains contested. Russo cites Denon's letters to Landolina in support of an initial Neapolitan diplomatic appointment in 1779. Gabriel Chevallier, "Denon chargé d'affaires à Naples, 1782–1785," *Mémoires de la société d'histoire et d'archéologie de Chalon-sur-Saône* 38 (1964/65): 106, note 2, suggests a tentative date of spring 1778 for Denon's appointment, because the previous *sécretaire de l'ambassade*, the Comte de Moustier, had resigned on the first of January. As further evidence Chevallier cites the dates given in Denon's pension award preserved at the AAE, *Dossiers du personnel*, vol. 22, fol. 328. According to this document, Denon served the French government for a total of seven years at the court of Naples, approximately three of them as *chargé d'affaires* (July 1782 to June 1785). Counting back from June 1785, one would arrive at spring/summer 1778 as a rough date for the original appointment as the *sécretaire de l'ambassade*, which he held prior to his promotion to *chargé d'affaires*. Possibly Denon was hired in 1778 but had to wait for his official confirmation, which meant that he could not exercise his functions until 1779.

35. Henry Swinburne, *Travels in the Two Sicilies in the Years 1777, 1778, 1779, 1780*, 2 vols. (London: Elmsly, 1783–85). On Laborde's role as organizer of the Swinburne edition, see Martine Reid, "Denon écrivain," in *L'Oeil de Napoléon*, 69, no. 9; Couty, *Jean-Benjamin de Laborde*, 221–22.

36. Vivant Denon, *Voyage en Sicile* (Paris: Didot, 1788). See also Reid, "Denon écrivain," 70, no. 70.

37. For an insightful social and political history of eighteenth-century Naples from the perspective of Enlightenment travel literature, see René Bouvier and André Laffargue, *La Vie napolitaine au XVIIIe siècle* (Paris: Hachette, 1956).

38. Michel Lacour-Gayet, *Marie-Caroline reine de Naples: Une Adversaire de Napoléon* (Paris: Tallandier, 1990), 21–41. On Marie-Caroline's patronage of Freemasonry, see Fulvio Bramato, *Napoli massonica nel settecento: Dalle origini al 1789* (Ravenna: Longo, 1980), 36–37.

39. Chevallier, "Denon chargé d'affaires," 105–14; Fedi, "Diplomatie et franc-maçonnerie," 196.

40. Antonella Scibilia, "Domenico Caracciolo," in *Dizionario biografico degli Italiani*, ed. Alberto Maria Ghisalberti, 62 vols. (Rome: Istituto della Enciclopedia italiana, 1960), 19:337–47.

41. Giuseppe Gorani, *Mémoires secrets et critiques des cours, des gouvernemens, et des moeurs des prinicipaux États de l'Italie*, 3 vols. (Paris: Buisson, 1793), 1:42–45. The peripatetic German chronicler of the Italian Masonic scene, Friedrich Münter, who met Caracciolo in Palermo in November 1785, described the viceroy in similar terms as a friend of d'Alembert and Diderot. See Friedrich Münter, *Aus den Tagebüchern Friedrich Münters: Wander- und Lehrjahre eines dänischen Gelehrten*, ed. Øjvind Andreasen, 3 vols. (Copenhagen and Leipzig: Haase, 1937), 2:48.

42. Gorani, *Mémoires secrets*, 1:165–66: "He retained a great predilection for France, and on every occasion felt obliged to draw comparison with the customs in Paris and at Versailles. His eulogies of the French nation could never be exhausted. It pleased him to imitate the French in his gestures, his way of speaking, his way of conducting business. Sometimes he modeled himself after Choiseul [secretary of state for foreign affairs, 1758–61 and 1766–70], sometimes after Vergennes [minister of foreign affairs under Louis XVI, 1774–87], or some other minister at Versailles. . . . Whether it be the fault of advanced age or whether the nature of Neapolitan government had an influence on him, one could no longer recognize this amiable philosopher, endowed with all the graces of *esprit* and a taste for play, who for so long had been high society's delight. His joyfulness degenerated into clownery, and his humor, though present, turned somber and severe. His manners lost their elegance. He even neglected to a revolting degree the appearance of his person."

43. The decoded inscription of Denon's Dauptain portrait reads as follows: "C[harles]. F[rançois]. Dauptain. Of[ficier]. D[u]. G[rand]. O[rient]∴ Elu V[énérable]∴ De La [Loge] De La DOUCE UNION, A L'O[rient] De Paris le 23 X 1780." On Dauptain, see Albert LeBihan, *Francs-maçons parisiens du Grand-Orient de France (Fin du XVIIIe siècle)* (Paris: Bibliothèque Nationale, 1966), 150.

44. Couty, *Jean-Benjamin de Laborde*, 204.

45. Dalbian, *Le Comte de Cagliostro*, 98–102, 230–31.

46. During his most prosperous days in Strasbourg and Paris, for instance, Cagliostro rented separate apartments to administer his miracle healings. See Brunet, *Cagliostro*, 147.

47. Giacomo Casanova, *The Memoirs of Jacques Casanova de Seingalt*, tr. Arthur Machen, 6 vols. (New York and London: Putnam, 1959–61), 6:250.

48. On the economic and aesthetic aspects of the passion for Rembrandt prints in eighteenth-century Venice, see for example: Bettina Erche, "Zu Rembrandt-Radierungen: Im Labyrinth der Reproduktion," *Kunst und Antiquitäten* 9 (September 1994): 20–21; Ulrich Finke, "Venezianische Rembrandtstecher um 1700," *Oud Holland* 79, no. 2 (1964): 111–21. Denon's *Resurrection of Lazarus* is mentioned in a letter the artist addressed to the Neapolitan scholar and antiquarian Tommaso Puccini on February 24, 1784: "I am glad to hear that you are satisfied with the way I designed the Lazarus plate, since it was you who imposed the commission on me. If some details that escaped my attention betray my hand, it is because I copied from a mirror so as to capture the effect of the original and not every single line." Biblioteca Forteguerriana, Pistoia, *Fondo Puccini*, cart. V, No. 4, E412.

49. LaFizelière, *L'Oeuvre originale*, 1:25. It is interesting to compare this plausible episode with an anecdote, according to which Denon once borrowed a Rembrandt etching from the connoisseur, collector, and art historian Jean-Baptiste-Louis Séroux d'Agincourt to copy it. Upon completion of the plate, he submitted to d'Agincourt both the original and his copy, printed on the blank flyleaf of an old volume printed in Leiden. Unable to distinguish between his print and Denon's copy, the connoisseur was even more baffled by the fact that Denon left him both prints for free, without, however, telling the experienced antiquarian which one was which. Finally, d'Agincourt enlisted the opinion of an outside specialist in Rembrandt's prints to identify his original etching. A.-D. Artaud, "Vivant Denon," in *Biographie universelle ancienne et moderne*, ed. Louis Michaud, 85 vols. (Paris: Michaud, 1811–62), 10:422.

50. Michele Mainardi, "Le incisioni dalle acquaforti di Rembrandt di Francesco Novelli" (Ph.D. diss., University of Venice, 2 vols., 1985–86), 1:10–58 (one copy in Venice, Biblioteca del Museo Civico Correr, coll. 0273.4); Giannantonio Moschini, *Dell'incisione in Venezia* (Venice: Zanetti, 1924), 163–75; Pier Antonio Novelli, *Memorie della vita di Pietro Antonio Novelli, scritte da lui medesimo* (Padua: Minerva, 1834), 42–45; Léon G. Pélissier, "Notes et documents: Vivant Denon suspect à Venise," *Bulletin de la Société de l'Histoire de l'Art français* 3 (1912): 260–89; Giambattista Perini, *Della vita e delle opere di Francesco Novelli pittore ed incisore veneziano* (Venice: Ex Cordella, 1888), 20–23; Udolpho van de Sandt, "Spicilège vénitien," in *Les Vies de Vivant Denon*, 1:253–77. The soaring number of Rembrandt reproductions Denon printed and sold in Venice between 1788 and 1793 can be explained by his acquisition of the prestigious Zanetti collection of old master drawings and prints, which included an almost complete set of original Rembrandt etchings: Alessandro Bettagno, "Anton Maria Zanetti, collezionista di Rembrandt," in *Scritti in onore di Giuliano Briganti*, ed. Marco Bona Castellotti, Laura Laureati, et al. (Milan: Longanesi, 1990), 241–46. See also Denon's Venetian sales catalog: [Vivant Denon], *Catalogo di incisioni di Mr. Denon* [Venice, ca. 1792–93]; one copy at BN-EST, Yb.3.338. The catalog is also discussed by Adrien Goetz, "Denon et l'estampe," in *L'Oeil de Napoléon*, 80, no. 14, who incorrectly gives the place of publication as Florence, while the currency used is in fact Venetian. The sales prices for Denon's Rembrandt reproductions—six to twelve *paoli* (a small silver coin) for middle-sized etchings—was roughly ten times higher than those of his three students, who were permitted to copy the Zanetti impressions in their master's collection. The quoted catalog prices for Denon's Rembrandt etchings would have approached the market value of Rembrandt originals, if one takes Finke's estimates ("Venezianische Rembrandtstecher um 1700," 119) as a benchmark.

51. Philippe-Auguste Hennequin, *Mémoires de Philippe-Auguste Hennequin*, ed. Jenny Hennequin (Paris: Calmann-Lévy, 1933), 107–16. See also Bruno Marty, "Des Artistes lyonnais franc-maçons dans le procès du Comte de Cagliostro (1789–1790)," *Travaux de l'Institut de l'Art de l'Université de Lyon* 14 (1991): 125–36; Crow, *Emulation*, 125–26.

52. *In Eminenti* issued by Clement XII in 1738, and *Providas Romanorum Pontificium* issued by Benedict XIV in 1751.

53. Van de Sandt, "Spicilège vénitien," 256–58. For Isabella Teotochi-Marini and her Salon, see also Cinzia Giorgetti, *Ritratto di Isabella: Studi e documenti su Isabella Teotochi Albrizzi* (Florence: Le Lettere, 1992); Vittorio Malamani, *Isabella Teotochi Albrizzi: I suoi amici, il suo tempo* (Turin: Locatelli, 1888). In July 1795 she divorced Carlo Antonio Marini, only to remarry Giuseppe Albrizzi about a year later.

54. Franco Venturi, "Venise et, par occasion, de la liberté," in *The Idea of Freedom: Essays in the Honour of Isaiah Berlin*, ed. Alan Ryan (Oxford and New York: Oxford University Press,

1979), 195–206. On Angelo Querini, see also Bruno Brunelli, "Un riformatore mancato: Angelo Querini," *Archivio Veneto*, series 5, 48–49, nos. 83–84 (1951): 185–200; Antonio del Piero, "Angelo Querini e la correzione del Consiglio dei X nel 1761–1762," *Ateneo Veneto* (1896): 280–303; Jean Georgelin, *Venise au siècle des Lumières* (Paris: École des hautes études en sciences sociales, 1978), 764–70.

55. The *Avogaria* was one of the oldest and most important administrative appointments in the Venetian Republic. It consisted of three members charged with supervising the correct application of the law in both the civil and criminal courts of the city. See Del Piero, "Angelo Querini," 280–81, note 2.

56. Brunelli, "Un riformatore mancato," 191; Venturi, "Venise," 200–201.

57. Giuliana Ericani, "La storia e l'utopia nel giardino del senatore Querini ad Alticchiero," in *Piranesi e la cultura antiquaria: Gli antecedenti e il contesto. Atti del convegno, 14–17 Novembre 1979*, ed. Anna Lo Bianca (Rome: Multigrafica, 1983), 178. Other sources confirming Querini's involvement with the lodge are: Fabio Mutinelli, *Memorie storiche degli ultimi cinquant'anni della Repubblica Veneta tratte da scritti e monumenti contemporanei* (Venice: Grimaldo, 1854), 9–17; Renata Targhetta, *La massoneria veneta dalle origine alla chiusura delle logge (1729–1785)* (Udine: Del Bianco, 1988), 32, 147, 150, 154, 158, 207; Renata Targhetta, "Ideologia massonica e sensibilità artistica nel Veneto settecentesco," *Studi veneziani* 16 (1988): 177–84.

58. Mutinelli, *Memorie*, 7, 13, 16.

59. *Massoni scoperti in Venezia 1785 e Napoli*, Gabinetto di Disegni e di Stampe, Museo Civico Correr, Venice, Ms. Cicogna 3058/7. See especially the *Lettera di WW ad NN* (March 11, 1785), describing the raid, and the *Nota degl'effetti ritrovati nella loggia dei Libri Muratori, o sia Franç Maçons, nella casa in Rio Marin in contrada di S. Simon Piccolo apportata dal Fante Cristofoli per ordine del Supremo Tribunali, e fatti abbrucciare pubblicam. e nella corte de Palazzo Ducale la mattina 5ste 9to* [1785], listing the objects to be publicly burned. The *Nota* refers to the raid in March, and enumerates several paintings on the theme of *pensata alla morta*, along with pieces of furniture, thrones, baldachins, triangles, compasses, and vases.

60. Ericani, "La storia e l'utopia nel giardino," 171–94. For the importance of Alticchiero in Querini's life after his forced retirement from politics, see Brunelli, "Un riformatore mancato," 193–200.

61. J.[ustiniana] W.[ynne] C.[omtesse] D.[e] R.[osenberg], *Alticchiero*, 2nd ed. (Padua, 1787). Her account of the estate is subdivided into detailed descriptions and analyses of each of the monuments to be found in the park. The basic sources for Wynne's life are Bruno Brunelli's biography *Un amica del Casanova* (Palermo: Remo Sandron, 1924), as well as Giuseppe Ortolani's essay "L'amore di Giustiniana Wynne," in his *Voci e visioni del settecento veneziano* (Bologna: Zanichelli, 1926), 251–65.

62. Casanova, *Memoirs*, 3:169–281.

63. W.[ynne] C.[omptesse] D.[e] R.[osenberg], *Alticchiero*, 44–45, §.XXIII.

64. Jean-Marie DuBoisaymé, *Marie-Thérèse de Bouès* (Paris: Prudhomme, 1838), chapter 22, 4, note 1. See also Denon's letter to Isabella Teotochi-Albrizzi of Floréal 2, year VI (April 22, 1798), in Vivant Denon, *Lettres à Bettine*, ed. Fausta Garavini (Arles: Actes Sud, 1999), 486–87 (Letter no. 1798-2): "You will doubtless be very surprised, my dear friend, to learn that I depart to who-knows-where. My acquaintance with General Bonaparte led me to commit myself to an expedition that he is about to under-take. . . . It is being said that we will only be away for six months, but I am counting on a year. . . . You have never been loved from Egypt—possibly it will be on the pyramids that I get to inscribe your name." The French fleet left Toulon on May 19, 1798 (Floréal 30, year VI).

65. Arthur Chuquet, *La Jeunesse de Napoléon*, 3 vols. (Paris: Colin, 1897–99), 2:237–40. The record of Napoleon's unflagging devotion to Volney is well documented even beyond October 1799. During the short interval between the general's return to France and the 18th of Brumaire, when public enthusiasm for Napoleon bordered on hysteria, the military commander publicly reiterated his admiration for Volney. On October 27, 1799, (Brumaire 5, year VIII), readers of the *Moniteur universel* encountered the following note: "Bonaparte has made great compliments to Volney on his *Voyage d'Égypte et de Syrie* [sic, *Voyage en Syrie et en Égypte pendant les années 1783, 1784, et 1785*]. He told him that he was almost the only traveler who did not lie, and that he knew how to combine the merit of fidelity with the greatest talent for observation." *Le Moniteur Universel* 35 (Brumaire 5, year VIII—October 27, 1799): 134. In referring to the travelers who lied, Napoleon was probably alluding to Claude-Étienne Savary's *Lettres d'Égypte*, which had deluded many of the common soldiers. Although Denon provided Napoleon with no fewer than forty-six copies of his *Voyage* in 1802, Volney's book still remained his reading of choice in his final exile on St. Helena. See the "Noms des souscripteurs" in Denon's *Voyage*, 1:319, and Ambroise Firmin-Didot, *Notes d'un voyage fait dans le Levant en 1816 et 1817* (Paris: Firmin-Didot, 1826), 191.

66. Carré, *Voyageurs*, 1:101. Citing Clément de Ris, *Les Amateurs d'autrefois* (Paris: Plon, 1877), 424, Nowinski, *Baron Dominique Vivant Denon*, 75, suggests that Josephine introduced Denon to Napoleon's "literary gathering (on the rue Chantereine) at which she hoped to entice distinguished men of letters and the arts to accompany the expedition." Another version maintains that Josephine met Denon when he was exhibiting François Gérard's *Belisarius*, and Denon's old painter-friend Jean-Baptiste Isabey introduced the general's consort to the courtier (Pastoret, *Éloge*, 15–16). A third theory, proposed by Antoine-Vincent Arnault in his *Souvenirs d'un sexagénaire*, (1833; repr., Paris: Champion, 2003), 602 (later to be embellished in a slightly altered version by LaFizelière, *L'Oeuvre originale*, 1:37), states that Denon and Napoleon first met at a ball given at the home of the Foreign Minister Charles-Maurice de Talleyrand-Périgord, the most influential political backer of the Egyptian campaign, where Denon offered the thirsty-looking young general a glass of lemonade. Later it was thanks to Mme de Beauharnais that the two men became reacquainted at Bonaparte's home on the rue de la Victoire. Denon's letters to Isabella Teotochi-Albrizzi confirm his close contacts with Josephine since June 1797; see his letter of Messidor 1, year V (June 20, 1797), in *Lettres à Bettine*, 476–77 (Letter no. 1797-11). Teotochi-Albrizzi's financial support is revealed in one of Denon's subsequent letters (Floréal 2, year VI—April 22, 1798), which he mailed to Venice shortly before his departure for Egypt: "Aubourg [Denon's caretaker in Paris] will receive the letters that you write and will forward them to me. I told him to open the one which he feels to contain the *lettre de change* over 1200 *livres* that I am expecting from you." Denon, *Lettres à Bettine*, 486–87 (Letter no. 1798-2).

67. Denon's membership in the Sophisian order was affirmed by Roger Cotte's article on Vivant Denon for Ligou's *Dictionnaire de la franc-maçonnerie*, 356. This opinion found an echo later in Fedi's article "Diplomatie et franc-maçonnerie," 1:195–96.

See also Philippe Sollers, *Le Cavalier du Louvre: Vivant Denon, 1747–1825* (Paris: Plon, 1995), 29–30.

68. Guerrier de Dumast, *La Maçonnerie*, 173:

In our midst, war and its clarion, the departed and their anguish,
Have troubled for too long already the charming sex.
Ah! In order to rally the élite of the French,
In order to plant here [the seed for] glory and new successes,
Is there not a single of those names left that connote glory?
There is one . . . our vows of allegiance point out *Belle et Bonne.*

Mme de Villette was Voltaire's niece. In 1778, while she was still a young girl, Voltaire presented her with his white gloves at the closing of his reception ceremony at the *Neuf Soeurs* lodge. He addressed his audience on this occasion by saying, "Since you wish that these gloves be the pawn of a pure affection founded on esteem, I will give them to *Belle et Bonne.*" Guerrier de Dumast, *La Maçonnerie*, 223. In November 1818 Mme de Villette founded the *Belle et Bonne* lodge in memory of this event. Her aim was to assemble women "who have belonged to diverse 'adoption workshops' and who have directed their works with wisdom." See the "Travaux du Sup∴ Conseil du 33e degree du rite écossais, ancien et accepté," in *Bibliothèque maçonnique, ou Recueil des matériaux propres à l'histoire de la maçonnerie* 1 (1818): 56. This openness made it possible for several male lodges to claim *Belle et Bonne* as their adopted lodge, including the *Amis des Lettres et des Arts* and possibly the *Frères Artistes.* It is also noteworthy that the foundation of the *Belle et Bonne* lodge coincided with the revival of Cuvelier de Trie's groups in 1818.

69. Sydney Lady Morgan, *Passages from My Autobiography* (London: Richard Bentley, 1859), 255–56, 263–64.

70. *Le Camp-Volant, journal des spectacles de tous les pays* 32 (February 21, 1819): 2: "Talma, covered with Masonic decorations, and Mlle Duchesnois, dressed for a ball, recite the fourth act of *Oedipe* in front of the statue of Voltaire, at the lodge *Belle et Bonne*, presided over by Mme de Villette. This is the second performance of this type that has taken place in the last couple of days; it was no less effective than the first one. This cursed author of *la Henriade* will long continue to be the cause of similar events." Talma was the most celebrated French actor at the turn of the nineteenth century and an intimate of Jacques-Louis David and his students. See Étienne-Jean Delécluze, *Louis David: Son École & son temps* (1855; reprint, Paris: Macula, 1989), 22-23.

2. THE LABORATORY OF REASON

1. *Livre d'or* [BN], fol. 14v.

2. Letter cited in Commandant Guitry, *L'Armée de Bonaparte en Égypte, 1798–1799*, Collection nouvelle de Mémoires militaires (Paris: Flammarion, 1898), 20. After citing Monge's letter, the editor continued to say that "Monge's friends told him that his wife was right. He agreed. But, when replying to her letter, he added: 'I have promised Bonaparte to follow him; I am too strongly engaged to withdraw.'"

3. La Jonquière, *L'Expédition*, 1:503.

4. Napoleon Bonaparte, *Correspondance de Napoléon Ier*, 32 vols. (Paris: Plon, Dumaine, 1858–70), 4:383, no. 3083.

5. Originally brought to Egypt in the wake of the fall of the Byzantine empire by the Turkish conquerors and mercenaries, the Mamelukes formed a group apart from the native Arabic, Jewish, and Coptic population of Egypt. The Mamelukes distinguished themselves by their non-sedentary lifestyle and their military system based on slaves organized in "households." The ethnic background of the slaves was very diverse. Most members of the warrior caste were Georgians and Circassians, Mongols, Turkomans, Kurds, or Albanians, but there were also Croats, Serbs, Greeks, and Western Europeans, who once had passed through the slave markets of the Black Sea region. On the colorful history of the Mamelukes in Egypt, see: Jean-Louis Bernard, *Histoire secrète de l'Égypte* (Paris: Albin Michel, 1983), 31–311; William Muir, *The Mameluke Slave Dynasty of Egypt, 1260–1517 A.D.* (London: Smith, Elder, 1896); Donald P. Little, *History and Historiography of the Mameluks* (London: Variorum, 1986).

6. La Jonquière, *L'Expédition d'Égypte*, 2:182.

7. Meulenaere, *Bibliographie raisonnée*, 173.

8. Jean-Louis-Ebénézer Reynier, *De l'Égypte après la bataille d'Héliopolis et considérations générales sur l'organisation physique et politique de ce pays* (Paris: Pougens, 1802), 85–87.

9. Denon, *Voyage*, 1:62, 146–47, 170; Denon, *Travels*, tr. Aikin, 1:170, 2:70–71, 127–28.

10. Jonathan I. Israel, *Radical Enlightenment: Philosophy and the Making of Modernity* (Oxford: Oxford University Press, 2001), 111, 152–53, 193, 218–22, 359–63, 371, 381, 589–90, 691, 701. Among many others, Israel mentions Spinoza, Anthonie Van Dale, Bernard de Le Bovier de Fontenelle, Balthasar Bekker, and Jean-Baptiste de Boyer Marquis d'Argens as proponents of these ideas.

11. Guerrier de Dumast, *La Maçonnerie*, 54–56, 59–60. The author admits, however, that "the pyramids in themselves were a crazy idea," but that Pharaoh Cheops and not the priests was to be held accountable for their construction. Furthermore, he insists that the felicitous ancient "Egyptian despotism has nothing but the name in common with the one that rules in our days in the Orient."

12. Djuvara, *Cent projets*; Ghorbal, *The Beginnings*, 1–4.

13. Laurens, *Les Origines*, 21–62.

14. Gottfried Wilhelm Freiherr von Leibniz, "Consilium Aegyptiacum," in *Die Werke von Leibniz*, 11 vols. (Hannover: Klindworth, 1864–84), Series 1, 2:175–207. For a French translation, see Ahmed Youssef, *La Fascination d'Égypte: Du Rêve au projet, avec 'Consilium Aegyptiacum,' le texte inédit que Leibniz présenta à Louis XIV* (Paris: L'Harmattan, 1998), 35–41, 194–224.

15. Adolf Hasenclever, *Geschichte Ägyptens im 19. Jahrhundert, 1798–1914* (Halle: Niemeyer, 1917), 20–21.

16. Laurens, *Les Origines*, 35–82. On the trope of "Oriental despotism" in Enlightenment literature, see Alain Grosrichard, *Structure du Sérail: La Fiction du despotisme asiatique dans l'occident classique* (Paris: Seuil, 1979).

17. Voltaire, *Essai sur les moeurs et l'esprit des nations et sur les principaux faits de l'histoire depuis Charlemagne jusqu'à Louis XIII*, ed. René Pomeau, 2 vols. (Paris: Garnier Frères, 1963), 1:263–64. Voltaire's comments do not apply to the Arabs, whom he praised for their advancement of sciences.

18. Anne-Robert-Jacques Turgot, "Plan du second discours sur les progrès de l'esprit humain," in *Oeuvres de Turgot et documents le concernant, avec biographie et notes*, ed. Gustav Schelle, 5 vols. (Paris: Alcan, 1913–23), 1:320. Turgot arrived at these conclusions from an analysis of linguistics.

19. Turgot, "Plan de deux discours sur l'histoire universelle," in ibid., 1:294.

20. Montesquieu, *Esprit des lois* XVII.3, in *Oeuvres complètes*, 2 vols. (Paris: Gallimard, 1949–51), 2:525–26.

21. Ibid., XVII.5-5, 2:526–27.

22. Claude-Étienne Savary, *Lettres d'Égypte, où l'on offre le parallèle des moeurs anciennes et modernes de ses habitans, où*

l'on décrit l'état, le commerce, l'agriculture, le gouvernement, l'ancienne religion du pays, et la descente de St. Louis à Damiette, tirées de Joinville et des auteurs arabes, 3 vols. (Paris: Onfroi, 1785–86).

23. Carré, *Voyageurs*, 1:87.

24. Ibid., 1:101–2.

25. Charles-Nicolas-Sigisbert Sonnini de Manoncour, *Voyage dans la Haute et Basse Égypte fait par l'ordre de l'ancien gouvernement (de 1777 à 1780) et contenant des observations de tous genres*, 3 vols. (Paris: Buisson, 1799).

26. Ghorbal, *The Beginnings*, 4.

27. Constantin de Volney, *Voyage en Syrie et en Égypte pendant les années 1783, 1784, et 1785*, 2 vols. (Paris: Volland, Desenne, 1787).

28. When he heard about the preparations for the Egyptian campaign, Volney immediately interrupted a stay in the United States to return to France to assist Bonaparte's staff. However, he did not join the Armée de l'Orient. Laurens, *L'Expédition*, 185; Ghorbal, *The Beginnings*, 9–10. Volney was not the only celebrity from the artistic/literary world to decline the offer to embark for Egypt. Jacques-Louis David, for instance, was even less inclined than Volney to exchange the comfort of his Parisian studio for the deserts of Egypt. Lelièvre, *Vivant Denon, homme des Lumières*, 99–100.

29. Volney, *Voyage*, 1:256–57. When reading Denon's *Voyage*, on the other hand, the reader arrives at the opposite conclusion: it was only because of the monuments and Egypt's past, not because of the Egyptian people, that France conquered the country. In Denon's eyes, the French army was primarily conquering history, not a colonial asset.

30. Ibid., 1:212, 224.

31. Ghorbal, *The Beginnings*, 5; Charles-Roux, *Les Origines*, 213–15. Volney, Corsica's former deputy at the Assemblée Nationale, had met Napoleon for the first time in 1792 on their home island, where the writer had retired to operate an experimental farm for the acclimatization of tropical plants. See Chuquet, *La Jeunesse*, 2:237–40. Thanks to the success of his *Voyage en Syrie et en Égypte*, Volney was by then a prominent figure in French society and a recognized national authority on all questions concerning Egypt. The encounter was the beginning of a lifelong friendship with Bonaparte, and there can be no doubt that Volney's thoughts about Egypt helped shape Napoleon's strategy on how to conquer North Africa.

32. Voltaire, *Essai sur les moeurs*, 1:83–84.

33. Erik Hornung, *L'Égypte ésotérique: Le Savoir occulte des Égyptiens et son influence en Occident*, tr. Nathalie Baum (Monaco: Rocher, 2001), 13.

34. Ibid., 13.

35. Étienne-François de Lantier, *Voyages d'Antenor en Grèce et en Asie avec des notions sur l'Égypte: Manuscrit grec trouvé à Herculanum*, 15th rev. ed., 2 vols. (1797; repr., Brussels: Wahlen, 1821). The last reedition of the book was published in Paris in 1836.

36. Baltrušaitis, *La Quête d'Isis*, 59.

37. Boucher de la Richarderie, "Notice sur l'abbé Terrasson," in *Séthos, histoire ou vie tirée des monumens anecdotes de l'ancienne Égypte: Traduction d'un manuscript grec*, rev. ed., 6 vols. (1731; repr., Paris: d'Hautel, 1813), 1:11–12. Subsequent quotes from Terrasson's novel are taken from this edition. On the impact of Terrasson's novel on Egyptian-rite Freemasonry, see also Jacques Brengues, "Une triple hypothèse prospective," *Humanisme* 124 (September 1978): 35–38.

38. Terrasson, *Séthos*, 1:17.

39. Jean Terrasson, *Dissertation critique sur L'Iliade d'Homer, où à l'occasion de ce poëme on cherche les règles d'une poëtique fondée sur la raison, & sur les exemples des anciens & des modernes* (Paris: Fournier et Coutstelier, 1715); Diodorus of Sicily, *Histoire universelle*, tr. Jean Terrasson, 7 vols. (Paris: De Bure, 1737–44). See also Boucher de la Richarderie, "Notice," 1:8.

40. Terrason, *Séthos*, 1:17, 29.

41. Ibid., 2:11.

42. Ibid., 2:19.

43. Ibid., 2:24–29.

44. Ibid., 1:50–54, 118–22; 2:29–50.

45. Ibid., 2:14.

46. Ibid., 1:54–55; 2:17.

47. Ibid., 1:104–48.

48. François de Salignac de La Mothe-Fénelon, *Les Aventures de Télémaque, fils d'Ulysse* (Paris: Barbin, 1699). Numerous reprints and translations of the novel appeared in European cities, including Brussels, The Hague, and London, within the same year. Dozens of other editions and translations into almost every European language followed over the course of the eighteenth century.

49. Boucher de la Richarderie, "Notice," 1:12.

50. Guerrier de Dumast, *La Maçonnerie*, 63.

51. Terrasson, *Séthos*, 1:23–24.

52. Jean Thiry, *Bonaparte en Égypte, Décembre 1797–24 Août 1799* (Paris: Berger-Levrault, 1973), 41; Laissus, *L'Égypte*, 35–36, 107.

53. Laissus, *L'Égypte*, 135–44.

54. Abd-al-Rahman al-Jabartî, *Merveilles biographiques et historiques, ou Chroniques du Cheikh Abd-el-Rahman el Djabarti, traduites de l'arabe*, tr. Chefik Mansour bey, Abdulaziz Kalil bey, Gabriel Nicolas Kalil bey, and Iskender Ammoun effendi, 9 vols. (1888–96; repr., Nendeln/Liechtenstein: Kraus, 1970), 6:66.

55. Laissus, *L'Égypte*, 175–76. On the reaction of the native population at the last hot air balloon launch in December 1798, which ended in an accident, see the *Courier [sic] de l'Égypte* 20 (Frimaire 18, year VII—December 8, 1798): 2: "The view of this experiment made the greatest impression on the natives of this country. Their disbelief continued through the time of the preparations; but they were moved by admiration once they saw this great globe moving by itself. When the machine began its ascent, those who were in the neighborhood from where it was launched took flight with an expression of bewilderment. When they saw the machine's debris and the firing stove tumbling back to earth, they concluded that it was a war engine we knew how to operate as we pleased so as to burn the towns of our enemies."

56. Louis-Antoine Fauvelet de Bourrienne, *Mémoires de Bourrienne, ministre d'État, sur Napoléon, le Directoire, le Consulat, l'Empire, la Restauration*, ed. Désiré Lacroix, 5 vols. (Paris: Garnier Frères, 1899–1900), 1:315–16. The event came in the aftermath of a native fortuneteller's visit to Napoleon's headquarters, which inspired his secretary, Bourrienne, to conceive of Berthollet's scientific demonstration as the Western response in a contest "opposing sorcerers with sorcerers."

57. F. Marouis, article "Ganteaume (Henri-Joseph-Antonin)," in *Dictionnaire de biographie française*, 15:351–53.

58. Émile Franceschini, article "Caffarelli ou Caffarelli du Falga (Louis-Marie-Joseph-Maximilien)," in *Dictionnaire de biographie française*, 7:812–13; La Jonquière, *L'Expédition*, 1:122, note 2.

59. Charles Thoumas, *Les Grands cavaliers du Premier Empire: Les Trois Colbert*, 3 vols. (Paris and Nancy: Berger-Levrault,

1890–1909), 1:183–231; Antoine-Vincent Arnault, article "Colbert (Édouard-Pierre-David)," in *Biographie nouvelle des contemporains*, 20 vols. (Paris: Librairie historique, 1820–25), 4:465–66.

60. Laissus, *L'Égypte*, 303–400; Laurens, *L'Expédition*, 225–326.

61. Galland, *Tableau*, 1:288–89.

62. Cuvelier de Trie, *La Mort de Kléber*, 32, note 1.

63. É. Franceschini, article "Destaing (Jacques-Zacharie)," in *Dictionnaire de biographie française*, 11:95; Meulenaere, *Bibliographie raisonnée*, 72.

64. For a complete list of members of the Institut and the Commission des sciences et des arts, see Meulenaere, *Bibliographie raisonnée*, 233–44, and Laissus, *L'Égypte*, 521–26.

65. Étienne-Louis Malus de Mitry, *L'Agenda de Malus: Souvenirs de l'expédition d'Égypte* (Paris: Champion, 1892), 140–41: "I was charged with making the arrangements for establishing the plague hospital, which was located in the Greek convent. For ten days I attended assiduously to this job and spent the mornings in the infected odor of this cloaca, where every last corner was filled with the sick. It was not until the eleventh day that I felt myself indisposed; a burning fever and violent headaches forced me to take rest."

66. Ibid., 25–26.

67. Ibid., 19–24, 109–11.

68. Laissus, *L'Égypte*, 256; Solé, *Les Savants*, 108-9; Meulenaere, *Bibliographie raisonnée*, 66.

69. Laissus, *L'Égypte*, 57, 326–27; Solé, *Les savants*, 220–21; Meulenaere, *Bibliographie raisonnée*, 99–100.

70. Letter by Geoffroy Saint-Hilaire to the Professors of the Muséum d'histoire naturelle in Paris of December 22, 1799 (Nivôse 1, year VIII), cited in Étienne Geoffroy Saint-Hilaire, *Lettres écrites d'Égypte à Cuvier, Jussieu, Lacépède, Monge, Desgenettes, Redouté jeune, Norry, etc., aux professeurs du Muséum et à sa famille*, ed. Ernest-Théodore Hamy (Paris: Hachette, 1901), 149, no. xxxvi.

71. Ibid., 103–10, no. xxv; 138–44, no. xxxiv. On Lacépède, see Henri Tribout de Morembert, article "Lacépède (Bernard-Germain-*Étienne* de La Ville-sur-Illon de)," in *Dictionnaire et biographie française*, 18:1476–77; Amiable, *Une loge maçonnique*, 293–95. Lacépède's claim to fame in the Masonic world was that he had joined the lodge *Les Neuf Soeurs* the same year, 1778, as the aged philosopher Voltaire. In the aftermath of Napoleon's reorganization of the Grand Orient, in 1804, Lacépède was appointed Great Administrator General of all lodges. A renowned musicologist and natural scientist, he wrote operas and published a five-volume ichthyological study. Because of his rallying to the Napoleonic cause during the *cent jours*, Lacépède was stripped of all his positions and honors during the Restoration.

72. Laissus, *L'Égypte*, 36, 245; Solé, *Les Savants*, 214–15; Meulenaere, *Bibliographie raisonnée*, 38–39.

73. Laissus, *L'Égypte*, 80–81, 117–18, 165–66; Meulenaere, *Bibliographie raisonnée*, 158–59.

74. Laissus, *L'Égypte*, 201–2, 360; Solé, *Les Savants*, 232; Meulenaere, *Bibliographie raisonnée*, 197–98; Georges Legrain, "Guillaume-André Villoteau, musicographe de l'expédition française d'Égypte (1759–1839)," *Bulletin de l'Institut égyptien* [Cairo] 11 (1917): 1–30.

75. Ghorbal, *The Beginnings*, 97.

76. *Moniteur universel* 161 (Ventôse 11, year VII—February 29, 1799): 657. The *Moniteur universel* was the most widely read daily newspaper during the Directory. Since it closely reflected the views of the government, it was not directly threatened by the censorship measures soon to be enacted, and was published continuously during the Empire. Unfortunately, no systematic study of the press during the Directory is available to date. On the structure and history of the French press after Napoleon's rise to power, see André Cabanis, *La Presse sous le Consulat et l'Empire, 1799–1814* (Paris: Société des études robespierristes, 1975).

77. See Talleyrand-Périgord's letter in *Le Rédacteur* 1314 (Thermidor 5, year VII—July 23, 1799): 2–3. Delacroix's response appeared first in the *Moniteur universel* 309 (Thermidor 9, year VII July 27, 1799): 1256, and was later reprinted in *Le Rédacteur* 1317 (Thermidor 8, year VII—July 26, 1799): 1–3. The publication of the letters occurred only a few days after Talleyrand-Périgord's resignation as foreign minister on July 20, 1799, which was at least partly triggered by the persistent controversy over the planning of the campaign. See also the following notice in the *Moniteur universel* 311 (Thermidor 11, year VII—July 29, 1799): 1263: "We take note that it was on the 5th of Thermidor, year 6, that Napoleon and his army entered Cairo, and that it was on the 5th of Thermidor, year 7, that the impeachment proceedings against those who ordered the expedition were opened."

78. *Moniteur universel* 319 (Thermidor 19, year VII—August 6, 1799): 1295.

79. *Moniteur universel* 346 (Fructidor 16, year VII—September 2, 1799): 1403: "We are assured, for example, that the [British] chancellor has taken to the project of forwarding to Egypt printed copies of the opinions professed in France against the expedition so as to demoralize General Bonaparte, who, having thus far braved the plague, illness, and combined British and Turkish attacks, might fear the blame spread by his compatriots."

80. A typical example is the following anecdote about the youthful bravura of the son of the president of the Directors, Merlin, who participated in the campaign, which appeared in the *Moniteur universel* 6 (Vendémiaire 6, year VIII—September 28, 1799): 7: "The following anecdote has been reported about the son of Merlin, age 18: Bonaparte gave him orders to explore a village located at several days' distance in the sands of the desert. He was the only one on horseback, accompanied by 25 chasseurs on foot. Not far from the army camp he encountered a detachment of Mamelukes stronger than his. He stops, dismounts, and lets the enemy advance without attacking him. The surprised Mamelukes also stop, but their chief tries to get hold of the horse of young Merlin; the latter blows his brains out, and orders the pursuit of the enemy, who is put in disarray." Letters and orders of the day appeared in the *Moniteur universel* 14 (Vendémiaire 14, year VIII—October 6, 1799): 49–50, and 15 (Vendémiaire 15, year VIII—October 7, 1799): 54.

81. *Le Thé, ou Le Contrôleur général* 9 (Thermidor 22, year VII—August 9, 1799): 4: "News that arrived almost at the same time from Genoa and Amsterdam agrees that Bonaparte has taken Acre and Damascus and is now marching on Constantinople. These notices are from a later date than those which have arrived from Vienna or London." In a similar vein, *Le Grondeur, ou Le Flambeau* 251 (Thermidor 28, year VII—August 15, 1799) wrote: "We have learned from the navy administration about the taking of Acre and Bonaparte's triumphant march on Constantinople." On the three invalid soldiers, see *Moniteur universel* 362 (Second complementary day, year VII – September 18, 1799): 1468: "Three soldiers from Bonaparte's army have come back from Egypt. Two are at the Invalides, the third is at the Val-de-Grace hospital. Several deputies and the citizen Volney, author of the *Voyage en Égypte*, paid a visit to the third soldier in order to question him concerning Bonaparte's situation when he left. This man,

who had had great difficulty speaking clearly, let it be understood that Bonaparte's attacks on Acre were pushed back three times. Irritated by the obstacle and determined to die before the fortress rather than not enter it, he led the charge a fourth time. This soldier saw Bonaparte take the flag out of the hands of the standard bearer so as to be the first to throw himself against the ramparts. The heroes of Lodi rallied to his side, charged against the besieged, fought for the place, caused terrible carnage, and let fly the tricolor flag. The description given by this soldier of the area adjacent to Acre has been recognized as correct by the citizen Volney, which makes one believe in the truthfulness of the report."

82. *Le Thé, ou Le Contrôleur général* 1 (Thermidor 15, year VII—August 2, 1799): 2.

83. A product of the post-Thermidorian reaction, the first series of Richer-Serizy's *L'Accusateur public* was published between 1795 and 1797. As Eugène Hatin noted, the paper was "a pamphlet rather than a journal," which was "written with passion, and one finds therein pages of true eloquence. One feels the emotions, the convictions of a man of good intentions, who believes that France cannot find a remedy for the ill that threatens to crush her, except by the re-establishment of religious and monarchic doctrines, and who tries to guide the nation towards this goal." Eugène Hatin, *Histoire politique et littéraire de la presse en France, avec une introduction historique sur les origines du journal et la bibliographie générale des journaux depuis leur origine*, 8 vols. (Paris, 1859–61), 7:301–5. The second series of the *Accusateur public*, which concerns us here, is a curiosity in its own right. The catalog of the Bibliothèque Nationale lists it as a "counterfeit" of Richer-Serizy's original *Accusateur public*, published by one Auguste Danican in a single issue in 1799. This issue deals almost exclusively with the Egyptian campaign. The political orientation of Danican's short-lived attempt to revive the defunct paper closely parallels that of the Richer-Serizy original, i.e., the journal embraced an exceedingly polemic tone to press its Catholic and monarchist agenda.

84. *L'Accusateur public*, Series 2, 1, no. 2 (Thermidor 6, year VII—July 24, 1799): 11–13.

85. Régis Michel, "L'Art des Salons," in *Aux Armes et aux Arts! Les arts de la Révolution, 1789–1799*, ed. Philippe Bordes and Régis Michel, exh. cat. (Paris: Adam Biro, 1988), 54–56.

86. *L'Accusateur public*, Series 2, 1, no. 2 (Thermidor 6, year VII—July 24, 1799): 13.

87. Briot developed these ideas in a lengthy speech before the Legislative Assembly on August 29, 1799 (Fructidor 12, year VII). The speech was reprinted in full over two issues of the *Moniteur universel*, nos. 346 (Fructidor 16, year VII—September 2, 1799): 1404, and 349 (Fructidor 17, year VII—September 3, 1799): 1409.

88. *Moniteur universel* 348 (Fructidor 18, year VII—September 4, 1799): 1412, and 349 (Fructidor 19, year VII—September 5, 1799): 1416. It comes as no surprise that *Le Thé, ou Le Contrôleur général* and the *Accusateur public* were on the list of newspapers to be shut down. After Napoleon's return to France these measures would even be tightened, and three-quarters of the French newspapers were suppressed entirely. See also Cabanis, *La Presse*, 12–24.

89. This series opens with two personal reports by Napoleon himself in No. 18, and is continued over the following days by General Berthier: *Moniteur universel* 18–32 (Vendémiaire 18 through Brumaire 2, year VIII—October 10 through October 24, 1799): 65–7, 69–70, 73–4, 78–9, 81–2, 86, 89–90, 94, 97, 101, 105–6, 110, 113, 118, 121–2.

90. See chapter 4, pages 115–16. According to the *Rédacteur* 1401 (Vendémiaire 27, year VIII—October 19, 1799): 2, Napo-

leon's itinerary from Fréjus to Paris after his landing on October 9, 1799, was a genuine march of triumph through France: "The courier riding in advance to prepare the horses demanded them for Bonaparte, and everywhere in the towns and villages the population assembled by the wayside to greet him; he would be accompanied even beyond the boundaries of the communities. The throngs were so thick that, even on the highways, the carriages advanced only with great difficulty. All the places through which Bonaparte traveled from Fréjus to Paris were illuminated at night."

91. *Moniteur universel* 30 (Vendémiaire 30, year VIII—October 22, 1799): 113, and 38 (Brumaire 8, year VIII—October 30, 1799): 145.

92. See for example the *Moniteur universel* 43 (Brumaire 13, year VIII—November 4, 1799): 165: "Although one cannot cast doubt on the taking of Aboukir and the destruction of 18,000 Turkish forces, one cannot help but notice that the French remaining in Egypt find themselves in a very precarious situation, if their hope depends on but a partial success [in these operations]."

93. *Moniteur universel* 44 (Brumaire 14, year VIII—November 5, 1799): 171. The disaffection of the French soldiers left behind by Bonaparte in Egypt is also described in Bourrienne, *Mémoires*, 2:119.

94. On the elevation of the *Moniteur universel* to the "only official newspaper," see Cabanis, *La Presse*, 11. The *Moniteur* was owned by the descendants of Charles-Joseph Panckoucke, publishers of an abbreviated, mass-marketed *Description de l'Égypte*, also called the "Panckoucke edition," which appeared between 1821 and 1829.

95. Significantly, Denon's name appeared for the first time twelve days after Napoleon's coup d'état in the first paragraph of the front page of the *Moniteur universel* 60 (Brumaire 30, year VIII—October 21, 1799): 233, in the context of a letter by the chemist Hippolyte-Victor Descotils, member of the Institut d'Égypte, who wrote about the ruins of Denderah. More short notices about Denon's archeological discoveries followed in December 1799. In 1801 the *Moniteur universel* 215 (Floréal 5, year IX—April 25, 1810): 903–4, reprinted the prospectus of Denon's book, written by Amaury Duval and Jacques-Guillaume Legrand, in full length to stir interest in the publication. Sometime between 1800 and 1801 the newspaper must have succeeded in securing exclusive rights to publish excerpts from the travel account. In August 1802, upon the completion of the printing of Denon's *Voyage*, Legrand was again called in to write an *Analyse et extraits du Voyage dans la Basse et la Haute Égypte*, introducing the series of excerpts from Denon's book which spread over a sequence of seven issues: *Moniteur universel* 340 (Fructidor 10, year X—August 28, 1802): 1388–89; 342 (Fructidor 12, year X—August 30, 1802): 1396–98; 343 (Fructidor 13, year X—August 31, 1802): 1401–2; 348 (Fructidor 18, year X—September 5, 1802), 1421–22; 353 (Fructidor 23, year X—August 10, 1802): 1453–54; 358 (Fructidor 28, year X—September 15, 1802), 1461–62; 359 (Fructidor 29, year X—September 16, 1802), 1464–65. The first two or three of these excerpts absorbed approximately two-thirds of the entire newspaper. The series concluded with a complete list of all 141 plates contained in the atlas of engravings that accompanied Denon's travel description.

3. UNDER THE PYRAMIDS OF PARIS

1. Heraclitus, *Fragments* B.CXXIII, in *Les Présocratiques*, ed. and tr. Jean-Paul Dumont, (Paris: Gallimard, La Pléiade, 1988), 173.

2. *L∴ & Ch∴ Frères Artistes: Tableaux*, BN-MSS, FM 2.78, nos. 9–14, 57. The artist provided his address in the critical years between 1818 and 1819 as "rue des Juifs No. 1, au Marais," an indication that he lived during this time in the Jewish quarter at the heart of the Marais. By 1822 he had moved to the Ile St. Louis in Paris. The most succinct biography of Ponce-Camus's life and work can be found in Arnault, article "Ponce-Camus (Marie-Nicolas)," *Biographie nouvelle des contemporains*, 11:449–50 (Supplement). See also Charles Gabet, *Dictionnaire des artistes de l'école française au XIXe siècle: Peinture, sculpture, architecture, gravure, dessin, lithographie et composition musicale* (Paris: Vergne, 1831), 566.

3. Daniel and Guy Wildenstein, *Documents complémentaires au catalogue de l'oeuvre de Louis David* (Paris: Fondation Wildenstein, 1973), 257, no. 2151; 34–38, nos. 283–320.

4. AN, F 17/1241, no. 42, cited after Wildenstein, 135–36, no. 1227.

5. ENSBA, Ms. 318, no. 55. See also Wildenstein, 230, no. 1968. In February 1816 Ponce-Camus was also one of the fifty-six signatories of a petition to the Minister of Police, Comte Decazes, asking to grant David an exceptional permission to return from his exile in Belgium. The request was approved, but David chose to stay in Brussels of his own volition. Louis Hautecoeur, *Louis David* (Paris: La table ronde, 1954), 260, note 65. On David's *Alexander, Apelles, and Campaspe* and the exclusion of Ponce-Camus's interpretation of the subject from the 1819 Salon, see Philippe Bordes, *Jacques-Louis David: Empire to Exile* (New Haven and London: Yale University Press, 2005), 225–30, no. 31.

6. Apparently, Ponce-Camus painted the *Napoleon Meditating before the Coffin of Frederick II of Prussia* at his own expense and, upon the completion of the canvas, received the state commission for *Napoleon in Osterode* from Vivant Denon. The art administration had originally only asked for a drawing of an unspecified subject. *Vivant Denon, Correspondance*, 2:1345, no. AN 75; 2:1347, no. AN 76, note 29.

7. On Bonaparte's visit in Potsdam, see Ilja Mieck, "Napoléon et Berlin," *Études napoléoniennes: Bulletin historique de la Société de sauvegarde du château impérial de Pont-de-Briques* 29, no. 3 (1993): 553–76.

8. Ibid., 560–62. Mieck pointed out a number of factual errors in Ponce-Camus's composition, the most salient of which concern the number of Napoleon's companions and the pattern of the floor. Only two men accompanied Napoleon to the crypt, Prince Gérôme and the local sacristan named Geim, instead of an entourage of ten as in Ponce-Camus's picture. Napoleon is said to have uttered the words "Death, Glory has survived you," and then to have asked the two men to withdraw so that he could contemplate the tomb alone. Mieck noticed that the floor of the Garnisonkirche features no pattern of the type depicted in Ponce-Camus's painting, but the connotations of this detail in Freemasonry escaped him. The Mosaic Pavement in a Masonic temple marks symbolically the ground floor or sanctuary of the Temple of Solomon. Further examples of Masonic checkerboard patterns of this type can be found for example in *Images du patrimoine maçonnique*, ed. Ludovic Marcos and Pierre Mollier, 2 vols. (Paris: Éditions maçonniques de France, 2002), 1:23, 27–29, 32-33, 57, 59, 61, 110, 113, 135–36, 154.

9. Hornung, *L'Égypte ésotérique*, 155. These accounts stand in striking contrast to historical reality, since Napoleon always seems to have kept a safe distance from the pyramids. For instance, when the members of the Institut undertook an expedition on September 24, 1798 (Vendémiaire 3, year VII) to explore the pyramids of Gizeh, Bonaparte preferred to observe the exploits of his colleagues from a distance. Despite his age, Monge arrived first at the summit, whereas Berthier did not manage to succeed but for the catcalls of Bonaparte, who preferred to stay down below. Laissus, *L'Égypte*, 205. Likewise, when it came to exploring the interior of the Cheops pyramid, Napoleon stayed outside, as noted by Villiers du Terrage: "On the descent, I still had time to enter the Pyramid. Bonaparte declined because doing so would have required crawling on his stomach in order to get around the stone blocking the entryway." Edouard de Villiers du Terrage, *L'Expédition d'Égypte: Journal et souvenirs d'un jeune savant engagé dans l'état-major de Bonaparte (1798–1801)*, ed. Alain Pigeard (1899; repr., Paris: Cosmopole, 2001), 81–82.

10. Thibaudeau, *Histoire générale*, 5:70–71, 5:489–93. Bourrienne, *Mémoires*, 1:403–4, knew about this legendary conversation, but dismissed it as "pure invention" and "a bad joke." According to him, Napoleon had set out for the pyramids because of a "military operation flavored with a little bit of curiosity," but he had "neither the desire nor the intention" of entering the pyramids.

11. *Description de l'Égypte, ou Receuil des observations et des recherches qui ont été faites en Égypte pendant l'expédition de l'armée française*, 20 vols. (Paris: Imprimerie impériale/Imprimerie royale, 1809–22). The work contains over nine hundred plates, which kept up to four hundred engravers busy at a time. On the publishing history of these volumes, see for example *The Napoleonic Survey of Egypt, Description de l'Égypte: The Monuments and Customs of Egypt, Selected Engravings and Texts*, ed. Terence M. Russel, 2 vols. (Aldershot and Burlington: Ashgate, 2001); Carré, *Voyageurs et écrivains*, 1:159–62; Meulenaere, *Bibliographie raisonnée*, 66–70.

12. *Description*, vol. 5, pl. 13.

13. Alain Pougetoux, "L'Empereur Napoléon au tombeau de Frédéric," in *L'Oeil de Napoléon*, 380–81, no. 409.

14. *Collection Deloynes: Collection de pièces sur les beauxarts imprimées et manuscrites*, vol. XLV, no. 1157, 647. BN-EST, Ya3.27 (1157)-8.

15. In spring 1807, for example, Ponce-Camus had made his bid, together with twenty-six competitors, for the monumental *Napoleon at Eylau* composition. The competition was won by Antoine-Jean Gros. See Lelièvre, *Vivant Denon: Homme de Lumière*, 170–71; Marc Gerstein, "Concours de la bataille d'Eylau: Enregistrement des esquisses, état des concurrents," in *L'Oeil de Napoléon*, 332–33, no. 342.

16. Vivant Denon, *Correspondance*, 2:1376–77, no. AN 89.

17. John McCormick, *Popular Theater in Nineteenth-Century France* (London and New York: Routledge, 1993), 152–54.

18. Mme Camus, for instance, played Euterpe and sang the *Conseils de Mentor*, set to music by Louis-Alexandre Piccinni, in Cuvelier de Trie's play *L'Asile du Silence, ou Gloire et Sagesse* (Paris: Barba, 1811), given in honor of the birth of Napoleon's son, the King of Rome. Themes and contents of the play show strong Sophisian overtones. On this play, its context, and positive reception, see Louis-Henry Lecomte, *Napoléon et l'Empire racontés par le théâtre, 1797–1899* (Paris: Raux, 1900), 251. In 1811 Mme Camus also played the Princess Lisca in Cuvelier de Trie's *L'Entrée des chevaliers français dans Serica* (Paris: Barba, 1811), given at the Jeux Gymniques.

19. ADPC, 6 Fi C965.

20. On Ponce-Camus's title *chevalier du Lion de Bavière*, see *L∴ & Ch∴ Frères Artistes: Tableaux*, BN-MSS, FM 2.78, no. 10. Testu's *Almanach Impérial pour l'année M.DCCC.XIII* (Paris: Testu, 1813), 175, lists eleven French recipients of the decoration—

seven members of the military and four civilians. The roster is apparently incomplete and does not mention Ponce-Camus's name among those of other Frenchmen who are known to have received the decoration.

21. Nicolas Buanic, "Portraits de legionnaires du Boulonnais," in *Deux siècles de Légion d'honneur à Boulogne-sur-Mer* (Arras: Conseil général du Pas-de-Calais, 2004), 66–67; Cardevacque, *Dictionnaire biographique*, 114–15; Dondey-Dupré, *Paroles funèbres*, 4–7; Mahul, *Annuaire nécrologique*, 5:68–70.

22. Anonymous, *Le Cirque Franconi: Détails historiques sur cet établissement hippique et sur ses principaux écuyers, recueillis par une chambrière en retraite avec quelques portraits gravés à l'eau-forte par Frédéric Hillemacher* (Lyon: Perrin & Marinet, 1875), 14.

23. See for instance Crow, *Emulation*, 239–40, for Gros's case.

24. Between 1807 and 1808 Cuvelier listed his address as "rue du Temple No. 22" or "enclos du Temple No. 22." He then moved to the northern extension of the same street, the rue du Faubourg du Temple No. 26, where he could have been found between 1809 and 1813. By the time of the Restoration he had moved a few houses down the rue du Faubourg du Temple, and was now at No. 9, where he still lived at the time of his death in 1824. For a short period in 1813 Cuvelier may also have occupied an apartment on the boulevard Bonne Nouvelle No. 2. See *L∴ & Ch∴ Frères Artistes: Tableaux*, BN-MSS, FM 2.78, nos. 4–13, 53–55, 57–58.

25. The tableaux of the *Frères Artistes* in the manuscript department of the Bibliothèque Nationale are teeming with addresses in and surrounding the Temple enclosure and the Marais. On the Marais, see Alfred Fierro, *Histoire et dictionnaire de Paris* (Paris: Laffont, 1996), 971–72. On the Temple enclosure and its history, see Jacques Hillairet, *Dictionnaire historique des rues de Paris*, 2 vols. (Paris: Minuit, 1963), 2:546–47. Demolished in the early nineteenth century, the Temple enclosure coincided roughly with the trapezoid formed by the modern-day rue du Temple, rue de Bretagne, rue de Picardie, and rue Béranger.

26. [André-Joseph-Étienne Lerouge], "Historique, Lettres de Convocation," in *Mélanges Lerouge*, CMC, Kloss Collection, Ms. 240.B.74.

27. See the biographies of Holtz, Norry, Royanez, and Villoteau in the appendix. On Norry during the Egyptian campaign, see also his memoirs, *Relation de l'expédition d'Égypte, suivie de la description de plusieurs des monumens de cette contrée, et ornée de figures* (Paris: Pougens, Year VII—1799).

28. Jean-Pierre Zimmer, *D'Orient en Occident: Histoire de la loge Les Vrais Amis Réunis d'Égypte, 1799–1845* (Paris: ÉDIMAF, 2001).

29. Ponce-Camus was an active member (i.e., signed the tableaux of the *Frères Artistes*) between 1813 and 1824. No other painters, draftsmen, or printmakers can be found in the group until after 1821, when two painters Pierre Dumay and Francisque-Martin-François Grenier de Saint-Martin, a student of David and Pierre-Narcisse Guérin, joined. Both seem to have been marginal figures within the hierarchy of the order, compared to Ponce-Camus.

30. *L∴ & Ch∴ Frères Artistes: Tableaux*, BN-MSS, FM 2.78, no. 11.

31. *Livre d'or* [BN], fol. 2v. Masonic conventions add four thousand years to the Christian calendar in order to express symbolically that Freemasonry started with the beginning of the world according to the Bible. By adding yet another ten thousand years, the Sophisians indicate that they are of an even more ancient derivation, namely that of Pharaonic Egypt.

32. *L∴ & Ch∴ Frères Artistes: Tableaux*, BN-MSS, FM 2.78, no. 12. The invitations to the *Fête Sophisienne (Hommage aux Dames)* and the *Agape Sophisienne* are bound together with the *Mélanges Lerouge* in The Hague, CMC.

33. Daniel Rabreau, "L'Architecture et la fête," in *Aux Armes et aux Arts!*, 265; Baltrušaitis, *La Quête d'Isis*, 31. On the *fête revolutionnaire* in general, see Mona Ozouf, *La Fête revolutionnaire, 1789–1799* (Paris: Gallimard, 1976).

34. Vivant Denon, *Correspondance*, 1:757–58, no. 2199; 1:767–68, no. 2233.2; 2:862–63, no. 2467; 2:880, no. 2524; 2:898, nos. 2579–80; 2:900, no. 2586.

35. W. Wynn Westcott, *The Isiac Tablet, or The Bembine Table of Isis* (1887; repr., Los Angeles: The Philosophical Research Society, 1976); Enrica Leospo, *La Mensa Isiaca di Torino* (Leiden: Brill, 1978); Ernesto Scamuzzi, *La "Mensa Isiaca" del Regio Museo di Antichità di Torino* (Rome: Bardi, 1939).

36. On the display of the Bembine Tablet in the Bibliothèque Nationale, see Alexandre Lenoir, *Nouvel essai sur la Table Isiaque* (Paris, 1809), x; Leospo, *La Mensa Isiaca*, 25–26; Scamuzzi, *La "Mensa Isiaca,"* 9. The tablet was returned to Italy after Napoleon's fall from power. Athanasius Kircher's analysis can be found in his *Oedipus aegyptiacus: Hoc est uniuersalis hierolglyphicae veterum doctrinae temporum iniuria abolitae instauratio. Opus ex omni orientalium doctrina & sapientia conditum, nec non viginti diuersarium linguarum, authoritate stabilitum*, 3 vols. (Rome: Mascardi, 1652–54), 3:79–100. His essay was preceded by Luigi Pignoria's *Vetustissimae tabulae aeneae sacris aegyptiorum simulachris coelatae accurata explication, in qua antiquissimarum superstitionum origines, progressiones, ritus ad Barbaram, Graecam, Romanamque historiam illustrandam enarrantur & multa scriptorum veterum loca qua explanantur, qua emendantur* (Venice: Franco, 1605), among other such treatises with small circulations. It was primarily Kircher's publication that earned the tablet international fame in antiquarian and scholarly circles. See Leospo, *La Mensa Isiaca*, 3; Baltrušaitis, *La Quête d'Isis*, 76–78; Scamuzzi, *La "Mensa Isiaca,"* 13; Hall, *The Secret Teachings of All Ages*, 162–77.

37. Patricia Rigault, "Coffret funéraire," in *L'Oeil de Napoléon*, 408–9, no. 450.

38. Gertrude Jobes, *Dictionary of Mythology, Folklore, and Symbolism*, 2 vols. (New York: Scarecrow Press, 1962), 1:99. The symbol of the Christian cross is believed by Egyptosophists to have evolved from the Egyptian *ankh*.

39. Plutarch, *De Iside et Osiride* 9, 354c, ed. Griffith, 130–31; 283–85 (commentary).

40. Proclus, *In Timaeum* II, 98.13–22, in *Proclus: Commentaire sur le Timée*, ed. and tr. André-Jean Festugière, 5 vols. (Paris: Vrin, 1966–68), 1:139–40; Lantier, *Voyages d'Antenor*, 1:115, 245.

41. Plutarch, *De Iside et Osiride* 12–19, 355d–358e, ed. Griffith, 134–47; Helmut Koester, *Introduction to the New Testament: History, Culture, and Religion of the Hellenistic Age*, 2 vols. (Philadelphia: Fortress Press, 1982), 1:183–91.

42. Herodotus, *Historiae* II.42, ed. and tr. Alfred Denis Godley, 4 vols. (Cambridge and London: Harvard University Press, Loeb Classical Library, 1920–25), 1:326–27; Apuleius, *Metamorphoseon* 11.1–30, in *Apuleius: Metamorphoses*, ed. and tr. John Arthur Hanson, 2 vols. (Cambridge: Harvard University Press, Loeb Classical Library, 1989), 2:290–359; Diodorus of Sicily, *Bibliotheca historica* I.11.1–V.69.1, ed. and tr. Charles Henry Oldfather (Cambridge and London: Harvard University Press, Loeb Classical Library, 1946–52), vols. I–III.

43. On this milieu, see for example Alain Faure, *Champollion: Le savant déchiffré* (Paris: Fayard, 2004), 10, 14, 157, 170–76.

44. See Introduction, 21–22.

45. August-Prosper-François Guerrier de Dumast, *Discours prononcé le 28 avril 5821, à la Loge des Artistes (Orient de Paris)* (Paris: Dondey-Dupré, 1821), 6–7. See also Rétat, "Initiations, initiatives," 35. Of the four Greeks received on that day, three were Sophisians: Demetrios N. Photilas, Nicolos Sava Piccolos, and Athanasias Vogorides.

46. *Livre d'or* [BN], fol. 2v.

47. The "Law of Silence" is of "fundamental importance" to all Masonic teachings. See Gilbert Kaluski, article "Silence," *Dictionnaire de la franc-maçonnerie*, ed. Ligou, 1140–41.

48. Plutarch, *De Iside et Osiride* 68, 378c, ed. Griffith, 224–25; 110, 354, 535 (commentaries).

49. "Hermes Trismegistus to His Son Tat: Secret Discourse on the Mountain about Regeneration and the Rule of Silence," in *Corpus Hermeticum* XIII.2, ed. and tr. Arthur Darby Nock and André-Jean Festugière, 4 vols. (Paris: Belles Lettres, 1945–54), 2:200–201. The connection between sowing and wisdom is also alluded to in the fourth Sophisian *Apophthegm* discussed below. Many similar references to silence can be cited in the *Corpus Hermeticum*, for instance I.30–31 ("From Hermes Trismegistus: Poimandres," 1:17, 1:19); X.5, 10 ("From Hermes Trismegistus: The Key," 1:115, 1:118); XIII.8 ("Hermes Trismegistus to His Son Tat: Secret Discourse on the Mountain about Regeneration and the Rule of Silence," 2:203).

50. *Livre d'or* [BN], fol. 16r.

51. Ibid., fol. 51r, no. 15.

52. See for instance the "Stele of Horus on a Crocodile" from about the fourth century B.C. in the Louvre, inv. E10902.

53. Jean-Jacques Boissard and Theodor de Bry, *VI. Pars antiquitatum romanorum, sive IIII. tomus, inscriptionum & monumentorum, quae Romae in saxis & marmoribus visuntur*, 3 vols. (Frankfurt: de Bry, 1597–1602), 3/II (Pt. VI), Plate 78; Bernard de Montfaucon, *L'Antiquité expliquée et représentée en figures*, 5 vols. (Paris: Delaulne, 1719), 2/II:312–13 (Book XIV, §. II–IV); Alexandre Lenoir, *Nouvelle explication des hieroglyphes, ou Des Anciennes allégories, sacrées des Égyptiens, utile à l'intelligence des monuments mythologiques des autres peuples suivie d'un résumé alphabétique ornée de dix-huit planches* (Paris: Musée des monumens français, 1809), 35–36. Montfaucon's commentary was based on Apuleius's *Metamorphoses*, wherein the author described a reveling, dog-headed Anubis as messenger in the procession of Isis, brandishing a palm branch and a caduceus. *Metamorphoseon* 11.11, in *Apuleius: Metamorphoses*, ed. Hanson, 2:312–13. Lantier in his *Voyages d'Atenor*, 2:202–3, conflates the dog-headed Anubis with Osiris, "father and husband of Isis." His canine appearance was due to the fact that "one fed in his [Anubis's] temple sacred dogs, before which one fell prostrate."

54. Alexandre Lenoir, *La Franche-Maçonnerie rendue à sa véritable origine, ou L'Antiquité de la Franche-Maçonnerie prouvée par l'explication des mystères anciens et modernes* (Paris: Fournier, 1814), 150.

55. *Livre d'or* [BN], fols. 18r, 22r.

56. Ibid., fol. 51r, no. 16.

57. Ibid., fols. 23r–26v, 29r–30v.

58. Ibid., fols. 31r–31v, 51v, nos. 1–2 ("Hyéroglyphes particuliers de l'aspiration des Sophisiennes").

59. Ibid., fol. 33r, §.3 ("Réglement").

60. Ibid., fol. 52v, no.1.

61. Ibid., fol. 67v ("Lieu de Rassemblement et Matériel").

62. Ibid., fols. 24r–24v, Section 1, Article 14; fol. 25v, Section 3, Article 6.

63. Lepeletier's vengeful royalist daughter is believed to have acquired the original in the early nineteenth century for the purpose of destroying it. See Antoine Schnapper, *David* (New York: Alpine, 1982), 151–53. The theme of the suspended sword also appears to have inspired Cuvelier de Trie's play *Le Phénix, ou L'Ile des Vieilles, comédie-féerie en quatre actes, mêlée de chants, pantomimes, combats et danses* (Paris: Barba, Year VI—1797), 20, in which the hero Zépherin, in order to earn the love of Nicette, has to set free her father Carambo, kept by "The Phantom" in an underground prison where he is "tied to a truncated column [while] a chevalier in full armor holds a knife against his throat. A shiny saber glitters above the head of the Enchanter [Carambo] and hangs from the ceiling, suspended on nothing more than a thread, which a second chevalier is about to cut with long scissors (the little blue light wanders across the stage and disappears). Zépherin arrives and, shaken by realizing Carambo's horrible situation, cuts the arm of the chevalier holding the scissors so that the arm drops to the floor."

64. *Livre d'or* [BN], fols. 69r–70r.

65. *Metamorphoseon* 11.11, in *Apuleius: Metamorphoses*, ed. Hanson, 2:312–13.

66. *The Jerusalem Bible*, 2 Samuel 6:5–16; 1 Kings 8:1–9; 1 Maccabees 1:1–25. On Cuvelier's play *Les Machabées, ou la prise de Jérusalem*, and its inspiration by 1 Maccabees, see chapter 4. Allusions to and symbolic representations of the Ark of the Covenant could be found in a variety of Masonic rituals in eighteenth- and nineteenth-century France. See F. Delon, articles "Arche" and "Arche d'Alliance Maçonnique," in *Dictionnaire de la franc-maçonnerie*, ed. Ligou, 66–67.

67. *Livre d'or* [BN], fol. 70r.

68. A similar "hair sacrifice" is described in Lantier, *Voyages d'Antenor*, 1:22–23.

69. *Trésor de la langue française: Dictionnaire de la langue du XIXe au XXe siècle (1789–1960)*, ed. Paul Imbs, 16 vols. (Paris: CNRS, 1971–94), 14:1275. The term syringe has Greek roots, as attested by the fourth-century A.D. Greco-Syrian historian Ammianus Marcellinus, in *Ammiani Marcellini Rerum Gestarum Libri qui supersunt* XVII.7.11, ed. and tr. John Carew Rolfe, 3 vols. (Cambridge and London: Harvard University Press, Loeb Classical Library, 1950–52), 1:346–47: "Now earthquakes take place (as the theories state, and among them Aristotle is perplexed and troubled) either in the tiny recesses of the earth, which in Greek we call σύριγγαι [=syringes; the term is cited in Greek in the original Latin text], under the excessive pressure of surging waters; or at any rate (as Anaxagoras asserts) through the force of the winds, which penetrate the innermost parts of the earth; for when these strike the solidly cemented walls and find no outlet, they violently shake those stretches of land under which they crept when swollen."

70. *Livre d'or* [BN], fols. 52v–53r.

71. Denis Diderot, "Égyptiens," in *Oeuvres complètes: Encyclopédie III (Lettres D–L)*, ed. John Lough and Jacques Proust, 25 vols. (Paris: Herman, 1975), 7:119. Alternatively, Lenoir, *La Franche-Maçonnerie*, 74, described the hierophant as head of the college of priests in ancient Egypt.

72. Diderot, "Égyptiens," 7:119, mentions explicitly "Moses, Orpheus, Linus, Plato, Pythagoras, Democritus, Thales; in a word all the philosophers of Greece."

73. Diderot, "Égyptiens," 7:122. Diderot was careful enough to point out that he did not invent this genealogy but resorted to a

text by Eusebius, which he quoted in the Latin original (7:132–33): "Thoth, the first Mercury, had engraved the sacred characters in sacred language on the columns erected on Syrian soil. After the deluge, these inscriptions were remade at the same spot in sacred characters, but translated from the sacred language into Greek, then reproduced in Egyptian sanctuaries by Agathos Daimon, upon the order of the second Mercury, father of Tat; this is why Tat declares that the books were written by his ancestor Mercury [Hermes] Trismegistus." Diderot probably quoted this text after the chapter *de philosophia aegyptiorum* in Johann Jakob Brucker's *Historia critica philosophiae a mundi incunabilis*, 2nd ed. (Leipzig: Weidemann & Reich, 1767), 251, where Eusebius is cited as original source for the Latin text. The figure of Tat is a genuine Hermetic invention that evolved from a Greek misspelling of Thoth; in due course, Tat became the son of Thoth in the Hermetica. See Garth Fowden, *The Egyptian Hermes: A Historical Approach to the Late Pagan Mind* (Princeton: Princeton University Press, 1993), 32–33.

74. Pseudo-Manetho, "From Syncellus," in *Manetho*, ed. and tr. William Gillan Waddell (Cambridge and London: Harvard University Press, Loeb Classical Library, 1940), 208–9. For a correct interpretation of the Hermetic genealogy in this fragment, see Walter Scott, *Hermetica: The Ancient Greek and Latin Writings Which Contain Religious or Philosophical Teachings Ascribed to Hermes Trismegistus*, 4 vols. (Oxford: Clarendon Press, 1924–36), 3:491–92. My corrected translation is taken from Fowden, *The Egyptian Hermes*, 30.

75. Fowden, *The Egyptian Hermes*, 22–31.

76. Iamblichus of Apamea, *De Mysteriis Aegyptiorum* I.2.5–6, in *Les Mystères d'Égypte*, ed. and tr. Édouard des Places (Paris: Belles Lettres, 1966), 40–41. The Neoplatonic editor Marsilio Ficino invented the title of Iambichus's treatise, *De Mysteriis Aegyptiorum*, during the Renaissance; the text was not known under this title in antiquity. See also Fowden, *The Egyptian Hermes*, 134.

77. Ammianus Marcellinus, *Ammiani Marcellini Rerum Gestarum Libri qui supersunt* XXII.15.30, ed. Rolfe, 2:294–95. My translation is taken from George Robert Stow Mead, *Thrice-Greatest Hermes: Studies in Hellenistic Theosophy and Gnosis*, 3 vols. (London: Watkins, 1964), 1:77–78. Mead points out that the passages and chambers in this description were hewn out of solid rock, a feature the Sophisians attempted to mimic in their insistence that their cavern walls, tables, and benches all be roughly hewn and unpolished.

78. *Hymne Sacré des Anciens Mystères, mis en musique par l'initié Foignet père, pour la Fête d'Isis célébrée à la L∴ des Artistes O∴ de Paris le 30 Aout 1821 (E_ V_), chanté par les aspirants Martin, Prévost et Trevaux, Professeurs, accompagné sur Harpe par l'aspirant Gabriel Foignet, Professeur, et sur le Piano par l'initié Alexandre Piccini, Professeur, à l'usage de la grande Pyramide de France et dédié au Souverain Patriarche de l'Ordre Sacré des Sophisiens, le Chevalier Cuvelier de Trie Vén∴ d'H∴* One copy at the BN-MUS, RÉS. F.1223. A printed invitation to the same event is preserved with the *Mélanges Lerouge* in The Hague, CMC. Both the musical score and this invitation to the *Agape Sophisienne pour la Fête d'Isis* refer to the same date, August 30, 1821. Despite their different titles, the texts of the *Hymne Sacré pour l'Initiation* in the BN Golden Book (fol. 38r) and the *Hymne Sacré des Anciens Mystères* at the *Fête d'Isis* are identical.

79. *Conseils de Mentor dans l'Asile du Silence, ou Gloire et Sagesse; Couplets chantés par Mme Camus, Paroles de J.G.A. Cuvelier, Musique d'Alex. Piccini* (Paris: Imbault, 1811). One copy

at the BN-MUS, Vm 7.89701. The score was written for Cuvelier de Trie's play *L'Asile du Silence, ou Gloire et Sagesse* of 1811.

80. *Livre d'or* [BN], fol. 38v.

81. Brian Juden, *Traditions Orphiques et tendances mystiques dans le Romantisme français, 1800–1855* (Paris: Klincksieck, 1971), 73.

82. Terrasson, *Séthos*, 2:34–42. Lantier, *Voyages d'Antenor*, 2:240–44, apparently copied the story from Terrasson. Antoine Abbé Pluche, *Histoire du ciel, où l'on recherche l'origine de l'idolâtrie et les méprises de la philosophie sur la formation et sur les influences des corps célestes*, 2nd ed., 2 vols. (Paris: Veuve Estienne, 1740), 1:157.

83. See for example *Courrier de l'Égypte* 21 (Frimaire 21, year VII—December 11, 1798): 4: "It is said amongst the Muslims of Cairo that a holy person was informed by means of a revelation about an encounter between Mohammed and his Destiny. The credibility that this revelation has attained made us resolve to reprint it in this paper: When Mohammed saw the French fleet approaching the coasts of Egypt, he looked for Destiny and told him: 'Oh, Destiny, how ungrateful you are! I have made you the sovereign judge of the world yet you want to deliver the most beautiful of all the regions subject to my laws to the French.' Destiny anwered him: 'Oh, Mohammed, now that the decree has been issued, it must be fulfilled. The French will arrive on Egyptian soil and will conquer it. I no longer have the power to prevent them from doing so. I have decided that these conquerors will turn themselves into Muslims.' Mohammed was completely satisfied with this answer and withdrew filled with satisfaction." See also Thibaudeau, *Histoire générale*, 5:68–69, on the French policy towards Islam. These accounts contrast sharply with the observations of the native chronicler Al-Jabartî, who pointed out that the French "are opposed to both Christians and Muslims, and do not hold fast to any religion. You see that they are materialists, who deny all God's attributes, the Hereafter and Resurrection, and who reject Prophethood and Messengership. They believe that the world was not created, and that the heavenly bodies and the occurrences of the Universe are influenced by the movement of the stars." Cited after *Napoleon in Egypt: Al-Jabarti's Chronicle of the First Seven Months of the French Occupation of Egypt, 1798*, ed. and tr. Robert L. Tignor and Shmuel Moreh (Princeton and New York: Markus Wiener, 1993), 32. The passage was omitted from the French standard edition of Al-Jabartî's Chronicles, the *Merveilles biographiques*.

84. Koester, *Introduction to the New Testament*, 1:161–62.

85. Apostolos N. Athanassakis, *The Orphic Hymns: Text, Translation and Notes* (Missoula: Scholars Press for the Society of Biblical Literature, 1977), ix.

86. Ibid., 22–23.

87. Like the Sophisian texts in the Golden Book, Orphic literature is a very flexible genre. As a scholar of Orphism has underscored, "it is a fallacy to suppose that all 'Orphic' poems and rituals are related to each other or that they are to be interpreted as different manifestations of a single religious movement. Of course, in some cases there are connections between different poems, between separate rituals, or between certain poems and certain rituals. But the essential principle to remember is that a poem becomes Orphic simply by being ascribed to Orpheus. By the same token, Orphics are simply people who in their religious beliefs and practices, whatever these may be, accord a place of honour to texts ascribed to Orpheus. There was no doctrinal criterion for ascription to Orpheus, and no copyright restriction. It was a device for conferring antiquity and authority upon a text that

stood in need of them." Martin Litchfield West, *The Orphic Poems* (Oxford: Clarendon Press, 1983), 3.

88. Juden, *Traditions Orphiques*, 70–87, 170–74.

89. *Livre d'or* [BN], fol. 53r, no. 2.

90. Torgny Säve-Söderbergh, article "Götterkreise," in *Lexikon der Ägyptologie*, ed. Wolfgang Helck, Eberhard Otto, et al., 7 vols. (Wiesbaden: Harrassowitz, 1975–92), 2:692–93. Triadic formulations are also a commonplace in the Hermetica. See *Corpus Hermeticum* VIII.2–3 and 5, ed. Nock and Festugière, 1:87–89: God, the First in His image, and Man; *Corpus Hermeticum* XIII.2, 2:200–201: God's will, intelligent Wisdom, the All in the All; *Asclepius* 10, in *Corpus Hermeticum*, 2:308: God, the World, and Man; Zosimus of Panopolis, *On the Letter Omega* 7, ed. and tr. Howard M. Jackson (Missoula: Scholars Press for the Society of Biblical Literature, 1978), 24–25, and 44–45, note 26 (commentary): Father (Mind), Son (Logos, born of Mind), and the material cosmos (man as possessing mind). As Jackson rightly points out, the idea of the triad is already implied in Trismegistus's name, the Thrice-Greatest.

91. Guerrier de Dumast, *La Maçonnerie*, 53. He goes on to explain that "one single and identical god (Jehovah) was considered [in the Ptah-Kneph-Neith trinity] under three aspects: [re]creative force, goodness, and intelligence or wisdom. Some say that Ptah was born from Kneph, because they did not understand by Ptah the eternal sun of justice, but the material star created in fact by *divine goodness*. Kneph was then reputed to be the Demiurge or *grand architect*; one gave him as attributes a blue dress and a golden scepter (blue and gold—today's colors of Freemasonry). Greek popular mythology, modified by the overly worldly notions concerning the divinities it borrowed from other nations, turned Ptah into Vulcan and Neith into Minerva. This is what led to the saying that Vulcan was the principal god of the Egyptians." In support of these ideas he cited Iamblichus of Apamea, Eusebius, and Pawel Ernest Jabłonski, among others.

92. Unless they looked at Alexandre Lenoir for guidance, the Sophisians probably jumbled together fragments from various Hermetic or hermetically inspired authors without much sense of how they all fit together. Possible candidates include Manetho's *Egyptiaca* Fr.1, I.1, ed. Waddell, 2–5, taken from his lost *History of Egypt*: "The first man (or god) in Egypt is Hephaestus [Ptah], who is also renowned among the Egyptians as the discoverer of fire. His son, Helios (the Sun), was succeeded by Sôsis: then follow, in turn, Cronos, Osiris, Typhon, brother of Osiris, and lastly [H]Orus, son of Osiris and Isis. These were the first to hold sway in Egypt"; or Iamblichus of Apamea, *De Mysteriis Aegyptiorum* VIII.2–3, 261–64, ed. des Places, 195–97: "Before the true beings and universal principles, there is a god who is the One, the First above everything else, even with respect to God and the First King; he remains immobile in the solitude of his uniqueness. [The One] is established after the model of a god who is himself a father and a son, and is the unique father of true Blessings, because he is larger, first, and the source of everything, base of the beings who are the intelligible Ideas. . . . These are the principles of the most ancient of all things, which Hermes ranks before the gods of the ether and the empyrean and before those [gods] of the sky. . . . On the next level [Hermes] proposes as god Emeph [Kneph], the head of the celestial gods, of whom he made an intellect that thinks itself and turns its thoughts upon itself. . . . Other powers have been put in charge of the creation of visible beings. The demiurgic intelligence, master of truth and wisdom, when it comes into the sphere of generation and leads into the light the invisible power of the hidden words, is called Amun in the language of the Egyptians;

but when it executes everything unfailingly and artfully according to the truth of everything, then it is called Ptah (a name the Greeks translate as Hephaestus, applying it only to [the god's] abilities as an artisan); while as a giver of Blessings, it is called Osiris, and it has other names according to its diverse virtues and activities."

93. Herman te Velde, article "Ptah," in *Lexikon der Ägyptologie*, 4:1177–80.

94. Robert Schlichting, article "Neith," in ibid., 4:392–95.

95. Winfried Barta, article "Kematef," in ibid., 3:382–83; and Philippe Derchain, article "Agathos Daimon," ibid., 1:94.

96. On the world egg, see for example Diodorus of Sicily, *Bibliotheca historica* I.27.3–5, ed. Oldfather, 1:86–89: "Now I am not unaware that some historians give the following account of Isis and Osiris: The tombs of these gods lie in Nysa in Arabia . . . And in that place there stands also a stele of each of the gods bearing an inscription in hieroglyphs. . . . And on the stele of Osiris the inscription is said to run: 'My father is Cronus, the youngest of all the gods, and I am Osiris the king, who campaigned over every country as far as the uninhabited regions of India and the lands to the north, even to the sources of the river Ister, and again to the remaining parts of the world as far as Oceanus. I am the eldest son of Cronus, and being sprung from a fair and noble egg I was begotten a seed of kindred birth to Day. There is no region of the inhabited world to which I have not come, dispensing to all men the things of which I was the discoverer." On the association of the world egg with Orpheus in the Hermetica, see Mead, "XI. Concerning the Aeon-Doctrine," in *Thrice-Greatest Hermes*, 1:271. On the importance of egg symbolism in Egyptian mythology in general, see Ricardo A. Caminos, article "Ei," in *Lexikon der Ägyptologie*, 1:1185–88: "Egyptian theologians speculating about the creation of the world spoke of a miraculous egg placed upon a hill surrounded by the primeval waters. The egg hatched and from it flew a bird that was a god and brought forth light, ending chaos and marking the beginning of things. Such was the gist of the myth; opinions differed as to how the world egg was formed, its location, and the identity of the god born from it. We have no coherent, self-contained version of the myth; the story must be pieced together from scattered, unconnected statements and ambiguous allusions."

97. See for example the parody of Orphic cosmogony in Aristophanes, *The Birds* (vs. 693–702): "There was Chaos at first, and Darkness, and Night, and Tartarus vasty and dismal; / But the Earth was not there, nor the Sky, nor the Air, till at length in the bosom abysmal / Of Darkness an egg, from the whirlwind conceived, was laid by the sable-plumed Night. / And out of this egg, as the Seasons revolved, sprang Love, the entrancing, the bright, / Love brilliant and bold with his pinions of gold, like a whirlwind, refulgent and sparkling! / Love hatched us, commingling in Tartarus wide, with Chaos, the murky, the darkling, / And brought us above, as the firstlings of love, and first to the light we ascended. / There was never a race of Immortals at all till Love had the universe blended; / Then all things commingling together in love, there rose the fair Earth, and the Sky, / And the limitless Sea; and the race of the Gods." *Aristophanes*, ed. and tr. Benjamin Bickley Rogers, 3 vols. (Cambridge and London: Harvard University Press, Loeb Classical Library, 1924), 2:198–201.

98. Lenoir, *La Franche-Maçonnerie*, 55. For the Diderot reference, see entry "Égyptiens" in *Oeuvres complètes*, 7:130–31: "[The Egyptians] used to have two theologies, one esoteric and the other exoteric. The first consisted in not admitting other gods but the Universe; no other origins of being but matter and movement were recognized. Osiris was the sun, the moon was Isis.

They said: at the beginning everything was confounded; heaven and earth were but one, but with time, the elements separated. Air started to move: the fiery part, drawn to the center, formed the stars and set ablaze the sun. Its base sediments did not remain unmoved. They spun around themselves and the earth appeared. The sun heated up this inert mass; the seeds it contained germinated, and life manifested itself in an infinity of diverse forms." In a footnote to Lenoir's text (*La Franche-Maçonnerie*, 56, note 1), the author describes, with typical syncretistic bravura, the cult of the world egg as a transcultural phenomenon: "The cult of the mystical egg, considered as emblem of the world, was widespread amongst the people of Asia and even amongst those of Europe. In the mysteries of Osiris and of those of Bacchus, the egg played a role; likewise we see it figuring in the Isiac festivities. This famous egg is the one of Leda, who gives birth to Castor and Pollux; it is the Orphic egg, which was suspended in Sparta from the vault of the temple; it is the one that gave life to Amor. Thus, Osiris was born from an egg in Egypt. Likewise Phanes, Chumong, etc. came into being. Among the Gauls, the Druids had introduced to their mysteries the cult of the egg, which they assumed had been formed by the slime from their sacred snake, since they also had a particular cult in honor of the serpent. Orpheus's respect for eggs was such that he not only refused to eat them, but he also refused to touch them. Finally, as one had seen the egg giving birth to the major part of the animal population, one assumed that the world had sprung forth from an egg."

99. *Livre d'or* [BN], fol. 53r, no. 3.

100. Plutarch, *De Iside et Osiride* 36, 365c, ed. Griffith, 174–75.

101. Kendrick, *The Secret Museum*, 6–7, 14–16. Kendrick underlines how social, economic, educational, and gender stratification determined access to sexually explicit imagery and shows how such stratification helped define modern notions of pornography. A watershed in this development was the excavations at Pompeii and Herculaneum during the 1750s: "From very early in the excavations, objects were being unearthed that presented a special problem to authorities. Already in 1758, for example, rumors circulated that 'lascivious' frescoes had been found; not long thereafter, a particularly outrageous artifact turned up—a small marble sculpture, highly naturalistic in style, representing a satyr in sexual congress with an apparently undaunted goat. This distressing artwork, under special orders from King Charles, was entrusted to the royal sculptor, Joseph Canart, with the 'strict injunction that no one should be allowed access to it.' . . . No doubt the procedure was already in operation, as it remained two centuries later, that a gentleman with appropriate demeanor (and ready cash for the custodian) would be admitted to the locked chamber where controversial items lurked; women, children, and the poor of both sexes and all ages were excluded."

102. Eusebius, *Preparation for the Gospel*, ed. and tr. Edwin Hamilton Gifford, 2 vols. (Oxford: Clarendon Press, 1903), 1:47–52.

103. See note 1 above. On the legend of Heraclitus's book *On Nature*, see Diogenes Laertius, *Vitae philosophorum* IX.6, in *Lives of Eminent Philosophers*, ed. and tr. Robert Drew Hicks, 2 vols. (Cambridge and London: Harvard University Press, Loeb Classical Library, 1970), 2:412–13. See also the commentary in Pierre Hadot, *Le Voile d'Isis: Essai sur l'histoire de l'idée de la Nature* (Paris: Gallimard, 2004), 19–21.

104. Hadot, *Le Voile d'Isis*, 105–12. The quote by Francis Bacon is from his *Novum Organum* I.98: "So the secrets of nature betray themselves more readily when tormented by experiment than when left to their own course." For the Latin version, see *The*

Works of Lord Bacon with an Introductory Essay, and a Portrait, 2 vols. (London: Ball, 1838), 2:449. English translation taken from Francis Bacon, *The Advancement of Learning and Novum Organum*, ed. and tr. James Edward Creighton (New York: Colonial Press, 1899), 351.

105. Hadot, *Le Voile d'Isis*, 141.

106. Iamblichus of Apamea, *De Mysteriis Aegyptiorum* VIII. I.261, ed. des Places, 195–96. According to Iamblichus, "since there existed many strongly different essences, tradition has assigned them a multiplicity of principles that carried a great many degrees and changed according to the diverse accounts of ancient priests; the totality has been completely expounded by Hermes in his books, twenty thousand according to Seleucus, or thirty-six thousand five hundred and twenty-five after the history by Manetho." Manetho, a temple priest, was one of the earliest native Egyptian writers to express himself in Greek. His *Sacred Book*, today lost, is only known in excerpts from other authors, such as Iamblichus. Although it is surprising that the Sophisians apparently possessed very specific knowledge of these obscure Hellenized Egyptian historians (Cuvelier and his group mostly stand mute as to their sources), the intellectual appeal of Manetho's *Sacred Book* is easily comprehensible.

107. *Livre d'or* [BN], fol. 54r. The solutions manual uses the name *Canicule*, dog-star, rather than the modern designation Sirius, to establish the association with Sothis. On the equivalence of *Canicule* and Sirius, see *Trésor de la langue française*, 5:108.

108. *Livre d'or* [BN], fol. 53v, no. 5.

109. Diodorus of Sicily, *Bibliotheca historica* I.11.3–5, ed. Oldfather, 1:38–41.

110. *Livre d'or* [BN], fols. 77r–77v.

111. Ibid., fols. 76r–76v.

112. Théodore Muret, *L'Histoire par le théâtre, 1789–1851*, 2 vols. (Paris: Amyot, 1865), 2:100; McCormick, *Popular Theaters*, 125, 154.

113. See note 78 above. The full text of Foignet's *Hymne Sacré des Anciens Mystères* reads: "In vain, Demiurge [Isis], you veil your presence, every being recognizes your law; even Time could not have given you birth, but the Universe received birth from you: You govern the Gods that the vulgar worship. You render the sky nebulous and serene so that, because of you, in Spring the earth takes on color and in Winter all dies at her bosom. Hell sees its audacity expiring at your feet; its fireballs, as they roll across space, being launched on their course by your hand."

114. *Livre d'or* [BN], fols. 78r–79r. The passage concludes with the following provision in case the female initiate refuses to slash herself: "Note: If the neophyte refuses to take the dagger, the Mystagogue, who administers the Test, makes the bouquet of flowers shoot out. She is blamed for her fears and small amount of confidence. The Emblem is explained to her, and she is forgiven."

115. Louis Amiable and Paul Guieysse, *L'Égypte ancienne et la franc-maçonnerie*, ed. Christian Lauzeray (Paris: Trédaniel, 1988), 34–36. This publication is a reprint of the text originally published under the title "L'Égypte ancienne et la franc-maçonnerie, conférence par le F∴ Paul Guieysse, discours préliminaire par le F∴ Louis Amiable, Conseil de l'Ordre, tenue du 4 février 1887" in the 1887 edition of the *Bulletin du Grand Orient de France*. Amiable analyzed the following publications by Louis Guillemain de Saint-Victor: *Recueil précieux de la Maçonnerie Adonhiramite: contenant les catéchismes des quatre premiers grades, et l'ouverture et clôture des différentes loges, l'instruction de la table, les santés générales et particulières, ainsi que les devoirs des premiers officiers eu [sic] charge; enrichi d'une infinité*

de demandes et de réponses symboliques, de l'explication des em-blêmes, et d'un grand nombre de notes aussi curieuses qu'utiles ("Philadelphia" [Paris]: Philarète, 1783), with subsequent editions in 1787 and 1789; *Origine de la maçonnerie adonhiramite, ou, Nouvelles observations critiques et raisonnés, sur la philosophie, les hieroglyphes, les mystères, la superstition et les vices des mages; précédée d'un chapitre sur l'Égypte ancienne et moderne; avec des remarques et des notes sur les historiens et la chronologie du monde* ("Heliopolis" [Paris], 1787); *Recueil élémentaire de la franc-maçonnerie adon-hiramite . . . par un chévalier de tous les ordres maçonniques* ("Jerusalem, 5803" [Paris, 1803]).

116. Henri Cauchois, *Cours oral de franc-maçonnerie symbolique en douze séances* (Paris: Dentu, 1863), 80–81. Significantly, Cauchois cites Lantier's *Voyages d'Antenor*, 2:231–33, as his source of inspiration.

117. *Livre d'or* [BN], fol. 26r, Section 4, Article 1. The Sophisian emphasis on the distribution of bread clearly derives from the Christian Eucharist, as is evident from the following passage (fol. 73v): "After this ceremony, they wet the index finger of their right hand in water and salute, one by one, the four cardinal points while saying: 'Male (or female) initiate, may you be purified by water.' Then they break the bread and distribute it to the right and to the left while saying: 'Share the bread of life; the powerful and the weak, the poor and the rich have a common right to it.'"

118. Ibid., fol. 26v. The Sophisian oath formula required every initiate "to consider as a brother any Sophisian and to save, without distinction, any mortal stricken by misfortune, since I owe to my fellow man bread, fire, and water."

119. Ibid., fol. 74r.

120. Ibid., fol. 79r. This passage was apparently added to the manuscript as an afterthought by a hand other than Ponce-Camus's.

121. "Nomenclature des officiers," Chapter IV, Article III, in Ordre Sacré des Sophisians, *Règlement de l'A-*[spirance], 14.

122. [Cuvelier de Trie], *Prix proposé sur une question philantropique L∴ des artistes O∴ de Paris: Extrait du Registre du Tribunal Suprême, Scéance du 3me. jour 5me. mois, an de la V∴ L∴ 5819* (Paris, 1819). One copy in Paris, BN-MSS, Baylot FM2.41, no. 1. This small printed pamphlet is in fact a Sophisian document, as the reference to the Supreme Tribunal reveals. It opens with the transcript of a speech by Cuvelier de Trie in a new guise as "Great Conservator" (pp. 1–2): "Whereas the ancient tree of Masonry, more vigorous and flowering than ever, extends its protective foliage over the peaceful grounds of France, true Masons observe with regret that no Institution of Beneficence, no establishment for the utility of humanity, grows in its shadow to serve our unfortunate brothers and to rally the profane to our altars, thereby spreading the word of the sacred goals of our mysteries. What good, outsiders say, are these small contributions collected at the end of our meetings? What use can there be in these infinitely split-up relief contributions, doled out without making informed choices? Will they not become an encouragement for laziness, rather than nourishment in the case of true need? Is it not time to finally dissipate this cloud of good-for-nothing bums who make it a profession to assail our outer sanctuaries and who drive away the truly deserving poor; those who strip orphans and widows of our aid by force of intimidation? Is it truly impossible to replace isolated and insignificant collections by a different organization, larger, more efficient, more useful for suffering humanity? Should one not assemble in one place all the donations which would otherwise get lost in a thousand obscure channels? Could we not, finally, by launching a Masonic Tontine, perhaps

create for ourselves a source of relief in times of misfortune, and sow, so to speak, on the field of beneficence a fistful of seeds to enjoy an abundant harvest? . . . It is with these intentions that, confining myself to a simple and modest reunion of Artists, I propose to the Tribunal to invite, in the name of the Lodge and following its approval, all regular Masons in France and all other Orients to submit proposals on the following question: PROGRAM FOR A COMPETITION. 'What would be the new form of organization to adopt, resulting in the suppression of the customary requests and replacing them by other voluntary donations, perhaps even through fixed annual payments delivered by all brothers, so as to bundle the charitable offers? How can we form a general welfare fund and establish across France central beneficence lodges, where, as in the ancient hospices of the Chivalric Orders, whose members dedicated themselves to the service of the less fortunate, Masons can find an honorable asylum in their old age? How can the interest on the imposed annual contributions be multiplied a hundredfold so as to create accommodations for travelers and a fraternal hospital for the sick, where they can be cared for with the greatest attention? . . . Resolution as follows: ARTICLE 1. The proposition above . . . shall be printed and sent to all regular lodges in France and in foreign countries, with an invitation to submit proposals. . . . ARTICLE 3. The competitors may write their submissions in French, Latin, Italian, German, and in English; they are to be in the form of memoirs or speeches." The jury was to consist almost entirely of Sophisians, including the Comte de Lacépède, the Baron Joseph Fauchet, Nicolas-Éloi Lemaire, Albert Taviel, Antoine-Louis-Germain Dutilleul, and Cuvelier himself as humble "secretary." The competition has the flavor of a brazen attempt to freeboot other lodges in order to spread Sophisian teachings, a strategy initially pioneered by Cagliostro.

123. Auguste-Prosper-François Guerrier de Dumast, *Rapport fait à la Loge des Artistes, le 19 juillet 1821, . . . sur l'établissement dit Manufacture des Apprentis Pauvres et Orphelins* (Paris: Dondey-Dupré, 1821).

124. *Livre d'or* [BN], fol. 80v.

125. Ibid., fol. 54r.

126. Karl-Theodor Zauzich, article "Hierogrammat," in *Lexikon der Ägyptologie*, 2:1199–201.

127. On Cagliostro's dabbling in alchemy, see for example Dalbian, *Le Comte de Cagliostro*, 56–70. The story of Casanova's life is filled with similar anecdotes; see for example his manipulation of Mme d'Urfé's credulity in his alchemical abilities, *Memoirs*, 3:91–113, 4:373–413.

128. Zosimus, *On the Letter Omega*, ed. Jackson. On Zosimus as originator of chemistry, see Julius Ruska, "Zosimos," in *Das Buch der grossen Chemiker*, ed. Günther Bugge, 2 vols. (Berlin: Verlag Chemie, 1929), 1:1–17; on his biographical details, see Fowden, *The Egyptian Hermes*, 120.

129. Zosimus, *On the Letter Omega* 1, ed. Jackson, 16–17.

130. Fowden, *The Egyptian Hermes*, 116.

131. Lenoir, *La Franche-Maçonnerie*, 127–29. See also a variation of the description in Lantier, *Voyages d'Antenor*, 2:207–9: "Following [the sacrifices of a bull and piglets] the [Isis] procession starts, in which one carries figures of about an ell in height, made to be moved by ropes; the phallus of these figures is as big as the rest of the body. Setting them in motion, women parade [the figures] through the boroughs and villages. A flute player marches at their head—they follow him while chanting in praise of Bacchus." On another occasion, 2:265, Lantier also imagined that the "famous Isis Tablet" (the Bembine Tablet, fig. 23) was carried in one such procession.

132. *Livre d'or* [BN], fols. 81r–81v.

133. Ibid., fols. 83r–83v: "1ˢᵗ hypothesis to be developed. From the hyssop [herb used in Mosaic rites of purification] to the oak, from the ant to the elephant, Nature seems to strive to march from perfection to perfection. Is not the single stem of the polyp the first sketch, the primordial type of the marvelous interior of man, at once the most complex and the most perfect being? Why did perfection stop at this point? Was the creator incapable? That would be impossible, if man is the last echelon of the sublunary beings. Does the ladder end with man? Why does it not lead step by step from the good to the better by rendering matter diaphanous and striving towards aerial intelligence, up to the level of pure spirit, the perfect point of its immersion in the source of life, of mixing and aggregation of divine essence, of the reunion of the soul of all things with nature? Man always hopes: this vague hope, is it not the word for the enigma of death? 2ⁿᵈ hypothesis to be developed. If life is nothing but a test, a passage; if Nature's great movements are to destroy and reconstruct in preparation for things to come; if death is the true guide; if every bit of matter returns inevitably to feed on the mass of its similars: Why does the spark called spirit or soul not enjoy the same privilege? If it did, it would return to its mass, and the soul is but a portion of god; if not, it will animate new aggregations, and in the first as in the second case, this spark is immortality. May some meditate on these high thoughts, while others, carried away by the force of their imagination towards mysteries no less incomprehensible, elevate themselves in a courageous flight towards regions where thunder attends more than just one sacred adept."

134. On the Seven Invisible Sages and the other Sophisian administrative bodies mentioned, see the "Charte Constitutionelle" in *Livre d'or* [BN], fols. 23r–26v. *Livre d'or* [GODF] contains an earlier and simplified version of the charter, presumably copied after the untraced first Golden Book. The charter in the *Mélanges Lerouge*, CMC, was apparently copied after the later BN version of the *Livre d'or*.

135. Plato, *Protagoras* 343a–b, in *Plato*, ed. and tr. Walter Rangeley Maitland Lamb, 12 vols. (Cambridge: Harvard University Press, Loeb Classical Library, 1924–35), 4:196–97. Plato identifies the Seven Sages by name: "Thales of Miletus, Pittacus of Mytilene, Bias of Priene, Solon of our city, Cleobulus of Lindus, Myson of Chenae, and, last of the traditional seven, Chilon of Sparta. All these were enthusiasts, lovers and disciples of the Spartan culture; and you can recognize that character in their wisdom by the short, memorable sayings that fell from each of them." Article 10 of the Constitutional Charter (fol. 23v) makes it clear that the Sophisian Seven Invisible Sages indeed had their Platonic homonyms as a model: "The Seven Sages are not known to the members of the order (except for those initiated to the Grand Mysteries) but under the names of Solon, Thales, Chilon, Pittacus, Cleobulus, Bias, and Periandros. In the case of death or resignation of one of them, it is the president of the Conclave who alone designates the successor to the vacant place."

136. Roman d'Amat, article "Fauchet (Jean-Antoine-*Joseph*)," in *Dictionnaire et biographie française*, 13:669–70.

137. *Livre d'or* [BN], fol. 23r-24v, Section 1, Articles 1–14.

138. Ibid., fols. 84r–84v.

139. Ibid., fol. 49v.

140. See Kolpaktchy, "Introduction," 34–35: "The comprehension of Egyptian writings, taken by itself, leads nowhere. The wisdom of this strange people resembles a fortress of the Middle Ages with fortification walls arranged in concentric circles. Once conquered, the outer fortification—hieroglyphics—gives way to a second wall, even more insurmountable: that of esoteric deciphering."

141. Fowden, *The Egyptian Hermes*, 14–22.

142. Ibid., 99–112, 148–50, 156–58.

143. In this regard, see also Guerrier de Dumast, *La Maçonnerie*, 192: "Since a reception is, or might be, at the same time tragedy, comedy, and opera, it is a drama where all the arts can unite their illusions; a drama that can assume many guises, even that of humor; a drama, finally, where the inventive genius of the ones who direct it can enlist the inspiration all the ages, all famous places, all the stories from the beginnings of the world, of antiquity, and the Middle Ages. And all the riches of allegory, of history, and of novels merge skillfully with the use of machinery [to awaken] the emotions of the recipient and to attain the perfection of his/her soul."

144. [Hermes Trismegistus,] *Liber de protestate et sapientia Dei, corpus hermeticum*, ed. and tr. Marsilio Ficino (Treviso: Gerardus de Lisa, 1471). On the history of the *Corpus Hermeticum* manuscript, see Mead, *Thrice-Greatest Hermes*, 1:4–6.

145. Gabriel du Préau, *Devx livres de Mercvre Trismegiste Hermés tres ancien theologien, et exzellent philozophe: L'Un de la puissance & sapience de Dieu; l'autre de la volonté de Dieu; avecq'un dialogue de Loys Lazarel, poëte chrestien, intitulé La Bassin d'Hermés* (Paris: Estiene Groulleau, 1557). Ficino's Latin edition of the Corpus had become available as early as 1505 in a Parisian reprint with an afterword by a certain Loys Lazarel, *Pimander Mercurii liber de sapienta et protestate Dei: Asclepius, ejusdem Mercurii liber de voluntate divina, item crater Hermetis a Lazarelo Septempedano* [i.e., Loys Lazarel]. Another Latin version was edited and published in 1574 under the title *Mercurii Trimegisti Pimander sive Poemander* by Franciscus Flussas Candalle in Bordeaux. The same editor also published in Bordeaux a second translation of the Corpus into French, *Le Pimandre de Mercure Trismegiste de la philosophie chrestienne, cognoissance du verb divin, et de l'excellence des oeuvres de Dieu*. On the history of Hermes Trismegistus editions through the ages, see also Mead, *Thrice-Greatest Hermes*, 1:6–11.

146. Isaac Casaubon, *De rebus sacris et ecclesiasticis exercitationes XVI* (London: Norton, 1614). On the genesis of Hermes Trismegistus's name, see Fowden, *The Egyptian Hermes*, 216–17.

147. Nevertheless, Champollion, even while still a teenager, had nothing but derision to spare for Lenoir. When, in 1808, the museum director published his *Nouvelle Explication des hiéroglyphes ou des figures symboliques et sacrées des Égyptiens et des Grecs, utile à l'intelligence des monuments mythologiques des autres peuples*, Champollion commented on the book in his private correspondence as follows: "We laughed a lot together with Jomard, since I had the good luck to read the inestimable book that proves to us that the Egyptians had no other supreme gods but Horus, Harpocrates, Typhon, and the entire astronomical gang from the myths of Egypt." Cited after Faure, *Champollion*, 134.

148. Dominique Poulot, "L'Égypte imaginaire d'Alexandre Lenoir," in *L'Égypte imaginaire de la Renaissance à Champollion*, ed. Chantal Grell (Paris: Presses de l'Université de Paris-Sorbonne, 2001), 127–49; Edouard Pommier, "La théorie des arts," in *Aux Armes et aux Arts!*, 188–91.

149. Lenoir, *La Franche-Maçonnerie*, 4–7.

150. Ibid., 50.

151. *Le Néo-Classicisme français: Dessins des musées de Province*, exh. cat. (Paris: Éditions des musées nationaux, 1974), 104–5, no. 105; Poulot, "L'Égypte imaginaire d'Alexandre Lenoir," 136–37, note 42.

152. Lenoir, *La Franche-Maçonnerie*, 16–18, 26, 65–66, 116, 125, 142.

153. Ibid., 8, 10, 21–22, 163–78.

154. Ibid., 18, 95, 125–26.

155. Jean-Guillaume-Augustin Cuvelier de Trie, *La Fête de l'Être Suprême: Scène patriotique* (Paris: L'Imprimerie des Écoles Républicaines, Year II [1794]), 6, 8. The role of the military commander was played by Guillaume-André Villoteau, the musicologist in residence at the Institut d'Égypte in Cairo during the Napoleonic campaign, and later a Sophisian. The play was performed for the first time on Prairial 20, year II (June 8, 1794), i.e., less than two months before Robespierre's fall.

156. François-Alphonse Aulard, *Le Culte de la raison et le culte de l'Être Suprême (1793–1794)* (Paris: Alcan, 1892), 1–2.

157. Baltrušaitis, *La Quête d'Isis*, 81–148; Hornung, *L'Égypte ésotérique*, 150.

158. Guerrier de Dumast, *La Maçonnerie*, 123–24.

159. Henri d'Almeras, *La Vie parisienne sous la Restauration* (Paris: Michel, 1910), 8–20; Guerrier de Dumast, *La Maçonnerie*, ii.

4. THE SOPHISIANS ON STAGE

1. Quintus Curtius Rufus, *Historiae Alexandri* IV.9.7, ed. and tr. John C. Rolfe, 2 vols. (Cambridge and London: Harvard University Press, Loeb Classical Library, 1946), 1:254–55; Jean-Guillaume-Augustin Cuvelier de Trie, *L'Enchanteur Morto-Vivo, prologue cabalistique; suivi de L'Isle de Silence, ou L'Arlequin malgré lui, féerie mélodramatique, mêlée de scènes pantomimes, en trois actes, à grand spectacle, metamorphoses, transformations, changemens de décoration, marches, combats, etc.* (Paris: Maldan, 1806), 15. Interestingly, the original passage by the Latin author, whose identity Cuvelier de Trie hid in the imprint of his play, complains about Egyptian soothsayers (*Aegyptiosque vates*) manipulating the casting of astrological spells before the credulous masses under Alexander's rule for reasons of political opportunism.

2. MacCormick, *Popular Theaters*, 13–15; Pao, *The Orient of the Boulevards*, 22–23.

3. MacCormick, *Popular Theaters*, 134–47.

4. Jean-Guillaume-Augustin Cuvelier de Trie, *L'Entrée des chevaliers français dans Sérica* (Paris: Barba, 1811), 12. Even the actors pretended to be taken by surprise: "But, that's a kind of marvel; a troubadour who can neither speak nor sing!"

5. Maurice Albert, *Les Théâtres des boulevards, 1789–1848* (Paris: Société française d'imprimerie et de librairie, 1902), 5, 76, note 1; McCormick, *Popular Theaters*, 15; Pao, *The Orient of the Boulevards*, 19–20. As both McCormick and Pao point out, the "slumming" appeal of boulevard theaters was a literary trope in itself. In fact, audiences of the secondary theaters were thoroughly heterogeneous. The interest of the upper classes in the material presented on these stages was mostly genuine and driven by the same search for carefree entertainment that was typically portrayed in official statements as a cultural preserve of the popular classes.

6. Thomas Crow, *Painters and Public Life in Eighteenth-Century Paris* (New Haven and London: Yale University Press, 1985), 45–74.

7. August-Aubin Millin de Grandmaison, *Sur la liberté du théâtre* (Paris: Lagrange, 1790), 3.

8. Ibid., 11.

9. Ibid., 16. See also Muret, *L'Histoire par le théâtre*, 1:19, who wrote that "the history of spectacles [in the late eighteenth century] is also that of the Revolution."

10. Nicolas Brazier, *Chroniques des petits théâtres de Paris*, 2 vols. (1837; repr., Paris: Rouveyre et Blond, 1883), 2:425–26, notes that fifty-one new theaters opened in 1791 as a direct consequence of the declaration of the freedom of theaters. Muret, *L'Histoire par le théâtre*, 1:227, puts the figure at fifty, of which only half remained in business by 1807. See also McCormick, *Popular Theaters*, 15.

11. Victor Couailhac, *La Vie de théâtre: Grandes et petites aventures de Mlle Montansier* (Brussels: Parent, 1863), 114–15, 156–60.

12. Privat-Joseph-Claramond Pelet de la Lozère, *Opinions de Napoléon sur divers sujets de politique et d'administration, recueillies par un membre de son conseil d'état, et récit de quelques événements de l'époque* (Paris: Firmin Didot, 1833), 284–85.

13. Dondey-Dupré, *Paroles funèbres*, 4–5; Bertrand, *Précis*, 2:596–97; Morand, *L'Année historique*, 11.

14. Bertrand, *Précis*, 2:597.

15. Cuvelier's first play written for a specific establishment, a legal comedy of June 1793 entitled *Le Codicille, ou Les Deux héritiers*, was conceived for the Théâtre Montansier. See Mahul, *Annuaire nécrologique*, 5:70. Unfortunately, as is the case with many of Cuvelier's early theatrical imprints of the 1790s, no copy of the play could be located in French public libraries. On the history of the Théâtre du Palais Royal in general, see Nicole Wild, *Dictionnaire des théâtres parisiens au XIXe siècle* (Paris: Amateurs de livres, 1989), 268–70, 351–53.

16. Couailhac, *La Vie de théâtre*, 28–42.

17. Ibid., 70–75.

18. Letter by Jean-Guillaume-Augustin Cuvelier of October 27, 1810, in *Dossier personnel "Cuvelier, Jean-Guillaume-Augustin,"* SHD-DAT, 2 Yf 4852. On the *Compagnie des Artistes Dramatiques*, see also Charles-Louis Chassin and Léon-Clément Hennet, *Les Volontaires nationaux pendant la Révolution*, 3 vols. (1899–1906; repr., New York: AMS, 1974), 1:337, 2:319–23. Chassin and Hennet cite a document of January 1793 that mentions Cuvelier as captain of the *1re Compagnie des Artistes Dramatiques*. Cuvelier himself referred to the unit in a handwritten curriculum vitae of 1810, preserved at Vincennes, as "1st free company of Paris, known as that of artists or theater people [1ère compagnie franche de Paris, dite des artistes ou théâtrale]." Unfortunately, no file on the Montansier unit as such exists in the archives at Vincennes.

19. Chassin and Hennet, *Les Volontaires nationaux*, 1:422, cite the figure of two hundred; Ragueneau de La Chainaye and Armand Henri, article "Montansier (Marguerite Brunet, dite)," in *Annuaire dramatique* 17/18 (1821/22): 386, cite eighty men in Mlle Montansier's "free company."

20. Alexandre Duval, *Oeuvres complètes*, 4 vols. (Paris: Barba, 1822), 3:66–70. Duval referred to the unit in the following terms "Having been the plaything of circumstances and events, I reached that terrible epoch when all the citizens were called upon to defend the *patrie*. All entities, all sections formed battalions, and those formed companies: I associated myself with that of the artists, several of whom had been the companions of my student days. All knew that I loved theater, and before I knew it I became their orator and troubadour." On Duval in Mlle Montansier's *compagnie franche*, see also Arthur de La Broderie, *Alexandre Duval et son théâtre* (Rennes: Caillière, 1893), 15.

21. Couailhac, *La Vie de théâtre*, 72.

22. Auguste-Philippe Herlaut, *Le Colonel Bouchotte: Ministre de la Guerre en l'an II*, 2 vols. (Paris: Poisson, 1946), 1:56, 66, 73, 77, 82–83.

23. Antoine-Étienne Carro, *Santerre, général de la République française: Sa vie politique et privée, écrite d'après les documents originaux*, 2nd ed. (Meaux: Carro, 1869); Raymonde Monnier, *Un Bourgeois sans-culotte: Le Général Santerre, suivi de 'L'Art du brasseur'* (Paris: Publications de la Sorbonne, 1989).

24. Letter by Cuvelier of October 27, 1810, SHD-DAT; Carro, *Santerre*, 200–228; Monnier, *Un Bourgeois sans-culotte*, 52–58.

25. McCormick, *Popular Theaters*, 99.

26. Albert, *Les Théâtres des boulevards*, 173–74; Muret, *L'Histoire par le théâtre*, 1:94–95, 160–62, 326–28. Albert pointed out that the Directory government had made preparations to introduce a legislation similar to Napoleon's 1807 decree, which would have limited the number of theaters to four principal and two secondary stages, but the Conseil des Anciens refused to ratify the proposal.

27. Letter by Cuvelier de Trie to the Ministry of the Interior (4th Division [*Arts et Belles Lettres*], 1st Bureau), demanding a pension or reemployment, dated August 7, 1822, AN, F 21/1008 (contained in dossier "Veuve Cuvelier"). See also the previously cited letter by Cuvelier of October 27, 1810, in his *dossier personnel*, SHD-DAT, and Albert, *Les Théâtres des boulevards*, 152. Censorship of the theater was typically administered by the same division in the Ministery of the Interior to which Cuvelier de Trie used to report. See McCormick, *Popular Theaters*, 99–100.

28. Jean-Guillaume-Augustin Cuvelier de Trie, *Le Damoisel et la bergerette, ou La Femme vindicative, historiette du XVI siècle* (Paris: Cailleau, 1795).

29. Letter by Cuvelier of October 27, 1810, SHD-DAT.

30. Mahul, *Annuaire nécrologique*, 5:71–76.

31. See for example the extensive production of *pièces de circonstance* written to celebrate Bonaparte's arrival in Paris that is discussed in Lecomte, *Napoléon et l'Empire*, 45–47. Lecomte also lists dozens of other plays, written over the course of nineteenth century, that apotheosize Napoleon's deeds in Egypt; the last Egyptian-themed drama he mentions dates from 1882.

32. Charles-Maurice Descombes, *Histoire anecdotique du théâtre, de la littérature et de diverses impressions contemporaines, tirée du coffre d'un journaliste, avec sa vie à tort et à travers*, 2 vols. (Paris: Plon, 1856), 1:57–60.

33. *Moniteur universel* 43 (Brumaire 13, year VIII—November 4, 1799), 165.

34. See for example the poem entitled *Au Général Bonaparte, à son retour d'Égypte en France*, published in *Le Rédacteur* 1404 (Vendémiaire 30, year VIII—October 22, 1799), 3:

> Return, wise conqueror of Egypt and Italy,
>   Come to put an end to your exploits:
> Return with the agreeable and sweet reign of Law,
>   To give peace to the *Patrie*.
> See, sensitive hero, the abysmal suffering,
>   Where your brothers the French are:
> And think that you, by your valiant success,
>   may make a paradise of France.
> Your compassion, your valor, your wisdom
>   come together, and one by one,
> Amidst the drive of a joyful optimism,
>   Establish our happiness and guide our love.
>   By citizen Guyot (from the North)

Concerning the call for vaudeville plays, see *Le Rédacteur* 1403 (Vendémiaire 29, year VIII—October 21, 1799), 3.

35. *Le Rédacteur* 1406 (Brumaire 2, year VIII—October 24, 1799), 3. The author of the letter possibly made reference to the vaudeville play *La Fin du monde, ou La Comète, comédie-parade en 1 acte* (1798) by Barré, Radet, Desfontaines, Duant, Bourgueil, and Desfougerais. The day Bonaparte returned to Paris another comet was reportedly seen in the sky, and the play was revised accordingly. See Lecomte, *Napoléon et l'Empire*, 31–32.

36. *Moniteur universel* 34 (Brumaire 4, year VIII—October 26, 1799), 130.

37. *Moniteur universel* 44 (Brumaire 14, year VIII—November 5, 1799), 171.

38. Étienne Maurel de Chédeville, Louis XVIII, Comte de Provence, and André-Ernest-Modeste Grétry, *La Caravane du Caire, opéra-ballet. Représenté à Fontainebleau, devant leurs Majestés, le 30 Octobre 1783 et pour la première fois sur le Théâtre de l'Académie royale de musique le lundi 12 janvier 1784* (Paris, 1784). Set to music by the composer André-Ernest-Modeste Grétry, the text for the *Caravane du Caire* is thought to have been written by the Comte de Provence, future king Louis XVIII, but was often published under the name of his private secretary, Étienne Maurel de Chédeville.

39. Albert, *Les Théâtres des boulevards*, 184, 187.

40. Muret, *L'Histoire par le théâtre*, 1:232–33; McCormick, *Popular Theaters*, 13.

41. Louis-Henry Lecomte, *Napoléon et le monde dramatique* (Paris: Daragon, 1912), 74.

42. Millin de Grandmaison, *Sur la liberté du théâtre*, 20, 53, note 15.

43. *Correspondance de Napoléon Ier*, 14:462, no. 12,068.

44. Ibid., 14:519, no. 12,156.

45. Muret, *L'Histoire par le théâtre*, 1:335–41; Léon de Lanzac de Laborie, *Paris sous Napoléon: Spectacles et Musées*, 2nd ed., 8 vols. (Paris: Plon-Nourrit, 1905–13), 8:146–48.

46. McCormick, *Popular Theaters*, 13.

47. Lanzac de Laborie, *Paris sous Napoléon*, 8:139; Jean Verzat, *Le Comte Regnaud de Saint-Jean-d'Angély (1760–1819): 'L'éminence grise' de l'Empereur* (Saint-Jean-d'Angély: Bordessoules, 2000), 5.

48. Ibid., 8:178–80; Brazier, *Chroniques*, 1:51–82; Wild, *Dictionnaire des théâtres*, 32–39; McCormick, *Popular Theaters*, 18–20; Arnault, *Biographie nouvelle*, 1:296.

49. Brazier, *Chroniques*, 1:69.

50. On Boilly's painting, see also Pao, *The Orient of the Boulevards*, 27–29.

51. On the social, egalitarian, and educational aspects of the "représentations gratis," see also Muret, *L'Histoire par le théâtre*, 1:53–54.

52. Theater riots were not uncommon in the early nineteenth century and all buildings housing stages were under special surveillance by the gendarmerie. See ibid., 2:194, 198.

53. See for instance Horace Vernet's *The Duc d'Orléans Proceeds to the Hôtel-de-Ville, July 31, 1830* (1833) at the Musée de Versailles, which depicts an episode from the aftermath of the July Revolution in which the Duc d'Orléans leaves the Palais Royal on horseback. The Revolutionary crowd, united in its political goals, is spatially divided along class lines: on the left, the blue-collar workers and craftsmen in their aprons and workman's caps are concentrated; the right side of the picture is the domain of the bourgeoisie dressed in redingote and top hat.

54. Jean-Guillaume-Augustin Cuvelier de Trie, *Les Machabées, ou La Prise de Jérusalem, drame sacré à grand spectacle* (Paris: Fages, 1817).

55. Ibid., 14–15.

56. Brazier, *Chroniques*, 1:69, 71–72. See biographies in the appendix of Mme de Puisaye mère, Louis-Antoine le Marquis de Puisaye, and Audinot D'Aussi.

57. Jean-Guillaume-Augustin Cuvelier de Trie, *C'est le diable, ou la Bohémienne, drame en cinq actes à grand spectacle, mêlé de pantomime, evolutions, combats, chants et danses* (Paris: Barba, 1797/98); idem., *Les Hommes de la nature et des hommes policés, pantomime en trois actes, dédié à ceux qui n'entendent pas, précédée et suivie des Deux Silphes* (Paris: Barba, 1800/1801); idem., *Les Machabées, ou la prise de Jérusalem.*

58. See biographies in the appendix of Amédée, Chaussier, Laroche, Ponce-Camus, and Varez.

59. Hillemacher, *Le Cirque Franconi*, 5–20; Brazier, *Chroniques*, 1:147–71; Lanzac de Laborie, *Paris sous Napoléon*, 8:201–4; Wild, *Dictionnaire des théâtres parisiens*, 79–86; McCormick, *Popular Theaters*, 30; Pao, *The Orient of the Boulevards*, 25.

60. Albert, *Les Théâtres des boulevards*, 266–67.

61. Muret, *L'Histoire par le théâtre*, 1:229.

62. Ibid., 268.

63. Jean-Guillaume-Augustin Cuvelier de Trie, *La Lanterne de Diogène, pantomime équestre, à grand spectacle, avec marches, evolutions et tournois, formant quatre petits tableaux de quatre siècles* (Paris: Barba, 1808). On this play, see also Lecomte, *Napoléon et l'Empire*, 170–71.

64. Ibid., 15.

65. McCormick, *Popular Theaters*, 29; see also Albert, *Les Théâtres des boulevards*, 268.

66. Jean-Guillaume-Augustin Cuvelier de Trie, *Nouvelles, contes, historiettes, anecdotes et mélanges*, 2nd rev. ed., 2 vols. (Paris: Le Teletier, 1808), 2:12. The allusions on the title page of this rare volume to an alleged first edition and an alleged first part of the *Nouvelles* may have been a literary pretension by Cuvelier de Trie. I could only locate one copy of the second part of this publication in Troyes, MAT, Desguerrois, D. G. 7774.

67. Jean-Guillaume-Augustin Cuvelier de Trie, *La Gloire et la Paix, dialogue dramatique en vers libres, fait à l'occasion des victoires en Espagne, de son Altesse Royale Monseigneur le Duc d'Angoulême, et ses fêtes données à l'armée par la ville de Paris en décembre 1823* (Paris: Dondey-Dupré, 1823). In his previously mentioned letter to the Beaux-Arts administration in the Ministry of the Interior (AN, F 21/1008) of August 7, 1822, Cuvelier audaciously presented himself as a diehard Bourbon supporter, who, "for ten years already, has made his lyre resound in favor of the Bourbons on any suitable occasion [à toutes les époques intéressantes]." By his own admission, it was above all when it came "to singing the song of the Bourbons" that he was "inspired to the utmost." The letter indeed cites a number of pieces written by Cuvelier during the Restoration that celebrate Bourbon rule: *L'Entrée d'Henri Quatre à Paris; La Fête d'un bon roi; La Jeunesse du Grand Condé, 1814; La Médaille, ou Le Retour de Chilperie; L'Union des Lys, Les Trois Âges de Henri Quatre; Le Berceau de Henri Quatre.* With the exception of *La Jeunesse du Grand Condé*, no trace remains of the other plays, attesting to the significant losses that Cuvelier's literary output has suffered over time.

68. Albert, *Les Théâtres des boulevards*, 250–312; Muret, *L'Histoire par le théâtre*, 2:124–26; McCormick, *Popular Theaters*, 101.

69. Hillemacher, *Le Cirque Franconi*, 19–21, McCormick, *Popular Theaters*, 30.

70. Jean-Guillaume-Augustin Cuvelier de Trie, *Cavalo-Dios, ou Le Cheval génie bienfaisant* (Paris: Barba, 1808).

71. Jean-Guillaume-Augustin Cuvelier de Trie, *Le Volcan, ou L'Anchorète du val des laves, pantomime magique en trois actes* (Paris: Barba, 1812). On the special effects cited, see in particular pages 10–12, 15, 18–19, 21–24. Cuvelier was not the first author to exploit volcanic settings as a pretext for melodramatic effects; see Muret's description of the scenography in Sylvain Maréchal's play *Le Jugement dernier des Rois* of 1793 in *L'Histoire par le théâtre*, 1:85–87.

72. Pao, *The Orient of the Boulevards*, 43.

73. Muret, *L'Histoire par le théâtre*, 2:100; McCormick, *Popular Theaters*, 125, 154.

74. Julien Deschamps, *Biographie de M. Comte, physicien du roi, suivie de la biographie en miniature des acteurs et actrices du théâtre Comte* (Paris: Desloges, 1845); Francis Roch, *Notice biographique sur M. Comte*, 2nd ed. (Paris: Bureau de la Revue, 1846); Wild, *Dictionnaire des théâtres parisiens*, 103–5.

75. Françoise Waquet, *Les Fêtes royales sous la Restauration, ou L'Ancien Régime retrouvé* (Geneva: Droz, 1981), 62; Invitation to the *Fête Sophisienne* (February 27, 1821), in *Mélanges Lerouge*, CMC, Kloss Collection, Ms. 240.B.74.

76. Couailhac, *La Vie de théâtre*, 280.

77. Cuvelier de Trie, *Nouvelles, contes, historiettes*, 2:172.

78. Brazier, *Chroniques*, 1:265, 2:90. Jean-Guillaume-Augustin Cuvelier de Trie, *L'Empire de la folie, ou La Mort et l'apothéose de Don Quichotte* (Paris: Imprimerie à Prix-Fixe, 1798/99); Jean-Guillaume-Augustin Cuvelier de Trie, *Les Tentations, ou Tous les diables, pantomime allégorique en trois actes, précédée du Conseil du Lucifer, prologue en un acte et en vers* (Paris: Barba, Year VIII—1799/1800). The Théâtre de la Cité was not located on the boulevard du Temple, but on the Ile de la Cité, across from the Palais de Justice.

79. Brazier, *Chroniques*, 1:277, 2:369; Lanzac de Laborie, *Paris sous Napoléon*, 8:137.

80. Jean-Guillaume-Augustin Cuvelier de Trie, *La Fille sauvage, ou L'Inconnu des Ardennes, mélodrama en trois actes et à grand spectacle* (Paris: Barba, 1812).

81. Ibid., 5–6.

82. Ibid., 10.

83. Clavel, *Histoire pittoresque de la franc-maçonnerie*, 362, 397–98; Jean Vidalenc, articles "Charbonnerie" and "Fendeurs," in *Dictionnaire de la franc-maçonnerie*, ed. Ligou, 226–32, 463. Despite similarities in rituals and symbolic content, it is important to distinguish the *Fendeurs-Charbonniers* from the secret society of the *Charbonnerie*, which, under its Italian name *Carbonari*, gained infamy for its nationalist and/or anti-Bourbon political conspiracies in the kingdom of Naples and in France from the 1810s through 1830.

84. Cuvelier de Trie, *La fille sauvage*, 17–18.

85. Cuvelier de Trie, *Nouvelles, contes, historiettes*, 2:12.

86. Jean-Guillaume-Augustin Cuvelier de Trie, *Le Tribunal invisible, ou Le Fils criminal* (Paris: Barba, 1802).

87. Ibid., 10.

88. Ibid., 40.

89. McCormick, *Popular Theaters*, 113, 157–79; Lanzac de Laborie, *Paris sous Napoléon*, 8:180–82.

90. Lanzac de Laborie, *Paris sous Napoléon*, 8:181.

91. Pao, *The Orient of the Boulevards*, 78–80.

92. Armand Charlemagne, *Le Mélodrame aux boulevards: Facétie littéraire, historique et dramatique* (Paris: Imprimerie de la rue Beaurepaire, 1809), 2, 20–21. Charlemagne's history of boulevard melodrama is delivered in the form of a prose poem with extensive annotated commentaries. He introduces Cuvelier with

a play on words modeled after a stanza in the *chant premier* of Boileau's *Art poétique*—the famous expression "Enfin Malherbe vint, et, le premier en France, / Fit sentir dans les vers une juste cadence [Finally Malherbe came, and, for the first time in France, / Gave verses the feeling of correct rhythm]" becomes "Enfin Cuvelier vint, et, le premier en France, / Montra le melodrama en sa magnificence [Finally Cuvelier came, and, for the first time in France, / Showed melodrama in all its magnificence]." Later, Charlemagne cites Cuvelier's *C'est le diable, ou la Bohémienne* (1798) as the first modern melodrama.

93. William Driver Howarth, "Word and Image in Pixérécourt's Melodramas: The Dramaturgy of the Strip-Cartoon," in *Performance and Politics in Popular Drama: Aspects of Popular Entertainment in Theater, Film, and Television, 1800–1976*, ed. David Bradby, Louis James, and Bernard Sharratt (Cambridge: Cambridge University Press, 1980), 17–32.

94. Lanzac de Laborie, *Paris sous Napoléon*, 8:180–82, 205–28.

95. Pao, *The Orient of the Boulevards*, 45–61.

96. See for instance the "Extrait d'une lettre de Caire, du 22 brumaire" signed by a "Citizen Attached to Bonaparte," in *Moniteur universel* 161 (Ventôse 11, year VII—February 29, 1799), 657. Many of the metaphors in the propaganda letter were probably derived from Claude-Étienne Savary's sanitized description of Egypt as a land of plenty in his *Lettres d'Égypte*.

97. Cuvelier de Trie, *Les Machabées*, 5–16. Cuvelier's *L'Enfant prodigue, ou Les Délices de Memphis, pantomime en trois actes et à grand spectacle* (Paris: Barba, 1812) is an example of an Orientalist play with an even more ancient historical setting than the *Machabées*. The play is mostly concerned with a conflict between two members of the displaced Jewish community, Judas and Benjamin, whose struggle is staged against a backdrop of an "Egypt, under the reign of a Pharaoh before Moses, at Memphis and its environs." Arabs only play a passing role as bandits and henchmen of the villain Judas, who intends to steal Benjamin's inheritance. Ostensibly an adaptation of Old Testament themes, Benjamin's adventures in the *Enfant prodigue* were in fact mostly modeled after themes from Abbé Terrasson's *Séthos*. Although the stage directions prescribe a décor of "an arid landscape" with fig trees and date palms or a tent, stagecraft and special effects in the *Enfant prodigue* seem to have been lackluster compared to *Les Machabées*.

98. Cuvelier de Trie, *Les Machabées*, 43–44.

99. Jean-Guillaume-Augustin Cuvelier de Trie, *Le Rénégat, ou La Belle Géorgienne, pantomime chevalresque en trois actes* (Paris: Barba, 1812).

100. Jean-Guillaume-Augustin Cuvelier de Trie, *Le Vieux de la montagne, ou Les Arabes du Liban, melodrama en trois actes, en prose et à grand spectacle* (Paris: Barba, 1815).

101. Jean-Guillaume-Augustin Cuvelier de Trie, *Le More de Venise, ou Othello, pantomime entremêlée de dialogue, en trois actes, imitée de la tragédie anglaise* (Paris: Fages, 1818), 16.

102. Ibid., 36.

103. Jean-Guillaume-Augustin Cuvelier de Trie, *Le Chat botté, ou Les 24 heures d'Arléquin, opéra pantomime-féerie en quatre actes* (Paris: Barba, 1802), 47–54.

104. Jean-Guillaume-Augustin Cuvelier de Trie, *L'Enfant du malheur, ou Les Amans muets, pantomime féerie, en trois actes et à grand spectacle*, 2nd ed. (Paris: Barba, 1817), 14, 17, 23.

105. Cuvelier de Trie, *Cavalo-Dios*.

106. Jean-Guillaume-Augustin Cuvelier de Trie, *La Belle Espagnole, ou L'Entrée triomphale des Français à Madrid, scènes équestres, militaires et historiques, à grand spectacle, en trois parties* (Paris: Barba, 1809).

107. Cuvelier de Trie, *La Bataille d'Aboukir, ou Les Arabes du désert* (Paris: Barba, 1810). On this play, see also Lecomte, *Napoléon et l'Empire*, 179–81.

108. Cuvelier de Trie, *La Mort de Kléber*, 3–4. The only censorship requirement imposed on the presentation of this play was that the actors not be allowed to wear the Revolutionary tricolor cocarde, which historical circumstances would have required for the costumes. Casts for plays in this genre were typically staffed with actors specializing in military roles. See Muret, *L'Histoire par le théâtre*, 2:128–29. On the divergent opinions of Restoration censors with regard to representations of the Egyptian campaign on stage, see Pao, *The Orient of the Boulevards*, 72–73.

109. Cuvelier de Trie, *L'Enchanteur Morto-Vivo*, 3–8.

110. Ibid., 3.

111. Ibid.

112. Ibid., 21.

113. On the violet as symbol for Bonapartist sympathies and its use on stage, see Muret, *L'Histoire par le théâtre*, 2:63–65. Originally chosen for its connotations with modesty, the violet came to be regarded as the "imperial flower" during the Empire. In 1814, when rumors spread prior to the *cent jours* that Bonaparte was about to return from Elba, his partisans asserted that he would "come back [to France] with violets." Henceforth, it was considered a symbol of resistance against Bourbon rule.

114. Peter Brooks, *The Melodramatic Imagination: Balzac, Henry James, Melodrama, and the Mode of Excess* (1976; repr., New York: Columbia University Press, 1984), 14–15.

115. Cuvelier de Trie, *Les Hommes de la nature, et les hommes policés*, 3–8.

116. Ibid., 24.

117. Some examples of Cuvelier's plays where "the people" make an appearance include: *Le Petit Poucet, ou L'Orphélin de la forêt, drame en cinq actes, en prose, mêlée de chants, pantomimes et danses* (Paris: Fages, 1801), 48; *Jeanne d'Arc, ou La Pucelle d'Orléans, pantomime en trois actes et à grand spectacle* (Paris: Théâtre de la Gaîté, 1803), 13; *Le Chef écossais, ou La Caverne d'Ossian, pantomime en deux actes, à grand spectacle* (Paris: Barba, 1815), 24; *Les Machabées* (1817), 17, 29, 46; *Le More de Venise* (1818), 17.

118. European Enlightenment literature of the eighteenth century teemed with titles celebrating the pursuit of happiness. Paul Hazard, *La Pensée européenne au XVIIIe siècle: De Montesquieu à Lessing*, 2 vols. (Paris: Boivin, 1946), 1:17–33, enumerates the following examples among many other such titles: *Réflexions sur le bonheur; Epître sur le bonheur; Sur la vie heureuse; Système du vrai bonheur; Essai sur le bonheur; Della felicità; L'arte di essere felici; Discorso sulla felicità; Versuch über die Kunst stets fröhlich zu sein; Über die menschliche Glückseligkeit; Of happiness.*

CONCLUSION

1. Antoine-Laurent-Apollinaire Fée, *Le Darwinisme, ou Examen de la théorie relative à l'origine des espèces* (Paris: Masson, 1864), 15.

2. Pluche, *Histoire du ciel*, 1:168.

3. Ibid., 1:xx.

4. Ibid., 1:xvi.

5. Ibid., 2:8–9.

6. Ibid., 1:xxix, 132, 137–38.

7. Ibid., 1:75, 80, 182–83, 199, 397–98, 423; 2:346.

8. Ibid., 1:3, 25–26, 31, 37.

9. Ibid., 1:42–44, 418–19.

10. Ibid., 2:16–17.

11. *Livre d'or* [BN], fols. 39v–40r.

12. Aristotle, *De generatione animalium* II.2, 716a; IV.1, 765b, in *Generation of Animals*, ed. and tr. Arthur Leslie Peck (Cambridge and London: Harvard University Press, Loeb Classical Library, 1943), 10–13, 384–85. Sophisian admiration for the Aristotelian concept of Nature is attested by Guerrier de Dumast, for example, who wrote in *La Maçonnerie*, 21: "In the eyes of the ancients, this beautiful title of lover of nature, inseparable from [the reputation] of a truly virtuous man, ranked even higher than we rank it today. Nature, says Aristotle, is nothing but a complement to perfection. Thus, when an organism of whatever sort, whether man, horse, or family, is perfect, we say that it is in Nature."

13. Cuvelier de Trie, *Nouvelles, contes, historiettes*, 2:38.

14. Guerrier de Dumast, *La Maçonnerie*, 321: "[Freemasonry] of course predates Christian religion, and is contemporary with ethnic beliefs; it shares some of the forms of popular cults, but only as a veil that it used to cover itself and that it knew when to lift at the right time." See also Lenoir, *La Franche-Maçonnerie*, 7, 12–13.

15. Guerrier de Dumast, *La Maçonnerie*, iii.

16. Anonymous, *Testament de Mort et Déclarations faites par Cagliostro, de la secte des Illuminés, & se disant chef de la Loge Égyptienne; condamné à Rome, le 7 avril 1791, à une prison perpétuelle, comme perturbateur du repos public, traduit de l'Italien* (Paris, 1791), 4, 6–7.

17. Ibid., 21–23.

18. Guerrier de Dumast, *La Maçonnerie*, 298.

19. J.-B.-L. Germond, "Notice nouvelle sur la vie et les ouvrages de Sylvain Maréchal," in *Dictionnaire des athées anciens et modernes*, 2nd revised and expanded ed. (Brussels: Balleroy, 1833), [15].

20. Maréchal, *Dictionnaire des athées*, 79–80.

21. Ibid., 128–29.

22. Ibid., 199.

23. Guerrier de Dumast, *La Maçonnerie*, 190–91.

24. Cuvelier de Trie, "Anecdote," in *Nouvelles, contes, historiettes*, 2:165.

25. Nicolas Vagner, *Notice sur M. Guerrier de Dumast, envisagé au point de vue religieux* (Nancy: Imprimerie et Librairie catholiques, 1883), 5.

26. Bernard Van Rinsveld, "Une Égyptomanie anti-bonapartiste: Le Journaliste Jean-Gabriel Peltier," *Chronique d'Égypte* 66, nos. 131–32 (1991): 5–22. The most complete set of Peltier's newspapers can be found in the Fonds Brouwet of the Musée royal de l'Armée et d'Histoire militaire in Brussels.

27. Jean-Gabriel Peltier, *The Trial of John Peltier, esq., for a Libel against Napoleon Bonaparte, First Consul of the French Republic, at the Court of the King's-Bench, Middlesex, on Monday the 21ˢᵗ February, 1803, Taken in Short-Hand by Mr. Adams, and the Defence Revised by Mr. Mackintosh* (London: Peltier, 1803), 234–35.

28. Fabien Richelme, *Mémoire relatif aux monumens de l'Égypte, considérés dans le sens hermético-maçonnique* (Saint-Pierre Martinique: Roques, 1807), 100–01. Richelme's book is exceedingly rare, since most copies were presumably lost during the 1902 volcanic eruption that destroyed Saint-Pierre Martinique completely. The only available copy I could locate is at the BN-RDJ, RÉS. P. R. 1084. The author explicitly denied being a Freemason, but admitted having taken an interest in the Denderah scene because of his fascination with esoteric speculations. In contrast to Pugnet's evolutionist interpretation, he saw the illustration as an alchemical allegory of the philosopher's stone. See also Jean-François-Xavier Pugnet's medical treatise *Mémoires sur les fièvres pestilentielles et insidieuses du Levant, avec un aperçu physique et médical du Sayd* (Lyons and Paris: Reymann and Périsse, 1802), 43–44, for the original description and analysis of the composition, passages of which were appropriated by Richelme.

29. Richelme, *Mémoire*, 4–6.

30. *Livre d'or* [BN], fol. 53r.

31. Richelme, *Mémoire*, 6.

32. Bernard-Germain-Étienne de la Ville-sur-Illion Comte de Lacépède, *Histoire naturelle de l'homme* (Paris and Strasbourg: Levrault, 1827); Bernard-Germain-Étienne de la Ville-sur-Illion Comte de Lacépède, *Les Âges de la nature*, 2 vols. (Paris and Strasbourg: Levrault, 1830).

33. Lacépède, *Les Âges de la nature*, 1:vi.

34. Ibid., 1:94–96.

35. Ibid., 1:64, 138.

36. Ibid., 1:184–225.

37. Ibid., 1:231, 226–96.

38. Paolo Rossi, *La Naissance de la science moderne en Europe*, tr. Patrick Vighetti (Paris: Seuil, 1999), 269–79.

39. *Forerunners of Darwin: 1745–1859*, ed. Bentley Glass, Owsei Temkin, and William L. Straus, Jr. (Baltimore: Johns Hopkins University Press, 1968), 79, 357.

40. Étienne Geoffroy Saint-Hilaire, *Principes de philosophie zoologique, discutés en Mars 1830 au sein de l'Académie Royale des Sciences* (Paris: Pichon, Didier and Rousseau, 1830), 53–110. The title makes reference to Lamarck's famous treatise *Philosophie zoologique* published in 1809. Geoffroy's "theory of analogy" stands in opposition to the theory of the "degradation of form," according to which all elements in animal anatomy derived from their perfected form in man. Geoffroy refrained from such value judgments and focused on objective anatomical comparisons instead.

41. Étienne Geoffroy Saint-Hilaire, "Le Degré de l'influence du monde ambiant pour modifier les formes animales: Question intéressant l'origine des espèces télésauriennes et successivement celle des animaux de l'époque actuelle," *Mémoires de l'Académie Royale des Sciences de l'Institut de France* 12 (1833): 89–90, note 1.

42. On vitalism in general, see Hans Driesch, *The History and Theory of Vitalism*, tr. Charles Kay Ogden (London: Macmillan, 1914) and Leonard Richmond Wheeler, *Vitalism: Its History and Validity* (London: Witherby, 1939).

43. Étienne Geoffroy Saint-Hilaire, "Loi universelle (Attraction de soi pour soi), ou Clef applicable à l'interprétation de tous les phénomènes de la philosophie naturelle: Découverte faite à la suite d'études incessantes concernant les arrangements, les complications, les mouvements, et généralement toutes les actions des êtres organisés," in *Études progressives d'un naturaliste pendant les années 1834 et 1835, faisant suite à ses publications dans les 42 volumes des Mémoires et Annales du Muséum d'Histoire Naturelle* (Paris: Roret, 1835), 125, note 1. Another noteworthy anti-vitalist statement can be found on page 176: "Rejecting all unfounded ideas deficient in thought and grounded in occult forces, we shall deny any belief in ambiguous life-force [*animation indéfinie*] as absolutely impossible to define. We are partisans of the line [of reasoning] that considers the medley of the vitalists and their compilation of incomprehensible ideas, supported by fictional structures, as opposed to common sense." See also pages

132–39 for Geoffroy's analogy of life with a watch, and pages 144–87 for his explanation of the principle of "mutual attraction" (*attraction de soi pour soi*). The trope of the "admirable machine" for living matter is first used on page 127.

44. Wheeler, *Vitalism*, 51–64.

45. Geoffroy, *Principes de philosophie zoologique*, 127–28; Geoffroy, "Loi universelle," 147–51, 154–55. He concludes the latter treatise on page 189 by saying that: "Definitively, the cause of the observable facts of the universe is attraction conceived according to the principle of reciprocal affinity (*le principe de l'affinité de soi pour soi*). But beyond that, incontestably, the cause of all causes is GOD."

46. Fée, *Le Darwinisme*, 5, 7, 24, 54–56, 102–5.

47. Ibid., 114–15.

48. Ibid., 3.

49. Ibid., 13.

50. *Livre d'or* [BN], 83r–83v.

51. Fée, *Le Darwinisme*, 46. Geoffroy, "Loi universelle," 171, also thought of Nature in legal terms, since "Nature cannot fail; her laws are nothing but a generalized expression of all her manifestations observed. . . . Other laws but [her] general laws are not admissible."

52. Fée, 12. Fée's statement is a variation on Pascal's saying in the *Pensées* that "Man is but a reed, the most feeble thing in nature, but he is a thinking reed." Blaise Pascal, *Pensées*, ed. Brunschvicg (1669; repr., Paris: Garnier, 1964), 162, no. 347.

53. Rossi, *La Naissance*, 40–46.

54. Guerrier de Dumast, *La Maçonnerie*, 215–16. The Sophisian author appropriated the esoteric-versus-exoteric distinction from either Diderot or Lenoir, who had previously used this terminology to discuss the status of scientific knowledge in ancient Egypt.

55. Ibid., 169: "During our meetings, where harmony rules, . . . / one often finds a soldier whose honor, whose valor, / make one forget the imperatives of an illustrious birth; / a magistrate faithful to ancient virtue, / who has long held the highest functions; / next to a timid young man, / who looks for guidance in this world; / a merchant, who passes unnoticed but whose activities are of importance; / a lover of fine arts, / proud of his poverty: / Thus under the power of an unknown force, / the distance of ranks effaces itself . . . or at least diminishes. / The powerful and the weak have established ties, / and this new relationship will ennoble both of them."

56. Baltrušaitis, *La Quête d'Isis*, 46, 79.

57. Israel, *Radical Enlightenment*, 83.

58. Cuvelier de Trie, *Nouvelles, contes, historiettes*, 2:15–16, 146, 166–72. The rape scene was apparently copied from the travel description by another Sophisian, Milfort, who had lived for many years with the Creek Indians. See *Chef de guerre chez les Creeks*, 204–6.

59. Israel, *Radical Enlightenment*, 93. For eulogies of innocence and sexual "virtue" in Cuvelier's literary work, see for example *Nouvelles, contes, historiettes*, 2:13, 145.

60. Hivert-Messeca, *Comment la franc-maçonnerie vint aux femmes*, 105.

61. Gérard de Nerval, *Les Filles du feu: Angélique, Sylvie, Jemmy, Octavie, Isis, Émilie, Pandora* (Paris: Le Divan, 1927); Auguste Comte de Villiers de L'Isle-Adam, *Isis* (Brussels: Librairie Internationale, 1900); Helena Petrovna Blavatsky, *Isis Unveiled: A Master-Key to the Mysteries of Ancient and Modern Science and Theology*, 2 vols. (1877; repr., Pasadena: Theosophical University Press, 1972); Philippe Lavergne, *André Breton et le mythe* (Paris:

Corti, 1985), 53–54, 59–62; Umberto Eco, *Foucault's Pendulum*, tr. William Weaver (New York: Harcourt Brace Jovanovich, 1988). Moreover, the Egyptian rite of Memphis-Misraïm, whose origins goes back to about 1810, continues to attract to present Egyptophile followers not only in France, but also in Great Britain and the United States, among other countries. See Serge Caillet, *La Franc-maçonnerie égyptienne de Memphis-Misraïm*, 2nd revised, corrected, and expanded ed. (Paris: Dervy, 2003).

Appendix

1. The BN Golden Book lists members' last names (listed here in bold) and their professions only. By supplementing this information with the annual *tableaux* of the lodge and the chapter of the *Frères Artistes* (BN-MSS, FM 2.78), one can recover first names, birth dates, places of birth, and addresses for about half of the Sophisian members. Compared to the selective and elitist Sophisians, the *Frères Artistes* had a much broader membership pool. Based on this collation of sources, it becomes possible to reconstruct the activities and historical importance of the Sophisians with standard biographical tools. In this respect, Antoine-Vincent Arnault's *Biographie nouvelle des contemporains*, 20 vols. (Paris: Librairie historique, 1820–25), proved to be a true gold mine. Arnault, who came from a theater background and accompanied the Egyptian expedition as far as Malta in 1798, knew everybody who was anybody during the Empire and the Restoration. Arnault's dictionary, however, needs updating with Michel Prevost and Roman D'Amat's modern-day *Dictionnaire de biographie française*, 19 vols. to date (Paris: Letouzey, 1933–), which, as of this writing, unfortunately stops with the letter L. For the second half of the alphabet, I consulted the Firmin Didot Brothers' *Nouvelle biographie générale*, ed. Jean-Chrétien-Ferdinand Hoefer, 46 vols. (Paris: Firmin-Didot, 1855–66). In addition, a number of specialized biographical dictionaries treating specific sub-sets of the Sophisian membership population turned out to be very helpful: on British members (Cobb, Goldsmith), see H. C. G. Matthew and Brian Harrison's *Oxford Dictionary of National Biography*, 60 vols. (Oxford: Oxford University Press, 2004); on German members (Gürlich, Iffland), see *Neue Deutsche Biographie*, ed. Historische Kommission bei der Bayerischen Akademie der Wissenschaften, 22 vols to date. (Berlin: Duncker & Humblot, 1953–); on Napoleon's marshals (Bessières, Brune), see David G. Chandler, *Napoleon's Marshals* (New York: Macmillan, 1987); on Napoleon's generals (Aubry, Bessières, Brune, Caffarelli, Colbert, Delmas, Desbureaux, Destaing, Ganteaume, Gratien, Guillemet, Lacrosse, Lasalle, Lorge, Magon, Menou, Reynier, Taviel, Verdier), see Georges Six, *Dictionnaire biographique des généraux & amiraux français de la Révolution française et de l'Empire, 1792–1814*, 2 vols. (Paris: Saffroy, 1934); on Napoleon's colonels (Dumolard, Holtz, Sarraire), see Danielle and Bernard Quintin, *Dictionnaire des colonels de Napoléon* (Paris: S.P.M., 1996); on admirals and members of the navy (Destaing, Ganteaume, Lacrosse, Magon), see Joseph-François-Gabriel Hennequin's *Biographie maritime, ou notices historiques sur la vie et les campagnes des marins célèbres français et étrangers*, 3 vols. (Paris: Regnault, 1835–37); on members of the Institut d'Égypte and participants in the Egyptian campaign in general (Bessières, Caffarelli, Colbert, Denon, Ganteaume, Geoffroy, Lancret, Lasalle, Malus, Menou, Monge, Norry, Verdier, Villoteau), see Laissus, *L'Égypte, une aventure savante*; on members associated with the popular theaters (M. and Mme Audinot-D'Aussy, Chaussier,

Comte, Cuvelier, Foignet, Mme Dengremont, Ponce-Camus, M. and Mme de Puisaye, Varez), see Nicolas Brazier, *Chroniques des petits théâtres de Paris*; on musicians (Amédée, Foignet, Lemière, Piccinni, Villoteau), see Ludwig Finscher's *Die Musik in Geschichte und Gegenwart: Allgemeine Enzyklopädie der Musik, Personenteil*, 2nd rev. ed., 13 vols. (Kassel and New York: Bärenreiter, 1994), along with Stanley Sadie's *The New Grove Dictionary of Music and Musicians*, 2nd ed., 29 vols. (London and New York: Macmillan, 2001); on artists and architects (Norry, Ponce-Camus, Grenier de Saint-Martin), see Ulrich Thieme and Felix Becker's *Allgemeines Lexikon der bildenden Künstler*, 37 vols. (Leipzig: Seeman, 1907–50); on the philhellenes from the Princely Academy in Bucharest (Photilas, Piccolos, Sakellarios, Vogorides), see Camariano-Cioran, *Les académies princières de Bucarest*; on doctors and pharmacists (Fée, Chaussier), see Achille Chereau, *Le Parnasse médical français, ou Dictionnaire des médecins-poètes de la France, anciens ou modernes, morts ou vivants* (Paris: Delahaye, 1874); on Freemasonic biographies (Brune, Cassabois, Cuvelier de Trie, Denon, Fauchet, Ganteaume, Guerrier de Dumast, Iffland, Lacépède, Lemaire, Lion, Magon, Menou, Monge, Piccinni, Régnaud), see Ligou's *Dictionnaire de la franc-maçonnerie*. I have also consulted a number of personnel dossiers in the French military archives at Vincennes in compiling these biographies; at the SHD-DAT: Balluet (2 Yf 104220), Brouilhony (2 Yf 86954), Cuvelier de Trie (2 Yf 4852), Desbureaux (7 Yd 106), Destaing (7 Yd 363), Girard (2 Yf 156247), Gratien (7 Yd 551), Lorge (7Yd 311), Milfort (8 Yd 692), Taviel (7 Yd 524), Verdier (7 Yd 359); at the SHD-DM: Noiseux (CC7 Alpha, Carton 1862), Rotrou (CC7 Alpha, Carton 2190), Tempié (CC7 Alpha, Carton 2340). Finally, the records of the Légion d'honneur at the AN in Paris revealed a wealth of information on the following individuals: Beaufils (LH 154/350), Cuvelier de Trie (LH 642/93), Dalmas de Pracontal (LH 649/29), Delaberge (LH 693/76), Desbureaux (LH 743/44), Fauchet (LH 936/6), Fauchon d'Henneville (LH 936/36), Fée (LH 951/58), Girard (LH 1143/76), Guerrier de Dumast (LH 1223/25), Holtz (LH 1306/62), Jacqueminot (LH 1342/10), Lacépède (C 38), Langlois de Septenville (LH 1471/16), Lemaire (LH 1574/25), Levy (LH 1630/9), Lion (1659/22), Magon (LH 1688/15), Norry (LH 2003/31), Pariset (LH 2053/70), Piccinni (LH 2146/38), Pigault-Maubaillarcq (LH 2158/65), Prisette (LH 2229/35), Trichon (LH 2629/39), Sarraire (LH 2460/38).

2. *Livre d'or* [BN], fols. 2v–3r. The list was mostly compiled in 1819, but new names may have been added as late as 1821. All entries were written in Ponce-Camus's handwriting and do not contain original signatures, like the *Frères Artistes* records. Testimonials concerning Sophisian ranks (*Isiarque, Harpocrate, Philisiarque*) often have to be gleaned from sources other than the *Livre d'or* [BN] or the archives of the *Frères Artistes*. The richest document in this regard is the invitation for the *Fête Sophisienne* of 1821, bound with the *Mélanges Lerouge*, which lists more than twenty Sophisian officers by name and rank. The records of the *Frères Artistes* include Sophisian ranks only once, in 1812, when Cuvelier de Trie is mentioned as *Grand Isiarque* and Dalmas de Pracontal as *Isiarque* (BN-MSS, FM 2.78, No. 8). Some Sophisian ranks for 1819 (or earlier for deceased members) are also alluded to in the description of the funerary rites for Paul-Louis Mariton, published as "L∴ †∴ des Artistes, O∴ de Paris," in *Hermès, ou Archives maçonniques par une Société de F∴ M∴*, 2 vols. (Paris: Renard, 1818–19), 1:324–34. Some such ranks can be confirmed

for the period prior to 1813 with the help of *Livre d'or* [GODF], where dignitaries signed with their names and symbolic representations of their ranks. The meaning of these symbols can be decoded by consulting Fig. 44.

3. *Livre d'or* [BN], fol. 27r. Some signatures cannot be fully deciphered, and only a fraction can be identified with the help of the *Frères Artistes* archives.

4. Joseph-Marie Quérard, *Les Supercheries littéraires dévoilées: Galerie des auteurs apocryphes, supposés, déguisés, plagiaires, et des éditeurs infidèles pendant les quatre derniers siècles*, 5 vols. (Paris, 1847–53), 3:202 (No. 4569).

5. Henry Yule, *Hobson-Jobson: A Glossary of Colloquial Anglo-Indian Words and Phrases*, 2 vols. (London: Murray, 1903), 2:809–11; John R. Elting, *Swords Around a Throne: Napoleon's Grande Armée* (New York and London: The Free Press and Macmillan, 1988), 223.

6. Cuvelier de Trie, *Les Hommes de la nature et les hommes policés*, 16.

7. Thomas-Xavier Bianchi, "Notice historique sur M. Ruffin," *Journal asiatique* 6 (January–June 1825): 337–48.

8. *Fastes de la Légion d'honneur: Biographie de tous les décorés, accompagnée de l'histoire législative et réglementaire de l'ordre*, ed. A. Lievyns, Jean-Maurice Verdot, and Pierre Bégat, 5 vols. (Paris, 1842–47), 2:187.

9. Geoffroy Saint-Hilaire, *Lettres écrites d'Égypte*, 103–10, 138–44.

10. The double entry in the Golden Book obviously refers to one and the same individual. See specifically Holtz's files from the Légion d'honneur, AN, LH 1306/62, and Georges Rigault, *Inventaire des États de service des officiers de l'armée d'Égypte* (Paris: Plon-Nourrit, 1911), 42, 181. On the Légion nautique, see Barallier, "Souvenirs d'un marin de la Légion nautique: Expédition d'Égypte, ans VII et VIII," in *Souvenirs et cahiers sur la campagne d'Égypte: Extraits du Carnet de La Sabretache années 1903–1906–1931–1932* (Paris: Teissèdre, 1997), 127; on Holtz's service under General Friant, see Jean-François Friant, *Vie militaire du lieutenant-général comte Friant* (Paris: Dentu, 1857), 76, 90–91, 108, 126, note 2.

11. Adolphe Robert, Edgar Bourloton, and Gaston Cougny, *Dictionnaire des parlementaires français*, 5 vols. (Paris: Bourloton, 1891), 4:165.

12. Malus de Mitry, *L'Agenda de Malus*, 11–26.

13. ADG, 3 E/22390 to 3 E/23303.

14. AN, F 7/3271 and F 7/9868.

15. Lascaris, "L'Académie Ionienne," 206–7.

16. Geoffroy Saint-Hilaire, *Lettres écrites d'Égypte*, 103–10.

17. Jean Verzat, *Le Comte Regnaud de Saint-Jean-d'Angély*, 13–16, 27–29.

18. *Kléber en Égypte, 1798–1800*, ed. Jacques and Henry Laurens, 4 vols. (Cairo: IFAO, 1995), 3:301.

19. AN, Minutier Central, ET XLIII/506 (January 8, 1811).

20. Bourrienne, *Mémoires*, 2:178–79.

21. B. Vendryes, *Mémoire pour M. B. Vendryes, directeur à Paris de la Société dite du Brésil contre M. le lieutenant-général Montmarie et le lieutenant-colonel Roise, actionnaires se disant mandataires, mais étant de fait cessionnaires à titre gratuit des autres actionnaires* ([Paris:] Vinchon, [1839]).

22. Brazier, *Chroniques*, 2:483.

Bibliography

Manuscript Archival Sources

Frères Artistes [Lodge]. *L∴ & Ch∴ Frères Artistes: Tableaux* [1796/97–1840]. BN-MSS, FM 2.78.

Ordre Sacré des Sophisiens. *Livre d'or: Institution de l'Ordre Sacré des Sophisiens dans la France*. BN-MSS, FM 4.15.

———. *Livre d'or, ou Institution de l'Ordre Sacré des Sophisiens dans la République française*. GODF, Ms. AR. Coll. Meyer, pièce 20.

———. *Mélanges Lerouge*. CMC, Kloss Collection, Ms. 240.B.74.

In addition, the series in the following archives were of particular relevance for research on the Sophisians:

- AN: Series F 21 (Beaux-Arts) and LH (Légion d'honneur)
- SHD-DAT: Series Yd (Dossiers d'officiers généraux), Yf (Dossiers de pensions militaires), and Xr (Non-combattants)
- SHD-DM: Series CC7 Alpha (Dossiers individuels des officiers de Marine)

Printed Primary Sources

Fictitious and presumed places of publication are given in quotation marks. In the case of rare works and editions the location of the copy used is indicated by the relevant abbreviation.

L'Accusateur public. Series 2. 1799. BN-RDJ

Al-Jabartî, Abd-al-Rahman. *Merveilles biographiques et historiques, ou Chroniques du Cheikh Abd-el-Rahman el Djabarti, traduites de l'arabe*. Translated by Chefik Mansour bey, Abdulaziz Kalil bey, Gabriel Nicolas Kalil bey and Iskender Ammoun effendi. 9 vols. 1888–96. Repr., Nendeln/Liechtenstein: Kraus, 1970.

Ammianus Marcellinus. *Ammiani Marcellini Rerum Gestarum Libri qui supersunt*. Edited and translated by John Carew Rolfe. 3 vols. Cambridge and London: Harvard University Press, Loeb Classical Library, 1950–52.

Anonymous. *Testament de Mort et Déclarations faites par Cagliostro, de la secte des Illuminés, & se disant chef de la Loge Égyptienne; condamné à Rome, le 7 avril 1791, à une prison perpétuelle, comme perturbateur du repos public, traduit de l'Italien*. Paris: 1791. BN-RDJ

———. "Travaux du Sup∴ Conseil du 33e degree du rite écossais, ancien et accepté." *Bibliothèque maçonnique, ou Recueil des matériaux propres à l'histoire de la maçonnerie* 1 (1818): 53–56. BN-RDJ

Apuleius. *Apuleius: Metamorphoses*. Edited and translated by John Arthur Hanson. 2 vols. Cambridge: Harvard University Press, Loeb Classical Library, 1989.

Aristophanes. *Aristophanes*. Edited and translated by Benjamin Bickley Rogers. 3 vols. Cambridge and London: Harvard University Press, Loeb Classical Library, 1924.

Aristotle. *Generation of Animals*. Edited and translated by Arthur Leslie Peck. Cambridge and London: Harvard University Press, Loeb Classical Library, 1943.

Arnault, Antoine-Vincent. *Biographie nouvelle des contemporains*. 20 vols. Paris: Librairie historique, 1820–25.

———. *Souvenirs d'un sexagénaire*. 1833. Repr., Paris: Champion, 2003.

Athanassakis, Apostolos N. *The Orphic Hymns: Text, Translation and Notes*. Missoula: Scholars Press for the Society of Biblical Literature, 1977.

Bacon, Francis. *The Advancement of Learning and Novum Organum*. Edited and translated by James Edward Creighton. New York: Colonial Press, 1899.

———. *The Works of Lord Bacon with an Introductory Essay, and a Portrait*. 2 vols. London: Ball, 1838.

Barruel, Augustin Abbé. *Mémoires pour servir à l'histoire du jacobinisme*. London: Le Boussonier, 1797/98.

Blavatsky, Helena Petrovna. *Isis Unveiled: A Master-Key to the Mysteries of Ancient and Modern Science and Theology*. 2 vols. 1877. Repr., Pasadena: Theosophical University Press, 1972.

Boissard, Jean-Jacques, and Theodor de Bry. *VI. Pars antiquitatum romanorum, sive IIII. tomus, inscriptionum & monumentorum, quae Romae in saxis & marmoribus visuntur*. 3 vols. Frankfurt: de Bry, 1597–1602.

Bonaparte, Napoleon. *Correspondance de Napoléon Ier*. 32 vols. Paris: Plon, Dumaine, 1858–70.

Bourrienne, Louis-Antoine Fauvelet de. *Mémoires de Bourrienne, ministre d'État, sur Napoléon, le Directoire, le Consulat, l'Empire, la Restauration*. Edited by Désiré Lacroix. 5 vols. Paris: Garnier Frères, 1899–1900.

Brazier, Nicolas. *Chroniques des petits théâtres de Paris*. Rev. ed. 2 vols. 1837. Repr., Paris: Rouveyre et Blond, 1883.

Brucker, Johann Jakob. *Historia critica philosophiae a mundi incunabulis*. 2nd ed. Leipzig: Weidemann & Reich, 1767.

Le Camp-Volant, journal des spectacles de tous les pays. 1818–20. BN-RDJ

Cagliostro: Dokumente zu Aufklärung und Okkultismus. Edited by Klaus H. Kiefer. Munich, Leipzig, and Weimar: Beck, 1991.

Casanova, Giacomo. *The Memoirs of Jacques Casanova de Seingalt*. Translated by Arthur Machen. 6 vols. New York and London: Putnam, 1959–61.

Casaubon, Isaac. *De rebus sacris et ecclesiasticis exercitationes XVI.* London: Norton, 1614.

Catalogue de livres manuscrits et imprimés sur la franc-maçonnerie et les sociétés secrètes provenant du cabinet de feu M. Lerouge . . . dont la vente aura lieu . . . le 7 janvier 1835 . . . rue des Beaux-Arts, no. 6. Paris: Leblanc, 1834. BN-MSS, FM.

Cauchois, Henri. *Cours oral de franc-maçonnerie symbolique en douze séances.* Paris: Dentu, 1863.

Charlemagne, Armand. *Le Mélodrame aux boulevards: Facétie littéraire, historique et dramatique.* Paris: Imprimerie de la rue Beaurepaire, 1809.

Chateaubriand, François-René de. *Oeuvres complètes.* 22 vols. Paris: Pourrat, 1833–35.

Collection Deloynes: Collection de pièces sur les beaux-arts imprimées et manuscrites. BN-EST

Corpus Hermeticum. Edited and translated by Arthur Darby Nock and André-Jean Festugière. 4 vols. Paris: Belles Lettres, 1945–54.

Courier [sic] de l'Égypte. 1798–1801. See *The Journals of Bonaparte in Egypt.*

Curtius Rufus, Quintus. *Historiae Alexandri.* Edited and translated by John C. Rolfe. 2 vols. Cambridge and London: Harvard University Press, Loeb Classical Library, 1946.

Cuvelier de Trie, Jean-Guillaume-Augustin. *L'Asile du Silence, ou Gloire et Sagesse.* Paris: Barba, 1811. BN-ASP, BN-RDJ

———. *La Bataille d'Aboukir, ou Les Arabes du désert.* Paris: Barba, 1810. BN-ASP, BN-RDJ

———. *La Belle Espagnole, ou L'Entrée triomphale des Français à Madrid, scènes équestres, militaires et historiques, à grand spectacle, en trois parties.* Paris: Barba, 1809. BN-ASP, BN-RDJ

———. *Cavalo-Dios, ou Le Cheval génie bienfaisant.* Paris: Barba, 1808. BN-ASP, BN-RDJ

———. *C'est le diable, ou la Bohémienne, drame en cinq actes à grand spectacle, mêlé de pantomime, evolutions, combats, chants et danses.* Paris: Barba, 1797/98. BN-ASP, BN-RDJ

———. *Le Chat botté, ou Les 24 heures d'Arléquin, opéra pantomime-féerie en quatre actes.* Paris: Barba, 1802. BN-ASP, BN-RDJ

———. *Le Chef écossais, ou La Caverne d'Ossian, pantomime en deux actes, à grand spectacle.* Paris: Barba, 1815. BN-ASP, BN-RDJ

———. *Le Damoisel et la bergerette, ou La Femme vindicative, historiette du XVI siècle.* Paris: Cailleau, 1795. BN-ASP

———. *L'Empire de la folie, ou La Mort et l'apothéose de Don Quichotte.* Paris: Imprimerie à Prix-Fixe, 1798/99. BN-ASP, BN-RDJ

———. *L'Enchanteur Morto-Vivo, prologue cabalistique; suivi de L'Isle de Silence, ou L'Arlequin malgré lui, féerie mélodramatique, mêlée de scènes pantomimes, en trois actes, à grand spectacle, metamorphoses, transformations, changemens de décoration, marches, combats, etc.* Paris: Maldan, 1806. BN-ASP, BN-RDJ

———. *L'Enfant du malheur, ou Les Amans muets, pantomime féerie, en trois actes et à grand spectacle.* 2nd ed., Paris: Barba, 1817. BN-ASP

———. *L'Enfant prodigue, ou Les Délices de Memphis, pantomime en trois actes et à grand spectacle.* Paris: Barba, 1812. BN-ASP, BN-RDJ

———. *L'Entrée des chevaliers français dans Serica.* Paris: Barba, 1811. BN-ASP, BN-RDJ

———. *La Fête de l'Être Suprême: Scène patriotique.* Paris: L'Imprimerie des Écoles Républicaines, Year II [1794]. BN-ASP

———. *La Fille sauvage, ou L'Inconnu des Ardennes, mélodrama en trois actes et à grand spectacle.* Paris: Barba, 1812. BN-ASP, BN-RDJ

———. *La Gloire et la Paix, dialogue dramatique en vers libres, fait à l'occasion des victoires en Espagne, de son Altesse Royale Monseigneur le Duc d'Angoulême, et ses fêtes données à l'armée par la ville de Paris en décembre 1823.* Paris: Dondey-Dupré, 1823. BN-RDJ

———. *Les Hommes de la nature et des hommes policés, pantomime en trois actes, dédié à ceux qui n'entendent pas, précédée et suivie des Deux Silphes.* Paris: Barba, 1800/1801. BN-ASP

———. *Jeanne d'Arc, ou La Pucelle d'Orléans, pantomime en trois actes et à grand spectacle.* Paris: Théâtre de la Gaîté, 1803. BN-ASP, BN-RDJ

———. *La Lanterne de Diogène, pantomime équestre, à grand spectacle, avec marches, evolutions et tournois, formant quatre petits tableaux de quatre siècles.* Paris: Barba, 1808. BN-ASP, BN-RDJ

———. *Les Machabées, ou La Prise de Jérusalem, drame sacré à grand spectacle.* Paris: Fages, 1817. BN-ASP, BN-RDJ

———. *Le More de Vénise, ou Othello, pantomime entremêlée de dialogue, en trois actes, imitée de la tragédie anglaise.* Paris: Fages, 1818. BN-ASP, BN-RDJ

———. *La Mort de Kléber, ou Les Français en Égypte: Mimodrame historique et militaire en deux actes.* Paris: Fages, 1819. BN-ASP, BN-RDJ

———. *Nouvelles, contes, historiettes, anecdotes et mélanges.* 2nd rev. ed. 2 vols. Paris: Le Teletier, 1808. MAT

———. *Le Petit Poucet, ou L'Orphélin de la forêt, drame en cinq actes, en prose, mêlée de chants, pantomimes et danses.* Paris: Fages, 1801. BN-ASP, BN-RDJ

———. *Le Phénix, ou L'Ile des Vieilles, comédie-féerie en quatre actes, mêlée de chants, pantomimes, combats et danses.* Paris: Barba, Year VI – 1797. BML

———. *Le Rénégat, ou La Belle Géorgienne, pantomime chevalresque en trois actes.* Paris: Barba, 1812. BN-ASP

———. *Les Tentations, ou Tous les diables, pantomime allégorique en trois actes, précédée du Conseil du Lucifer, prologue en un acte et en vers.* Paris: Barba, Year VIII—1799/1800. BN-ASP, BN-RDJ

———. *Le Tribunal invisible, ou Le Fils criminel.* Paris: Barba, 1802. BML

———. *Le Vieux de la montagne, ou Les Arabes du Liban, melodrama en trois actes, en prose et à grand spectacle.* Paris: Barba, 1815. BN-ASP, BN-RDJ

———. *Le Volcan, ou L'Anchorète du val des laves, pantomime magique en trois actes.* Paris: Barba, 1812. BN-ASP, BN-RDJ

[Cuvelier de Trie, Jean-Guillaume-Augustin]. *Prix proposé sur une question philantropique L∴ des artistes O∴ de Paris: Extrait du Registre du Tribunal Suprême, Scéance du 3me. jour 5me. mois, an de la V∴ L∴ 5819.* Paris, 1819. BN-MSS, FM

Cuvelier de Trie, Jean-Guillaume-Augustin, and Louis-Alexandre Piccinni. *Conseils de Mentor dans l'Asile du Silence, ou Gloire et Sagesse; Couplets chantés par Mme Camus, Paroles* de J.G.A. Cuvelier, Musique d'Alex. Piccini. Paris: Imbault, 1811. BN-MUS

Delécluze, Étienne-Jean. *Louis David: Son École & son temps.* 1855. Repr., Paris: Macula, 1989.

Denon, Vivant. *Lettres à Bettine*, Edited by Fausta Garavini. Arles: Actes Sud, 1999.

———. *Travels in Upper and Lower Egypt.* Translated by Arthur Aikin. 2 vols. London: Longman, Rees, and Phillips, 1803.

———. *Voyage dans la Basse et la Haute Égypte.* 2 vols. Paris: Didot, 1802.

———. *Voyage en Sicile.* Paris: Didot, 1788.

[Denon, Vivant]. *Catalogo di incisioni di Mr. Denon.* [Venice, ca. 1792–93]. BN-EST

Description de l'Égypte, ou Receuil des observations et des recherches qui ont été faites en Égypte pendant l'expédition de l'armée française. 20 vols. Paris: Imprimerie impériale/Imprimerie royale, 1809–22.

Desgenettes, René-Nicolas Dufriche. *Histoire médicale de l'armée d'Orient par le médecin en chef R. Desgenettes.* 2 vols. Paris: Croullebois et Bossange, 1802.

Diderot, Denis. *Oeuvres complètes.* Edited by John Lough and Jacques Proust. 25 vols. Paris: Herman, 1975.

Diodorus of Sicily. *Bibliotheca historica.* Edited and translated by Charles Henry Oldfather. 3 vols. Cambridge and London: Harvard University Press, Loeb Classical Library, 1946–52.

———. *Histoire universelle.* Translated by Jean Abbé Terrasson, 7 vols. Paris: De Bure, 1737–44.

Diogenes Laertius. *Lives of Eminent Philosophers.* Edited and translated by Robert Drew Hicks. 2 vols. Cambridge and London: Harvard University Press, Loeb Classical Library, 1970.

Dondey-Dupré fils, P[rosper]. *Paroles funèbres prononcées à la tombe de notre ami J.-G.-A. Cuvelier de Trie, capitaine de cavalerie en retraite, chevalier de l'ordre royal de la légion d'honneur, cons.∴ ad vitam de la R.∴ L.∴ des Artistes O.∴ de Paris.* Paris: Dondey-Dupré, 1824. BN-RDJ

DuBoisaymé, Jean-Marie. *Marie-Thérèse de Bouès.* Paris: Prud-homme, 1838.

Du Préau, Gabriel. *Devx livres de Mercvre Trismegiste Hermés tres ancien theologien, et exzellent philozophe: L'Un de la puissance & sapience de Dieu; l'autre de la volonté de Dieu; avecq'un dialogue de Loys Lazarel, poëte chrestien, intitulé La Bassin d'Hermés.* Paris: Estiene Groulleau, 1557.

Duval, Alexandre. *Oeuvres complètes*, 4 vols. Paris: Barba, 1822.

Eusebius. *Preparation for the Gospel.* Edited and translated by Edwin Hamilton Gifford. 2 vols. Oxford: Clarendon Press, 1903.

Fée, Antoine-Laurent-Apollinaire. *Le Darwinisme, ou Examen de la théorie relative à l'origine des espèces.* Paris: Masson, 1864.

Fénelon, François de Salignac de La Mothe-. *Les Aventures de Télémaque, fils d'Ulysse.* Paris: Barbin, 1699.

Firmin-Didot, Ambroise. *Notes d'un voyage fait dans le Levant en 1816 et 1817.* Paris: Firmin-Didot, 1826.

Frères Artistes [Lodge]. *Hymne Sacré des Anciens Mystères, mis en musique par l'initié Foignet père, pour la Fête d'Isis célébrée à la L.∴ des Artistes O.∴ de Paris le 30 Aout 1821 (E_V_), chanté par les aspirants Martin, Prévost et Trevaux, Professeurs, accompagné sur Harpe par l'aspirant Gabriel Foignet, Professeur, et sur le Piano par l'initié Alexandre Piccini, Professeur, à*

l'usage de la grande Pyramide de France et dédié au Souverain Patriarche de l'Ordre Sacré des Sophisiens, le Chevalier Cuvelier de Trie Vén.∴ d'H.∴ [Paris: 1821]. BN-MUS

Frères Artistes [Lodge]. *Proposition faite à la scéance du quatorzième jour du premier mois de l'an D.∴ L.∴ V.∴ L.∴ 5826 (14 Mars 1826) par le F.∴ E.∴ J.∴ Thayer, troisième Or.∴, et imprimée par ordre de la ⸬ des FF Artistes à l'Or.∴ de Paris.* Paris: Dondey-Dupré, 1826. BN-MSS, FM

———. *Rapport fait à la R.∴ L.∴ des FF.∴ Artistes, dans sa scéance du 31 mai 1820 (ère vulg.∴), par le F.∴ Orateur Lemaire, professeur de poésie latine à la Faculté des Lettres de Paris, Chevalier de la Légion d'honneur.* [Paris, 1820.] BN-RDJ, RÉS

———. *Scéance du Conseil des Conservateurs, du 5 mai 1820 (ère vulg.∴).* [Paris, 1820.] BN-RDJ, RÉS

Gabet, Charles. *Dictionnaire des artistes de l'école française au XIXe siècle: Peinture, sculpture, architecture, gravure, dessin, lithographie et composition musicale.* Paris: Vergne, 1831.

Galland, Antoine. *Tableau de l'Égypte, pendant le séjour de l'armée française.* 2 vols. Paris: Galland, 1804.

Geoffroy Saint-Hilaire, Étienne. "Le Degré de l'influence du monde ambiant pour modifier les formes animales: Question intéressant l'origine des espèces télésauriennes et successivement celle des animaux de l'époque actuelle." *Mémoires de l'Académie Royale des Sciences de l'Institut de France* 12 (1833): 63–92.

———. *Lettres écrites d'Égypte à Cuvier, Jussieu, Lacépède, Monge, Desgenettes, Redouté jeune, Norry, etc., aux professeurs du Muséum et à sa famille.* Edited by Ernest-Théodore Hamy. Paris: Hachette, 1901.

———. "Loi universelle (Attraction de soi pour soi), ou Clef applicable à l'interprétation de tous les phénomènes de la philosophie naturelle: Découverte faite à la suite d'études incessantes concernant les arrangements, les complications, les mouvements, et généralement toutes les actions des êtres organisés." In *Études progressives d'un naturaliste pendant les années 1834 et 1835, faisant suite à ses publications dans les 42 volumes des Mémoires et Annales du Muséum d'Histoire Naturelle,* 125-89. Paris: Roret, 1835.

———. *Principes de philosophie zoologique, discutés en Mars 1830 au sein de l'Académie Royale des Sciences.* Paris: Pichon, Didier and Rousseau, 1830.

Gorani, Giuseppe. *Mémoires secrets et critiques des cours, des gouvernemens, et des moeurs des prinicipaux États de l'Italie.* 3 vols. Paris: Buisson, 1793.

Le Grondeur, ou Le Flambeau. 1799. BN-RDJ

Guerrier de Dumast, Auguste-Prosper-François. *A mon ami Piccolo, quarante vers sur deux rimes (rêne et li).* Nancy: Vagner, 1861. BN-RDJ

———. "Un Chapitre de l'histoire littéraire française: Renaissance de la rime riche." *Mémoire de l'Académie de Stanislas,* 4th series, 12 (1880), 1–28.

———. *Chios, la Grèce et l'Europe, poème lyrique, accompagné de notes explicatives, suivi de la traduction, avec le texte en regard, d'une épitre grecque-moderne, adressée, en 1820, par N. S. Piccolos à G. Glaracés.* Paris: Schlesinger, 1822. BN-RDJ

———. *Discours prononcé le 28 avril 5821, à la Loge des Artistes (Orient de Paris).* Paris: Dondey-Dupré, 1821. BN-RDJ

———. *La Maçonnerie, poème en trois chants avec des notes historiques, étymologiques et critiques.* Paris: Arthus Bertrand, 1820. BN-RDJ, RÉS

————. *Rapport fait à la Loge des Artistes, le 19 juillet 1821, . . . sur l'établissement dit Manufacture des Apprentis Pauvres et Orphelins.* Paris: Dondey-Dupré, 1821. BN-MSS, FM

Guillemain de Saint-Victor, Louis. *Origine de la maçonnerie adon-hiramite, ou, Nouvelles observations critiques et raisonnés, sur la philosophie, les hieroglyphes, les mystères, la superstition et les vices des mages; précédée d'un chapitre sur l'Égypte anci-enne et moderne; avec des remarques et des notes sur les histo-riens et la chronologie du monde.* "Heliopolis" [Paris], 1787.

————. *Recueil élémentaire de la franc-maçonnerie adon-hiramite . . . par un chévalier de tous les ordres maçonniques.* "Jerusa-lem," 5803 [Paris, 1803].

————. *Recueil précieux de la maçonnerie adonhiramite: conten-ant les catéchismes des quatre premiers grades, et l'ouverture et clôture des différentes loges, l'instruction de la table, les santés générales et particulières, ainsi que les devoirs des premiers of-ficiers eu [sic] charge; enrichi d'une infinité de demandes et de réponses symboliques, de l'explication des emblêmes, et d'un grand nombre de notes aussi curieuses qu'utiles.* "Philadelphia" [Paris]: Philarète, 1783.

Guitry, Commandant. *L'Armée de Bonaparte en Égypte, 1798–1799.* Collection nouvelle de Mémoires militaires. Paris: Flam-marion, 1898.

Hennequin, Philippe-Auguste. *Mémoires de Philippe-Auguste Hen-nequin.* Edited by Jenny Hennequin. Paris: Calmann-Lévy, 1933.

[Hermes Trismegistus.] *Liber de protestate et sapientia Dei, corpus hermeticum.* Edited and translated by Marsilio Ficino. Treviso: Gerardus de Lisa, 1471.

————. *Mercurii Trimegisti Pimander sive Poemander.* Edited by Franciscus Flussas Candalle. Bordeaux: Millanges, 1574.

————. *Pimander Mercurii liber de sapienta et protestate Dei: Asclepius, ejusdem Mercurii liber de voluntate divina, item cra-ter Hermetis a Lazarelo Septempedano.* Edited by Loys Lazarel. Paris: Stephani, 1505.

————. *Le Pimandre de Mercure Trismegiste de la philosophie chrestienne, cognoissance du verb divin, et de l'excellence des oeuvres de Dieu.* Edited by Franciscus Flussas Candalle. Bor-deaux: Millanges, 1579.

Herodotus. *Historiae.* Edited and translated by Alfred Denis God-ley. 4 vols. Cambridge and London: Harvard University Press, Loeb Classical Library, 1920–25.

Iamblichus of Apamea. *Les Mystères d'Égypte.* Edited and trans-lated by Édouard des Places. Paris: Belles Lettres, 1966.

The Jerusalem Bible. Garden City: Doubleday, 1966.

The Journals of Bonaparte in Egypt, 1798–1801. Edited by Salah al-Din al-Bustani. 10 vols. Cairo: Al-Arab Bookstore, 1971.

Kircher, Athanasius. *Oedipus aegyptiacus: Hoc est uniuersalis hierolglyphicae veterum doctrinae temporum iniuria abolitae instauratio. Opus ex omni orientalium doctrina & sapientia con-ditum, nec non viginti diuersarium linguarum, authoritate sta-bilitum.* 3 vols. Rome: Mascardi, 1652-54.

Kléber en Égypte, 1798–1800. Edited by Jacques and Henry Lau-rens. 4 vols. Cairo: IFAO, 1995.

Laborde, Jean-Benjamin de. *Choix de chansons mises en musique.* 2nd ed. 4 vols. Rouen: Lemonnyer, 1881.

————. *Lettres sur la Suisse adressées à Mme M.*** par un voya-geur françois en 1781.* 2 vols. Geneva and Paris: Jombert, 1783.

Lacépède, Bernard-Germain-Étienne de la Ville-sur-Illion Comte de. *Les Âges de la nature.* 2 vols. Paris and Strasbourg: Levrault, 1830.

————. *Histoire naturelle de l'homme.* Paris and Strasbourg: Levrault, 1827.

La Chainaye, Raguneau de, and Armand Henri. Article "Montan-sier (Marguerite Brunet, dite)." In *Annuaire dramatique* 17/18 (1821/22): 383–97.

Lacorre, Alexandre. *Journal inédit d'un commis aux vivres pendant l'expédition d'Égypte: Voyage à Malte et en Égypte, expédition de Syrie.* Bordeaux: Crugy, 1852.

Lantier, Étienne-François de. *Voyages d'Antenor en Grèce et en Asie avec des notions sur l'Égypte: Manuscrit grec trouvé à Her-culanum.* 15th rev. ed. 2 vols. 1797. Reprint, Brussels: Wahlen, 1821.

Latour-Chatillon de Zur-Lauben, Beatus Fidelis Anton Johann Dominik Baron de. *Tableaux topographiques, pittoresques, phy-siques, historiques, moraux, politiques, littéraires de la Suisse.* 2 vols. Paris: Clousier, 1780–86.

Laujon, Pierre. *Oeuvres choisies, contenant ses pieces [. . .], ses fêtes [. . .], ses chansons et autres opuscules, avec des anec-dotes, remarques et notices relatives à ces divers genres.* 4 vols. Paris: Patris, 1811.

Leibniz, Gottfried Wilhelm Freiherr von. "Consilium Aegyptia-cum." In *Die Werke von Leibniz.* Series 1, 2:175–207. Hannover: Klindworth, 1864–84. 11 vols.

Lenoir, Alexandre. *La Franche-Maçonnerie rendue à sa véritable origine, ou L'Antiquité de la Franche-Maçonnerie prouvée par l'explication des mystères anciens et modernes.* Paris: Fournier, 1814.

————. *Nouvel essai sur la Table Isiaque.* Paris, 1809.

————. *Nouvelle explication des hieroglyphes, ou Des Anciennes allégories, sacrées des Égyptiens, utile à l'intelligence des mon-uments mythologiques des autres peuples suivie d'un résumé alphabétique ornée de dix-huit planches.* Paris: Musée des mon-umens français, 1809.

Malus de Mitry, Étienne-Louis. *L'Agenda de Malus: Souvenirs de l'expédition d'Égypte* Paris: Champion, 1892.

Maréchal, Sylvain. *Dictionnaire des athées anciens et modernes.* 2nd rev. and expanded ed. Brussels: Balleroy, 1833.

Mariton, Louis. "L∴ †∴ des Artistes, O∴ de Paris." In *Hermès, ou Archives maçonniques par une Société de F∴ M∴,* 1:324–34. Paris: Renard, 1818–19. 2 vols.

Marmontel, Jean-François. *Mémoires.* Edited by John Renwick. 2 vols. Clermont-Ferrand: Bussac, 1972.

Maurel de Chédeville, Étienne, Louis XVIII, Comte de Provence, and André-Ernest-Modeste Grétry, *La Caravane du Caire, opéra-ballet. Représenté à Fontainebleau, devant leurs Majestés, le 30 Octobre 1783 et pour la première fois sur le Théâtre de l'Académie royale de musique le lundi 12 janvier 1784.* Paris, 1784.

Mead, George Robert Stow. *Thrice-Greatest Hermes: Studies in Hel-lenistic Theosophy and Gnosis.* 3 vols. London: Watkins, 1964.

Milfort, Louis. *Mémoire, ou Coup-d'oeil rapide sur mes différents voyages et mon séjour dans la nation crèck.* Paris: Giguet et Mi-chaud, Year XI—1802. BN-RDJ

————. *Memoirs, or a Quick Glance at My Various Travels and My Sojourn in the Creek Nation.* Edited and translated by Ben C. McCary. Kennsaw: Continental Book Company, 1959.

———. *Milford's Memoirs, or a Cursory Glance at My Different Travels and My Sojourn in the Creek Nation.* Translated by Geraldine De Courcy. Edited by John Francis McDermott. Santa Barbara: The Narrative Press, 2000.

[Milfort, Louis.] *Chef de guerre chez les Creeks.* Edited by Christian Buchet. Paris: France-Empire, 1994.

Millin de Grandmaison, August-Aubin. *Sur la liberté du théâtre.* Paris: Lagrange, 1790.

Mme B***. *Les Animaux savants, ou exercises des chevaux de MM. Franconi, du cerf Coco, du cerf Azor, de l'éléphant Baba, des serrins hollandois, du singe militaire.* Paris: Didot, 1816. BN-RDJ

Le Moniteur Universel. 1789–1871.

Montesquieu. *Oeuvres complètes,* 2 vols. Paris: Gallimard, 1949–51.

Montfaucon, Bernard de. *L'Antiquité expliquée et représentée en figures.* 5 vols. Paris: Delaulne, 1719.

Morgan, Sydney Lady. *Passages from My Autobiography.* London: Richard Bentley, 1859.

Münter, Friedrich. *Aus den Tagebüchern Friedrich Münters: Wander- und Lehrjahre eines dänischen Gelehrten.* Edited by Øjvind Andreasen. 3 vols. Copenhagen and Leipzig: Haase, 1937.

Mutinelli, Fabio. *Memorie storiche degli ultimi cinquant'anni della Repubblica Veneta tratte da scritti e monumenti contemporanei.* Venice: Grimaldo, 1854.

Napier, William Francis Patrick. *The Life and Opinions of General Sir Charles Napier, G.C.B.* 4 vols. London: Murray, 1857.

Napoleon in Egypt: Al-Jabarti's Chronicle of the First Seven Months of the French Occupation of Egypt, 1798. Edited and translated by Robert L. Tignor and Shmuel Moreh. Princeton and New York: Markus Wiener, 1993.

Nerval, Gérard de. *Les Filles du feu: Angélique, Sylvie, Jemmy, Octavie, Isis, Émilie, Pandora.* Paris: Le Divan, 1927.

Norry, Charles. *Relation de l'expédition d'Égypte, suivie de la description de plusieurs des monumens de cette contrée, et ornée de figures.* Paris: Pougens, Year VII—1799. BN-RDJ

Novelli, Pier Antonio. *Memorie della vita di Pietro Antonio Novelli, scritte da lui medesimo.* Padua: Minerva, 1834.

Ordre Sacré des Sophisiens. *Règlement de l'A-[spirance]/Nomenclature des officiers.* Paris: Year IX—1800/1801. BN-MSS, FM, BVP, CMC

Pelet de la Lozère, Privat-Joseph-Claramond. *Opinions de Napoléon sur divers sujets de politique et d'administration, recueillies par un membre de son conseil d'état, et récit de quelques événements de l'époque.* Paris: Firmin Didot, 1833.

Pélissier, Léon G. "Notes et documents: Vivant Denon suspect à Venise," *Bulletin de la Société de l'Histoire de l'Art français* 3 (1912): 260–89.

Peltier, Jean-Gabriel. *The Trial of John Peltier, esq., for a Libel against Napoleon Bonaparte, First Consul of the French Republic, at the Court of the King's-Bench, Middlesex, on Monday the 21ˢᵗ February, 1803, Taken in Short-Hand by Mr. Adams, and the Defence Revised by Mr. Mackintosh.* London: Peltier, 1803.

Pignoria, Luigi. *Vetustissimae tabulae aeneae sacris aegyptiorum simulachris coelatae accurata explicatio, in qua antiquissimarum superstitionum origines, progressiones, ritus ad Barbaram, Graecam, Romanamque historiam illustrandam enarrantur & multa scriptorum veterum loca qua explanantur, qua emendantur.* Venice: Franco, 1605.

Plato. *Plato.* Edited and translated by Walter Rangeley Maitland Lamb. 12 vols. Cambridge: Harvard University Press, Loeb Classical Library, 1924–35.

Pluche, Antoine Abbé. *Histoire du ciel, où l'on recherche l'origine de l'idolâtrie et les méprises de la philosophie sur la formation et sur les influences des corps célestes.* 2ⁿᵈ edition. 2 vols. Paris: Veuve Estienne, 1740.

Plutarch, *De Iside et Osiride.* Edited and translated by John Gwyn Griffith. Cardiff: University of Wales Press, 1970.

Les Présocratiques. Edited and translated by Jean-Paul Dumont. Paris: Gallimard, La Pléiade, 1988.

Proclus, *Commentaire sur le Timée.* Edited and translated by André-Jean Festugière. 5 vols. Paris: Vrin, 1966–68.

Pseudo-Manetho. *Manetho.* Edited and translated by William Gillan Waddell. Cambridge and London: Harvard University Press, Loeb Classical Library, 1940.

Pugnet, Jean-François-Xavier. *Mémoires sur les fièvres pestilentielles et insidieuses du Levant, avec un aperçu physique et médical du Sayd.* Lyons and Paris: Reymann and Périsse, 1802.

Quérard, Joseph-Marie. *Les Supercheries littéraires dévoilées: Galerie des auteurs apocryphes, supposés, déguisés, plagiaires, et des éditeurs infidèles pendant les quatre derniers siècles.* 5 vols. Paris, 1847–53.

Le Rédacteur. 1795–1800. BN-RDJ

Reynier, Jean-Louis-Ebénézer. *De l'Égypte après la bataille d'Héliopolis et considérations générales sur l'organisation physique et politique de ce pays.* Paris: Pougens, 1802.

Richelme, Fabien. *Mémoire relatif aux monumens de l'Égypte, considérés dans le sens hermético-maçonnique.* Saint-Pierre Martinique: Roques, 1807. BN-RDJ, RÉS

Rituel de la franc-maçonnerie égyptienne. Edited by Marc Haven. 1948. Repr., Paris: Télètes, 2003.

Russo, Salvatore. *Il viaggiatore curioso: Lettere di Denon e Houel a Landolina.* Palermo: Lombardi, 1993.

Saint-Non, Richard Abbé de. *Voyage pittoresque dans les royaumes de Naples et de Sicile.* 5 vols. Paris: Clousier, 1780–86.

Savary, Claude-Étienne. *Lettres d'Égypte, où l'on offre le parallèle des moeurs anciennes et modernes de ses habitans, où l'on décrit l'état, le commerce, l'agriculture, le gouvernement, l'ancienne religion du pays, et la descente de St. Louis à Damiette, tirées de Joinville et des auteurs arabes.* 3 vols. Paris: Onfroi, 1785–86.

Scott, Walter. *Hermetica: The Ancient Greek and Latin Writings Which Contain Religious or Philosophical Teachings Ascribed to Hermes Trismegistus.* 4 vols. Oxford: Clarendon Press, 1924–36.

Sonnini de Manoncour, Charles-Nicolas-Sigisbert. *Voyage dans la Haute et Basse Égypte fait par l'ordre de l'ancien gouvernement (de 1777 à 1780) et contenant des observations de tous genres.* 3 vols. Paris: Buisson, 1799.

Swinburne, Henry. *Travels in the Two Sicilies in the Years 1777, 1778, 1779, 1780.* 2 vols. London: Elmsly, 1783–85.

Terrasson, Jean Abbé. *Dissertation critique sur L'Iliade d'Homer, où à l'occasion de ce poëme on cherche les règles d'une poëtique fondée sur la raison, & sur les exemples des anciens & des modernes.* Paris: Fournier et Coutstelier, 1715.

———. *Séthos, histoire ou vie tirée des monumens anecdotes de l'ancienne Égypte: Traduction d'un manuscript grec.* Rev. ed. 6 vols. 1731. Repr., Paris: d'Hautel, 1813.

Testu. *Almanach Impérial pour l'année M.DCCC.XIII.* Paris: Testu, 1813. BN-RDJ

Le Thé, ou Le Contrôleur général. 1797–99. BN-RDJ

Toso Rodinis, Giuliana. *La commedia degli intrighi e degli amori: Le più belle lettere da Napoli di Dominique Vivant Denon (1782–1785).* Florence: Olschki, 1977.

Turgot, Anne-Robert-Jacques. "Plan du second discours sur les progrès de l'esprit humain," in *Oeuvres de Turgot et documents le concernant, avec biographie et notes,* edited by Gustav Schelle, 1:298–323. Paris: Alcan, 1913–23. 5 vols.

Vendryes, B. *Mémoire pour M. B. Vendryes, directeur à Paris de la Société dite du Brésil contre M. le lieutenant-général Montmarie et le lieutenant-colonel Roise, actionnaires se disant mandataires, mais étant de fait cessionnaires à titre gratuit des autres actionnaires.* [Paris:] Vinchon, [1839]. BN-RDJ

Villiers de L'Isle-Adam, Auguste Comte de. *Isis.* Brussels: Librairie Internationale, 1900.

Vivant Denon, directeur des musées sous le Consulat et l'Empire: Correspondance, 1802–1815. Edited by Marie-Anne Dupuy and Isabelle Le Masne de Chermont. 2 vols. Paris: Réunion des Musées Nationaux, 1999.

Volney, Constantin de. *Voyage en Syrie et en Égypte pendant les années 1783, 1784, et 1785.* 2 vols. Paris: Volland, Desenne, 1787.

Voltaire, *Essai sur les moeurs et l'esprit des nations et sur les principaux faits de l'histoire depuis Charlemagne jusqu'à Louis XIII.* Edited by René Pomeau. 2 vols. Paris: Garnier Frères, 1963.

Voltaire's Correspondence. Edited by Theodore Besterman. 107 vols. Geneva: 1953–65.

West, Martin Litchfield. *The Orphic Poems.* Oxford: Clarendon Press, 1983.

W.[ynne] C.[omtesse] D.[e] R.[osenberg], J.[ustiniana]. *Alticchiero.* 2nd ed. Padua, 1787.

Zosimus of Panopolis. *On the Letter Omega.* Edited and translated by Howard M. Jackson. Missoula: Scholars Press for the Society of Biblical Literature, 1978.

SECONDARY SOURCES

Albert, Maurice. *Les Théâtres des boulevards, 1789–1848.* Paris: Société française d'imprimerie et de librairie, 1902.

Almeras, Henri d'. *La Vie parisienne sous la Restauration.* Paris: Michel, 1910.

Amadou, Robert. *Cagliostro et le rituel de la maçonnerie égyptienne.* Paris: Sepp, 1996.

Amazons to Fighter Pilots: A Biographical Dictionary of Military Women. Edited by Reina Pennington and Robin Higham. 2 vols. Westport and London: Greenwood Press, 2003.

Amiable, Louis. *Une Loge maçonnique d'avant 1789: La R∴ L∴ Les Neuf Soeurs.* Paris: Alcan, 1897.

Amiable, Louis, and Paul Guieysse. *L'Égypte ancienne et la franc-maçonnerie.* Edited by Christian Lauzeray. Paris: Trédaniel, 1988.

Anonymous. *Le Cirque Franconi: Détails historiques sur cet établissement hippique et sur ses principaux écuyers, recueillis par une chambrière en retraite avec quelques portraits gravés à l'eau-forte par Frédéric Hillemacher.* Lyons: Perrin & Marinet, 1875.

Argyropoulos, Roxane D. "Nicolas Piccolos et la philosophie néo-hellénique." *Balkan Studies* 25, no. 2 (1984): 235–42.

Asse, Eugène. *Les Petits Romantiques: Antoine Fontaney, Jean Polonius, l'indépendance de la Grèce et les poètes de la Restauration, Jules de Rességuier, Edouard d'Anglemont.* Geneva: Slatkine, 1968.

Athanassoglou-Kallmyer, Nina. *French Images from the Greek War of Independence, 1821–1830: Art and Politics under the Restoration.* New Haven and London: Yale University Press, 1989.

Aulard, François-Alphonse. *Le Culte de la raison et le culte de l'Être Suprême (1793–1794).* Paris: Alcan, 1892.

Aux Armes et aux Arts! Les arts de la Révolution, 1789–1799. Edited by Philippe Bordes and Régis Michel. Exhibition catalog. Paris: Adam Biro, 1988.

Baltrušaitis, Jurgis. *La Quête d'Isis: Essai sur la légende d'un mythe.* 1967. Repr., Paris: Flammarion 1985.

Bernard, Jean-Louis. *Histoire secrète de l'Égypte.* Paris: Albin Michel, 1983.

Bertrand, Pierre-Jean-Baptiste. *Précis de l'histoire physique, civile et politique de la ville de Boulogne-sur-mer et de ses environs, depuis les Morins jusqu'en 1814.* 2 vols. 1828. Repr., Marseille: Lafitte, 1975.

Bésuchet de Saunois, Jean-Claude. *Précis historique de l'ordre de la franc-maçonnerie, depuis son introduction en France jusqu'en 1829.* 2 vols. Paris: Rapilly, 1829.

Bettagno, Alessandro. "Anton Maria Zanetti, collezionista di Rembrandt." In *Scritti in onore di Giuliano Briganti,* edited by Marco Bona Castellotti, Laura Laureati, et al., 241–46. Milan: Longanesi, 1990.

Bhabha, Homi K. *The Location of Culture.* London and New York: Routledge, 1994.

Bianchi, Thomas-Xavier. "Notice historique sur M. Ruffin." *Journal asiatique* 6 (January–June 1825): 283–97, 335–58 and 7 (July–December 1825): 90–104.

Biographie universelle ancienne et moderne. Edited by Louis Michaud. 85 vols. Paris: Michaud, 1811–62.

Bordes, Philippe. *Jacques-Louis David: Empire to Exile.* New Haven and London: Yale University Press, 2005.

Bossu, Jean. "Francs-Maçons d'autrefois—XXIII: Guerrier de Dumast, Catholique libéral." *Renaissance traditionelle* 62–63 (April–July 1985): 227–29.

———. "La Petite histoire maçonnique: Au Temps du mélodrama le F∴ Cuvier [*sic*] de Trie fut le 'Crébillon des Boulevards,'" *Les Lettres mensuelles: Revue de libre discussion philosophique et sociale,* new series 6, no. 4 (August-September 1958): 7–8.

Bouvier, René, and André Laffargue. *La Vie napolitaine au XVIIIe siècle.* Paris: Hachette, 1956.

Bramato, Fulvio. *Napoli massonica nel settecento: Dalle origini al 1789.* Ravenna: Longo, 1980.

Brengues, Jacques. "Une triple hypothèse prospective." *Humanisme* 124 (September 1978): 35–38.

Brooks, Peter. *The Melodramatic Imagination: Balzac, Henry James, Melodrama, and the Mode of Excess.* 1976. Repr., New York: Columbia University Press, 1984.

Brunelli, Bruno. *Un amica del Casanova*. Collezione settecentesca, vol. 22. Palermo: Remo Sandron, 1924.

———. "Un riformatore mancato: Angelo Querini." *Archivio Veneto*, series 5, 48–49, nos. 83–84 (1951): 185–200.

Brunet, Philippe. *Cagliostro: Biographie*. Paris: Bourin, 1992.

Cabanis, André. *La Presse sous le Consulat et l'Empire, 1799–1814*. Paris: Société des études robespierristes, 1975.

Caillet, Serge. *La Franc-maçonnerie égyptienne de Memphis-Misraïm*. 2nd rev. ed. Paris: Dervy, 2003.

Camariano-Cioran, Ariadna. *Les Académies princières de Bucarest et de Jassy et leurs professeurs*. Thessaloniki: Institute for Balkan Studies, 1974.

Cardevacque, Adolphe de. *Dictionnaire biographique du département du Pas-de-Calais*. Arras: Sueur-Charruey, 1879.

Carré, Jean-Marie. *Voyageurs et écrivains français en Égypte*. 2 vols. 1956. Repr., Cairo: IFAO, 1988.

Carro, Antoine-Étienne. *Santerre, général de la République française: Sa vie politique et privée, écrite d'après les documents originiaux*. 2nd ed. Meaux: Carro, 1869.

Chaconas, Stephen George. *Adamantios Korais: A Study in Greek Nationalism*. New York: Columbia University Press, 1942.

Chandler, David G. *Napoleon's Marshals*. New York: Macmillan, 1987.

Chaponnière, Paul. *Piron, sa vie et son oeuvre*. Paris: Jullien, 1910.

Chassin, Charles-Louis, and Léon-Clément Hennet. *Les Volontaires nationaux pendant la Révolution*. 3 vols. 1899–1906. Repr., New York: AMS, 1974.

Chatelain, Jean. *Vivant Denon et le Louvre de Napoléon*. Paris: Perrin, 1973.

Chereau, Achille. *Le Parnasse médical français, ou Dictionnaire des médecins-poètes de la France, anciens ou modernes, morts ou vivants*. Paris: Delahaye, 1874.

Chevallier, Gabriel. "Denon chargé d'affaires à Naples, 1782–1785." *Mémoires de la société d'histoire et d'archéologie de Chalon-sur-Saône* 38 (1964/65): 104–21.

Chuquet, Arthur. *La Jeunesse de Napoléon*. 3 vols. Paris: Colin, 1897–99.

Clavel, François-Timoléon Bègue. *Histoire pittoresque de la franc-maçonnerie et des sociétés secrètes anciennes et modernes*. 3rd ed. 1844. Repr., Paris: Veyrier, 1989.

Collaveri, François. *Napoléon franc-maçon?* Revised ed. Paris: Tallandier, 2003.

Couailhac, Victor. *La Vie de théâtre: Grandes et petites aventures de Mlle Montansier*. Brussels: Parent, 1863.

Coupin, Pierre-André. "Notice nécrologique sur M. le baron Denon," *Revue encyclopédique* 28 (July 1825): 30-41.

Couty, Mathieu. *Jean-Benjamin de Laborde, ou Le Bonheur d'être fermier-général*. Paris: Michel de Maule, 2001.

Crow, Thomas. *Emulation: Making Artists for Revolutionary France*. New Haven and London: Yale University Press, 1995.

———. *Painters and Public Life in Eighteenth-Century Paris*. New Haven and London: Yale University Press, 1985.

Curl, James Stevens. *The Egyptian Revival: An Introductory Study of a Recurring Theme in the History of Taste*. London and Boston: Allen & Unwin, 1982.

Dalbian, Denyse. *Le Comte de Cagliostro*. Paris: Laffont, 1983.

Del Piero, Antonio. "Angelo Querini e la correzione del Consiglio dei X nel 1761–1762." *Ateneo Veneto* (1896): 280–303.

Deschamps, Julien. *Biographie de M. Comte, physicien du roi, suivie de la biographie en miniature des acteurs et actrices du théâtre Comte*. Paris: Desloges, 1845.

Descombes, Charles-Maurice. *Histoire anecdotique du théâtre, de la littérature et de diverses impressions contemporaines, tirée du coffre d'un journaliste, avec sa vie à tort et à travers*. 2 vols. Paris: Plon, 1856.

Desnoiresterres, Gustave. *Iconographie Voltairienne: Histoire et description de ce qui a été publié sur Voltaire dans l'art contemporain*. Paris: Didier, 1879.

Deux siècles de Légion d'honneur à Boulogne-sur-Mer. Arras: Conseil général du Pas-de-Calais, 2004.

Dictionnaire de biographie française. Edited by Michel Prevost and Roman d'Amat. 19 vols. to date. Paris: Letouzey et Ané, 1933–.

Dictionnaire de la franc-maçonnerie. Edited by Daniel Ligou. New ed. Paris: Quadrige, Presses universitaires de France, 2004.

Dinaux, Arthur. *Les Sociétés badines, bachiques, littéraires et chantantes, leur histoire et leurs travaux*. Paris: Bachelin-Deflorenne, 1867.

Dizionario biografico degli Italiani. Edited by Alberto Maria Ghisalberti. 62 vols. Rome: Istituto della Enciclopedia italiana, 1960.

Djuvara, Trandafir G. *Cent projets du partage de la Turquie (1281–1913)*. Paris: Alcan, 1914.

Dominique Vivant Denon: L'Oeil de Napoléon. Exhibition catalog. Paris: Réunion des Musées Nationaux, 1999.

Driesch, Hans. *The History and Theory of Vitalism*. Translated by Charles Kay Ogden. London: Macmillan, 1914.

Dutrait, Maurice. *Étude sur la vie et le théâtre de Crébillon (1674–1762)*. 1895; repr., Geneva: Slatkine, 1970.

Eco, Umberto. *Foucault's Pendulum*. Translated by William Weaver. New York: Harcourt Brace Jovanovich, 1988.

Egyptomania: Egypt in Western Art, 1730–1930. Exhibition catalog. Paris, Ottawa, and Vienna: National Gallery of Canada and Réunion des Musées Nationaux, 1994.

Elting, John R. *Swords Around a Throne: Napoleon's Grande Armée*. New York and London: The Free Press and Macmillan, 1988.

Erche, Bettina. "Zu Rembrandt-Radierungen: Im Labyrinth der Reproduktion," *Kunst und Antiquitäten* 9 (September 1994): 20–21.

Ericani, Giuliana. "La storia e l'utopia nel giardino del senatore Querini ad Altichiero." In *Piranesi e la cultura antiquaria: Gli antecedenti e il contesto. Atti del convegno, 14–17 Novembre 1979*, edited by Anna Lo Bianca, 171–94. Rome: Multigrafica, 1983.

Fastes de la Légion d'honneur: Biographie de tous les décorés, accompagnée de l'histoire législative et réglementaire de l'ordre. Edited by A. Lievyns, Jean-Maurice Verdot, and Pierre Bégat. 5 vols. Paris: 1842–47.

Faure, Alain. *Champollion: Le savant déchiffré*. Paris: Fayard, 2004.

Fedi, Francesca. "Diplomatie et franc-maçonnerie dans la seconde moitié du XVIIIe siècle." In *Les Vies de Vivant Denon*, edited by Daniela Gallo, 1:193–214. Paris: La Documentation française, Musée du Louvre, 2001. 2 vols.

Ferriman, Z. Duckett. *Some English Philhellenes: VI. Lord Guilford.* London: The Anglo-Hellenic League, 1919.

Fierro, Alfred. *Histoire et dictionnaire de Paris.* Paris: Laffont, 1996.

Finke, Ulrich. "Venezianische Rembrandtstecher um 1700." *Oud Holland* 79, no. 2 (1964): 111–21.

Finscher, Ludwig. *Die Musik in Geschichte und Gegenwart: Allgemeine Enzyklopädie der Musik, Personenteil.* 2nd rev. ed. 13 vols. Kassel and New York: Bärenreiter, 1994.

Forerunners of Darwin: 1745–1859. Edited by Bentley Glass, Owsei Temkin, and William L. Straus, Jr. Baltimore: Johns Hopkins University Press, 1968.

Fowden, Garth. *The Egyptian Hermes: A Historical Approach to the Late Pagan Mind.* Princeton: Princeton University Press, 1993.

Friant, Jean-François. *Vie militaire du lieutenant-général comte Friant.* Paris: Dentu, 1857.

Friedlaender, Walter. "Napoleon as 'Roi Thaumaturge.'" *Journal of the Warburg and Courtauld Institutes* 4 (1940–41): 139–41.

Galtier, Gérard. *Maçonnerie égyptienne, Rose-Croix et néo-chevalerie: Les Fils de Cagliostro.* Monaco: Rocher, 1994.

Georgelin, Jean. *Venise au siècle des Lumières.* Paris: École des hautes études en sciences sociales, 1978.

Ghali, Ibrahim Amin. *Vivant Denon, ou La Conquête du bonheur.* Cairo and Paris: IFAO, 1986.

Ghorbal, Shafik. *The Beginnings of the Egyptian Question and the Rise of Mehmet Ali: A Study in the Diplomacy of the Napoleonic Era Based on Researches in the British and French Archives.* London: Routledge, 1928.

Giorgetti, Cinzia. *Ritratto di Isabella: Studi e documenti su Isabella Teotochi Albrizzi.* Florence: Le Lettere, 1992.

Goby, Jean-Edouard. "La Composition du premier Institut d'Égypte." *Bulletin de l'Institut d'Égypte* 29 (1948): 345–67, and 30 (1949): 81–99.

Granges de Surgères, Anatole Marquis de, and Gustave Bourcard. *Les Françaises du XVIIIe siècle: Portraits gravés.* Paris: Dentu, 1887.

Grigsby, Darcy Grimaldo. *Extremities: Painting Empire in Post-Revolutionary France.* New Haven and London: Yale University Press, 2002.

Grosrichard, Alain. *Structure du Sérail: La Fiction du despotisme asiatique dans l'occident classique.* Paris: Seuil, 1979.

Guimbaud, Louis. *Saint-Non et Fragonard d'après des documents inédits.* Paris: Le Goupy, 1928.

Hadot, Pierre. *Le Voile d'Isis: Essai sur l'histoire de l'idée de la Nature.* Paris: Gallimard, 2004.

Hall, Manly P. *The Secret Teachings of all Ages: An Encyclopedic Outline of Masonic, Hermetic, Quabbalistic, and Rosicrucian Symbolic Philosophy.* 1928. Repr., New York: Tarcher/Penguin, 2003.

Hasenclever, Adolf. *Geschichte Ägyptens im 19. Jahrhundert, 1798–1914.* Halle: Niemeyer, 1917.

Hatin, Eugène. *Histoire politique et littéraire de la presse en France, avec une introduction historique sur les origines du journal et la bibliographie générale des journaux depuis leur origine.* 8 vols. Paris, 1859–61.

Haven, Marc. *Le Maître inconnu Cagliostro: Étude historique et critique sur la haute magie.* 4th ed. 1964. Repr., Paris: Dervy, 1996.

Hazard, Paul. *La Pensée européenne au XVIIIe siècle: De Montesquieu à Lessing.* 2 vols. Paris: Boivin, 1946.

Hennequin, Joseph-François-Gabriel. *Biographie maritime, ou Notices historiques sur la vie et les campagnes des marins célèbres français et étrangers.* 3 vols. Paris: Regnault, 1835–37.

Herlaut, Auguste-Philippe. *Le Colonel Bouchotte: Ministre de la Guerre en l'an II,* 2 vols. Paris: Poisson, 1946.

Hillairet, Jacques. *Dictionnaire historique des rues de Paris.* 2 vols. Paris: Minuit, 1963.

Hivert-Messeca, Gisèle and Yves. *Comment la Franc-Maçonnerie vint aux femmes: Deux siècles de Franc-Maçonnerie d'adoption feminine et mixte en France, 1740–1940.* Paris: Dervy, 1997.

Hornung, Erik. *L'Égypte ésoterique: Le Savoir occulte des Égyptiens et son influence en Occident.* Translated by Nathalie Baum. Monaco: Rocher, 2001.

Howarth, William Driver. "Word and Image in Pixérécourt's Melodramas: The Dramaturgy of the Strip-Cartoon." In *Performance and Politics in Popular Drama: Aspects of Popular Entertainment in Theater, Film, and Television, 1800–1976,* edited by David Bradby, Louis James, and Bernard Sharratt, 17–32. Cambridge: Cambridge University Press, 1980.

Il y a 200 ans: Les Savants en Égypte. Edited by Marie-Noëlle Bourguet and Yves Laissus. Exhibition catalog. Paris: Nathan, 1998.

Images du patrimoine maçonnique. Edited by Ludovic Marcos and Pierre Mollier. 2 vols. Paris: Éditions maçonniques de France, 2002.

Isar, Nicolae. "Deux Correspondants de N. Rosetti-Roznovanu: Coray et Guilford. Une Lettre de Piccolo." *Revue des études sud-est européennes* 8 (1970): 365–72.

Israel, Jonathan I. *Radical Enlightenment: Philosophy and the Making of Modernity.* Oxford: Oxford University Press, 2001.

Jobes, Gertrude. *Dictionary of Mythology, Folklore, and Symbolism.* 2 vols. New York: Scarecrow Press, 1962.

Juden, Brian. *Traditions Orphiques et tendances mystiques dans le Romantisme français, 1800–1855.* Paris: Klincksieck, 1971.

Kadach, Dorothea. "Ein Aufklärer des Balkan: Dr. Atanas Bogoridi." *Südost-Forschungen* 34 (1975): 125–65.

Karathanassis, Athanassis E. "Ἀθανάσιος Βογορίδης: Βιογραφικά και εργογραφικά ενός εκπροδώπου τού Νεοελληνικού Διαφωτισμού." *Παρουσία* 7 (1991): 125–68.

Kendrick, Walter. *The Secret Museum: Pornography in Modern Culture.* New York: Viking, 1987.

Kirkova, Tatjana E. "Nicolas S. Piccolos—Sa vie, son oeuvre." *Bulgarian Historical Review* 5, no. 3 (1977): 18–37.

Kloss, Georg Franz Burkhard, *Geschichte der Freimaurerei in Frankreich aus ächten Urkunden dargestellt (1725–1830).* 2 vols. 1852–53. Repr., Graz: Akademische Druck- und Verlagsanstalt, 1971.

Koester, Helmut. *Introduction to the New Testament: History, Culture, and Religion of the Hellenistic Age.* 2 vols. Philadelphia: Fortress Press, 1982.

Kolpaktchy, Grégoire. *Livre des morts des anciens Égyptiens.* Paris: Ominum littéraire, 1954.

La Broderie, Arthur de. *Alexandre Duval et son théâtre.* Rennes: Caillière, 1893.

Lacour-Gayet, Michel. *Marie-Caroline reine de Naples: Une Adversaire de Napoléon.* Paris: Tallandier, 1990.

LaFizelière, Albert de. *L'Oeuvre originale de Vivant Denon*. 2 vols. Paris: Barraud, 1873.

Laissus, Yves. *L'Égypte, une aventure savante avec Bonaparte, Kléber, Menou, 1798–1801*. Paris: Fayard, 1998.

La Jonquière, Clément de. *L'Expédition d'Égypte 1798–1801*. 5 vols. Paris: Charles-Lavauzelle, 1899–1907.

Lanzac de Laborie, Léon de. *Paris sous Napoléon: Spectacles et Musées*. 2nd ed.. 8 vols. Paris: Plon-Nourrit, 1905–13.

Lascaris, Stamati Théodore. "L'Académie Ionienne: Un Institut littéraire à Corfou sous la domination napoléonienne." *Revue des études napoléonienne* 25 (July–December 1925): 203–16.

Laurens, Henry. *L'Expédition d'Égypte, 1798–1801*. Paris: Colin, 1989.

———. *Les Òrigines intellectuelles de l'expédition d'Égypte: L'Orientalisme islamisant en France, 1868–1798*. Istanbul and Paris: Éditions Isis, 1987.

Lavergne, Philippe. *André Breton et le mythe*. Paris: Corti, 1985.

LeBihan, Albert. *Francs-maçons parisiens du Grand-Orient de France (Fin du XVIIIe siècle)*. Paris: Bibliothèque Nationale, 1966.

Lecomte, Louis-Henry. *Napoléon et le monde dramatique*. Paris: Daragon, 1912.

———. *Napoléon et l'Empire racontés par le théâtre, 1797–1899*. Paris: Raux, 1900.

Legrain, Georges. "Guillaume-André Villoteau, musicographe de l'expédition française d'Égypte (1759–1839)." *Bulletin de l'Institut égyptien* [Cairo] 11 (1917): 1–30.

Lelièvre, Pierre. *Vivant Denon, homme des Lumières, 'ministre des arts' de Napoléon*. Paris: Picard, 1993.

Leospo, Enrica. *La Mensa Isiaca di Torino*. Leiden: Brill, 1978.

Lexikon der Ägyptologie. Edited by Wolfgang Helck, Eberhard Otto, et al. 7 vols. Wiesbaden: Harrassowitz, 1975–92.

Little, Donald P. *History and Historiography of the Mameluks*. London: Variorum, 1986.

Mahul, Alphonse. *Annuaire nécrologique, ou Complement annuel et continuation de toutes les biographies, ou Dictionnaires historiques*. 7 vols. Paris: Baudouin, 1821–26.

Mainardi, Michele. "Le incisioni dalle acquaforti di Rembrandt di Francesco Novelli." PhD dissertation, 2 vols. Venice: Università di Venezia, 1985–86.

Malamani, Vittorio. *Isabella Teotochi Albrizzi: I suoi amici, il suo tempo*. Turin: Locatelli, 1888.

Marty, Bruno. "Des Artistes lyonnais franc-maçons dans le procès du Comte de Cagliostro (1789–90)." *Travaux de l'Institut de l'Art de l'Université de Lyon* 14 (1991): 125–36.

Matthew, H. C. G., and Brian Harrison. *Oxford Dictionary of National Biography*. 60 vols. Oxford: Oxford University Press, 2004.

McCalman, Iain. *The Last Alchemist: Count Cagliostro, Master of Magic in the Age of Reason*. New York: Harper Collins, 2003.

McCormick, John. *Popular Theater in Nineteenth-Century France*. London and New York: Routledge, 1993.

Meulenaere, Philippe de. *Bibliographie raisonnée des témoignages oculaires imprimés de l'expédition d'Égypte (1798–1801)*. Paris: Chamonal, 1993.

Mieck, Ilja. "Napoléon et Berlin." *Études napoléoniennes: Bulletin historique de la Société de sauvegarde du château impérial de Pont-de-Briques* 29, no. 3 (1993): 553–76.

Monnier, Raymonde. *Un Bourgeois sans-culotte: Le Général Santerre, suivi de 'L'Art du brasseur.'* Paris: Publications de la Sorbonne, 1989.

Monuments des arts du dessin chez les peuples tant anciens que modernes, recueillis par le baron Vivant Denon. Edited by Pineu Amaury-Duval and Jacques-Charles Brunet. 4 vols. Paris: Brunet Denon, 1829.

Morand, François. *L'Année historique de Boulogne-sur-mer: Recueil de faits et des événements intéressant l'histoire de cette ville, et rangés selon leurs jours anniversaires*. Boulogne-sur-mer: Déligny, 1859.

Moschini, Giannantonio. *Dell'incisione in Venezia*. Venice: Zanetti, 1924.

Muir, William. *The Mameluke Slave Dynasty of Egypt, 1260–1517 A.D.* London: Smith, Elder, 1896.

Muret, Théodore. *L'Histoire par le théâtre, 1789–1851*. 2 vols. Paris: Amyot, 1865.

The Napoleonic Survey of Egypt, Description de l'Égypte: The Monuments and Customs of Egypt, Selected Engravings and Texts. Edited by Terence M. Russel. 2 vols. Aldershot and Burlington: Ashgate, 2001.

Le Néo-Classicisme français: Dessins des musées de Province. Exhibition catalog. Paris: Éditions des musées nationaux, 1974.

Neue Deutsche Biographie. Edited by the Historische Kommission bei der Bayerischen Akademie der Wissenschaften. 22 vols to date. Berlin: Duncker & Humblot, 1953–.

Nouvelle biographie générale. Edited by Jean-Chrétien-Ferdinand Hoefer. 46 vols. Paris: Firmin-Didot, 1855–66.

Nowinski, Judith. *Baron Dominique Vivant Denon (1747–1825): Hedonist and Scholar in a Period of Transition*. Rutherford: Fairleigh Dickinson University Press, 1970.

Ortolani, Giuseppe. *Voci e visioni del settecento veneziano*. Bologna: Zanichelli, 1926.

Ozouf, Mona. *La Fête revolutionnaire, 1789–99*. Paris: Gallimard, 1976.

Pao, Angela C. *The Orient of the Boulevards: Exoticism, Empire, and Nineteenth-Century French Theater*. Philadelphia: University of Pennsylvania Press, 1998.

Pastoret, Amédée-David de. *Éloge historique sur la vie et les ouvrages de M. le B.on Denon*. Paris: Firmin-Didot, 1851.

Perini, Giambattista. *Della vita e delle opere di Francesco Novelli pittore ed incisore veneziano*. Venice: Ex Cordella, 1888.

Portalis, Roger, and Henri Beraldi. *Les Graveurs du dix-huitième siècle*. 3 vols. Paris: Morgand et Fatout, 1880–82.

Porterfield, Todd. *The Allure of Empire: Art in the Service of French Imperialism, 1798–1836*. Princeton: Princeton University Press, 1998.

Poulot, Dominique. "L'Égypte imaginaire d'Alexandre Lenoir." In *L'Égypte imaginaire de la Renaissance à Champollion*, edited by Chantal Grell, 127–49. Paris: Presses de l'Université de Paris-Sorbonne, 2001.

Prevost, Michel, and Roman D'Amat. *Dictionnaire de biographie française*. 19 vols. to date. Paris: Letouzey, 1933–.

Quintin, Danielle and Bernard. *Dictionnaire des colonels de Napoléon*. Paris: S.P.M., 1996.

Ragon, Jean-Marie. *Orthodoxie maçonnique, suivie de la maçonnerie occulte et de l'initiation hermétique*. Paris: Dentu, 1853.

Rétat, Claude. "Initiations, initiatives: Prosper Guerrier de Dumast dans les 'mines de l'Orient.'" *Chroniques d'histoire maçonnique lorraine* 10 (May 2000): 8–54.

Richard, Roger. *Dictionnaire maçonnique: Le Sens caché des rituals et de la symbolique maçonnique*. Paris: Dervy, 1999.

Rigault, Georges. *Inventaire des États de service des officiers de l'armée d'Égypte*. Paris: Plon-Nourrit, 1911.

Ris, Clément de. *Les Amateurs d'autrefois*. Paris: Plon, 1877.

Robert, Adolphe, Edgar Bourloton, and Gaston Cougny. *Dictionnaire des parlementaires français*. 5 vols. Paris: Bourloton, 1891.

Roch, Francis. *Notice biographique sur M. Comte*. 2nd ed.. Paris: Bureau de la Revue, 1846.

Roux, François-Charles. *Les Origines de l'expédition d'Égypte*. Paris: Plon-Nourrit, 1910.

Ruska, Julius. "Zosimos." In *Das Buch der grossen Chemiker*, edited by Günther Bugge, 1:1–17. Berlin: Verlag Chemie, 1929. 2 vols.

Sadie, Stanley. *The New Grove Dictionary of Music and Musicians*. 2nd ed. 29 vols. London and New York: Macmillan, 2001.

Said, Edward. *Orientalism*. New York: Vintage, 1979.

Scamuzzi, Ernesto. *La "Mensa Isiaca" del Regio Museo di Antichità di Torino*. Rome: Bardi, 1939.

Schnapper, Antoine. *David*. New York: Alpine, 1982.

Schuster, Georg. *Die geheimen Gesellschaften, Verbindungen und Orden*. 1906. Repr., Wiesbaden: Fourier, 1995.

Six, Georges. *Dictionnaire biographique des généraux & amiraux français de la Révolution française et de l'Empire, 1792-1814*. 2 vols. Paris: Saffroy, 1934.

Solé, Robert. *Les Savants de Bonaparte*. Paris: Seuil, 1998.

Sollers, Philippe. *Le Cavalier du Louvre: Vivant Denon, 1747–1825*. Paris: Plon, 1995.

Souvenirs et cahiers sur la campagne d'Égypte: Extraits du Carnet de La Sabretache années 1903–1906–1931–1932. Repr., Paris: Teissèdre, 1997.

Spieth, Darius. "Michel Rigo and Bonaparte's Egyptian Campaign (1798–1801): Portraits of the Divan in Cairo." *1650-1850: Ideas, Aesthetics, and Inquiries in the Early Modern Age* 13 (2006): 133–63.

Targhetta, Renata. "Ideologia massonica e sensibilità artistica nel Veneto settecentesco." *Studi veneziani* 16 (1988): 171-211.

———. *La massoneria veneta dalle origine alla chiusura delle logge (1729–1785)*. Udine: Del Bianco, 1988.

Ten-Doesschate Chu, Petra. *The Illustrated Bartsch: French Masters of the Nineteenth Century, Vivant Denon*. 2 vols. New York: Abaris, 1985–88.

Thibaudeau, Antoine-Clair. *Histoire générale de Napoléon Bonaparte, de sa vie privée et publique, de sa carrière politique et militaire, de son administration et de son gouvernement*. 6 vols. Paris and Stuttgart: Ponthieu & Cotta, 1827–28.

Thieme, Ulrich, and Felix Becker. *Allgemeines Lexikon der bildenden Künstler*. 37 vols. Leipzig: Seeman, 1907–50.

Thiry, Jean. *Bonaparte en Égypte, Décembre 1797–24 Août 1799*. Paris: Berger-Levrault, 1973.

Thoumas, Charles. *Les Grands cavaliers du Premier Empire: Les Trois Colbert*. 3 vols. Paris and Nancy: Berger-Levrault, 1890–1909.

Toso Rodinis, Giuliana. *Dominique Vivant Denon, i fiordalisi, il berretto frigio, la sfinge*. Florence: Olschki, 1977.

Trésor de la langue française: Dictionnaire de la langue du XIXe au XXe siècle (1789–1960). Edited by Paul Imbs. 16 vols. Paris: CNRS, 1971–94.

Tulard, Jean. *Napoléon, ou Le Mythe du sauveur*. Paris: Fayard, 1977.

Vagner, Nicolas. *Notice sur M. Guerrier de Dumast, envisagé au point de vue religieux*. Nancy: Imprimerie et Librairie catholiques, 1883.

Van de Sandt, Udolpho. "Spicilège vénitien." In *Les Vies de Vivant Denon*, edited by Daniela Gallo. Vol. 1:253–77. Paris: La Documentation française, Musée du Louvre, 2001.

Van Rinsveld, Bernard. "Une Égyptomanie anti-bonapartiste: Le Journaliste Jean-Gabriel Peltier." *Chronique d'Égypte* 66, nos. 131–32 (1991): 5–22.

Venturi, Franco. "Venise et, par occasion, de la liberté." In *The Idea of Freedom: Essays in the Honour of Isaiah Berlin*, edited by Alan Ryan, 195–210. Oxford and New York: Oxford University Press, 1979.

Verzat, Jean. *Le Comte Regnaud de Saint-Jean-d'Angély (1760–1819): 'L'éminence grise' de l'Empereur*. Saint-Jean-d'Angély: Bordessoules, 2000.

Villebois-Mareuil, Commandant de. "Le Centenaire de l'expédition de l'Égypte: Comment se préparait une campagne coloniale en 1798." *Le Correspondant* 192, no. 860 (July 25, 1898): 209–29.

Villiers du Terrage, Edouard de. *L'Expédition d'Égypte: Journal et souvenirs d'un jeune savant engagé dans l'état-major de Bonaparte (1798-1801)*. Edited by Alain Pigeard 1899. Repr., Paris: Cosmopole, 2001.

Waquet, Françoise. *Les Fêtes royales sous la Restauration, ou L'Ancien régime retrouvé*. Geneva: Droz, 1981.

Westcott, W. Wynn. *The Isiac Tablet, or The Bembine Table of Isis*. 1887. Repr., Los Angeles: The Philosophical Research Society, 1976.

Wheeler, Leonard Richmond. *Vitalism: Its History and Validity*. London: Witherby, 1939.

Wild, Nicole. *Dictionnaire des théâtres parisiens au XIXe siècle*. Paris: Amateurs de livres, 1989.

Wildenstein, Daniel and Guy. *Documents complémentaires au catalogue de l'oeuvre de Louis David*. Paris: Fondation Wildenstein, 1973.

Wildenstein, Georges. *Fragonard aquafortiste*. Paris: Les Beaux-Arts, 1956.

Wright, Dudley. *Women and Freemasonry*. London: Rider, 1922.

Youssef, Ahmed. *La Fascination d'Égypte: Du Rêve au projet, avec 'Consilium Aegyptiacum,' le texte inédit que Leibniz présenta à Louis XIV*. Paris: L'Harmattan, 1998.

Yule, Henry. *Hobson-Jobson: A Glossary of Colloquial Anglo-Indian Words and Phrases*. 2 vols. London: Murray, 1903.

Zimmer, Jean-Pierre. *D'Orient en Occident: Histoire de la loge Les Vrais Amis Réunis d'Égypte, 1799–1845*. Paris: ÉDIMAF, 2001.

Index

Page numbers in italics refer to illustrations; the abbreviations pl. and pls. refer to color plates.